THE POETRY OF THE FO

THE POETRY OF
THE FORTIES

A.T. TOLLEY

**MANCHESTER
UNIVERSITY PRESS**

Published by Manchester University Press,
Oxford Road, Manchester MI3 9PL

 British Library Cataloguing in Publication Data

Tolley, A.T.
　Poetry of the Forties.
　1. English poetry—20th century—History
　and criticism
　I. Title
　821′.912′09　　PR601

　ISBN 0-7190-1708-4
　ISBN 0-7190-1709-2 Pbk

Printed and bound in Canada

To
MOTHER
and to
FATHER
in memory

By the same author

The Poetry of the Thirties

The Early Published Poems of Stephen Spender: a Chronology

CONTENTS

PREFACE

Philip Toynbee, reviewing the predecessor of this book, *The Poetry of the Thirties,* remarked: "Imagine a long critical work called 'The Poetry of the Forties'." The remark was very understandable. The poets of the thirties included writers who, despite very adverse criticism from *Scrutiny* and its associates, attained and held both affection and critical esteem among those who cared for contemporary poetry throughout the English speaking world. The same cannot be said for the poets who are associated with the change of taste in poetry in the nineteen-forties: though most of them gained easy and broad publication, they were not esteemed widely and many became objects of derision from the nineteen-fifties on. Even the most famous of them, Dylan Thomas, has been the subject of violent division of opinion. The poetry of the decade, indeed, left the arena of critical discussion to enter the mythology of literary politics. Robert Conquest, introducing *New Lines* in 1956, stated:

> In the 1940s the mistake was made of giving the Id, a sound player on the percussion side under a strict conductor, too much of a say in the doings of the orchestra as a whole. As it turned out, it could only manage the simpler part of melody and rhythm, and was completely out of its depth with harmony and orchestration. This led to a rapid collapse of public taste, from which we have not yet recovered.

He went on to describe the debilitating results: "men capable of moving work were encouraged to regard their task simply as one of making an arrangement of images of sex and violence tapped straight from the unconscious . . ., or to evoke without comment the *naivetés* and nostalgias of childhood."

In the first issue of Ian Hamilton's *The Review,* in 1962, two reviewers use the term "Apocalyptic" with the assured sense that it will not only be recognized as a reference to a poetic movement of the forties, but will also, without further ado, be taken as a term of abuse.

One purpose of this book is to take the poetry of the forties out of this context and subject it to a proper critical and historical appraisal. In doing this, there is no attempt to restore the forties as they appeared to readers or writers at the time. Indeed, the estimations aimed at will be seen to be very wide of those current in the forties; and "Apocalyptic" is not restored as a term of praise. Many of the writers who figure importantly in discussion here were little regarded or scarcely known at all during the decade. What is attempted is a discussion that takes into account the poetic orientations of the decade and does not dismiss its poetry out of hand because it was not something it never intended to be.

A second purpose of the book is to give a sense of what the poetry of the forties was like, and this involves giving some consideration to work that got attention in the period, even though it seems of little worth today. In this connection, one would give a poor sense of the period if one were to confine attention to those writers considered of first importance then or later. Few periods until the recent past can have seen more poetry published or poetry more widely read. Not all of the lesser writers, either, deserve to be forgotten, even if their work did not warrant the acclaim it received at the time. Among such poets are those killed in the war—a group larger than is generally remembered.

The poets whose work dominated poetic taste in the forties were writers who had gained early acclaim in the late thirties, that period so hospitable to the precocious recognition of talent: Dylan Thomas, George Barker, and David Gascoyne are the most notable of this group. These writers, who were born in or after 1912, and who came to maturity after the appearance of Hitler and during the growing critical acclaim of modernist poetry, constitute the earliest writers considered in this study. Their orientations were very different from those of Auden and his generation; and it is their work that gave the forties its poetic tone. The study closes with a consideration of writers born a decade later, some of whom, like Sidney Keyes, attained early success in the forties, and some of whom, like Philip Larkin, Keyes's contemporary, figure in this history only because of their frustrated attempt to find a congenial medium in the dominant idiom of the decade.

Quotations are from versions of poems published in the forties, generally from the source discussed in the context in which the quotation is made.

The following anthologies provide a good accompaniment to the reading of this book:

Poetry of the Forties ed. R. Skelton (London: Penguin, 1968)
Poetry of the Forties ed. H. Sergeant (London: Longmans, 1971)
The Poetry of War: 1939-1945 ed. I. Hamilton (London: Ross, 1968)
The Terrible Rain: The War Poets 1939-1945 ed. B. Gardner (London: Methuen, 1966).

ACKNOWLEDGEMENTS

I should like first of all to thank the Canada Council and the Social Science and Humanities Research Council of Canada for a leave fellowship and research grants to assist work on this book. I should also like to thank Carleton University and Dean James Downey (now President Downey of the University of New Brunswick) for the award of the Marston Lafrance Memorial Fellowship which gave me a year free of teaching for research and writing. In addition, I should like to thank Dean Naomi Griffiths for financial assistance related to the fellowship. Thanks are also due to the Canadian Federation for the Humanities for a grant in aid of publication; and to Michael Gnarowski of Carleton University Press, who arranged the joint publication of the book.

Mr. John Lehmann has given me valued encouragement to complete this book since the appearance of *The Poetry of the Thirties* in 1975. Professor Bernard Bergonzi and Frank Wilson both gave me the benefit of their discussion of the forties and their encouragement too. Professors Rob McDougall and George Johnston generously took time to write in support of my research to the granting bodies. Kevin Crossley-Holland has been a good friend of the book since its conception. It has benefited from correspondence with Mr. John Heath-Stubbs. Mr. Harvey MacGregor gave valued advice on legal problems.

I have derived considerable bibliographical information from the catalogues of Bertrand Rota and I.D. Edrich, both of whom found books that I needed. Mr. Charles Skilton, the owner of the Fortune Press, was kind enough to talk to me and write to me about the past of the Press, and sold me books from his small stock.

Miss Hilda Gifford, Carleton's Collections Librarian, sought books for me and gave me much appreciated leads to their purchase. The staff of the Carleton Library gave me valuable assistance, particularly the members of the Humanities Section and the Inter Library Loan Section. The librarians in the Literature Section of the Birmingham Reference Library were regularly helpful on my many visits there; and I am grateful to have been allowed to draw on the resources of the British Library and on its Manuscript Collection. Thanks are due again to the G.J. Wood Memorial Clipping Service for continued resourcefulness in a changing world.

My wife, Dr. Glenda M. Patrick, took time from her own research to read the book and to give valuable editorial assistance. Devon Sliwka and the staff of the English Department at Carleton University have given me frequent help.

Chapter 1

INTRODUCTORY

"I am going to keep a journal, because I cannot accept the fact that I feel so shattered that I cannot write at all."[1] These are the first words of a journal that Stephen Spender began on September 3rd, 1939, the day on which Britain declared war on Germany in answer to Hitler's invasion of Poland on September 1st. The hope of intellectual radicals like Spender that the anti-fascist political movements of the thirties could prevent a second world war was shattered: they felt that they had been betrayed into war by the cowardice and stupidity of a conservative establishment. Much more was to be shattered before the new decade ended—much more than could have been envisioned in even the most horrendous imaginings. The studied slaughter of the trench warfare of the first world war was avoided; but in the future lay the gas chambers, the thousand bomber raids, the atom bomb, the Japanese treatment of war prisoners, the twenty million Russian dead. It would be the beginning of the destruction of a traditional conception of human nature. The war was to last almost six years; and, at the end of 1947, there were still men being demobilised who had been called up while the war was on.

Compared with what happened abroad, the war in England, in spite of the bombing, seems in retrospect positively domestic. Yet the coming of total war was to affect indelibly life in Britain and the conception that the British people had of themselves. The collapse of France and the hair-breadth escape of the British army via Dunkirk shook an imbued and seldom questioned sense of superiority. The controls, the rationing, the direction of labour that followed changed life irremediably and affected all classes. Domestic servants, a privileged monopoly of higher education, and disparities of income that left many undernourished were largely to disappear.

The events and changes of the war affected British intellectual life decisively, but diffusely and in a general way. People felt humbled by the devastation they saw around them. "Human respect" was the feeling that John Lehmann found characteristic of those years. Though the nineteen-forties saw a decline in the support of organised religion (so much a part of the establishment in Britain) there grew up a strong leaning to older pieties. "God" was seldom referred to in poems of

the thirties: in the poetry of the forties he frequently received respectful mention. There arose a distrust of intellectual panaceas.

Victory and its surprises were, in some respects, as disconcerting to
many intellectuals as the war itself. On the one hand, Hitler and the
menace of fascism were suddenly gone for good; and a Labour government had been returned with a large majority and was proceeding with
what then seemed a radical programme of nationalisation and social
reform. On the other hand, the British Empire, on which the sun had
indeed not set in 1939, and which had been protected then by the
largest navy in the world, emerged, after winning the war, embarrassed by the costs of world power and secondary to the United States
and the Soviet Union in its influence. At the end of the war, Britain
had an external debt of nearly three thousand million pounds: over a
thousand million pounds of overseas assets had been sold to pay for
the war. Lend-lease, under which supplies had come to Britain from
the United States without payment as a transaction between allies,
ceased with the coming of peace. Rations of some commodities became smaller, and few of the luxuries looked forward to during the
war in fact reappeared.

The situation produced a stunned lack of any sense of direction.
For those on the Right, the old days were gone for good; for those on
the Left, it was hard to raise the banner for radical change when the
Labour government was beset by economic difficulties in the midst of
what it *had* done. There could be no return to things as they had
been. As Dorian Cooke wrote in "Poem on returning to England after
Six Years' Absence":

> . . . And who will dare
> To walk back six Decembers
> And dig the mud of that dark bed
> To the roots of these Summer wounds we bear?

British intellectuals and the British people entered a puzzled crisis concerning their identity. The sense of the centrality of British experience,
so firmly assumed for over a century, was falling away. Above all, it
would seem, there was a lack of any focussed pressure for change
that could have provided an impetus for fresh intellectual life. The
outlook of the enlightened elements of the British middle class had
been one of decency and a wish to do good to others. In a situation
where sweeping economic changes had been introduced and where
shortages and high taxation appeared to make any further redistribution
of wealth impossible, the prospects for further radicalism seemed un-
clear. It was to remain for intellectuals of the fifties, in writings like
Hugh Thomas's *The Establishment* (1959), to show that further radical
perspectives concerning social change were possible.

II

During the war there was a remarkable interest in nearly all cultural activities. People were thrown back upon themselves because the black-out and other features of the war inhibited social gatherings. Many of those in the forces or civil defence found themselves with a great deal of time on their hands far from any source of entertainment other than a book or the radio. Above all, in the face of the complete disruption of their lives and the possibility of sudden death, people began to think about fundamental things and to seek what would sustain them emotionally. Things as various as the B.B.C. "Brains Trust" and the revived interest in serious theatre and the ballet were symptoms of this.

The fact that the wartime shortages produced a seller's market in everything contributed to this. This was particularly true of books. Paper was rationed, and several million books, many of them middle-brow best sellers, were destroyed in the bombing. Editions of classics were hard to come by; and publishers could publish what they wished in confidence that their complete edition would sell out. Poetry took very little paper, and publishers were happy to be able to put out more of it than they would have been able to in more competitive days. Poetry was readily purchased: T.S. Eliot's *Little Gidding* appeared in 1942 in an edition of 16,775 copies. Not only did poetry provide suitable reading for short periods of free time; it also offered a consolation and an exploration of the important questions of life and death, so needed then. No doubt the same needs account for the large amount of poetry written during the war.

One of the seemingly never to be repeated phenomena of the period was the enormous sale of John Lehmann's *Penguin New Writing*—a "little magazine" that sold up to 100,000 copies an issue, and was probably seen by many more readers. Cyril Connolly's *Horizon*, aggressively highbrow, sold up to 10,000, and George Woodcock's anarchistic *Now* could regularly sell out its printing of 2,000 copies between 1943 and 1946. Although the principal verse periodicals of the thirties *New Verse* and *Twentieth Century Verse* had ceased with the outbreak of hostilities, the war years were a great time for literary periodicals. *New Writing,* the parent of *Penguin New Writing,* had always appeared as a miscellany in book form, and several other miscellanies appeared during the forties in an evasion of the restriction on the starting of new magazines: *New Road* from the Grey Walls Press; the rather middle-brow *Here and Now; Orion,* edited by C. Day Lewis and Dennis Kilham Roberts; Geoffrey Grigson's *The Mint;* and John Lehmann's last stand from his own publishing house, the two issues of *Orpheus.*

At the end of the war many publishers and editors looked forward to taking advantage of the cultural boom with ambitious programmes. At first the back-log of unsatisfied demand, particularly for editions of the classics, maintained the illusion of opportunity. However, the rising cost of book production and the decline of enforced leisure soon saw many publishers in difficulties. Poetry, particularly that of writers whose reputation was associated with the war, was severely hit. Alun Lewis's *Raiders' Dawn* is a signal example. It ran through five impressions from its publication in March, 1942 to the end of the war. A sixth impression was produced in 1946. That impression could still be purchased from the publisher in 1974. From 1946 until the end of the decade, alarmingly few first books of poetry appeared. Small magazines were almost eliminated. As John Lehmann remarked in the last issue of *Penguin New Writing*, ". . . soon there will hardly be any address at all to which a young poet or writer of short stories can send his MSS . . ." While publishing difficulties curtailed the appearance of literature, there was an accompanying literary hiatus. Innovative new work was not forthcoming, and even issues of periodicals that contained work of high quality seemed to exemplify a cultural listlessness.

There had not been as much life in the literary scene as the wartime activity in publishing suggested; and many associated with that activity had not been impressed by it. T.S. Eliot was no longer a force for literary change, and he virtually ceased to write non-dramatic poems after 1944. The movement in writing associated with W.H. Auden and *New Verse* and *New Writing* exerted an influence on the writing of the forties that was only grudgingly acknowledged, but these writers seemed themselves to be groping stylistically after the collapse of the movement with which they had been associated. Even Dylan Thomas, more of an emblem than an influence, wrote fewer and fewer poems as the decade closed. The "death of the novel" was widely discussed, and the work of writers like Elizabeth Bowen, Rosamond Lehmann, Elizabeth Taylor—or even of Henry Green, Graham Greene, Joyce Cary—was caught up with middle-class experience that was passing. Evelyn Waugh's *Brideshead Revisited* (1945) celebrated golden days of upper class life with a seductiveness that almost contradicted its nostalgic emphasis that all this had passed.

There was no one writer or group of writers who were felt to show the way that writing should go. Herbert Read had a considerable influence on the thinking of young writers of anarchistic or "neo-Romantic" leaning. The denigration of Romantic poetry, common in the nineteen-thirties, and derived from the critical notions of T.S. Eliot and T.E. Hulme, was replaced by an admiration of Romanticism and of visionary poetry. Yeats came into increasing respect, though he was a model for only a few. Through J.B. Leishman's translations, Rilke's work became widely known, and the *Duino Elegies*, which seemed to distil a transcendental meaning from transient experience, were greatly admired; though Rilke's influence on W.H. Auden, Stephen Spender and John Lehmann in the thirties had been far more pronounced than it was to be for any poet in the forties. Indeed, as Henry Reed remarked in 1943, ". . . young writers of to-day tend more and more to think that literature consists of their own generation and the one immediately before it . . ."[2]

This was strikingly true of the "New Romantic" writers who frequented the pubs of Fitzrovia, where nobody had any money and everyone lived out of everybody else's pockets. Fitzrovia comprised Soho and the adjacent area north of Oxford Street. It constituted England's only twentieth century Bohemia, glowingly remembered by John Heath-Stubbs, David Wright, Michael Hamburger and Alan Ross, who recall it as the place of their poetic education. Yet, cut off from widespread acceptance by the modernity of their art, the poets of Fitzrovia contributed to little magazines where they constituted their own public. Some seemed to belong nowhere and to have read little outside the periodicals to which they contributed. Nevertheless, through *Poetry London* and through a growing acceptance, they slowly asserted their non-ironic tone; and, by the second half of the decade, with the immense following of Thomas's *Deaths and Entrances,* their tone became the established one.

A sense of the milieu in which poetry developed during the forties is given by some important publishing events. T.S. Eliot's "Burnt Norton" of 1935 became *Four Quartets* (1943) with the successive publication of *East Coker* (1940), *The Dry Salvages* (1941) and *Little Gidding* (1942). These were undoubtedly the greatest poems published in Britain during the war—perhaps during this century; and their emphasis on acceptance and the irremediable spiritual imperfection of human beings answered concerns widely felt. Edith Sitwell, whose poetry in the twenties had seemed startlingly irreverent, began, with *Street Songs* in 1942, to publish poetry of anguished religious concern, placing the events of the war in a traditional spiritual context. "The Song of the Cold", concerning the London bombing, was widely acclaimed; though her poetry does not seem to deserve the high estimate given it by people like Sir Kenneth Clark or Maurice Bowra. More surely substantial was the poetry of Edwin Muir, which grew in stature in the forties and, as much as any other work of the period, moved contemporary experience into a realm suggestive of inescapable patterns of human conflict and reconciliation.

Many foreign writers, in exile from war or persecution, appeared in British periodicals. Among them were the Greek poets George Seferis and Demetrios Capetanakis. Capetanakis suffered from a killing disease through much of his time in England, and yet came to write striking poetry in English. Also of note was the Czeck poet, Fred Marnau, whose *The Wounds of the Apostles,* appearing in parallel German and English texts in 1945, was one of the more powerful works of the period.

The war separated England from the continent, and after the war much of Europe was shattered. News and books did come out of France during the war, and among these were new poems by Louis Aragon, two books of which Cyril Connolly published. After the war, the work of Jean-Paul Sartre and Albert Camus and many other new French authors was well published in England; yet it is one of the paradoxes of British cultural history that the Sunday papers could explain week by week how much better literary matters were ordered in France with almost no noticeable effect on the course of British writing.

The same cannot be said for the interest in American literature. As the decade progressed, American writing appeared more frequently in British little magazines, and the great American makers of twentieth century poetry became better known. Condescension was slowly replaced by admiration.

The forties saw an important expansion in the public for modern poetry. In 1939, the readership of the new poetry was still very small, and there were large numbers of "poetry lovers" who detested the ugly, modern poetry. By 1950, the acceptance of a contemporary idiom in poetry was widespread among literate people. The award of the Order of Merit and the Nobel Prize to T.S. Eliot in 1948 was a mark of that acceptance. Nevertheless, the decade closed with British poetic taste in an evident state of lassitude and indirection. For the Festival of Britain in 1951, the Arts Council offered prize money totalling over a thousand pounds for a Poetry Contest, and the winning entries were published by Penguin Books under the editorship of John Hayward. The winners were Jack Clemo, Clive Sansom, Gerald Bromhead Walker, T.P. Fletcher, Robert Conquest, J.C. Grant, Theodore Nicholl and L.A. Redford. Only Clemo and Conquest are now remembered.

III

Though the events of the forties affected British cultural life markedly and irreversibly, it would be wrong to imagine that all the new poets developed in direct response to those events. Many of the poets who achieved prominence during the decade had started to publish in the years immediately preceding the war. Roy Fuller, Julian Symons, H.B. Mallalieu, Ruthven Todd, D.S. Savage and George Woodcock had been associated with Symons's *Twentieth Century Verse;* and the writers of the Apocalypse movement—Henry Treece, J.F. Hendry, Dorian Cooke, G.S. Fraser and Norman McCaig had appeared in *Seven* and had published their anthology *The New Apocalypse* before the war began. Lawrence Durrell, Laurie Lee, Henry Reed and Anne Ridler had all been writing and (except for Lee) publishing before 1940. If to this number we add the names of other writers of the same age group who published extensively in the middle and late thirties—George Barker, Dylan Thomas, David Gascoyne—we have a high proportion of the poets who made their mark in the forties or who contributed to the characteristic tone of its poetry.

What had these poets in common? In the important, literary sense of the question, the answer, it is hoped, will appear from the book as a whole. However, certain facts emerge when we place these poets beside the poets of the thirties, with whose work there is sometimes a continuity but often a striking contrast. The poets of the thirties grew up during the first world war; the poets mentioned above were born between 1912 and 1918, and were just too young to remember the war. Auden and his contemporaries came to maturity before the depression began or Hitler came to power: the writers born between 1912 and 1918 did not. The poets of the thirties were nearly all educated at public schools and at Oxford or Cambridge: hardly any of the younger writers were of upper-middle class origin or had been to the older universities. Many, like Dylan Thomas, did not go to university at all. The attitudes of some of these writers to politics and to the generation of poets who preceded them was no doubt coloured by these facts. They were not haunted by the blimpish propaganda of the Great War, nor did they have any sense of guilt or relief at having missed the fighting. They did not have an intimate quarrel with the ruling class, because they were not from that class. The depression did not come to them as a shock, and Hitler was a fact of life when many of them came to political awareness. Though Auden and his generation had done much in adapting stylistically the new and shocking "modern" poetry and in getting some public acceptance for work in that idiom, there seems to have been an undercurrent of resentment that the Oxbridge writers had so effectively cornered the market with a taste for their kind of poetry.

It is easy to see the emergence of poets like Dylan Thomas and George Barker as a symptom of the greater accessibility of secondary education and the widening intellectual aspirations of the lower-middle classes from which they came. It is not clear why, when we turn to writers who were born in or after 1918, and who came to maturity as the second world war began, we find again that nearly all of them were products of Oxford or Cambridge: John Heath-Stubbs, Nicholas Moore, Keith Douglas, Alex Comfort, David Wright, Drummond Allison, Alan Ross, J.C. Hall, Hamish Henderson and Sidney Keyes. By the time these writers grew up, it was clear that their likely destiny was to be killed in war, as several of them were. They were the poets who should have left their mark as the new poets of the forties and of World War II. Even more enigmatic are the careers of other writers of the same age who were also at Oxford or Cambridge—D.J. Enright, Kingsley Amis, Philip Larkin, Donald Davie. They failed to discover their idiom in the forties, yet they showed much greater staying power than their more precocious contemporaries when they finally emerged as the *New Lines* poets of the late fifties.

Indeed the great puzzle is why so many poets who started publishing poetry after 1937 and who made a reputation out of it during the forties had stopped publishing poetry regularly by 1953. The number of such poets who went on to sustained careers was very small: Roy Fuller, Lawrence Durrell, John Heath-Stubbs, David Wright, Norman Nicholson, W.S. Graham and Alan Ross are among the few. Durable careers were to be made by poets whose early poetry, though powerful and characteristic of the authors, passed unnoticed in the forties: R.S. Thomas, Jack Clemo, Charles Causley. No simple answer can be given to the questions raised by this state of affairs. What is clear is that, despite the boom in the publication of poetry during the war, these years were bad ones for starters.

Chapter 2

THE NEW ESTABLISHMENT

The Thirties poets–*Horizon–New Writing–Scrutiny*–
Publishing in the Forties

Few literary events have been so dramatic as the collapse and dispersal of the literary movement that dominated the thirties. Left-wing, nostalgically critical of the dominant middle-class from which most of its writers came, ironic and preoccupied with the actual, it lost cohesion and direction when the war brought an end to any hope of a peaceful, political defeat of fascism. The departure of Auden and Isherwood for America, the closing down of *New Verse* and of *Twentieth Century Verse* and the temporary cessation of *New Writing,* reinforced the disorientation these writers felt.

Yet the forties were in fact to see them consolidate their positions as the literary establishment of their day. Cyril Connolly's *Horizon* and John Lehmann's revived *New Writing* (in its various forms) were to be leaders of literary taste in the decade. While a "new romanticism" was to be proclaimed by admirers of Dylan Thomas and George Barker, the secure and revered poets of the period were to be the big four of the thirties—Auden, Day Lewis, MacNeice and Spender. Their work was to have a far greater circulation in the forties than it had in the thirties, and many of the younger writers were to continue to look to it for a model.

It was indeed the volumes from the thirties that were widely read during the war. This was particularly the case with Auden. In *Poems* (1930) and *Look Stranger* (1936), he had shown his great feeling for what was English, and the settings of his poems seemed the natural exemplars of the reflections they gave rise to. In his later poetry, the outer world was to become merely the source of illustration for the stream of reflections that gave shape to his poems, and this change was already showing itself in the collection of short poems that appeared in 1940, *Another Time.* As John Lehmann wrote then "There is . . . a tendency . . . to lose the compactness and the vivid seeing which were characteristic of the best of his previous poetry; some of the Odes seem strangely prosy and sentential, and are full of dangerously vacant phrases . . ."[1] The dominance of abstract argument was oppressive in *New Year Letter* (1941), Auden's long philosophical poem in octosyllabic couplets—a poem that has never had many admir-

ers. Unfortunately, it was only Auden's long poems that were published in book form in England in the forties. *The Age of Anxiety*
(1948)—a "baroque ecloque" in alliterative meter set in a Manhattan
bar—was greeted as brilliant by those who wanted to see Auden as an
established master, but it seemed ill conceived in form and unengaging
in execution. The title poem in *For the Time Being* (1945) was unin-
spiring, but "The Sea and the Mirror" that made up the remainder of
the book contained some of Auden's finest poetry. Arranged as a poetic commentary on Shakespeare's *The Tempest,* it may have seemed at
the time too recondite to be recognised as the remarkable religious
work that it is. Auden wrote few shorter poems, mainly at the beginning of the decade. Several of them appeared in America in *Collected
Poems* (1945), but its British counterpart, *Collected Shorter Poems,*
was not published until 1950. British readers in the forties did not see
important poems like "Atlantis" or "Time will say nothing but 'I
told you so' ": before the appearance of "In Praise of Limestone" in
Horizon in August, 1948, Auden must have appeared to have lost his
way. His influence on British poetry in the forties—a pervasive one—
was hence mainly through his earlier books.

In the work of Stephen Spender in the forties we see the changing
stance of the poets of his generation and the defeating effect of that
change on their creative impulse. Spender's radicalism had seemed
more natural to him than that of Auden and Day Lewis. He had always been distrustful of "committed literature"; and, in 1942, in *Life
and the Poet,* he gave open expression to that distrust. "I am not
recanting," he wrote, "I am merely trying to understand . . . why our
position was ineffective, why we may even have betrayed our function . . ."[2] Nevertheless, his attitude to the role of the poet shows a
shift of emphasis that is fundamental: "Today the different attitudes
of the poets are different attempts to break beneath the surface of the
enormous solidified appearance of the age to the instincts, traditions
and fundamental nature of humanity beneath . . ."[3] "There is only
true or false poetry. No aesthetic or religious or political dogma can
dictate what is the subject for poetry in this or any future time."[4] His
Ruins and Visions (1942) was much praised when it appeared, particularly for the war poems like "June 1940". These poems seem in retrospect marred by Spender's recurrent shortcomings, diffuseness and
uncertainty of rhythm. There is only one powerful poem in the book—
perhaps the best poem Spender ever wrote—the haunting, introspective
"The Double Vision", which belongs with his previous volume, *The
Still Centre* (1939). Spender's work was already in decline. After the
war he wrote some touching and evocative poems, such as "Meeting"
(*Penguin New Writing* 27, Spring, 1946) which were brought together

in *Poems of Dedication* (1947); but *The Edge of Being* (1949)—his last collection for a quarter of a century—was disappointing. His best poems of the forties continued to reflect the personal and introspective side of his writing rather than the political. Nevertheless, like Auden, he remained an important influence through a handful of his earlier poems, with their powerful combination of the realistic and the visionary.

Cecil Day Lewis captured his generation's ambivalent attitude to poetry and the war in the dedicatory stanzas to his translation of *The Georgics of Virgil* (1940):

> Where are the war poets? the fools inquire.
> We were the prophets of a changeable morning
> Who hoped for much but saw the clouds fore warning:
> We were at war, while they still played with fire
> And rigged the market for the ruin of man:
> Spain was a death to us, Munich a mourning.

Day Lewis had found himself turning away from political poetry and political action in the late thirties, not out of a death of conviction, but because of the dismaying division between public and private concerns that it made in him. In *Word Over All* (1943), easily his best book, he explores personal themes, looking back, as did so many poets in the forties, into childhood for an earnest of innocence and authenticity in human experience. The sonnet sequence "O Dreams, O Destinations" and the evocative "Cornet Solo" are among those poems so characteristic of the decade:

> Thirty years ago lying awake,
> Lying awake
> In London at night when childhood barred me
> From livelier pastimes, I'd hear a street-band break
> Into old favourites—'The Ash Grove', 'Killarney'
> Or 'Angels Guard Thee'.

These poems showed a turning away from modernism. Day Lewis was not an important influence in the forties, and his *Poems 1943-1947* displayed the conventional and literary strain that had always been there.

After 1940, it was Louis MacNeice who, through his new poetry, continued to be an important example in his fine feeling for the actual, even though some of his best poems of the decade are on literary themes, like "Autolycus", or are purely descriptive, like "Street Scene". He was important to writers such as Alan Ross, who took their departure from immediate experience. MacNeice wrote a number of telling but characteristically unassuming poems about London in wartime and the raids. He captures superbly the bemused ideological stance of many of his generation in face of the war in ''Bottleneck'':

> Never to fight unless from a pure motive
> And for a clear end was his unwritten rule
> Who had been in books and visions to a progressive school
> And dreamt of barricades, yet being observant
> Knew that that was not the way things are:
> This man would never make a soldier or a servant.
>
> When I saw him last, carving the longshore mist
> With an ascetic profile, he was standing
> Watching the troopship leave, he did not speak
> But from his eyes there peered a furtive footsore envy
> Of these who sailed away to make an opposed landing—
> So calm because so young, so lethal because so meek . . .

MacNeice's poetry underwent less change than that of other poets of his generation. There was a toning down of imagery and a greater emphasis on subject. His writing had been less involved with the political movements of the thirties and proved a congenial and accessible model for many poets of the forties engaged in grappling with the unexpected experiences of wartime.

Of the other poets whom Michael Roberts had brought together in *New Signatures* (1932)—the defining anthology of the new poetry of the thirties—Julian Bell was dead, Richard Eberhart was in America and A.S.J. Tessimond published only the occasional poem. William Empson's *The Gathering Storm* (1940) was more uneven than his brilliant first book, *Poems* (1935), and it was to be his last volume of entirely new poetry. A *Selected Poems* by William Plomer appeared in 1940: but *The Dworking Thigh* (1945) confirmed the sense that poetry was not, at that time, the main avenue for his talents. Only John Lehmann and C. Day Lewis of the *New Signatures* poets seemed to find a renewal of inspiration in the wartime years. After a period when poetry did not come easily, Lehmann became aware of possibilities for experience that he had not imagined before; and, with the encouragement of the exiled Greek poet, Demetrios Capetanakis, began writing poetry again. The sense of a civilisation that had lost its way and of the distant historical antecedents of the war are powerfully conveyed in a poem like ''The Sphere of Glass'', which arose out of a walk with his sister Rosamond beside a Roman dyke:

> Within the wood, within the hour
> It seemed a sphere of glass had grown
> That glittered round their lives with power

To link what grief the dyke had known
With voices of their vaster war
The sun-shot bombers droning home.

As did Day Lewis, Lehmann seemed to find himself by turning away
from the contemporary, radical concerns of his earlier poetry. Though
these poems constitute perhaps the finest work of his career, his most
important influence on the new poetry of the forties was to be through
his work as editor.

The decade saw the poets of the thirties more and more securely
established with the reading public, with their earlier books frequently
reprinted; and, by the end of the forties, they had moved from being
innovators to being part of the body of work that gave the norm of
poetic expression. Such a view may seem odd in the light of the contention of many younger writers that they were reacting against the
work of the previous decade. Yet one of the significant things about
the forties is that the new writers did not produce a body of work that
was accepted in the sense that it came to exert a pressure on the writing of the future. Dylan Thomas was the only leading poet of the
forties at all imitated, and *Deaths and Entrances* (1946) was the one
book by a poet of the period to have a wide influence on taste—though
few, in fact, seem to have set out to imitate that book. Its adulation
among readers of poetry, especially younger ones, created a climate
that hindered creative change. This failure to generate work that would
have an immediate continuity with future writing is one of the saddening features of the forties. For all its various "movements", the forties
did not shake the literary ascendancy of the previous decade. This
was particularly true of the generation that came of age between 1940
and 1945.

II

The best known literary periodical of the forties, both in its day
and now, was *Horizon*. It provided a notable continuity with the previous decade in sustaining the upper-middle class literary and cultural
valuations of the thirties—values that survived the abandonment of Leftist positions. Elusive and enigmatic concerning what it stood for, it
vocally paraded a despair over the condition of the arts that came close
to self-denigration. Frequently outrageously emphatic, its principal
editor, Cyril Connolly, nevertheless often left the reader wondering
whether he really could mean what he had said as he shifted stance
from issue to issue. Later in life, with 10,000 pages of *Horizon* as
perhaps his principal achievement, he was to write: "My idea of Hell

is a place where one is made to listen to everything one has ever said. But if this punishment be more than one could bear, then to listen to everything one said during the war would be hell enough".[5]

Although *Horizon* began in January 1940 and ended exactly ten years later, giving the appearance that it had been conceived as a holding operation for culture during the war and in the parlous years that concluded the decade, it was in fact planned before the war began: " 'Favourite Daydream,' I wrote in 1933, 'to edit a monthly entirely subsidized by self. No advertisements. Harmless title. Deleterious contents.' In 1939 I found my friend Peter Watson was prepared to launch it . . . Peter Watson's main interests were modern painting and music, mine were literature and psychology . . ."[6] The first number contained a statement of policy that seemed to give to *Horizon* the task of providing a sustaining continuity in the face of the demise of the revolution of the thirties:

> A magazine should be the reflection of its time, and one that ceases to reflect this should come to an end. The moment we live in is anarchistic, conservative and irresponsible, for the war is separating culture from life and driving it back on itself, the impetus given by Left Wing politics is for the time exhausted, and however much we would like to have a paper that was revolutionary in opinions or original in technique, it is impossible to do so when there is a certain suspension of judgement and creative activity. The aim of *Horizon* is to give to writers a place to express themselves, and to readers the best writing we can obtain. Our standards are aesthetic, and our politics are in abeyance. (I, 1, 5)

Yet, as Stephen Spender, who soon left the editorial team, remarked: "The strength of *Horizon* lay not in its having any defined cultural or political policy, but in the vitality and idiosyncrasy of the editor . . ."[7] In the fourth issue, Connolly's "Comment" begins:

> The position of the artist to-day should occasion general concern were it not that the whole human race seems threatened by an interior urge to destruction. He occupies, amid the surrounding dilapidation, a corner even more dilapidated, sitting with his begging bowl in the shadow of the volcano. (I, 4, 229)

The note of sustained, public responsibility is not congenial to Connolly, and the tone of the self-pitying outsider caught in the telling phrase about the "begging bowl" is soon taken up again in a prophetic vignette: ". . . the artist is drifting into becoming a disreputable member of the lower middle classes waiting, in a borrowed mackintosh, for the pubs to open . . ." (I, 4, 235) Connolly occasionally rounded on himself for having no policy; and, in the sixtieth issue, announced: "By now we should have a policy. We have. Accused of 'aestheticism', 'escapism', 'ivory towerism', 'bourgeois formalism', 'frivolity' and 'preferring art to life', it pleads on all these counts 'guilty and proud of it'.'' (X, 60, 367) Nevertheless it is to the image of the artist as cast out from his place ''snug in the heart of the bourgeoisie, with a safe middle income'' (I, 4, 236) to which Connolly recurs with a kind of fervent despair. In August, 1946 he came out with the term ''Inflationary decadence'' to describe ''an age when rewards increase as standards decline'' (XIV, 80, 69); and followed this with a survey among a number of writers on ''The Cost of Letters'' (XIV, 81, September 1946). One of the best sustained series was ''Where shall John go?'', a total of nineteen travel reports running from 1943 to 1949 on places in the Sterling area that the writer might happily visit away from the controls and ravages of post-war England. Connolly, who himself made trips to France, Switzerland and America, seemed to think of the artist's difficulties only too readily in terms of food and food parcels—though it is not a square meal but the elusive *foie gras* and *Chablis* that one sees him in search of. His England is similar to that of his friend George Orwell's *1984* (1948) with its ''Victory gin'', so redolant of the substitutes on which good cheer had to be sustained in those austere days. The theme of decline preoccupied him more and more in the last years of the periodical, and he returns to it in the last sentence of his final ''Comment''—the most celebrated sentence he ever wrote, and characteristically a parody of Sir Edward Grey's classic words of 1914: ''. . . it is closing time in the gardens of the West and from now on an artist will be judged only by the resonance of his solitude or the quality of his despair.'' (XX, 120-121, 362)

It is easy enough to judge Connolly by ''the quality of his despair'', and to say that he lamented the decline of privileged middle class life. The inventor of ''The Theory of Permanent Adolescence''[8], he seems to have seen himself (as he was) equally at home with the insouciant aestheticism of the twenties as with the social responsibility of the thirties. Yet the attitudes that leave Connolly open to criticism were associated with and balanced by what he called ''wholesome blasphemy'' (XII, 72, 366)—a quality that benefited from a desistance of earnestness. When, in No. 100 he said, ''During the eight years I have edited *Horizon* we have witnessed a continuous decline in all the arts'', he was largely right; and very much to the point when he said that ''such a thing as *avant-garde* in literature has ceased to exist.'' (XVI, 96 (December 1947) 299)

A literary periodical is not, in any case, to be judged by the remarks in its editorials, but by the quality of what it publishes. *Horizon* was sub-titled ''A Review of Literature and Art''; and, while its coverage of painting and sculpture was exciting and comprehensive, it went beyond its own prescription to touch many fields of intellectual interest. Though it published poetry and stories steadily through its life, these did not have the predominance one would expect in a literary periodical. In 121 issues it published about half that number of stories—plus two short novels, Evelyn Waugh's *The Loved One* (XVII, 98, Feb 48) and Mary McCarthy's *The Oasis (A Source of Embarrassment)* (XIX, 110, Feb 49), the winner of the *Horizon* prize. The articles were "the core of the magazine", as Connolly saw:[9] by the end of 1943 there had been several issues consisting entirely of articles or recollections (for which Connolly evidently had a liking). Many of the articles were presented in series: "Novelist Philosophers" (15); "Studies in Genius" (10); "Contemporary Sculptors" (8). They were extensive (some, like Edward Glover's "Freud or Jung", were much too long and ran through more than one issue); and they prodded the reader into interest in artists and thinkers he may never have heard of: Chestov; Luigi Dellapiccola; Matta; St. John of the Cross; Unamuno; Italo Svevo. The answer to those who felt that the periodical was over their heads was, perhaps, that it was, and that was good for them.

The task of educating the reader carried over into the choice of literary contributions. After the liberation, *Horizon* had a special French number. It introduced its readers to Existentialism. Connolly went to America in 1947 and produced a special American issue; and from then on introduced readers to a number of exciting and new American writers: Lionel Trilling; Truman Capote; Donald Wyndham; J.F. Powers; Robert Lowry; and William Goyen. Yet the criticism was often voiced that *Horizon* lacked not only a policy but any definite editorial character, and it has to be admitted that this was true. Connolly's nucleus of contributors began by being associates of the thirties, and W.H. Auden, George Orwell and Louis MacNeice were among the most extensively featured. Yet there was always a veering towards the middle-brow, the slightly out of date or the conventional: Alfred Noyes; Logan Pearsall-Smith; the essays that became Peter Quennell's *Four Portraits* (1945). Augustus John's "Fragment of an Autobiography" ran through eighteen appearances between 1941 and 1949, and must hold the record for desultory serialisation without appearance in book form. There are only a few new prose writers whom Connolly can be said to have discovered and in any way steadily encouraged: J. Maclaren-Ross; Angus Wilson; and Philip Toynbee.

The same criticism may be made of *Horizon's* editorial showing in poetry. Almost every poet of any note discussed in this book—and many others—appeared in *Horizon,* but hardly any new poet was given sustained support: W.R. Rodgers was a not too creditable exception. There are few triumphs either; the one notable one being the publication of several of Dylan Thomas's most important poems of the decade. Another is the appearance of Auden's "In Praise of Limestone" (XVIII, 103, Jul 48). The editorial touch seems surer towards the end of the decade—perhaps because there were so few new writers appearing. The issue for April, 1940 contained Frederick Prokosch's "Sunburned Ulysses", W.R. Rodgers's "War Time", Laurie Lee's "A Moment of War", G.M. Brady's "On That Last Sigh", Adam Drinan's "The Gulls", F. Buchanan's "Not into Temptation", L.S. Little's "January", and Terence Heywood's "Notes for a Bestiary". Heywood was the author of *Architechtonic* (1953), one of the least readable books of poetry of the decade, and highly pretentious: he got into *Horizon* again that same year. Little was a rather prosey writer also favoured by John Lehmann. It is hard to see what sort of acumen could even let Buchanan and Brady by in a bad moment:

> On that last sigh
> The wind gave issue to another frisk of leaves,
> Pale butterflies accepting union
> With the mud-brown river,
> And there between the flutter and the frequent water
> The thought unblossomed round its wintry giver.
> (G.M. Brady "On That Last Sigh", I, 4, 246)

The early reviews by Kathleen Raine and the surveys of the previous year's poetry were a service to poetry at the time; but, in April 1947, *Horizon* announced, with some justification, that it would not be giving a survey because "we do not consider the volumes produced in 1946 to justify one." (XV, 87, 154) The editor's leaning was to the prosey but polite poem of reflection or observation, exemplified in Brian Howard's "Gone to Report", trotted out again in his retrospective *The Golden Horizon* in 1953.

> For twenty-one years he remained, faithful and lounging
> There, under the last tree, at the end of the charming
> evening street.
> His flask was always full for the unhappy, rich, or bold;
> He could always tell you where you wanted to go, what
> you wanted to be told,
> And during all the dear twenty-one years he remained
> exactly twenty-one years old.
> His eyes were the most honest of all, his smile the most
> naturally sweet.

Horizon did little to shape the course of poetry in the forties, other than publish some of it—which was perhaps a great deal. Its significant contribution to the life of literature (and hence of poetry) in the decade was that it proselytised aggressively for what was modern in all the arts, for a breadth and cosmopolitanism of interest against provincialism, for the highbrow and the difficult against what was conventional, comfortable and easy to understand. To return to it today is still a broadening experience.

Yet this achievement cannot be dissociated entirely from Connolly's continued and vocal concern with the fate of the upper-middle class and his sense of culture as a (justifiably) privileged accomplishment and enjoyment. After *Horizon* closed, he reviewed for the *Sunday Times,* a bastion then of literature as cultivated pleasure. During his editorship of *Horizon,* Connolly favoured, despite his catholicity, the writers of the thirties or that late twenties twilight of aestheticism from which he came. Though he lamented the absence of an *avant-garde,* he was not the man to foster one, and the influence of *Horizon* was strong in reinforcing the upper-middle class cultural values of the late twenties and the thirties.

III

The leading periodicals of the literary movement of the thirties had been Geoffrey Grigson's *New Verse* and John Lehmann's *New Writing.* *New Verse* had ceased publication in 1939, and a last issue of *New Writing* was in preparation when war broke out. It seemed to its editor that *New Writing,* like the literary ideology with which it had been associated, was at an end. However, as things settled down, Lehmann felt that there might still be a place for the half-yearly miscellany *New Writing* had been, but reduced from its pre-war 150,000 words to half that length. In Spring, 1940, *Folios of New Writing* appeared, to be followed by three further issues at six month intervals. For his first issue, Lehmann had many of his old contributors: Henry Green, André Chamson, B.L. Coombes, George Orwell and Stephen Spender. This continuity was to be maintained, though with a changed tone: Lehmann fostered an art largely realist, with an emphasis on the interaction of individual and society, but Left-wing assumptions were gone, even if a radical stance survived.

With the fall of France, there came an end to literary contributions from the continent, and *New Writing*'s old international character seemed about to be lost. However, in 1941, Lehmann brought out a new miscellany, *Daylight,* in collaboration with Czech writers in exile in London. This was successful, but ran for only one issue, after which it was combined with *Folios* under the title *New Writing and Daylight,* which endeavoured to maintain an international character through eight issues, until its close in 1946.

The most important *New Writing* venture started when Allen Lane suggested that his Penguin Books might bring out a selection from the pre-war *New Writing*. After investigation, it was decided that there should be two selections; but, before the second had appeared, it was decided that *Penguin New Writing* should be a monthly that would also include new contributions. The new features were initially mainly topical: "The Way We Live Now"; Stephen Spender's "Books and the War"; and "Shaving Through the Blitz" by "Fanfarlo" (G.W. Stonier). However, work by new writers, such as Alun Lewis and Laurie Lee, began to appear. After twelve issues, it was decided that *Penguin New Writing* should become a quarterly, reorganised to consist principally of new contributions. The first issue appeared in June, 1942, and it quickly became the most notable forum for new writers of the decade. It retained the old "reporting" flavour of the thirties with its "Report on Today"—(later "The Living Moment", until it was dropped after the war for lack of suitable material). "Books and the War" became "Book Front", a section of critical articles that was continued as "The Critical View" up to the last issue. Theatre, Dance, Film and Music criticism were introduced, as well as Art criticism, with supporting reproductions.

Penguin New Writing ran as a quarterly—or as near as production difficulties would permit—until 1950. By that time, its parent *New Writing and Daylight* had closed down; while *Orpheus,* a miscellany Lehmann brought out in 1948 and 1949 under his own imprint, had ceased after two issues. A volume of *Penguin New Writing* was about 150 pages in length and sold for sixpence, up to its nineteenth issue, when the price rose to ninepence. With a new and expanded format in 1946, the price was a shilling, and the last issues sold for one and sixpence. At the height of its success, in the immediate post-war period, the first printing was 100,000, and it no doubt had many more readers. When it closed, with its fortieth number in 1950, circulation was below 40,000, and insufficient to support a mass circulation miscellany of its type (though still extraordinary for a literary periodical).

It had had a remarkable reception, and the sudden decline was one of the saddening features of the coming of peace. It had no doubt been helped by the wartime shortage of reading material and the great demand among those isolated by the war for something to read. Yet much more is needed to explain the success of a periodical that made no attempt to cater to even middle-brow tastes. People had been thrown back on themselves, their lives had been disrupted, and sudden death had been a possibility for many. The demand for something that would afford a basis for personal reflection was what the war had created, and *Penguin New Writing* had met the demand.

Penguin New Writing was followed by other paper-back miscel-

lanies, such as Reginald Moore's *Modern Reading* or Robin
Maugham's *Convoy*. However, *Penguin New Writing* was something
more than an attempt to offer a quarterly collection of serious reading.
Lehmann, through his "Armoured Writer" series in *New Writing and
Daylight* and his "Forewords" in *Penguin New Writing*, showed a
developing editorial attitude that controlled what was printed in his
miscellanies and gave them the defined character that is needed to
exert influence. "If one compares," he wrote, "the stories and
sketches that are being written to-day with those that were typical of
ten years ago, one can by now see that the centre of balance has
shifted from a rather extravert, documentary type of realism, to something more introvert . . ." (*PNW*, 14, 7) He speaks of "the desire to
create a modern myth" (*NW&D*, Summer 1942, 160) and of "the
absence of a generally accepted myth or system of beliefs . . . a myth
whose wholeness would heal the wound between war and peace-time
occupation, between the past and present, between one class and
another. . . ." (*PNW*, 19, 7) In introducing his new miscellany in
1948, he wrote: "*Orpheus* will . . . choose what is visionary rather
than what is merely realistic . . . The deep need today is to assert the
lyrical and imaginative spirit against materialism and the pseudo-sci-
ences . . ." (*Orpheus I*, vi) He saw the wartime writing of his own
generation as containing "the suggestion of deeper and often terrifying
truths of our historic existence" (*NW&D*, Autumn 1944, 171).
Nevertheless, he found himself unable to hail many of the new generation writers in the way that Herbert Read had, and lamented "a rather
glib and cliché-ridden sentimentality." (*NW&D*, Winter 1942-43, 167)
In spite of his recognition of a growing visionary quality in the writing
of the forties, he had—correctly—a very low opinion of the poetry of
the Apocalypse movement, and felt too that even such comparatively
steady writers as Anne Ridler, G.S. Fraser, Norman Nicholson, Keidrych Rhys and Alun Lewis (all of whom he published) had "reached
a crossroads where their future development is in doubt." (*NW&D*
Winter 1942-43, 169-170) In the same piece he praised the work of
W.R. Rodgers, Laurie Lee, Peter Yates, Roy Fuller, Demetrious
Capetenakis and Terrence Tiller. Lee, Yates, Fuller and Tiller, along
with Henry Reed, Alan Ross and Lawrence Little, were to be the poets
whose work he consistently promoted, both in his miscellanies, and,
in the case of Lee, Fuller and Tiller, through publication by the
Hogarth Press, of which he was a partner.
   The list of poets defines the type of poetry that Lehmann supported:
controlled, unrhetorical, humanist, grounded in personal experience,
and, above all, perceptive and sensitive. The same may be said of the
new writers of fiction whom he most consistently encouraged: William

Sansom and Denton Welch. It was through this style of writing that so many contributors were to define their experience of the war. Its qualities are exemplified in H.B. Mallalieu's "Landscape" from *New Writing and Daylight* for winter 1942-43:

> So questioning, we pass
> From hill to road towards the village street;
> Planning our obstacles, laying traps to meet
> The possible enemy. We read the landscape thus.
> Yet as we leave, it has another word for us.
> The finches' chorus plays above the map:
> Light rains through trees like gold. A gap
> Between the pines leads back our martialled thought.
> The eye translates the features we have caught
> In the false language we are bound to speak.
> But dumb the sunlight falls across this peak.

Lehmann attempted to retain for *New Writing and Daylight* what he could of the pre-war European flavour by publishing the work of exiled writers. Among the most remarkable of these was the Greek writer, Demetrios Capetanakis, who died at the age of thirty-two in 1944. He wrote almost exclusively in English. He left a volume of powerful literary essays preceded by his few poems. In writing of Dostoevsky he said:

> There are two kinds of writers: those whose world is protected by a hedge, and whose truths are unambiguous, and those whose world is not protected by anything against the powers of nothingness, and whose truths are bound to be ambiguous, since, for them, there is no line of demarcation between the things which are and the things which are not.[10]

His poems are undoubtedly the work of a writer who senses himself unprotected "against the powers of nothingness"; and their "ambiguousness" seems to express with stark immediacy the ambiguous relation of victim and perpetrator that we all have to evil:

> My brother Cain, the wounded, liked to sit
> Brushing my shoulder, by the staring water
> Of life, or death, in cinemas half-lit
> By scenes of peace that always turned to slaughter.
>
> He liked to talk to me. His eager voice
> Whispered the puzzle of his bleeding thirst,
> Or prayed me not to make my final choice,
> Unless we had a chat about it first.
>
> And then he chose the final pain for me.
> I do not blame his nature: he's my brother;

Nor what you call the times: our love was free,
Would be the same at any time; but rather

The ageless ambiguity of things
Which makes our life mean death, our love be hate.
My blood that streams across the bedroom sings:
"I am my brother opening the gate!"

("Abel")

In their directness and economy, such poems remind one of Emily
Dickinson, whom Capetanakis was before his time in admiring. They
seem to arise from a feeling, which grew commoner as the war progressed, that the horror witnessed throughout Europe must spring from
something endemic to the human condition.

The achievement of the *New Writing* publications—and particularly
of *Penguin New Writing*—is perhaps greater in retrospect than it appeared at the time. It is not merely that a literary periodical of class
attained enormous circulation and was seriously read by an even
greater number of people than bought it: *Penguin New Writing,* like
the *New Writing* of the thirties, remains extremely readable today. It
did not bring together the work of an exciting and influential group of
new writers, as did its predecessor: in the thirties Lehmann was a
member of such a group; while, in the forties, one of the depressing
things was that such a group did not seem to exist. Yet Lehmann
could claim quite rightly, in introducing his anthology *Poems from
New Writing* in 1946, "that it contains . . . a high proportion of the
outstanding poems that were written between the beginning of the
Spanish Civil War and the end of the European War, perhaps higher
than any other single editor can proudly stick as feathers in his cap."[11]
He had published the continuing work of poets of his own generation;
he had encouraged by regular publication the work of some of the
better newer poets, particularly of Roy Fuller; and he had given publication, in the course of the decade, to the work of over a hundred
poets in all. The wartime selection of fiction had been less remarkable
and had included fewer new writers of notable talent—a reflection of a
situation in which few people had the leisure for extended writing.
During its years of publication, *Penguin New Writing* may have
seemed the intellectual poor relation of *Horizon,* because it did not set
out to frighten its readers into attention with extended articles on arcane foreign writers; but the large number of critical articles Lehmann
published have stood up very well.

An international flavour had been maintained throughout the years
of wartime isolation, and, after the war, new American writing was
introduced. Lehmann never showed signs of the "French 'flu" that
was a mark of *Horizon* and the Sunday papers and of the upper-middle

class cultural milieu with which they were associated. Indeed, the decided Englishness of *Penguin New Writing* stands out today. In this respect one can also perceive its limitations, which were the limitations of the period and of the middle class that produced nearly all the writers of the day. Perceptiveness and sensitivity gave the tone to the writing published in Lehmann's miscellanies. In England there were few of the devasting upheavals that resulted in a questioning of fundamental assumptions concerning human nature in continental Europe. An assured sense of the pattern of human behaviour led to writing in which sensitivity seemed cultivated for its own sake as the quality that differentiated artists from other members of society. What was absent was the circumspection and robustness that could come from a stance that permitted the questioning of assumptions concerning human decency and other values. Such questioning, in terms of a more radical sociological perspective, was to be a feature of the writing of the fifties. Lehmann reflected faithfully the decade in which he worked in a body of publication that is enduringly representative. His periodicals gave a powerful steering to the writing of the decade.

IV

It may seem perverse to consider *Scrutiny* part of the critical establishment of the forties. The sense of the beleaguerment of intelligent criticism in the modern world was with it from the start. The "Manifesto" in its first number had stated, "The general dissolution of standards is commonplace." (I, 1 (May, 1932) 2) Looking back, "After Ten Years", in 1942, its editor saw *Scrutiny* as "consciously appealing to the idea that it was more than ever the *raison d'etre* of the university to be, amid the material pressures and dehumanising complications of the modern world, a focus of humane consciousness." (X, 4 (Apr, 1942) 327) As the forties progressed, the feeling of beleaguerment was exacerbated by a sense that *Scrutiny* was deliberately ignored by the metropolitan literary establishment that saw the values guarded by *Scrutiny* as a danger to its influence: "the contemporary literary world is controlled by a system of personal and institutional relations that, pursuing its own ends, is inevitably hostile both to the play of criticism, and to the emergence and recognition of the new and significant." ("Mr. Pryce-Jones, the British Council and British Culture") (XVIII, 3 (Winter, 1951-52) 225) In fact, of course, as the "Valedictory" in the final number protested, *Scrutiny* had "an established classical status" and had had a wide academic influence. (XIX, 4 (Oct, 1953) 255) Indeed, by the late forties, there can have been no periodical with such influence on students of English literature, either directly, or through books like Leavis's *Revaluation* (1936) or L.C. Knights' *Explorations* (1947). Among those who felt the influence of *Scrutiny* were many of the poets who were to appear in the anthology *New Lines* (1956), and young critics and academics such as Laurence Lerner, A. Alvarez and W.W. Robson. By the time *Scrutiny* closed in October, 1953, its views were close to being an influential and widely received orthodoxy, a fact attested by a reading of almost any part of the seven volume *Pelican Guide to English Literature* that began publication in 1954.

The lack of standards in the metropolitan literary establishment was responsible, in *Scrutiny*'s view, for the increasingly unsatisfactory state of contemporary writing: "has there ever been a time when the young aspirant, graduating from his university group, could immediately and without any notable sense of change find himself in a fraternity that effectively 'ran' contemporary letters—'ran' them so effectively that he could make a name and career without even coming in sight of adult standards?" ("Retrospect of a Decade" IX, 1 (Jun, 1940) 72) This diagnosis was an extension of one of the periodical's initial positions that "there is no public of Common Readers with whom the critic can rejoice to concur" (I, 1 (May, 1932) 4)—no informed body of readers whose discernment would provide a resistance to the modish promotion of untried literary products. *Scrutiny* had been, initially, a champion of modern writing in the face of an establishment that dismissed the new with crass imperceptiveness. It had championed the work of T.S. Eliot—and would continue to do so. It had praised the early work of Ronald Bottrall, William Empson and W.H. Auden, and it had published poems by Bottrall and reviews by Auden. After 1933, with the publication of *New Country*, an anthology that made explicit the Left-wing orientation of many of the new poets and the Marxist criteria that were to be the basis of literary judgement among them, there was a disenchantment with the new poetry and a hardening of attitude towards it. By the end of the decade, *Scrutiny* could state: "there was never . . . any hesitation . . . about our anti-Marxism"; and, looking back on a "Marxist decade", it found that, although the "nineteen-thirties started with a Poetic Renascence . . . at their close one is driven to judge that the making available of Isaac Rosenberg . . . was a more important event in English poetry than any emergence of a new poet." (IX, 1 (Jun, 1940) 70-71)

It is not the judgement itself that is so disturbing, but the fact that, in *Scrutiny*'s influential decade, it was echoed by so many of its writers, as a noticeable element of ventriloquism entered into the reviewing. Established judgements were applied to new volumes; and new publications were often approached primarily as symptoms of shared diagnoses concerning the malaise of metropolitan culture quoted above. Exemplary is R.G. Leinhardt's review of Auden's *For the Time Being* (1945)—"Auden's Inverted Development".

> Few poets can have started writing with such superficial promise of accomplishment, have developed so completely their early weaknesses, and shelved so definitely their early strength . . . He has thus undergone an inverted process of development, natural enough in a poet impervious to criticism from outside the group which formed his ideal public, and which existed on a basis of mutual admiration which a more independent poet would have found an embarrassment.

"The Sea and the Mirror" is recognised as "the more successful" poem, but "the allegorical figures have such a wide possible field of reference" that they make "the meaning too dependent on individual construction." (XIII, 2 (Sep, 1945) 138-42) There is no suggestion of the religious nature of the poem, nor any sense of the power and brilliance of poems like "Alonso".

The watchdog approach is exemplified by the treatment of Henry Reed's *A Map to Verona* (1946). In Autumn 1944, Geoffrey Walton mentioned with approval Reed's "Iseult Blanchesmains"—in fact a rather precious, literary poem—in contrast to some poems he had under review. (XII, 4 (Autumn, 1944) 310-321) In December, 1946, Reed's book became the subject of a diagnostic analysis of its shortcomings, on the basis of the favourable comparisons that had been drawn between Reed's work and that of Eliot. (XIV, 2 (Dec, 1946) 141-5) It is certainly true that many of the volumes reviewed—such as Henry Treece's *Invitation and Warning* (1942) and Paul Potts' *Instead of a Sonnet* (1945)—warranted the dismissal they received. *Scrutiny* reviewers were right to see in Auden's *New Year Letter* (1941) and *The Age of Anxiety* (1948) a fatal gap between intention, form and artistic accomplishment. Yet it is not unfair to say that, taking the reviewing of poetry as a whole in *Scrutiny* in the nineteen-forties, the paucity of approval seems to point to a readiness to disapprove. When W.H. Mellers, throughout his review of Louis MacNeice's *Autumn Journal* (1939), refers to it as *Autumnal Journey*, one can only attribute the carelessness to disrespect and irritation. (VIII, 1 (Jun, 1939) 117-128) Bottrall continued to be treated with respect, though the reservations were more pronounced as the decade progressed.

Scrutiny's championing of "standards" was, by its nature, directed towards the reading public rather than towards the artistic community, in so far as they are separate. Had *Scrutiny* been, as it was first intended to be, an outlet for creative as well as critical writing, one wonders what the editors would have found to publish. Despite the subtlety with which the notion of "standards" is defined in relation to the innovative genius of artists like Eliot and Lawrence, there is not the overt acceptance that the nature and development of post-Romantic art has been such as to make the existence of shared standards unlikely. Indeed, in *Scrutiny's* nostalgic reverence for the seventeenth century, there is a recognition that the lamented decline is a symptom of deeper cultural changes. What is not recognised, as it is not recognised in even Eliot's most distinguished criticism, is that the absence of shared cultural assumptions is an inevitable condition of modern artistic life.

Scrutiny's stance was essentially conservative; and its immediate targets included the Northcliffe press, dedicated to nothing but the raising of circulation, and an upper-middle class literary establishment that it saw to be intent, above all, on retaining its own influence by the cultivation of the modishly acceptable. It looked back to the immediate past when a still affluent middle class supported journals of independent standards that could influence an opinion forming elite. In the forties one senses an unspoken recognition by *Scrutiny's* editors that little can be done for contemporary writing. With the end of the war, *Scrutiny,* like *Horizon,* ran articles on the work of Sartre and Camus; but the central achievement of the periodical in this decade is the consolidation and filling out of its sense of the canon of classic English literature, as seen in essays that came to make up volumes like Leavis's *The Great Tradition* (1948), L.C. Knights' *Explorations* (1947) and John Spiers' *Chaucer the Maker* (1951), and in the many articles on Shakespeare. It was this work, along with Leavis's earlier *Revaluation,* that was so influential and that led not merely to widespread admiration of *Scrutiny's* critical standards and methods, but also to the adoption of its critical valuations. This influence was a largely salutory one; and, in the case of the poets who appeared in *New Lines,* one that was fruitful creatively. The emphasis was a moral one, and the preference it elicited was for art that moved towards conscious elucidation. In this *Scrutiny* was in the main English tradition. Nevertheless, *Scrutiny's* influence, even where it did not give rise to a new orthodoxy, was ultimately unfriendly to any rich artistic development, just because of its innately puritanical demand that art should measure up, meet standards, provide resolutions, and be not self-indulgent but self-critical. Such demands seem impeccable. Yet, for all Leavis's sensitive awareness that the poem is "not thought of, but possessed imaginatively in its concreteness, so that, as it grows in specificity, it in turn possesses the poet's mind and commands expression" ("Tragedy and the Medium", XII, 4 (Autumn, 1944) 252), the insistence on "standards" seems to imply an artistic process altogether too deliberate. There is too little recognition of the situation of the artist, caught between what he feels impelled to do and the things he has talent to do, attempting to make his abilities and proclivities match a sense of things that must in part remain numinous.

V

While *Horizon* and the *New Writing* publications grew to dominate the periodical publication of new literature in the forties, no publisher came to have such an important role for books of poetry. The paper shortage made wartime book publication a sellers market, and poetry of quality appeared under many imprints. Nevertheless, a few publishers were responsible for the appearance of the majority of volumes of anything more than passing interest. Faber and Faber had, before the war, established a preeminence as publishers of contemporary poetry. Their director, T.S. Eliot, had encouraged and accepted the early work of W.H. Auden, Louis MacNeice, Stephen Spender, George Barker and Charles Madge (though he had passed over C. Day Lewis and Dylan Thomas). The Faber list continued to grow more impressive into the fifties, though largely not because of the newcomers. Indeed, after 1940, there was a decided conventionality in many of the editorial choices; and, in so far as Faber books carried prestige, the new publications asserted a conservative influence.

More adventurous was Herbert Read, an acknowledged influence on the new poets of romantic or anarchistic leaning, whom he published in the very slim volumes of wartime paper that appeared in Routledge's "Broadway House" series: J.F. Hendry, Norman McCaig, George Woodcock, Alex Comfort. He also encouraged the young poets at Oxford in the early forties, and put out books by John Heath-Stubbs and Sidney Keyes. The influence of *New Writing* was felt in the volumes published by John Lehmann, first from the Woolf's Hogarth Press and then under his own imprint. He published the work of writers strongly featured in his periodicals: Terence Tiller, Roy Fuller, Laurie Lee and Alan Ross.

The most voluminous publishers of poetry in the forties were two of the most outrageous: Tambimuttu of *Poetry London;* and R.A. Caton of the Fortune Press. Tambimuttu was a charismatic devotee of contemporary poetry; there is no evidence that Caton liked modern poetry at all. Tambimuttu, erratic in business to the point of losing manuscripts, accepted far more books than he or his early supporters Nicholson and Watson could handle. Nevertheless, he published volumes—in many cases the first—by Kathleen Raine, Nicholas Moore, David Gascoyne, G.S. Fraser, Keith Douglas, W.S. Graham, Michael Hamburger, Bernard Spencer, David Wright and Anne Ridler. His activities as publisher, less than successful financially, constituted the most extensive opportunity for new directions in poetry in the decade.

Caton, who began with fine printing and erotica, turned to publishing poetry on consignment in the late thirties. Fortune Press books were poorly produced, and their appearance in a variety of shades of binding for one book attests to their having been bound as occasion demanded. A standard arrangement was for an author to purchase 120 copies of his book, and the unbound sheets left when the press was sold might indicate that often few further copies got bound. Caton began the war with a large stock of paper and was able to use un-rationed hand-made paper for his short runs. Fortune Press poetry was seldom found in bookstores, though the books were often reviewed and wartime library purchases may have been good. However, among Caton's earliest volumes were Roy Fuller's *Poems* (1939) and Julian Symons's *Confusions about "X"* (1939). Books by other contributors to Symons's *Twentieth Century Verse* appeared as "The Fortune Poets". Caton also put out Henry Treece's *38 Poems* and the anthology, *The New Apocalypse* in 1939. In 1945 he produced *Poetry from Oxford in Wartime* and canvassed all the contributors for individual volumes. Perhaps this slate of beginners accounts for the fact that Caton's list eventually included Nicholas Moore, Tambimuttu, Gervase Stewart, Drummond Allison, William Bell, Kingsley Amis, Philip Larkin, Christopher Middleton, Arthur Boyars, Ronald Duncan and John Waller. He even bought *18 Poems* (originally published by David Archer's Parton Press) from the always down-in-the-pocket Dylan Thomas for £15, and continued to print it without any indication of how many impressions it went through. Caton died well to do: many of his publications are collectors' items. Yet most of them, when read, leave one unsurprised that regular commercial publishers were reluctant to take them.

None of these publishing ventures asserted the cultural influence that the Faber list had before the war, or that it continued to have during the war through its publication of Auden, MacNeice and Spender. The collapse of the wartime interest in poetry, along with rising costs of book production, left the publication of poetry in disarray when the war was over. Of all the series mentioned in this section, only Faber's continued actively after 1950.

VI

The conjunction in this chapter of Connolly, Lehmann and Leavis may seem a strange one. *Horizon* and *New Writing* came in for their share of *Scrutiny* disdain, if for no other reason than their considerable influence. Yet *Horizon* and *Scrutiny*, symptomatically, lament the parlous state of the arts in Britain in the forties, and both look back to better conditions that prevailed in the Edwardian era. While Connolly's conception of an ideal condition for the production of the arts would seem to epitomise the *rentier* role so despised by *Scrutiny*, both periodicals deplored the decline of serious literary journalism as a cultural support to creative literature and as an avenue of employment for the creative writer. They also both saw themselves as having a mission to maintain culture in a dark hour; and in this respect both were strongly concerned with the prevalent level of taste. Their importance for the poetry of the decade lay in the extent to which they conditioned its cultural ambience. *Horizon* published new writing extensively, while *Scrutiny* did not; but the power of *Horizon* lay very much in its implicit or explicit critical role.

This cannot be said to the same degree of Lehmann, whose readiness to encourage what was promising without hindrance of too many preconceived ideas has been one of his notable strengths as an editor. He published John Wain's essay on William Empson, a formative precursor of "Movement" orientations, in the last issue of *Penguin New Writing;* though he never published the Apocalypse poets. *New Writing and Daylight* and *Penguin New Writing* exerted an enormous influence through the quality of writing they published. The strength of the influence came from the esteem they generated: the nature of the influence came from the character of the writing Lehmann favoured. The same may be said of *Horizon,* though the British writing that it published had a less decided character. Between them, Connolly and Lehmann commanded the best contributions from writers of their generation—writers whose growing reputation in the forties made them increasingly the standard of judgement of all new writing. In this respect the two periodicals constituted an "establishment". The unacknowledged mutation of *Scrutiny* from outcast to "establishment" took place in the latter part of the decade: its influence on students of English literature was often evangelistic, and it was felt by younger writers like John Wain and D.J. Enright, who, for the greater part of the decade, struggled to find an idiom in a cultural environment whose antipathetic qualities were steadily defined by *Scrutiny*.

The role of *Horizon, New Writing and Daylight, Penguin New Writing* and *Scrutiny* contrasts with that of *Poetry London, Now* and *Wales* and many other "little magazines" of the forties. The policy of these periodicals derived from changes they wished to bring about in creative writing or the cultural situation in which it was produced. Their influence on the literature of the day was designedly and rightly partisan. The influence of *Scrutiny* and *Horizon* in contrast was on the reading public and was on the whole conservative. *Horizon* and the *New Writing* publications helped entrench literary valuations from the thirties. By 1950 the leading poets of that decade were established literary figures. The forties left no powerful group of writers to challenge them. Few of the poets who had started careers in the last years of the thirties or in the early forties were to publish books of poetry after 1953. Of those who came of age in the forties, several, like Sidney Keyes and Keith Douglas were dead by 1950, while others, like Philip Larkin, had still to establish a firm idiom. Only G.S. Fraser and Julian Symons, from their generation, were to make a lasting contribution to literary journalism in the fifties and after. Tambimuttu of *Poetry London* and George Woodcock of *Now* had both ceased their editorial work (and in fact had left England). *Horizon, Penguin New Writing* and *Scrutiny* saw the decade to its end; and, though they were all edited by writers whose stances had been formed in the nineteen-thirties, they continued to set the literary tone for the aspiring intellectual reader. They concerned themselves passionately, if often antagonistically, with the writing of the forties; yet they also constituted an establishment under whose shadow that writing developed.

In 1950, under the pressure of declining circulation and rising costs, *Horizon* and *Penguin New Writing* ceased publication, to be followed in 1953 by *Scrutiny*. There seemed nothing ready to replace them. It was a time of creative uncertainty for Auden and MacNeice; and, with the death of Dylan Thomas and the virtual cessation of publication of poetry by Stephen Spender, only writers of an older generation, Edwin Muir and Robert Graves, seemed to offer valuable creative examples. Scarcely any of the literary periodicals begun in the forties were still appearing; and no group of younger writers remained with established reputations to carry valuations into the succeeding period. F.R. Leavis, in the midst of growing acclaim, still contrived to speak like a disdained prophetic voice. It was the influence of *Scrutiny,* growing unnoticed in the forties, that carried over with power into the fifties.

Chapter 3

THE COURSE OF BRITISH MODERNISM

The Course of British Modernism—Lawrence Durrell
—Henry Reed, Terence Tiller—G.S. Fraser

The groupings of qualities associated with the modern movement in poetry at the beginning of this century are hard to delineate and have only recently begun to be characterised with dispassionate accuracy. In 1940 they were far from clear. Terms like "classical", "romantic", "traditional", "revolutionary", "objective", "imagistic" were used with a variety of meanings and were frequently slogans rather than terms of criticism. There was no clear picture of the English reaction to the new developments—as opposed to a French or German or American one—and no awareness of how American were many of the modernist tendencies in poetry written in English.

Since 1950 there has been a growing clarification of these matters. One can see a clear relationship between the poetry of T.S. Eliot and the poetry of the writers who came together in *New Signatures,* just as one can see an equally clear relationship between the poetry of the thirties and that written by some of the contributors of *New Lines.* The changes defined by these relationships help to characterise the peculiarly British developments from the Anglo-American revolution in poetry that, for a time, had its focus in the Imagist movement. Such a characterisation was made by A. Alvarez in *The Shaping Spirit* (1958).[1]

The poetry of the forties seems not to belong. The whipping boy of *New Lines,* it emerges as an aberration from an age of mistakes. This is in part due to the large quantity of inferior verse that got into print during the decade, and in part to the fact that many writers of the period adopted the slogan "A New Romanticism"—a phrase that recalled the literary disparagements of the early days of Anglo-American modernism. T.E. Hulme had associated Imagism with classicism, and had called Romanticism "spilt religion".[2] T.S. Eliot had characterised his views as "classicist in literature, royalist in politics, and anglo-catholic in religion"[3] in 1929 and had spoken in 1919 against the conception of poetry as "a turning loose of emotions".[4] W. H. Auden, Louis MacNeice and Geoffrey Grigson had emphasised the common sense element in poetry and had called for poetry to have a social or non-personal orientation. At the beginning of the war, Julian

Symons wrote in the *Kenyon Review:* ". . . the end of *New Verse* is
the end, for this time, of the movement towards commonsense standards in English letters. It is axiomatic that "commonsense" has little
chance in a war: and it is obvious too that inflation of language and
sentiment is as certain in wartime as inflation of prices."[5] It is true,
of course, that the forties did see an inflation of language and sentiment; but Symon's remarks are clearly polemical, as have been many
of the accepted characterisations of the poetry of the forties.

Unfortunately such a perspective is still assumed by many concerning the development of British poetry in the forties. Reaction to the
"political" poetry of the thirties is seen as leading to an unfortunate
return of "romanticism" (so out of fashion in the inter-war years). In
fact, it is impossible to regard the poetry of George Barker, Dylan
Thomas and David Gascoyne as a reaction to the poetry of *New Signatures* and *New Country,* the defining anthologies of the social-realist
poetry of the thirties. The second, and decidedly more political, of
these anthologies had been out only a short time when the first books
by Barker and Thomas appeared. Nor can the early work of these
writers be seen as discontinuous with early modernist poetry. Barker
remained a devoted admirer of T.S. Eliot; and one of Thomas's earliest published poems, "That sanity be kept . . ." (1933) is an imitation of Eliot. Barker, Thomas and Gascoyne all wrote imagistic poems
of distorted syntax, in accordance with early modernist precept and
example, to a degree that Auden and MacNeice did not. It was Mac-
Neice who, in 1939, wrote "Subject in Modern Poetry", recognising
his departure from the modernist dogma that a poem is not about anything.[6] Gascoyne, in his early poetry was an exponent of free verse
and of surrealism. In many respects, these young writers were more
"modern" than the *New Signatures* poets, though they did not aggressively employ non-traditional industrial images. It was for his traditional imagery and his preoccupation with the "eternal" topics of
poetry that Dylan Thomas was hailed by Edith Sitwell in 1936; though
anything less traditional, in some respects, than his "sonnets" in
Twenty-five Poems is hard to conceive.

A distortion of judgement arises from the identification of Anglo-
American modernism with one of its unstated prescriptions: that poetry
should be ironic. The estimation is reflected in some of Eliot's essays,
though in few from his formative period. Nevertheless, irony is a feature of the rhetoric and vision of much of the influential writing of
Eliot and Pound. The recognition of irony as the definitive modern
tone is found in the influential critical writing of I.A. Richards, Allen
Tate, Cleanth Brooks and F.R. Leavis, and throughout the post-war
years. Yet, in the broader perspective of European modernism, irony

is by no means an all pervasive feature. It is ever-present in the poetry of Cavafy, but it is inimical to most of Rilke's writing. The work of Apollinaire, Eluard and the surrealists, despite the associations with Da-Da, and despite the use, at times, of intentionally shocking imagery, does not proceed with the guarded sense of the possible other view, that readiness to protect or even puncture one's own afflatus, that we find in so much Anglo-American modernism.

European modernism had little influence on the development of poetry in England. This is true even of the Surrealist movement. Yet, if we characterise Surrealism and the type of writing out of which it grew as "visionary" modernism (in contrast with the "ironic" Anglo-American modernism) we can see the poetry of Barker, Thomas and Gascoyne as being in that stream. Gascoyne's early poetry is consciously surrealist; and, though Thomas, for instance, explicitly denied any likeness of his work to surrealism,[7] Gascoyne's work does not stand entirely alone in British poetry. Rodger Roughton's periodical, *Contemporary Poetry and Prose,* published from May, 1936 to autumn 1937, was one of Britain's few Surrealist periodicals. It contained work by Kenneth Allott, David Gascoyne, Dylan Thomas and Humphrey Jennings. It was published from Parton Street, the home of the communist publishers, Lawrence and Wishart, and of David Archer's famous bookshop. Parton Street is lovingly recalled by George Barker[8] as a place where one might encounter the younger writers of the *avant garde* like Gascoyne, Thomas and Charles Madge in the mid-thirties.

While it would be wrong to see *Contemporary Poetry and Prose* as seminal in the literature of the period, it is nevertheless symptomatic of the leanings of many younger writers of its day—those who were born between 1912 and 1918 and who came of age during the thirties. There is an interest in the irrational in the arts, and a personal, introspective orientation (though Roughton took a doctrinaire Communist stand in his few editorial statements). Several small periodicals of like character appeared towards the end of the thirties. *Janus,* edited by Reginald Hutchins and John Royston Morley, appeared for a couple of issues in 1936 with pieces by a number of *Contemporary Poetry and Prose* contributors. *Delta* (a continuation of *The Booster*—kidnapped by Henry Miller from the American Country Club in Paris) contained contributions by Lawrence Durrell (under a variety of names) as well as work by Miller, Alfred Perlès and Anaïs Nin; while *Seven,* published from summer 1938 to spring 1940 by Nicholas Moore and John Garland, also contained writing by Miller, Nin and Durrell (including excerpts from his surrealist, *The Black Book*), as well as work of the Apocalypse group. These periodicals contrast with *Twentieth Century Verse* and the wartime *Now,* which continued the orientation of *New Writing* and *New Verse*. Between them, these two groups of periodicals sum up important tendencies among younger writers at the end of the thirties.

Seven can be seen as the cradle of the Apocalypse movement, which one of its members G.S. Fraser called "a dialectical development of Surrealism".[9] These poets did see themselves as reacting against a poetic of the "object image", which they identified with *New Verse*. The movement included J.F. Hendry and Henry Treece—both older than Thomas, Barker or Gascoyne. With its notion of the transformation of man's relationship to society by a recognition of the role of myth in that relationship, Apocalypse was very much of the thirties. By 1943 it had finished as a movement, fading into what termed itself the "new romanticism".

"Romanticism" was invoked variously as an ideal by many poets of the forties who disliked the dominant poetry of the previous decade. Sidney Keyes, introducing a collection of new poets from Oxford in 1941—*Eight Oxford Poets,* said "we are all . . . Romantic writers"; Vernon Watkins and Kathleen Raine—writers of the previous generation who did not feel at home with the poetry of the thirties—saw their allegiances as "romantic"; Alex Comfort, in his essay, "Art and Social Responsibility", wrote in 1944:

> The classic sees man as master and the romantic as victim of his environment . . . It is as if awareness of death, the factor which, at root, determines the degree to which we feel masters of our circumstances, ebbed and flowed, alternatively emphasised and obscured as a factor in interpretive art . . . The active periods with their extroverted public alternate with ages when the realization of the Tragic Sense becomes general . . . The socialist poets attempted to deny the awareness and to turn to society, but in Spain the face of the unpleasant black figure was unveiled . . . Dylan Thomas knew it early in life, long before the Spanish defeat.[10]

Comfort's remarks point to fundamental changes of attitude that lay behind the change in literary orientation. In the thirties, the emphasis had been on the manipulation and improvement of the world: in the forties, in the face of the enormities of the war, it was on acceptance. This is exemplified in the acknowledged masterpieces of the period, such as Eliot's *Four Quartets,* as well as in the writing of new poets; it showed itself in the growing admiration for writers like Rilke, Yeats and Kierkegaard. C. Day Lewis, a decided Marxist in the thirties, explored childhood experience as an earnest of meaning in a wartime sonnet sequence, "O Dreams, O Destinations". Many had never liked modern poetry and were happy to welcome the return of more traditional styles and attitudes. Poets such as Anne Ridler and Norman

Nicholson, who wrote explicitly religious poetry, appeared. There was a resurgence of regionalist and rural writing. Wrey Gardiner's *Poetry Quarterly* and Tambimuttu's *Poetry London* championed the "new romanticism"; and Tambimuttu declared that "Poetry is an awareness of the mind of the universe." He complained that Geoffrey Grigson had persuaded writers "that poetry in which objects replace emotions . . . was the only poetry worth publishing."[11] This disparagement of *New Verse* and the poets associated with it became widely voiced. Kathleen Raine said that "The shallow blasphemy of the *New Verse* period is gone for good"[12] (though she had been a regular contributor to that periodical). Lawrence Durrell, hardly a self-designated "new romantic" asked, in 1939: "How many of us, turning from the pages of *New Verse* . . . have sighed for a bucket of liquid manure to dash over these elegant and epicene narcissi . . ."[13]

The call for a poetry that was more overtly emotional, that was not afraid to be prophetic, that dealt with the "eternal questions"—this was the common ground of the poets who took or were given the name "romantic" in the forties: Dylan Thomas, George Barker, David Gascoyne, Vernon Watkins, Kathleen Raine, the Apocalypse poets, Sidney Keyes. No doubt this accounted for the popularity with some of them of a very un-English writer, Henry Miller. His British admirers did not perceive Miller's Emersonian attitudes, but they saw his vitality and apprehended him as "a WHOLE man".[14] "Wholeness" and the "organic" was what the father figure of the "new romanticism", Herbert Read, had stood for. During the thirties, Read had been one of the few modernist proponents of Romantic literature. In the forties he encouraged and published the work of the Apocalypse writers—among them J.F. Hendry and Norman McCaig, and that of younger writers of "romantic" leaning, such as Alex Comfort, Sidney Keyes and John Heath-Stubbs. He wrote an introduction to the first "New Romantic" anthology, *Lyra*[15].

Contributors to *Lyra* included some of the Apocalypse poets, but also writers whose work gave a broader and even less defined stylistic sense to the term "new romanticism". Among them was Wrey Gardiner, a poet of Auden's generation, who, in the forties, ran the Grey Walls Press and edited *Poetry Quarterly*. *Poetry Quarterly* had early recognised the "new romanticism", and nearly all the newer poets who could be so designated appeared in it. However, in *Poetry Quarterly*, "new romanticism" got stretched until it almost spelled "old conventionalism". One cannot help feeling that even some of the better contributors were pleased to be able to feel in the forefront of poetry without having to turn their backs on old fashioned "beauty".

The forties are indeed remembered by many as the period of the

Apocalyptics and the "new romantics". The amount of writing produced by them is, on examination, greater even than one remembers.
Their influence was very little. Their sense of their own importance
was the most startling (and irritating) thing about them. A young poet,
Peter Baker, publishing a small set of conventional and rather poor
poems, *The Beggar's Lute,* could write, by way of introduction:
"Poetry should be universal. It should be in touch with the world and
with mankind. Auden, Day Lewis, MacNeice have realised this, but
they have mistaken the trappings and external characteristics of our
twentieth century civilisation for eternal elements of human existence."[16] Far from dominating the literary scene, these writers in fact
found themselves largely excluded from certain parts of it. *Horizon*
readily published the work of Thomas, Barker, Gascoyne, Raine and
Watkins; but hardly anything by their younger poet admirers. John
Lehmann spoke of "quite horribly feeble stuff . . . the sloppy jottings
and rantings of innumerable immature and incoherent pseudo-poets";
and found the Apocalyptics "among the worst offenders".[17] Julian Symons wrote: "I read all the poets of this phoney 'new Renaissance'
with a yawn or a shudder; a yawn for Mr. Litvinoff, a shudder for
Mr. Tambimuttu, a yawn *and* a shudder for Mr. Henry Treece . . ."[18]
Only Dylan Thomas had any marked influence, and that mainly on
the taste of poetry readers.

Indeed, the "new romanticism" was in no sense the vital movement
in British poetry that it proved to be in British art. In the work of
John Piper, Graham Sutherland, Henry Moore, Victor Pasmore and
Paul Nash, it was a central and revitalising development that redis-
covered for British painting its roots in the Romantic period; whereas,
in poetry, the commerce of the "new romanticism" with its Romantic
heritage led frequently to a stale conventionalism.

A more vital continuity in the forties was the continuity with the
poetry of the thirties, which is greater than has been allowed.
Throughout the decade there were those like Roy Fuller, Julian Symons and the poets associated with *Now,* who took as their starting
point the work of Auden and his generation. There were also those,
like Lawrence Durrell, whose work continued the ironic strain of
Anglo-American modernism. A great deal of the war poetry, when
not frankly traditional, takes as its starting point the poetry of the thirties; and irony is a central tone for Keith Douglas and Drummond
Allison. At the close of the decade, when British poetry found itself
in a doldrums, in the decadence of those impulses that had emerged
in the forties, it was in an ironic poetry, in *New Lines,* that renewal
was to be found.

II

The poet of the forties whose work best exemplifies the continuities of modernism is Lawrence Durrell—a friend and admirer of masters as various as T.S. Eliot, Henry Miller and George Seferis. It is hard to recapture how he must have appeared to readers who knew his work in 1949. *The Alexandria Quartet* had not been written, and *The Black Book,* published in Paris in 1938, was banned in England and known to many only from a derogatory remark by F.R. Leavis in *The Great Tradition* (1948). *Cefalu,* a not very distinguished novel, published by Editions Poetry London in 1947, had little circulation, and the existence of the two earliest novels, *Pied Piper of Lovers* (1935) and *Panic Spring* (1937), was hardly suspected. It was as the author of three books of poetry—*A Private Country* (1942), *Cities, Plains and People* (1946) and *On Seeming to Presume* (1948), together with a journal of life in Corfu, *Prospero's Cell* (1945), that Durrell was then known. He seemed an exponent of the sensitive, imagistic poetry produced by so many poets in the forties: to-day his poetry is often seen as the side product of a major novelist.

His earliest publications were poems, including two small collections, *Ten Poems* (1932) and *Transition* (1934), which, while showing a maturing talent, are coventional and without individual voice. It was in *The Black Book* that Durrell "first heard the sound of my own voice"[19]; and it was at about the same time that his authentic voice emerged in poems like "Carol in Corfu" and "Unckebuncke" [sic], contributed to *Seven* and to the Fortune Press anthology, *Proems* (1938).

It is interesting to see Durrell's early mature poetry in the light of his first two mature prose works. *The Black Book* and *Prospero's Cell* can be viewed as the Dionysian and Apollonian reflections of Durrell's preoccupation with what he called in *The Black Book* "the cultural swaddling clothes which I symbolized as the English Death"[20]—a death that involves "the terrible disintegration of action under the hideous pressure of the ideal".[21] This concern with the "English Death" involves themes that were to remain dominant throughout Durrell's work: "It is the endless duel with one's anonymity that weakens one"[22]; "Does the endless iteration of loneliness tire you? It is the one constant in our lives."[23]; "how seldom we realize time . . . it's going through us the whole time . . ."[24]. Durrell found an escape from the "English Death" in his life with his family in Corfu from 1933 on[25]: *Prospero's Cell* draws its material from that life. In "A Landmark Gone", written in 1940 and later incorporated in *Prospero's Cell,* he wrote:

Somewhere between Calabria and Corfu the blue really begins. You feel
the horizon beginning to stain at the rim, the sky seems to come nearer
and into deeper focus; the sea darkens as it uncurls its troughs round the
boat. You are aware not so much of a landscape coming to meet you
invisibly over those blue miles of water as of a climate. Entering Greece
is like entering a dark crystal; the form of things becomes irregular, re-
fracted. Mirages suddenly swallow islands and if you watch you can see
the trembling curtain of the atmosphere. Once in the shadow of the Alba-
nian hills you are aware of this profound change. It haunts you while you
live there, this creeping refraction of light altering with the time of day,
so that you can fall asleep in a valley and awake in Tibet, with all the
landmarks gone.[26]

The Black Book is a surrealist influenced exploration of the emptiness
and loneliness and suffocation of the self endemic in English life as
Durrell then saw it; *Prospero's Cell* offers a counterbalancing exultance in Greek life and the Greek landscape. These two patterns are
repeated in his first commercially published book of poems, *A Private
Country*.

"The Death of General Uncebuncke" [sic] ("Fourteen Carols"
followed by "Five Soliloquies upon the Tomb of Uncebuncke") celebrates the death of an English soldier and colonial administrator.
Durrell had been born in India, and his father had spent his life in the
service of the colonial administration. In its exploration of attitudes to
Durrell's British colonial roots, the poem is related to *The Black
Book*, and in places its tone reminds us of the prose:

> Deliver us from the trauma of death's pupil
> From the forked tongue of devil,
> Deliver us from the vicar's bubonic purple,
> From canine hysteria, the lethal smile
> O deliver us from botanical sleep . . .

But the overall tone is very different from that of *The Black Book:*

> My uncle sleeps in the image of death.
> In the greenhouse and in the potting-shed
> The wrens juncket: the old girl with the trowel
> Is a pillar of salt, insufferably brittle.
> His not to reason why, though a thinking man.

"Not satire but an exercise in ironic compassion", Durrell says in the
head note; and, in a review of *A Private Country* that he wrote himself
for *Personal Landscape*, he drew attention to this as an "adult quality".[27] There is nothing indeed quite like it, except perhaps in Kenneth
Allott's poetry of that period:

> Friends, Humans, Englishmen:
> Officer at the bar and gentleman in bed,
> Kings in your counting-houses, clerks at cricket,
> All you who play in the desperate game,
> Hopes of the side, the tenth wicket,
> Who will certainly be raised to the rank of aunt
> In the new millenium: permit
> The bromoid encomium of the harmonium . . .

The seemingly discordant association of lyricism, nonsense and bathos appears at first satirical, and, on acquaintance, disconcerting; but it is productively disconcerting, pressing us towards a multiple focus on its subject. It shows how fruitful was Durrell's early formed conception of poetic structure as non-logical and as akin to nonsense as to plain sense. No doubt the manner owes something to the small body of English surrealist writing, as found in periodicals like *Contemporary Poetry and Prose;* but the tone constitutes a singular and individual achievement.

Equally individual is the tone of the lyrical poems, so often occasioned by the Greek landscape, and to be found in all of Durrell's mature collections up to *The Tree of Idleness* (1955):

> I, per se I, I sing on.
> Let flesh falter, or let bone break
> Break, yet the salt of the poem holds on,
> Even in empty weather
> When beak and feather have done . . .
>
> O per se O, I sing on.
> Never tongue falters or love lessens,
> Lessens. The salt of the poem lives on
> Like this carol of empty weather
> Now feather and beak have gone.
>
> ("Carol on Corfu")

What is striking is the clarity and buoyancy of the writing. There is little modern English poetry that achieves such a tone of celebration without a trace of the unctuous or the ponderous. "Greek landscapes are, as it were, the co-authors of my poems."[28] In their lucid rendering of physical detail, the poems seem, as Durrell said of George Seferis's poetry, "transparent, seamless"[29]; and one is reminded of Seferis's remark: "There must be something about the light that makes us what we are."[30]

> This unimportant morning
> Something goes singing where

> The capes turn over on their sides
> And the warm Adriatic rides
> Her blue and sun washing
> At the edge of the world and its brilliant cliffs.

The power of these poems to explore experience while remaining so vividly with the sensuous is a reflection of Durrell's feeling of "the universality of the phenomenal world as it presented itself to the Greek thinkers—the universality of its application in thought, in paint, and in poetry."[31] "The salt of the poem lives on/Like this carol of empty weather": implicit in the rendering of the physical is the acceptance of transience as part of the complete experience, fundamental to Greek attitudes and to much modern Greek poetry.

> So the riders of the darkness pass
> On their circuit: the luminous island
> Of the self trembles and waits,
> Waits for us, all, my friends,
> Where the sea's big brush recolours
> The dying lives, and the unborn smile.
>
> ("Fangbrand")

The lyrical bitterness of transience is a note recurrent in Durrell's poetry and in his prose.

The period during which Durrell developed as a poet was a great age for Greek poetry—the period of George Seferis's maturity and of the appearance of Demétrius Antoníou, Odysseus Elytis and Nikos Gátsos. George Katsimbalis and Andreas Kavantonis edited *Ta Nea Grammatica,* in which Sikelianós's best work appeared. Durrell knew Seferis, Katsimbalis and Antoníou—the first two well—and we see him with them in Henry Miller's account of his visit to Greece in 1939, *The Colossus of Maroussi.* Yet his style seems to have been formed in early days in Corfu. Though he admired the gnomic quality that he felt Seferis's poetry shared with that of Valéry[32], his own work does not have the elegiac tone so characteristic of Seferis.

A modern Greek poet with whom Durrell had a good deal in common was Cavafy. Cavafy is a haunting presence in the sensibility of *The Alexandria Quartet.* The sceptical but pained irony of his lyricism must have been congenial to Durrell, who wrote of him:

> And here I find him great. Never
> To attempt a masterpiece of size—
> You must leave life for that. No
> But always to preserve the advantive
> Minute, never to destroy the truth,
> Amid the coarse manipulations of the lie.
>
> ("Cavafy")

Cavafy's spirit is felt in the poems that Durrell wrote in Alexandria, most notably in the "persona" poems, "Conon in Alexandria", where he shares Cavafy's sense of at once belonging and being exiled:

> Ash-heap of four cultures,
> Bounded by Mareotis, a salt lake,
> On which the winter rain rings and whitens,
> In the waters, stiffens like eyes.
>
> I have been four years bound here:
> A time for sentences by the tripod:
> Prophecies by those who were born dead,
> Or who lost their character but kept their taste.
>
> A solitary presumed quite happy,
> Writing those interminable whining letters,
> On the long beaches dimpled by rain,
> Tasting the island wind
>
> Blown against wet lips and shutters out of Rhodes.
> I say 'presumed', but would not have it otherwise.

Cavafy's poems of historical *personae* could have suggested Durrell's "Eternal Contemporaries":

> Four card-players: an ikon of the saint
> On a pitted table among eight hands
> That cough and spit or close like mandibles
> On fortunate court-cards or on the bottle
> Which on the pitted paintwork stands.
> Among them one whose soft transpontine nose
> Fuller of dirty pores pricked on a chart
> Has stood akimbo on the turning world,
> From Cimbalu to Smyrna shaken hands,
> Tasted the depths of every hidden sound:
> In wine or poppy a drunkard with a drunkard's heart
> Who never yet was known to pay his round.
>   ("Dmitri of Carpathos")

For Cavafy, Anthony and other historical figures of Alexandria become contemporaries; for Durrell, the inhabitants of contemporary Greece belong to the same family as characters of Homer: "Ulysses can only be ratified as an historical figure with the help of the fishermen who to-day sit in the smoky tavern of 'The Dragon' playing cards and waiting for the wind to change."[33] The mythical, "heraldic" significance such figures seem to have—contemporary yet eternal, defying time—was a source of reassurance to Durrell, for whom time is the destructive element.

Though the experience of Greece was so important for Durrell's poetry, he did not develop in isolation from the British poetry of his day. "My love on Wednesday letting fall her body/From upright walking won by weariness" ("In Crisis") is suggestive of the poetry of Durrell's friend, George Barker. In a number of poems there is a resemblance to the informal, meditative yet sensuous poetry of place that was Louis MacNeice's forte:

> At Corinth one has forgiven
> The recording travellers in the same past
> Who first entered this land of doors,
> Hunting a precise emotion by clues,
> Haunting a river, or a place in a book.
>
> ("At Corinth")

In *Cities, Plains and People,* it is Auden who is the strengthening (and admitted) influence. Indeed, "Heloise and Abelard", "Fabre" and "Poggio" follow too closely for their own good the pattern and mannerisms of the poems on historical and literary figures in *Another Time* (1940):

> For years slept badly—who does not?
> Took bribes, and drugs, ate far too much and dreamed.
> Married unwisely, yes, but died quite well.
>
> ("Poggio")

The oxymoron in "Took bribes, and drugs" is typical of Auden, though Auden would have omitted the comma, clinching the effect. However, "On First Looking Into Loeb's Horace" is a poem that owes a great deal to Auden and even looks forward to the urbane, meditative poetry of Auden's later years; yet, despite the rather mannered stance implied by the title, it has concerns of its own and a tone impressively individual and authentic:

> All the small-holder's ambitions; the yield
> Of wine-bearing grape, pruning and drainage
> Laid out by laws, almost like the austere
> Shell of his verses—a pattern of Latin thrift;
> Waiting so patiently in a library for
> Autumn and the drying of apples;
> The betraying hour-glass and its deathward drift.

At its most Audenesque, paradoxically, the poem touches Durrell's most lasting concerns:

> Describing clearly a bachelor, sedentary,
> With a fond weakness for bronze-age conversation,
> Disguising a sense of failure in a hatred for the young,

Who built in the Sabine hills this forgery
Of completeness, an orchard with a view of Rome;
Who studiously developed his sense of death
Till it was all around him, walking at the circus,
At the baths, playing dominoes in a shop—
The escape from self-knowledge with its tragic
Imperatives: *Seek, suffer, endure.*

The emptiness from which the Horacean tranquility is an attempted shelter is a central theme in Durrell's writing. The epigraph to *The Tree of Idleness* (1955) is "The notion of emptiness engenders compassion"; and the notion of emptiness is associated with the destructiveness of time: "time is . . . the measure of our death-consciousness"[34]. In "Alexandria", exiled by the war, he looks across the threatening, stormy Mediterranean to the Greek islands that are a continuing emblem of an emotional wholeness unimpaired by the consciousness of time as destroyer. The images of "whirling autumn leaves/Promontaries splashed by the salty sea" epitomise the threatened condition of human experience.

"Time and the ego are the two centres of focus for all contemporary poets with any pretentions to message."[35] "Yet the ego has become diffused, broken down by philosophic and scientific enquiry; what reintegration is possible for the poet in order to recompose the ego, to give it value and shape?"[36] He cites Rimbaud's 'Je est un autre' (used as a title for one of his own poems): "in its very dislocation of the grammatical form it prefigures much that is to come." He finds in the poetry of Rimbaud's time a " 'Semantic Disturbance'—the disturbance of meaning within the structure of language".[37] It is a reaction to "the general philosophic view of subject divorced from object, which is one of the beliefs that haunted" the Victorian age; and in "the Semantic Disturbance you see an attempt being made to join up subject and object, to marry the reality around them and renounce their individual isolation."[38]

This historical discussion illuminates the relation between Durrell's preoccupations with time, isolation and the unification of personality, and the techniques and imagery of his poems. The attainment of stillness and completeness is continually rehearsed in his work, particularly in his most lyrical poems. "In the Garden: Villa Cleobolus" presents the problem of "how to capture, praise or measure/The full round of this simple garden"—a common enough poetic ambition, but one that leads to

        somehow, yes,
To outflank the personal neurasthenia
That lies beyond in each expiring kiss:
Bring joy, as lustrous on this dish

> The painted dancers motionless in play
> Spin for eternity, describing for us all
> The natural history of the human wish.

There are poems too of the crumbling or shattering of unviolated experience, as in "The Swans":

> The procession is over and what is now
> Alarming is more the mirror split
> From end to end by the harsh clap
> Of wooden beaks, than the empty space
> Which follows them about,
> Stained by their whiteness when they pass.

"The ruling passion is for perfection", remarked his friend Alfred Perlès[39]; and the force of this is felt in Durrell's lyrics, some of which bring to mind his admiration for the poems of Paul Valery (in the following case, "Le Pas"):

> Yet as if rising from a still,
> Perfume whispered at the sill,
> All those discarded husks of thought
> Hanging untenanted like gowns,
> Rinds of which the fruit had gone . . .
>
> Still the long chapter led me on.
> Still the clock beside the bed
> Heart-beat after heart-beat shed.
>
>   ("Chanel")

The very loose syntax, giving a sense of the seamless reality he admired in Seferis, is also typical of Durrell, and in keeping with his idea of the "Semantic Disturbance". Several of his lyrics at their poetically most pellucid moments are baffling syntactically.

Against this urge for perfection one must place one of Durrell's earliest pronouncements on poetry (quoted earlier): "How many of us, turning from the pages of *New Verse* in the last year or so have sighed for a bucket of liquid manure to dash over these eloquent and epicene narcissi in the vain hope of making them sit up and look fruitful?"[40] This is the voice of the author of *The Black Book,* and one recalls Durrell's admiration of Henry Miller, of whom he wrote in 1949 "Miller . . . recognizes that sex is *both* a sacrament *and* also uproariously funny . . ."[41] An animal zest permeates Durrell's prose writings, and there is a spectrum of attitudes from the poetic to the comic. In the poetry there is less earthiness than in the prose, and a decided separation between the majority of his poetry and the few poems where "liquid manure" is an ingredient. "The Ballad of the Good

Lord Nelson'' is one of Durrell's best known pieces, partly because it is one of the few poems with this free-wheeling panache:

> 'England Expects' was the motto he gave
> When he thought of little Emma out on Biscay's wave,
> And remembered working on her like a galley-slave
> Aboard the Victory, Victory O.

One poem that attempts to bring rejected experience into the range of non-comic poetry is "Elegy on the Closing of the French Brothels", dedicated to his friends Henry Miller and George Katsimbalis, and published in George Woodcock's *Now* in 1949. It is an impressive poem, but only locally so. It has the air of seeking an ambitious resolution concerning the multiplicity of sexual experience, but the ambition is not sustained, despite some bold recognitions.

> Of all the sicknesses, autumnal Paris,
> This self-infection was the best, where friends
> Like self-possession could be learned
> Through the mystery of a slit
> Like a tear in an old fur coat,
> A hole in a paper lantern where the seeing I
> Looked out and measured one:
> The ferocious knuckle of sex
> Standing to acknowledge like a hambone
> Our membership in the body of a tribe
> Holy and ridiculous at once:
> Symbol of unrecognised desire, pain, pain.

Its failure seems to spring from a limited sense of the seriousness appropriate to such a poem: it is too steadily high toned for its subject.

Durrell's concern with time and the ego lie behind his thinking about modern art and his conception of his own art. He discusses these in terms of theories of Einstein, Freud and Groddeck. He remarks that "Einstein's theory joined up subject and object"[42] and quotes Freud that the "dream always turns temporal relations into spatial relations"[43]. "The new logic, borrowed from cosmology and expressed in poetry, yields one an original and bewildering syntactical scheme."[44] These ideas and concerns are utilised in his theory of the "heraldic universe"—a notion developed as early as 1937 (as his letters to Henry Miller show) and set out in *Personal Landscape* in 1942.

> Logic tries to describe the world; but it is never found adequate for the task. Logic is not really an instrument: merely a method.
>
> Describing, logic limits. Its law is causality.

Poetry by an associative approach transcends its own syntax in order not to describe but to be the cause of apprehension in others:

Transcending logic it invades a realm where unreason reigns, and where the relations between ideas are sympathetic and mysterious—affective—rather than causal, objective, substitutional.

I call this The Heraldic Universe, because in Heraldy [sic] the object is used in an emotive and affective sense—statically to body forth or utter: not as a victim of description.

The Heraldic Universe is that territory of experience in which the symbol exists—as opposed to the emblem or badge, which are the children of algebra and substitution.

It is not a 'state of mind' but a continuous self-subsisting plane of reality towards which the spiritual self of man is trying to reach out through various media: artists like antennae boring into the unknown through music or paint or words, suddenly strike this Universe where for every object in the known world there exists an ideogram.

Since words are inadequate they can only render all this negatively—by an oblique method.

'Art' then is only the smoked glass through which we can look at a dangerous sun.[45]

The poet can enter this Heraldic Universe only occasionally—a universe freed from the relativity of temporal vision, in which the temporal aspect of things becomes a fourth and fixed dimension: "an attitude of mind which consists in literally replacing Time by Space . . ."[46] This conception lies behind the four part structure of *The Alexandria Quartet*.

"Logic, syntax, is a causal instrument"[47]: the equation of "logic" and "syntax" is reflected in Durrell's poetry. Of William Empson, he said: "his real contribution to poetry is in the logical way in which he has disturbed syntax to force multiple meanings upon the structure of words. He is the real space-time poet."[48] Poetry, Durrell felt, is akin to nonsense—"like good sense with all the logic removed."[49] Distorted or incomplete syntax is frequent in Durrell's poetry. It is a step outside the bounds of "good sense", to allow "play"—or the play of the imagination.

> When from the Grecian meadows
> Responsive rose the larks,
> Stiffly as if on strings,
> Ebbing, drew thin as tops
> While each in rising squeezed
> His spire of singing drops

> On that renewed landscape
> Like semen from the grape.
> ("Patmos")

Durrell, more than most poets of his generation, shows a clear idea of the heritage of modernism and of the relation of his own work to it. His best poetry is among the finest of the period and is an achievement that reflects a sustained contemplation of the idiom of his day. Yet there is something hit or miss about a great deal of his work, as he has recognised. "Any poetic reputation" he had, he felt, was due to T.S. Eliot's "persuasion—to cut down poems, verbose ones, poems bulging with connective tissue."[50] There are still plenty of baggy poems in Collected Poems, such as "Cities, Plains and People" or "Byron". Durrell has named his poetry as the work "closest to his heart", but went on to say that he thought he had "missed his shot".[51] "To achieve great poetry, you must give up everything. Personally, I have been over-greedy about life."[52] The shortcoming of the poetry has not been an overabundance of life, such as one finds in a good deal of his prose. The pressure toward perfection has dominated too frequently in the poetry. What is noticeable is a drop in pressure in The Tree of Idleness in 1955, when The Alexandria Quartet was absorbing his creative energies. Above all, in spite of the extent and quality of Durrell's poetry, despite the unusual gift for rendering the combination of irony and tenderness, one seldom has the sense of feeling taking hold of one, of being carried into the heart of some central human emotion.

Durrell was an admirer of Jules Laforgue, one of the originators of the free verse and romantic irony that were so decisive in giving character to T.S. Eliot's early work. In Durrell's poetry, we see that irony perpetuated, along with other important "modernist" tendencies. "Syntax" (equated by Durrell with "logic") is for him the enemy of poetry; and twentieth century poetic theory and practice have been deeply influenced by the search for a mode quintessentially poetic, clearly distinct from "discourse" with its sequential logic of syntax. Durrell sees distortion (the "semantic disturbance") as a characteristic of modern writing in both prose and verse, and he makes it a part of his own work. Indeed, no British poet of the forties carries on so strongly the ironic inheritance of Anglo-American modernism as does Durrell. Yet Durrell's irony, as his distrust of logic might lead one to expect, is not the controlled, distanced irony of so much British writing. The Durrell of The Black Book remains. There is a responsiveness to disturbing and often alienating feelings below the rational level, and a recognition of the power of writers in whom control is not paramount. It is the combination of these two disparate tendencies that gives Durrell's writing its individual tone.

III

The way in which the pervasive influence of early modernist poetry could be at once liberating and distortive is seen in the careers of Henry Reed and Terence Tiller. Both gave the impression of brilliant and cultivated talents with their first books. They were among the few poets that John Lehmann encouraged by steady publication in his periodicals throughout the decade. Yet the work of each of them gives the impression of a talent in some ways led astray.

Reed produced only one book of poetry, *A Map of Verona* (1946): it contained the celebrated "Lessons of War"; and the telling parody of *Four Quartets*, "Chard Whitlow". A number of the poems were clearly written before the war; and the principal poems from the forties are the Arthurian suite, "Tintagel", and the classical monologues, "Chrysothemis" and "Philoctetes". A third monologue, "Antigone" later appeared in *Penguin New Writing*.

These poems attempt an exploration of the inner life through the use of myth: in "Tintagel" the protagonists become exemplars of states of mind; while in "Antigone" there is a probing of the myth for its psychological meaning. Like Reed's earlier poems, they are stylish, evocative and controlled. Their notable achievement is the skilfully modulated tone of voice, recognisably Reed's, even though the diction and movement of the poems are derivative from Eliot. There is a gift for the evocation of particular detail, with sensitivity of observation and discrimination.

> Somewhere beyond, and held in a dream of summer,
> Lies the familiar place, familiar,
> And desperately unknown. And high or low,
> Under that sky, through every branch and bracken,
> In every fibre of the sunflower-hedge, in every ripple
> Of air among the grasses, silent glint
> Of light on leaf, the sense of prearrangement,
> And the sense of a new death. Forever and forever,
> This place has waited for you, created leaf and flower,
> Has shaped the stream in its course for you to remember,
> Forever waiting.
>
> ("Tintagel III—King Mark")

Yet the effect of this delicacy of delineation is sometimes to overwhelm the poems, rather than to bring feeling into focus. Indeed, the tentative questionings and characterisations become the mannerisms of a sensitivity at times seemingly factitious, because it has no object. The parody of "Chard Whitlow" shows an acute recognition of the mannerisms of *Four Quartets,* but these same mannerisms become a staple of Reed's poetry without the firm resonance of inner meaning that redeems them in Eliot's poems. "I have changed my mind; or my mind is changed in me" ("Philoctetes"): the play on words through the correction of the customary phrase does not alert the reader in any important way. Characteristic is the puzzled cultivation of local sensitivity in the attractive title poem, "A Map of Verona", in which the speaker lingers over a map of the city he has never visited:

> But I remember, once your map lay open,
> As now Verona's, under the still lamp-light.
> I thought, are these the streets to walk in in the mornings,
> Are these the gardens to linger in at night?

Reed's poems show a serious attempt to cultivate an individual talent of considerable potentiality. Their over-insistence on sensitivity is symptomatic of the high valuation placed on that quality in the forties. Yet the failure of some poems can also be seen as symptomatic of the modernist preoccupation with style—a concern that leaves Reed very much at the mercy of his chief admiration, Eliot. It is hard to imagine what Reed's poetry would have been without the example of Eliot; but Eliot becomes (in the phrase he used of Milton) a "Chinese Wall"[53] for Reed's poetry. The very accomplishment of Reed's cultivation of the Eliotean manner seems to hinder the development of a personal voice, heard authentically and enduringly in congenial but minor poems like "A Map of Verona" or "Lessons of War".

Terence Tiller's poetry, at its best, gives a subtle introspective exploration in a manner that derives from the seventeenth century metaphysical poets:

> Being oneself: the last and worst exclusion,
> unit's enclosure of communal nothing.
>> There is a prison,
> or a deserted village, in my breathing:
>> where is your strength, soft bitter *one,*
>> to hurl stones at another stone,
> breaking its windows? or to break your own?

His most enduring concern is with the remoteness of the self within the individual, a theme encountered in the work of W.S. Graham and the early Dylan Thomas. Isolated in Egypt by the war, he gave this preoccupation a contemporary perspective in his second book, *The Inward Animal* (1943):

> Now that the war has taken millions from their familiar environment and associates, its impact and the impact of strangeness must have shaken, and perhaps destroyed, many a customary self. There will have been a shocked and defensive rebellion; reconciliation must follow; the birth of some mutual thing in which the old and the new, the self and the alien, are combined after war . . . The "inward animal" is this child, so unwillingly conceived and carried, so hardly brought forth.

Like the metaphysical poets, he often stays with an image, elaborating his argument in terms of it; but, as with so many twentieth century writers, there is a pressure to render everything in imagistic terms, and the imagery often takes over the poem. The weakness of Tiller's less good poetry is its excessive obliqueness. There is an overelaboration of sensitive observation and the appearance of subtlety of distinction that is not sustained by further acquaintance. This goes along with a syntactical elusiveness.

> Four elements, black angels, walk this ground;
> no god; no beckoning halo roams
> these empty cold and captive tombs
> arid as rock, as the split bone beyond,
> four elements and their possessing Moloch, battle
> of blind or innocent, the wasting fire
> whose murderous embers bar
> the hopeless turning in the ring of metal.
>
> ("Elegy I")

Tiller is one of the few poets of his generation to owe anything to William Empson. It was through the example of Empson that the influence of the metaphysicals was transmitted to Tiller. Tiller often proceeds as Empson did with a series of sententious phrases:

> The star and the burnt insect under glass,
> sharing the fact, must share the word of flame;
> there is no point less infinite than space.

> Sun and electron, circles are the same:
> if you and love outstretch the universe,
> what shall I apprehend without your name?

However, he does not have Empson's toughness of argument, and this is not his most successful vein. Indeed, his best writing has often a disarming and unpretentious lyricism:

A poem for a minute
for the embracing smiling
light upon a planet
sown flower swelling
where there is no time being
waiting or double seeing
is the budding of bells
in the happy pulse.

("Song")

Such lyrics in their clarity and poise can remind one of Durrell. There is a same tightening of the lyricism through the elusive syntax, as with Durrell; but the effect is somewhat static and cold. Indeed, so many modernist devices, so rewardingly utilised by Durrell, seem impediments to Tiller.

In Tiller's second and third books, *The Inward Animal* and *Unarm, Eros* (1947), there are poems that take for their material a scene, incident or individual, such as "Egyptian Dancer", "Beggar" or "Camels", and they show Tiller at his best. Like similar poems by Louis MacNeice, they are constructed of a sequence of images and observations, with only a muted resolution, if any, at the conclusion. One of the most effective is "Lecturing the Troops":

Waiting for my announcement, I feel neat and shy,
    foreign before their curious helplessness,
innocence bought by action, like the sea's amnesty:
all my clean cleverness is tiny, is a loss;
and it is useless to be friendly and precise
            —thin as a hornet in a dome
        against the cries of death and home.

He bequeaths an image very characteristic of the period: the intellectual, alienated from the main life of action of the time, isolated in his own sensitivity.

Tiller's poetry is not always so rewarding. As Alan Ross remarked, reviewing *Unarm, Eros* in 1948.

Mr. Tiller has penetrated to the roots of his own predicament—a feeling of ineffectuality despite his surface abilities . . . Where one hoped for a whole human personality growing from the poetry, Mr. Tiller has produced simply the poems as isolated things in themselves—charming, full of grace and of a metaphysical fluidity that is reminiscent of Donne, but still without cohesion or impact . . . [54]

Tiller himself remarked, in a series of gnomic observations in *Personal*

Landscape: "Poetry's reality, then, is the knowledge and calculation of effects."[55] An impression of contrived imagery, conventionally beautiful in character, but often cold and inhuman in impact, is what can remain from a reading of the whole body of his poetry, despite its "finish" and distinction of manner. We seem to encounter one of the elements of modernism carried to the point of self-defeat: the life of the surface is over-developed, with the consequence that feeling is less effectively brought into focus. In addition, in key with much writing of the decade, there is a parade of sensitivity in the details that is not conjunctive to larger rewards of insight through the poems as wholes. Exemplary of his gifts and his shortcomings, in its brilliance and its coldness, is one of his last poems of the decade, "Swords of Glass", published in *Penguin New Writing* in 1949:

> Their twin smooth tips are sharp
> as briars; the blades though flute and twist and warp
> like barley-sugar if it glittered, or the gold
> shafts of a roundabout. Self-enclosed and cold,
> they creep with childhood's nausea for the too
> richly-confected plane which is not quite true.
> As these are not: not toys, yet they would smash
> to sharp confetti round the fighter; never a flash
> in beauty or gallantry; they have never been
> crossed, but in mocking rest, the blue and green.

Impressively memorable, it is not moving in terms of deeper human concerns. It epitomises Tiller's very real gifts—but, unhappily, his limitations.

IV

Few poets have had a reputation more distorted by the comings and goings of literary fashion than had G.S. Fraser. Born in Glasgow and educated at St. Andrews, he spent the war in the middle-east. During the early forties he was associated with the Apocalypse movement; he appeared in Cairo in *Personal Landscape* and other middle-east collections; and he was presented as a Scots poet in *Poetry Scotland* and other nationalistic compilations. During the last years of the decade, in his association with Peter Russell's periodical, *Nine,* he was seen as a "neo-classicist". Fraser was Scottish in a sense that is natural to anyone who grew up in Scotland, and one or two of his poems in *The White Horseman* (the only Apocalypse collection in which he appeared) showed the influence of the company he was keeping. Yet his urbane, quiet poetry owes little to the movements into which he was inducted and had none of their strident partisanship. His work is more at home beside that of Bernard Spencer or Louis MacNeice:

> The traveller has regrets
> For the receding shore
> That with its many nets
> Has caught, not to restore,
> The white lights in the bay,
> The blue lights on the hill . . .
> ("The Traveller Has Regrets")

Fraser produced three books of poetry in the forties, *The Fatal Landscape* (1941), *Home Town Elegy* (1944) and *The Traveller Has Regrets* (1948). *Home Town Elegy* is often prosey and self-important, and several of the poems are immaturely literary in inspiration. He is most touching and most at ease in those in which he remembers Scotland, such as the powerful poem on "The Death of my Grandmother", or the poem that John Waller found "so moving that when reading it I had to separate myself entirely from my voice . . . to avoid breaking into tears . . ."[55]

> Drifting and innocent and like snow,
> Now memories tease me, wherever I go,
> And I think of the glitter of granite and distances
> And against the blue air the lovely and bare trees,
> And slippery pavements spangled with delight
> Under the needles of a winter's night,
> And I remember the dances, with scarf and cane,
> Strolling home in the cold with the silly refrain
> Of a tune by Cole Porter or Irving Berlin
> Warming a naughty memory up like gin,
> And Bunny and Sheila and Joyce and Rosemary
> Chattering on sofas or preparing tea,
> With their delicate voices and their small white hands
> This is the sorrow everyone understands.
> More than Rostov's artillery, more than the planes
> Skirting the cyclonic islands, this remains,
> The little, lovely taste of youth we had:
> The guns and not our silliness were mad . . .
> ("Christmas Letter Home")

The unpretentious truthfulness reminds one that Fraser (one of the few notable critics of his generation) was the inventor of the phrase "evasive honesty" for Louis MacNeice. The rhythm of the poem is delicate and individual; but if it evokes the memory of any other poet, it is MacNeice, a master of the long lined couplet with rhythms carefully broken to produce a natural effect.

As Fraser modestly remarked in 1948, "I am not a very original writer myself; I am lost, on the whole, without a convention of some sort . . ."[56] A care for form and a dependence on tone and movement (qualities not notable in much poetry of the forties) were and remained a feature of his poems.

Fraser's poetry belongs (unassertively and not very adventurously) in the mainstream of twentieth century British poetry—ironic, urbane, colloquial, with a tempered debt to the great modernist revolution. It is symptomatic of the ethos of the forties that Fraser's best poems were not recognised as having these central qualities, but that he was induced to find support in movements out of keeping with his talents and to keep company with writers considerably less gifted than himself. His modest but treasurable success typfies the strengths of a great deal of British poetry in this century—strengths whose cultivation is not enhanced by doctrinaire positions. In this it provides a salutary footnote to the course of British modernism.

V

The development of British poetry in the nineteen-forties could be seen as a set of attempts to come to terms with Anglo-American modernism, which Auden and his generation had found so liberating. There were those who continued the developments of Auden, such as Roy Fuller, Julian Symons and Ruthven Todd; there were those who reacted at once to modernism and the poetry of Auden, in the cultivation of a "new romanticism", in tune with a growing admiration for the work of Yeats and the great Romantic poets. There were others who deliberately turned back to more traditional forms of poetry that in the thirties would have been scorned as old fashioned. And finally there were those who had, in many cases, been nurtured on modernism and its dogmas, and who could find themselves only by breaking free. This last group was to make its mark only in the fifties, in what came to be known as the Movement.

Indeed the modifications and dilutions of modernism that are encountered in the poetry of the thirties and of the forties constitute adaptations of Anglo-American modernism to a more native idiom. By the late forties we see an end of an impulse, an end of the vitality that the encounter with modernism had brought to the early poetry of Auden and of Dylan Thomas. From then on the adaptations of the thirties and forties seem to stand in the way of innovation and a revitalisation of the idiom; and the work of the great modernists, no longer possible direct models for British poets, becomes an influence to be avoided. This was the situation as it was very painfully sensed by many younger writers in the late forties.

Chapter 4

KEEPING LEFT

The Left in Wartime—*Now*—George Woodcock,
Julian Symons, Ruthven Todd, H.B. Mallalieu,
D.S. Savage

While most British poetry in the nineteen-forties did not have a Left-wing political orientation, a Leftist ideology still remained a powerful force in British intellectual life, and certain younger poets, who had been associated with Julian Symons's *Twentieth Century Verse* in the late thirties, continued to write under the influence of that ideology and in a manner that derived from the literary Left of the thirties.

The war and events leading up to it produced considerable changes in the face of British radicalism. Spain, the cliche goes, was the graveyard of the hopes of the British Left-wing intellectual and literary movement of the thirties. This is largely true. The battles for Madrid had given support to the hope that political action and the will of the people could stop the advance of fascism and prevent a second world war. The British and French policy of non-intervention, under which they continually met in committee with Germans and Italians who were intervening, contributed strongly to the overthrow of the Republican government, and demonstrated how unlikely it was that conservative politicians would whole-heartedly face the menace that Hitler presented. This feeling was reinforced by the Munich agreement of 1938, when Britain and France agreed with Hitler and Mussolini on the carving up of Czechoslovakia. After that war seemed, quite rightly, inevitable.

The behaviour of the Communists in Spain had also been disturbing to Communists and fellow-travellers in Britain. Because of the policy of non-intervention, Russia became the sole important source of arms for the Republican side; and, as the Communists became increasingly dominant, they used their position forcibly to eliminate opposition, as they did in the case of the Trotskyite P.O.U.M. in Barcelona, whose liquidation was described by George Orwell in *Homage to Catalonia* (1938). At the same time, reports of the Moscow trials of 1938, in which Stalin brought to extorted confession and execution those opposed to him in the Soviet hierarchy, grated on the essentially liberal views of justice held by the intellectual Left. The pact between Hitler and Stalin in 1939, which resulted in a Russian invasion of half of Poland in September, was the final disorienting blow for many. As

George Woodcock was to write, in 1943: "The Russian-German alliance on the eve of the war destroyed Communism as an influence . . . The intelligentsia began an aimless intellectual trek into the wartime wilderness . . ."[1]

The war produced ideological embarrassment on all sides. Many of the Right did not view the war readily as a struggle to destroy fascism: for them the "bogey" of the inter-war years had been the "bolshies". Such attitudes were evidently sufficiently manifest in government policy and private talk for Left-wingers like George Orwell to feel in 1940 that "bankers, generals, bishops, kings, big industrialists" were "willing to do a deal" with Hitler.[2] Labour was suspicious of a war in which the representatives of British capitalism called on them for patriotic sacrifice and national unity while unemployment continued throughout the first year of war. Communist embarrassment with the Hitler-Stalin pact was heightened by the Russian invasion of Finland in November, 1939. Further emotional "quick changes" would be called for when Germany invaded Russia, and, later, as the totalitarian nature of Communist Russia became clear after the war.

Stephen Spender, representative of the anti-fascist movement of the thirties, said of the war: "It is not a conflict between God and the Devil, Christ and Judas, but between the systems represented by Hitler and Chamberlain."[3] Julian Symons, whom George Woodcock called "a kind of dissident Trotskyite" termed it "the second capitalist war"[4]. George Woodcock felt that "The significant war is not the horizontal one between England and Germany, but the vertical one between the rulers of England and Germany, America, Russia on the one side, and on the other the ruled throughout the world."[5] The strong pacifist tendencies of the thirties continued during the war, and pacifists throughout the period refused to fight.

The Peace Pledge Movement was prominent in the thirties; but, as D.S. Savage stated, "By 1940, only a hard core of conscientious objectors and veteran socialists, anarchists and Christian pacifists remained."[6] Nevertheless, some sixty thousand people asked to be registered as conscientious objectors, and fifty thousand were. Most of them accepted non-combatant duties in or out of the forces. Among them, at various times, were Julian Symons, George Woodcock, D.S. Savage, Nicholas Moore, John Bayliss and Derek Stanford—all poets who spent their adolescence in the depression. George Woodcock's *Now* for Fall, 1940 contains the tribunal statements of himself, Symons and Savage. The American *Partisan Review* for September-October, 1942 printed letters from Savage, Woodcock and Alex Comfort, taking sides against George Orwell's criticism of pacifism.

Dissidence on the Left was not confined to Communists (up to

1942), anarchists, Trotskytites and pacifists. Even though there was a coalition government and leaders of the Labour party were members of the War Cabinet, the more radical members of the Labour movement continued to be critical of the government, the conduct of the war, war aims, and promises for the future after the war. *Guilty Men* by "Cato" (Michael Frost, Frank Owen and Peter Howard), published by Victor Gollancz in 1940, blamed the war on Chamberlain and the "appeasers", and went through nineteen reprints in a month. Gollancz edited a volume called *The Betrayal of the Left* in 1941, to which George Orwell contributed two chapters. Another book to which Orwell contributed, *Victory or Vested Interest?* (1942), indicates, in its title, the drift of much of the criticism. This was the theme of *Why Not Trust the Tories?* (1944) by "Celiticus" (Aneurin Bevan), later to be Minister of Health in the post-war Labour Government: it gives voice to the common feeling that the working class would again be cheated after winning the war.

Bevan was, at that time, one of the directors of the independent radical weekly, *Tribune*. It was more trenchant in its politics than the intellectual and rather academic *New Statesman and Nation*. Orwell became its literary editor in November, 1943, and contributed a column, "As I Please", regularly until February, 1945, and after that irregularly until April, 1947. Julian Symons, who contributed to *Tribune,* said of Orwell at that time: ". . . we were both what might be called premature anti-Stalinists."[7] Orwell was the leading voice of the dissident democratic Left in the England of his day—a voice whose dissidence was not always welcome to fellow radicals. When Russia was attacked by Germany in 1941, he wrote that "All really depends on whether Russia and Britain are ready really to cooperate . . ."; but ten days later an entry in his diary ran: "One could not have a better example of the moral and emotional shallowness of our time, than the fact that we are now all more or less pro-Stalin. This disgusting murderer is temporarily on our side, and so the purges etc. are suddenly forgotten."[8] An admired and increasingly influential figure, he still had difficulty in getting his masterpiece *Animal Farm* published when he completed it in 1944. This was presumably because its fable of criticism of Soviet Communism was felt to be out of keeping when the allies were about to invade Europe.

Orwell's work provides an important continuity in British radicalism. A contemporary of Cyril Connolly at Eton and a lifelong friend, he embarrassed the Left with *Homage to Catolonia* (1939) and "Inside the Whale" (1940), where he exposed sentimentalities and inconsistencies in Left-wing positions. A continuing embarrassment in the forties, he was a revered mentor for writers like Julian Symons and

George Woodcock. For the Movement of the fifties, his perceptive honesty became a touchstone.

II

A major legacy of the Left-wing radicalism of the thirties was the feeling that the war was a capitalist blunder. This, combined with the discredit into which Communism had fallen, no doubt had a great deal to do with the attraction that some form of anarchism had for younger intellectuals during the war. A protest against *organised* killing by a society that abominates killing by individuals is the essence of a great deal of pacifism. As Alex Comfort, an anarchist himself, wrote in 1944, ". . . I sat smoking last week with a great personal friend of mine who had just helped to exterminate, under orders, the population of a city where he has a good many acquaintances:"[9]

Comfort's essay, "Art and Social Responsibility", gives classic expression to the wartime anarchist position:

> . . . one of the properties common to humanity . . . is a congenital inability to form a community which does not involve the abuse of power.

> There are no corporate allegiances. All our politics are atomised.

> Society is a flight *from* responsibility, an attempt to exercise it towards a non-existent scarecrow rather than to real people.

> It is with the whole idea of society as a super-person that we are at war, and class struggles are superseded by this struggle.[10]

A good deal of Comfort's thinking derives from the work of Herbert Read, as Comfort pointed out:

> I do not think that it is possible to overestimate Read's personal influence through his writings on the development of poetry since 1938. He has stood in much the same relation to the younger writers as Godwin did to the earlier romantics. In 'The Politics of the Unpolitical' he has coined a phrase which will play as great a part in the struggle between anarchism and authoritarianism which will follow the war . . . The indissoluble alliance between art and anarchism, was virtually his own discovery.[11]

Read's influence was felt by several groups of poets in the late thirties and early forties, and in Read's writing we can see the interconnection between ideas that were important in that period. Wrey Gardiner, who edited *Poetry Quarterly*, wrote "In politics I follow Read"[12]; and Henry Treece, a spokesman for the Apocalypse movement said, "The only way Left . . . is that of anarchism . . ."[13]. Read discovered and published Sidney Keyes and John Heath-Stubbs. He also published, in Routledge's "Broadway House" series, Julian Symons,

George Woodcock, Alex Comfort, J.F. Hendry, Norman McCaig, D.S. Savage and Derek Stanford. A supporter of surrealism in the mid-thirties, he moved beyond the connection that the surrealists had made between surrealism and Marxism to develop, particularly in *Poetry and Anarchism* (1938) and *The Politics of the Unpolitical* (1943), his sense of the relationship between Romanticism, organic form, freedom, individuality, anarchism, socialism, and the education of the sensibility—a spectrum of ideas influential in the early forties both with writers of overtly political orientation and with the "new romanticism". In *Poetry and Anarchism* he wrote: "Engels describes the State as 'withering away'—it is one of the key passages in the formulation of Marxism . . ." "The inevitable is the classless society—the society without a bureaucracy, without an army, without any closed grade or profession . . . there would be no work done in excess of immediate needs, except such as may be required to insure against the risks of natural calamities"; ". . . to live according to natural laws—this is also to release the imagination."[14]

Among the many younger writers whom Read influenced or encouraged was George Woodcock, who edited the periodical *Now* from 1940 to 1947. Woodcock gave the following account of it in 1943.

Three years ago, during the first winter of the war, I realised the need for a magazine that might in some degree replace the small literary reviews, such as New Verse, Twentieth Century Verse and Wales, which had vanished as early casualties in this war of our rulers against culture and freedom. I also felt there was a need for a forum of unpopular and minority views, a medium for what is termed "free expression" on social matters.

The magazine, NOW, appeared in the spring of 1940 as a cyclo-styled sheet, containing contributions from a number of the more capable young writers, including Charles Madge, Kathleen Raine, Roy Fuller, H.B. Mallalieu, D.S. Savage and Keidrych Rhys. Two further numbers, printed, appeared in the autumn of 1940, including, among other new contributors, Frederic Prokosch, Julian Symons, Ruthven Todd and Nicholas Moore.

In March 1941 NOW was restarted on a more ambitious scale, with a wider range of contributors, including Herbert Read, Rhys Davies, James Hanley, John Middleton Murry, Roy Campbell, Hugh Ross Williams, Hugh I'Anson Fausset, Francis Scarfe and Julian Huxley.

Four numbers appeared. By the last, No. 7, I had come to realise the justice of a criticism made by Julian Symons, in which he attacked the 'free expression' policy, which had united in one review so many imcompatible opinions, and contended that a small magazine was only justified if it represented a defined attitude.

When, this year, I decided to collaborate with the Freedom Press in preparing a series of volumes of literary and social writings the title of NOW was transferred to the new venture, which, in many ways, is the natural conclusion of the line of development represented by the review.

So far as social content is concerned, the volumes of NOW will be edited from an anarchist point of view. So far as their literary content is concerned, our criterion will be the quality of writing. Nor do we intend to exclude poets, essayists, story writers, because their political views do not coincide with our own.

(*Now*, New Series, 1)

Subsequent contributors to *Now* were to include, in addition to those already mentioned, George Orwell (whose "How the Poor Die" was one of the most powerful pieces published by Woodcock), George Barker, Lawrence Durrell, W.S. Graham, D.S. Savage, Alex Comfort and Emanuel Litvinoff, along with an increasing number of American contributors, including Henry Miller, Paul Goodman and Kenneth Rexroth. *Now* came to grief when the editor (like many others in publishing) misread the signs in 1947, and felt that the time was propitious for bi-monthly issues that the lifting of restrictions permitted.

Woodcock started *Now* because he believed that there was still a place for a periodical that recognized "the interdependence of poetry and politics."[15] His own political position was anarchist, as set out in his numerous contributions, and most particularly in "The Writer and Politics" (*Now*, New Series, 4). In particular, he remarks of the turning of the intellectuals from Communism after the 1930's: "They have repudiated political methods, and have realised once again the need for individual freedom as a basic factor in social organisations"; and goes on to say, "The really independent writer, by the exercise of his function, represents a revolutionary force." In an essay on Graham Greene, he spoke of ". . . the fraud of politics . . ." (*Now*, New Series, 6). Political action and organisation had implicit in them the possibility of oppression. In 1947 he wrote: "In almost every country, no less in Labour England than in Communist Russia, there is a steady increase in totalitarian method, and, what is worse, totalitarian thought." (*Now*, New Series, 7,5). During the forties Woodcock wrote a study of William Godwin, and essays on the nineteenth century anarchists, Proudhon, Herzen and Kropotkin. As he showed in a later essay, "Anarchism Revisited" (1968)[16], the roots of the anarchism of the forties were, for him, in a long tradition of European thought. In that same essay he characterises the appeal of that tradition in a distinction that in fact epitomises a change in political outlook that took place around 1940: "What the anarchist tradition has to give . . . is . . . the vision of a society in which every relation would have a moral rather than political characteristic."[17]

With its abundance not only of political and sociological commentary but of literary discussion with a similar emphasis, *Now* resembled the American *Partisan Review*, which Woodcock admired. While it emphasised the anarchist position in the discussions it printed, it nevertheless did include radical articles that had a different point of view, such as Julian Symons's "Freedom and Reality" (*Now*, New Series, 7), a decidedly Marxist analysis, which took the position that "The reality behind the word 'freedom' . . . is power."

Now offered an important opportunity for the expression of serious radical ideas that would have got little hearing in more established periodicals. Many of its interesting pieces were by Americans. It stood up for Henry Miller and it published him. It included work by William Everson (Brother Antonius) and Philip Lamantia—poets who were not to be recognised in the United States for many years, let alone in Britain. It provided a focus for a type of radicalism and protest that was much more widely diffused than was recognised—either then or now.

III

Woodcock had published poems in Julian Symons's *Twentieth Century Verse* before the war, and Symons was a frequent contributor to *Now*. In *Now* Woodcock drew on the poets who had been the main contributors to *Twentieth Century Verse:* Symons, Ruthven Todd, D.S. Savage, H.B. Mallalieu, Roy Fuller and Francis Scarfe. *Twentieth Century Verse,* while advertising no political viewpoint, had nevertheless been responsive to the relationship between politics and poetry characteristic of its decade; and the stylistic influence of Auden was most noticeable among its poets.

These continuities with the previous decade were maintained in *Now*. *Now* was not the only periodical of the nineteen-forties to publish poetry of a "social realist" orientation—to use the language of the time. The majority of the poetry of the decade—especially the poetry of war—took as its mode the exploration of actual experience presented in realistic terms. Yet *Now* was the one periodical of consequence to maintain the connection with radical politics. The type of poetry striven for by the poets associated with *Twentieth Century Verse* and *Now* has been characterised by George Woodcock: "poetry should strive for the maximum possible intellectual clarity compatible with the relation of its essentially intuitive elements, and a poem that did not explain itself to a sensitive reader seemed to us a spoiled poem."[18] His own poetry at its best, plain and direct, exemplifies these qualities:

The days grow dim. Melancholy chrysanthemums
Wilt under dank shrubberies where roses
Still open, niggardly, to the winter sun
Cramped flowers like slum women's faces.

Traditional Sundays falling on villages
Set the harmonium measure, tea at the manse,
Song and the thudding darts at the public,
Dark empty lanes returning from the dance.

The farmer walks home drunk across his acres
Beneath whose hedges rabbits and virgins scream,
And the uniformed shadows darken in corners—
Putting to time the riddle of their doom.

                    ("November"—*Now*, New Series, 1, 1943)

The most gifted of these poets were Roy Fuller and Julian Symons.
Symons's first book, *Confusions about 'X'* (1939), was one of the
few to show the marked influence of Auden's *Poems* (1930); while,
in the early forties, the influence of Auden's rhetorically more expan-
sive manner of the late thirties was obvious in the work of Symons,
Fuller, Todd and Mallalieu.

The glasses are raised, the voices drift into laughter,
The clock hands have stopped, the beer in the hands
                                    off the soldiers
Is blond, the faces are calm and the fingers can feel
The wet touch of glasses, the glasses print rings on
                                    the table,
The smoke rings curl and go up and dissolve near the
                                    ceiling,
            This moment exists and is real.

                    . . . . . .

The houses are shut and the people go home, we are left in
Our islands of pain, the clocks start to move and the
                                    powerful
To act, there is nothing now, nothing at all
To be done: for the trouble is real: and the verdict is
                                    final
Against us. The clocks go round faster and faster. And
                                    fast as confetti
            The days are beginning to fall.

These are the first and last stanzas of Julian Symons's "Pub", from
his second book of poems, *The Second Man* (1943). A common feature of many of the best poems in *Twentieth Century Verse* had been

the subjugation of rhetorical effects to the direct presentation of a scene or event, in contrast to the figurative deployment of imagery in the poetry of Auden or Spender, or to the construction of poems from a sequence of images that seemed to have their own aesthetic validity, as was characteristic of many contributions to *New Verse*. "Pub" provides a good example of the change. Its first stanza presents a scene with considerable brightness of visual perception. Yet the very extent to which the perceptual sensitivity is paraded produces a feeling of expectation, a sense of the portentous. This is explicit in "The clock hands have stopped"—something of a thirties cliché; and the effect is rammed home by the Audenesque final line; "This moment exists and is real." The gratuitous dead-pan "exists"—what else can the moment do—suggests that we have little to hold on to; while "real" not only reinforces this feeling, but casts a questioning but unfocussed glance at anything else that might pretend to claim a greater significance. The abracadabra of thirties portentousness—largely out of Auden— supplies virtually all the material for the final stanza. The clock now moves; "real", poorly defined by the poem, is again overworked, teetering between "actual" and "important"; something—presumably "history", a favourite thirties abstraction, is giving an irrevocable "verdict"; the "powerful" (in contrast, it seems to be implied, to everyone else) begin to "act". "Our islands of pain" suggests the vision of Auden's "September 1st, 1939"; while, "The houses are shut and the people go home" is clearly reminiscent of the end of Auden's "August and the people for their favourite islands". The poem does not move from its perception of a particular scene to an enhanced vision of it; instead, when it leaves the purely perceptual, it offers a worn rhetorical gesture rather than a valid extension of experience. Yet "Pub" is not to be despised. In its low-toned movement and in its evocation of the actual it has a decided distinction, and it has been at least twice anthologised since the forties. There are grosser poems in *The Second Man*, and they are often ones that commit themselves to some doctrinaire expression, such as "Homage to our Leaders" with the phrase "Churchill the moonface moocow".

A similar coarsening seems to have occurred in the work of Ruthven Todd, who wrote poems in the late thirties that measured up to his own description of his work: "My poems try to be poems, and to be simple."[19] During the forties he wrote a few personal poems of some strength; but those written in the early part of the war tended to be crude in their emotional stance. In his sonnets, Todd had been too obvious an imitator of Auden; and his book of 1943, *The Acreage of the Heart*, contains over a dozen poems on literary and artistic topics— mainly sonnets giving quick epitomies of their subjects, as Auden did in sonnets in *Another Time* (1940). Indeed, where Todd is bad, the malaise of "the Audenesque" (to use the phrase after Bernard Bergonzi) is generally felt: "History, alas, is past" (from "Love is no Ghost") combines derivative rhetoric (Auden's *Spain*) with inanely obvious sentiment; "Only the dreamer really can manage to be free" (from "Exiles") has Auden's "all-or-nothing" use of "only" and the sloppy use of "really" for reinforcement.

Of the *Twentieth Century Verse* regulars only Fuller (and in a minor way, Todd) survived the forties as poets. H.B. Mallalieu wrote a few attractive poems during the war; Francis Scarfe's work did not develop what promise his first book had; while D.S. Savage seems to have published little poetry after 1943—though his book, *The Personal Principle* (1944), gave a valid and individual discussion of the development of twentieth century poetry in England.

We can see in this the demise or subjugation of the political impulse that had dominated new writing in the thirties. Woodcock has described how, in the late forties, he felt "a sudden diminution in the urge to write poetry. This happened, at about the same time, to many poets who, like me, had begun to appear at the end of the thirties. Julian Symons . . . himself a victim of a loss of power, has suggested that it sprang from a disillusionment at finding the world unchanged after the great war ended . . ."[20] (though for Mallalieu and Savage the change had come earlier). Even for Fuller, whose poetry expanded under the impact of the war, the post-war years brought a taxing reorientation.

IV

The end of the war produced further discouragements for the radical left. A Tory victory at the polls, followed by a betrayal of wartime promises and a return to the pre-war economic pattern of society had been expected, and a recession after the wartime full employment and full production was predicted by economists of a variety of persuasion. Instead there came a resounding victory for the British Labour Party, a programme of social and industrial nationalisation, and the more or less steady continuation of the phenomenal wartime demand for labour for the rest of the decade. The main economic problem was to counter the devastating effect that the war had had on Britain's position in the world. Class distinction did not return to the extent that it had been prevalent before the war; educational opportunities, particularly for many returning from the war, were much better than they had been; domestic service seemed then largely a thing of the past.

There was not much opportunity for radical pressure from the democratic Left; and, after the elections and the demobilisation, there was less and less audience for such radicalism. Among intellectuals, Communism was further discredited by the Russian usurpation of democratic processes in the occupied countries of Eastern Europe. The Communist Party of Great Britain was largely active in attempting to get controlling positions in the leadership of Trade Unions.

The effect in brief was a muting of radicalism as a force in British intellectual life. Radicalism, for the literary left, had been the basis for a commentary on what it meant to be English. The poetry of the war sustained a protest that was radical and often pacifist, even from those who fought. Any further radical orientation to British experience was undermined by the conclusion of the war and the decline of Britain's position in the post-war world, which took away from the sense of the centrality of British experience. Inevitably there was a collapse of the idiom that had been associated with such an orientation. British writing was thrown back for its basic strength on a rudderless decency and sensitivity, and a puzzled indirection characterised the end of the decade. An effective radicalism was not to be found again until the mid-fifties, when it emerged in books like *Declaration*[21] (with contributions from John Wain, Doris Lessing, John Osborne and others), or in the work of the Movement. By then its relation to the older Leftist alignments was such that it was no longer "political" in the traditional sense of the word.

Chapter 5

THREE RHETORICIANS
George Barker—W.S. Graham—W.R. Rodgers

In 1938, Louis MacNeice wrote: "I consider that the poet is a blend of the entertainer and the critic or informer; he is not a legislator, however unacknowledged, nor yet, essentially, a prophet."[1] He expressed, somewhat abrasively, a view widely held in the nineteen-thirties. In the forties there was an openness to a more self-important role for the poet and to a less guarded and naturalistic deployment of language than is found in the work of MacNeice and many poets of his generation. "Rhetorical" was no longer a term of denigration, and a relishing of colour and sonority was no longer suspect. Indeed, a demand for a poetry that was unguarded in the expression of emotion came as a reaction to the poetry of the thirties. Three proponents of the self-consciously rhetorical were George Barker, W.S. Graham and W.R. Rodgers.

George Barker published his first book of poems, *Thirty Preliminary Poems,* at the age of twenty in 1933. By 1940 he had published three more volumes: *Poems* (1935), *Calamiterror* (1937) and *Lament and Triumph* (1940)—all with an unmistakable rhetoric that combined the colloquial with the orotund, and a distorted syntax with traditional "poetic" imagery. *Poems* was decidedly introspective, but *Lament and Triumph* contained visionary political poems extremely individual in tone.

Barker was brought up a Catholic. Like many lapsed Catholics, he retained modes of feeling characteristic of his former religion; and, as is so often the case, a haunting sense of original sin. However, Barker is by no means the former Catholic who continues to apply Catholic standards to experience. His poetry is a prolonged wrestle with the religion he has abandoned—a wrestle whose outcome can be direct and strident blasphemy. He has a virulent sense of guilt; yet—or perhaps because of this—a compulsive attachment to a way of life (particularly of sexual behaviour) that is a desecration of the Catholic view. His poetry is at every turn strongly moral, but in a way that leads him back compulsively to the fallen condition.

Barker's prose work of 1950, *The Dead Seagull,* offers a powerful and often astounding rehearsal of his positions and preoccupations of that time. It tells the story of a newly married writer who is at a seaside cottage with his wife, awaiting the birth of a son. As time goes by, he becomes jealous of his unborn son. They are visited by a predatory and voluptuous friend of the wife, Marsden. The writer becomes her lover on a visit to London, and stays with her. The son is born dead—it seems to the writer, in compliance with his wish. His wife dies, cursing him and Marsden.

The events of the story seem to be received by the writer in a state of horrified mesmerisation. He is fascinatedly incapable of turning away from a course of action that fills him with guilt and despair. The book is as much a meditation as a story; and nothing can better give its quality than some of the very explicit products of that meditation.[2]

> Love, with no blood on its knife, does not sleep easily, if it sleeps at all, until every one of its devotees lies dead. The great destroyer.(10)
>
> . . .
>
> And what we are caged in is, in the end, the locked and barred box of zoological sex.(80)
>
> . . .
>
> For freedom is the knowledge of necessity, and the necessity of the human is love, and the necessity of love is existence, and the necessity of existence is two sinning in a bed, and the necessity of two sinning in a bed is to be forgiven. It is thus that our only freedom is to be damned.(141-2)

Sexuality, a recurrent theme of Barker's poetry, is inextricably involved with sin and guilt in his writing of this time: ". . . a garden in which a snake and a tree stand coiled in a perpetual convulsion of realisation." (The Dead Seagull, 138-9) In his essay "The Philadelphia Train", Barker makes use of the distinction between "Profane Love" and "Sacred Love"—between Eros and Agape. The distinction is utilised in Eros in Dogma (1944), with its sequences of Sacred Elegies and Secular Elegies, and it is embodied in The Dead Seagull in the contrast between the wife, Theresa (whose name suggests purity and long suffering) and the Circean Marsden. Barker is the servant of Eros, "Pig to the Circean Muse's honour" (The True Confessions of George Barker (1950), II).

Barker's erratic and tortured concerns with the sacred and the profane, the spiritual and the fleshly, emerge in his two important collections of poetry from the forties, Eros in Dogma and News of the World (1950). The title of the first announces his concerns: "eros" in "dogma"—the erotic in the framework of the religious or the moral; while News of the World was the name of the Sunday newspaper that had the largest circulation in Great Britain, and which supported that circulation on reports of titillating cases of divorce, rape, homosexuality and indecency as they appeared before the courts (court reports being uncensorable). Some of the poems have a very direct relation to passages in *The Dead Seagull:*

> Physical love is a sin because there, and not in the arguments of atheists, god has been rendered unnecessary: in the centre of the ovum is the atheistical void . . . And the blasphemy of two lovers, at the mutually sufficient moment of consummated love, when god, standing in the corner of the room, knows that, at that kiss, he is unnecessary . . .
>
> (The Dead Seagull, 101)

> The kiss is diagonals on which you die
>   Smiling in sweat because
> The turn of your face away would undo
>   The cross of a kiss.
>
> Who rubs our double destruction together
>   Save procreative fate
> So that we shed the fire, the child, each other?
>   Turn, turn away your face.
>
> ("The Bridal Nightmare II")

The act of love is, as traditionally, associated with original sin; and conception is seen as the passing on of the hereditary curse of evil, which separates god from man. The separation of god from man, of man from man, and of man from the world, is the explicit theme of the sequence of "Sacred Elegies" in *Eros in Dogma.* They are subtitled: I, "The Separation of Lovers"; II, "The Exile of Travellers, the Poor and the Invalids"; III, "The Isolation of the Great and all Historical Isolation"; IV "The Actual but Imperfect Union of the Lover, the Labourer and the Poet with the Object of their Love"; V, "The Separation of Man from God". This last poem concludes in despairing, pleading, blasphemy:

> Incubus. Anaesthetist with glory in a bag,
> Foreman with a sweatbox and a whip. Asphyxiator
> Of the ecstatic. Sergeant with a grudge
> Against the lost lovers in the park of creation,
> Fiend behind the fiend behind the fiend behind the
> Friend. Mastodon with mastery, monster with the ache
> At the tooth of the ego, the dead drunk judge:
> Wheresoever Thou art our agony will find Thee
> Enthroned on the darkest altar of our heartbreak
> Perfect. Beast, brute, bastard. O dog my God.

The same stance is taken up in the uncollected poem "Dog, dog in my Manger":

Dog, good dog, trick do and make me take
Calmly the consciousness of the crime
Born in the blood simply because we are here . . .
Dog, dog, your bone I am, who tear my life
Tatterdemalion from me. From you I have no peace,
No life at all unless you break my bone,
No bed unless I sleep upon my grief
That without you we are too much alone,
No peace until no peace is a happy home;
O dog my god, how can I cease to praise.

Barker's equivocal relationship to his theme is seen not merely in the
mixture of blasphemy and humility but in the ill taste of the rather
cocky word-play. "Secular Elegy V", which begins with a magnificent evocation of the serenity of erotic love, is torn by a similar rage—
a rage that, in its expression, again echoes Barker's ambivalence concerning erotic love as seen in *The Dead Seagull:*

O Golden Fleece she is where she lies tonight
Tramelled in her sheets like midsummer on a bed,
Kisses like moths flitter over her bright
Mouth, and, as she turns her head,
All space moves over to give her beauty room . . .

My nine-tiered tigress in the cage of sex
I feed with meat you tear from my side
Crowning your nine months with the paradox:
The love that kisses with a homicide
In robes of red generation resurrects . . .

In *News of the World,* Barker seems to be moving towards an acceptance of the world as a place in which the Ideal does not have its
habitat; yet the struggle, again, does not seem simply to be one of
taking an imperfect world and an imperfect self for what they are. In
"To My Son" he writes:

Underneath
The human heart, I believe,
Lives a god who cannot grieve
No matter how disastrous
The crimes our passion brings on us
Because this ungrieving god
Knows that either bad or good
Might look, from a better angle,
Like a double-headed angel.

In a slightly later poem, "Letter to a Young Poet", he speaks of his
experience of poetry:

> I speak of the whispering gallery
> Of all Dionysian poetry
> Within whose precincts I have heard
> An apotheosis of the word
>
> As down those echoing corridors
> The Logos rode on a white horse;
> Till every No that sense could express
> Turned to a transcendental Yes.

It is hard to reconcile the stance in the poems with the sentence in *The Dead Seagull,* where he paraphrases a celebrated phrase of Newman: "Yes, Love is the terrible aboriginal calamity." (128) The poems seem to reflect the Romantic position that, for those who can see fully and purely, all is pure; while the prose statement seems a tortured Byronic recognition of the irremediable flaw of original sin. The rage of Barker's writing of the forties is the rage of a man haunted by the irreconcilability of these two positions, and by a guilt that stems from his not being able to accept one or the other as the basis on which to order and judge his life.

                                    II

   Barker is always coming back to the subject of the Nature of Poetry in his essays: indeed, *Essays* (1970) might be regarded as an extended disquisition on poetry rather than the series of brief writings from four decades on a variety of subjects that it comprises[3]. Inevitably, Barker's conception of poetry reflects the pressing concerns already discussed. As one would expect from even a brief acquaintance with Barker's work, the poet is seen as "at heart anarchic" ("Introduction")—one whose relationship to society is that of "irreconcilable enmity" ("Poet as Pariah" 1948). Yet he is, as one would also expect, an "elector of moral categories" ("Poem in an Orange Wig" 1955); and "a poem without a sense of moral responsibility is really nothing more than the brilliant gibberish of a nut." ("How to Refuse a Heavenly Home" 1961).
   However, ". . . the moral vision . . . is the arithmetic upon which the Creator has constructed not, it would seem, Nature, but the lost Paradise." ("The Hippogryph and the Water Pistol" 1960). The role of the poet is "the exploitation, by the imagination, or process of poetry, of the sensual world of events and persons, in such a manner that an intuitive rather than rational evaluation of them is achieved . . ." ("Poetry and Reality" 1937); and to do this "the poet works to rid the head of all that is not ideal, and the heart of all that is not, truly, real." ("The Exacting God" 1949). Poetry is contrasted,

as traditionally, with History: ". . . myth takes the side of heaven against the Satanic battalions of facts, figures, diagrams, graphs, records, reports, eye-witness accounts and philosophical histories. For the compilers of the latter fail to see that facts function only by illuminating the fundamental element, namely the element of the inexperiential or perfect, which Myths, Poems, Religions, Mathematics perpetuate." ("A Letter to History" 1940).

A poem is "the metaphor of an event . . . an event stolen from temporal affairs and transferred to the altitude of the Ideal." ("The Face behind the Poem" 1948). The business of the poem is not to present reality for its own sake: ". . . I do not read poems in order to save myself the railway fare to a particular place so that I can examine a particular object: I read poems because . . . they really know much more than they seem to know." ("On the Image" 1948). It is through the image that the poet works: "The image is what the imagination ascertains about the hitherto unimaginable . . . The image is the first formula of the poem that the intellect can unconditionally modify." ("On the Image").

He cites Melville's description of Ahab, "A man with a crucifixion in his face", as an image "full of the features I seek for." ("On the Image"). The way in which the image operates for Barker is well exemplified in the following passage:

> The mistletoe by which Balduer died hangs over the mantlepieces of a hundred students of Nordic Mythology, but the gun that shot Abraham Lincoln has been relegated to a second-hand ironmongers or made into a razor blade. These are the dim and hazy forms of historical apprehension: Apollo kidnapping Chatterton, Ulysses encircling the world for the first time in a single engined monoplane, Mythrias performing miracles of healing in California . . . ("A Letter to History")

The mythical, which embodies the Ideal, is brought into play with the natural, so that the mythical is exemplified, imperfectly, in the natural, or the mythical is contrasted with the natural. There is always a fairly clear separation, nevertheless, of mythical and natural, metaphysical and actual, image and abstraction in Barker's thinking, for all his vociferations against realism. One cannot imagine him offering "explanations" of his poetry, such as Dylan Thomas offered, that were further adventures into poetry. Although his poetry owes a great deal to the developments begun by T.S. Eliot (Barker's first admiration in modern poetry) and the Imagists, it remains "rhetorical" in a rather old fashioned way, in that, behind the images, there lurk, fairly closely, traditional abstractions of moral, philosophical and religious thought. Indeed, Barker's images are often the well known images of religion or mythology:

This morning take a holiday from unhappiness because
It is the greatest day that ever was
When he stepped down out of the nuptial arch
With the cross in his face and he shall search
For ever for the wreath and not even at his death
Really regret this day that gave him birth.

O history be kind and time be short to him
Where he is anonymous and let him come to no harm
From the hammer of the diurnal, or the drum,
The sweatbox and the wheel where the dog's dream
Turns and is interminable. O be near always
You whom from far I shall not the less praise!

Let the gentle solstice, like the Fierral Bay
Where the Eleven Thousand Virgins keep
The fishes quiet in their arms, keep him asleep
All his life long in a long summer's day:
With the empty hourglass, the four-leafed clover,
The rock for the resurrection, and much love.

("First Cycle of Love Poems" I)

The poem strides out with a certainty and ease in its pronounced and decided placing of stress within a diction that is natural and tender, yet capable of grandeur, as at the beginning of the final stanza. The images of "the empty hourglass" and "the four-leafed clover" are of common use and require no explanation. The "search . . . for the wreath" and "the cross in his face" speak of the inexorable movement of life towards death, and of the fallen, tortured condition of human life. The mind moves easily from the images to the notions behind them, and is not engaged strongly by the images other than in their isolated, representational, sensuous and associative impact. The same may be said of the images of enclosure that are linked with "the dog's dream".

Barker does not, in Thomas's phrase, work "*out* of words"—at least, not to the extent that Thomas does. Indeed, one of his shortcomings is a tendency to preach in his verse—to embody a message too decidedly independent of the poem:

The armies of Hohenzollern, brooding on loss,
Know best that the real enemy is never there
Pinned akimbo on the gun-sight, but in the cause.
O sheeted in their horoscopes like togas
Under red stars strut the catchpenny Caesars.

("Secular Elegy I")

The poet here is decidedly the "elector of moral categories".

III

The earlier forties were one of the high points in Barker's career, if only for the continuously beautiful celebration of sexual love found in poem after poem—in "O Golden Fleece", in the three cycles of love poems, and in the following poem from *News of the World:*

> Turn on your side and bear the day to me
> Beloved, sceptre-struck, immured
> In the glass wall of sleep. Slowly
> Uncloud the borealis of your eye
> And show your iceberg secrets, your midnight prizes
> To the green-eyed world and me. Sin
> Coils upward into thin air when you awaken
> And again morning announces amnesty over
> The serpent-kingdomed bed. Your mother
> Watched with as dove an eye the unforgiveable night
> Sigh backward into innocence when you
> Set a bright monument in her amorous sea.
> Look down, Undine, on the trident that struck
> Sons from the rock of vanity. Turn in the world
> Sceptre-struck, spellbound, beloved,
> Turn in the world and bear the day to me.

The poem is remarkable in the way in which it conveys serenity, a sensuous richness, a majesty in its presentation of this moving scene. There is nothing particularised or unusual about the visual elements of the poem, which succeeds by the power of its generality. The framing phrase, "sceptre-struck", suggests at once magic and majesty; and the combination of power and serenity is also found in the images of "the glass wall", "the iceberg", the "monument" and the "trident", which all enter the poem casually but contribute strongly to its tone. Equally compelling is the movement, perfectly modulated, giving at once a sense of control and a richness and resonance to the poem as a whole.

The three cycles of "Love Poems" are remarkably sustained in their power, though more lyrical and simple in style:

> Lie still, lie still, here at my heart lie still
> Sleeping like thunderheads. Be over me dominant
> So I shall sleep as the river sleeps under the hill
> Kissing the foot and giving back the element.

This simplicity of style is found too in the sequence of "Pacific Sonnets", which arose out of Barker's experiences in Japan, where he was teaching at the outbreak of the war in Europe. A definite change in style in the direction of simplicity can be seen in Barker's poetry in the forties. The first two "Secular Elegies" in *Eros in Dogma* are on political themes, and, with their rhetorical and imagistic manner, can be grouped with the visionary social poems of the late thirties. In contrast, "To My Son" in *News of the World,* with its relaxed octosyllabic couplets and its subdued diction, looks forward to the directness of volumes like *Poems of Places and People* (1971).

In *Lament and Triumph,* in which he brings together his shorter poems of the late thirties, there is already a contrast in style between the rhetorical visionary poems and poems like "Battersea Park" that celebrate more personal and particular themes. A simple and more direct style is to be observed in the "Supplementary Personal Sonnets" in *Eros in Dogma.* Of these the most celebrated—and justly—is "To My Mother":

> Most near, most dear, most loved and most far,
> Under the window where I often found her
> Sitting as huge as Asia, seismic with laughter,
> Gin and chicken helpless in her Irish hand,
> Irresistible as Rabelais, but most tender for
> The lame dogs and hurt birds that surround her,—
> She is a procession no one can follow after
> But be like a little dog following a brass band.
>
> She will not glance up at the bomber, or condescend
> To drop her gin and scuttle to a cellar,
> But lean on the mahogany table like a mountain
> Whom only faith can move, and so I send
> O all my faith and all my love to tell her
> That she will move from mourning into morning.

This is a very characteristic Barker poem, fearlessly and successfully mixing hyperbole ("Sitting as huge as Asia") with understatement ("She is a procession no one can follow after"), the arcane with the ordinary ("seismic with laughter"), and sustaining a tone of dignity even in the face of the introduction of an ostensibly deflating image ("a little dog following a brass band"). The octet is one sentence that accommodates the demands of form with both sweep and naturalness. In Lines 5 and 6 the rhythm is allowed to crumble—a frequent trick of style with Barker—without damage to the cohesiveness of the movement, giving an added naturalness. As characteristic as anything in the poem is, however, the marring of the last line with a ghastly pun— a pun in fact imported from an earlier poem by Barker. He must have liked it.

The late forties were then a transitional period for Barker. *News of the World* is nowhere near so impressive as *Eros in Dogma,* and the large proportion of poems about literary personages seems to indicate a hesitation of impulse. The movement is clearly away from the rhetorical visionary style of the late thirties and early forties towards simpler and more relaxed diction and rhythm. At times elements of the earlier style jar with the new manner, as in "Channel Crossing", one of the last poems of the decade:

> The horror of the questionmark
> I looked back and saw stand over
> The white and open page of Dover
> Huge as the horn of the scapegoat. Dark
> It stood up in the English day
> Interrogating Destiny
> With the old lip of the sea:
> "What can a dead nation say?"

The visionary stance, the exaggerated imagery need the pomp of the older style to carry them: the more austere diction and subdued movement leave them starkly exposed as being over-done.

The change of style would seem to mark a radical change of attitude by Barker to his material—as indeed a change of style must in an artist of any stature. In *The True Confession of George Barker* (1950) he writes:

> To nineteen hundred and forty-seven
>   I pay the deepest of respects,
> For during this year I was given
>   Some insight into the other sex.
> I was a victim, till forty-six,
>   Of the rosy bed with bitches in it . . .

Though Barker's obsessive and compulsive concern with sin and sexuality were to remain a feature of his work, he seems to have attained a greater acceptance of the fallen nature of this world, its imperfections and dividedness.

Barker's obsessions get full play in *True Confession,* a poem evidently unwelcome to Faber and Faber and their director, T.S. Eliot, so that its first part appeared as a small pink pamphlet in Jack Lindsay's Fore Poets. In some respects, *True Confession* is one of Barker's most engaging pieces, and has the energy and panache of his best work. The model is Villon's *Testament,* and the same stanza pattern is used; while the dash and the sudden romantic deflations remind one of Auden's "Letter to Lord Byron" (1937). Barker nuzzles into his private hang-ups and gives full expression to his disgust with love;

in the words of one of his most disastrous puns: "I see phallic: you, cephalic." The poem concludes with a strongly moral, quasi-religious appeal:

> Enisled and visionary, mad,
>   Alive in the catacomb of the heart,
> O lonely diviner, lovely diviner, impart
>   The knowledge of the good and the bad
> To us in our need. Emblazon
>   Our instincts upon your illumination
> So that the rot's revealed, and the reason
>   Shown crucified upon our desolation . . .
>
> Get rags, get rags, all angels, all
>   Laws, all principles, all deities,
> Get rags, come down and suffocate
>   The orphan in its flaming cradle,
> Snuff the game and the candle, for our state
>   —Insufferable among mysteries—
> Makes the worms weep. Abate, abate
>   Your justice. Execute us with mercies!

However, its treatment of experience cannot, in all cases, be said to lead to that conclusion or level with it:

> The act of human procreation
>   —The rutting tongue, the grunt and shudder,
> The sweat, the reek of defecation,
>   The cradle hanging by the bladder,
> The scramble up the hairy ladder,
>   And from the thumping bed of Time
> Immortality, a white slime,
>   Sucking at its mother's udder . . .

It is easy enough to name Barker's shortcomings—the dreadful puns, the inane circumlocutions, the pomposities, the clashing images. They are there in *Eros in Dogma* and *News of the World,* as they were there in his collections of the thirties; but in the forties they are no longer so obtrusive, and his self-consciously rhetorical style attains at its best a new purity and serenity. "Flash Harry", G.S. Fraser called him, in a poem for his sixtieth birthday[4]; and Barker himself had written: "One must never become so engrossed in one's private miseries as to forget that their public presentation should be conducted in style." ("A Cripple and a Masher"). He went on to add, "Style is wonderful stuff if you know what to do with it. Like a handsome walk you have to learn how it's done and then forget all about it." Barker's faults are in the direction of too much swagger, and of uncontrolled compulsive treatment of material; and without his energy, Barker would be nothing. Much of his poetry is of the type in which the rhetoric may be conceived of as separate from the thought; though, in poems like ''O Golden Fleece'' or ''Turn on your side'', the rhetoric becomes the ''subject'' in the sense that the poems may be regarded as an occasion for the emotive deployment and exploration of words and images that have a special power and significance for the poet. In his earlier work in *Poems,* the independent life of the rhetoric sometimes permitted the tricky indulgence of tendencies only ostensibly ''contained'' by the poem; but in the forties, when rhetoric, energy and impulse come harmoniously together, the result is some of the most moving poetry of the decade.

IV

The publication of W.S. Graham's *Collected Poems* in 1979 revealed a poetic attainment subtle, individual, with a continuity and centrality of vision equalled by few poets of his generation. It was an achievement garnered slowly. In the previous thirty years, Graham had published three volumes of poetry: *The Nightfishing* (1955); *Malcolm Mooney's Land* (1970); and *Implements in their Places* (1977). These constitute Graham's patient and enduring achievement. Yet Graham, born in 1917, had produced four books of poetry between 1942 and 1947: *A Cage without Grievance* (1942); *Seven Journeys* (1944); *2nd Poems* (1945); and *The White Threshold* (1949). Indeed, the dates are a little deceptive: *The White Threshold* states that the poems were written between February 1944 and October 1946 (except presumably for the last three, dated 1948).

Some of Graham's earliest poetry, like the earliest poetry of George Barker, echoed Romantic poetry in a conventional way. The influence of Dylan Thomas was clearly a decisive one, and was to show itself soon in the mannered and distorted syntax, in the liking for portmanteau words, and in the very rhythm and vocabulary:

> Near farms and property of bright night-time
> By mileaway dogbark now there is means to say
> What unseen bargain makes heavier where I walk
> The meanwhile word here of this neighbourhood.
> Mileaway for answer tilling the fertile sky
> Direction's breakdown assembles my own heaven
> Builds up, breaks the dead quarter into miles
> With towering tongue of each discovering hour.
> Some loud means in the dark for my sake tells

> My journey manned and sailed but none so man,
> Bullhorned, treehorned from the heads of huntsmen.
>
> ("Explanation of a Map", *2nd Poems*)

It was Thomas's work of the thirties that was Graham's model, particularly the notorious sonnet sequence, "Altarwise by Owl-light", whose obscurity Thomas himself was to turn away from. While Graham does not build his poems out of the dialectical interplay of images, as did Thomas in his early poetry, he shows the egocentric orientation of the young Thomas. Indeed, concern with the "self", with the elusiveness of experience and a need to give it coherence, is behind most of Graham's seemingly incoherent poetry of the forties.

Seven Journeys, published in the Poetry Scotland series, contains an introduction by William Montgomerie:

> Without attacking the assumption in our minds, that in prose meaning is primary, W.S. Graham by *making* his poems out of words, as a cathedral is built out of squared stone, has assumed that we will ultimately approach his poems in a frame of mind from which meaning is not so much a practical question, as a metaphysical question, as we might say, What is the meaning of St. Mark's in Venice?

By the nineteen-forties, the notion that a poem should *be* and not *mean* had passed from critical novelty to received opinion. Graham employs conventional syntax in *Seven Journeys,* but seems to avoid giving his sentences coherent denotation by creating an apparent nonsense that depends on the things to which he refers failing to cohere into a meaning realisable in terms of experience. The result is that the reader feels bombarded by a series of images whose meaning and associations are *felt* but do not form an *understandable* sequence. *Seven Journeys* was not a rewarding book, and Graham did not reprint it in *Collected Poems*.

This way of writing might seem close to surrealism; and the interest in surrealism in the later thirties could have inspired Graham to take this direction. However, the strongly verbal orientation of Graham's writing displays a selection and control very much at odds with surrealism, which emphasises the elimination of control in the selection of images. Not to see this would be to miss the continuity between Graham's earlier work and his later. Indeed, the more one reads his work of the forties, the more one detects the presence of well defined concerns that contradict any attempt at impressionistic reading.

Graham's egocentric preoccupations begin to come together in a personal vision in *2nd Poems*. At the same time, a recognisable manner emerges:

Soon to be distances locked sound
In the day of travel my passing knows
The place across which I slowly move
With ease and the lonely stumble
Feeds day with dark and fastens me
Meaning no hurt or comfort
To parallels barbed in the brake and bramble.

What I learn turns barrier to voice.

The poetry, while seemingly impenetrable and heavy with uncontrolled suggestion, gets sparser in imagery. Its apparent clottedness comes increasingly from deliberate syntactic disorientation: "This day dies down to tell so never better/Begun than quietly to lie still lowly bragging . . ." ("Lying in Corn"). The temptation is to regard the writing as pretentious and obscurantist; and it must be admitted that a first reading of the hundred or so pages of poetry published by Graham in the forties leaves one with nothing quite so memorable as the effort involved in getting through it. Nevertheless, *The White Threshold* proves to be a rewarding book with singular unity of style, imagery and theme.

With all many men laid down in the burial heart,
Hearing spring fall and the joyfaring weather waken
Another thunder's arrival under my footfall,
I walk well over the hill of my listening dead.
I wear early April blessed in best innocence
Won from watched wonder and all my called people
Falling behind me into the look in my eyes.
With all my altering men, my messengers ranging
The never-still Aprils heading up from my first
Step started over shelter's threshold and throe,
And put into speed as green kindles into quickly
A flower in a snap of weather; I walk discovered
Up over the shepherd heart and containing hill
Earning the blood of my dead who lie down flowering.
With yes all wishes and my best men well alive,
Eyes turned to whinwork bright in the present time
And the skyward-worded morning, my word breaks way
After the shape of entering and leaving this welcoming
And lives handmouth on bread of the singing springside.

As soon as it is realised that the dead are equated, naturally enough, with the past and with the poet's past selves, this celebratory poem about a spring morning and the acceptance of the present comes alive with brightness and clarity, in spite of its rather too sustained homage to Dylan Thomas.

The focus of Graham's poetry is on the elusiveness of the present, seen as a fulcrum of future and past.

> Since all my steps taken
> Are audience of my last
> With hobnail on Ben Narnain
> Or mind on the word's crest
> I'll walk the kyleside shingle
> With scarcely a hark back
> To the step dying from my heel
> Or the creak of the rucksack.
> All journey, since the first
> Step from my father and mother
> Toward the word's crest
> Or walking towards that other,
> The new step arrives out
> Of all my steps taken
> And out of to-day's light.

Movement and journeying are recurrent images. Images from his childhood appear; and these are constantly set over against his strongest image, the sea: "Men Sign the Sea"; "Three Poems of Drowning"; "The Voyages of Alfred Wallis"; and the title poem, "The White Threshold". The sea seems to epitomise for him the elusiveness of experience and its inchoate nature; it is seen as a vast reservoir of all that is past or "drowned"; and, in this sense, the poet's identity, which can only find itself in the changing present, is literally drowned in the sea of the past.

Graham explores the relationship between the numinous, shifting nature of experience and the articulation of language: "Each word is but a longing/Set out to break from a difficult home. Yet in/Its meaning I am." ("The Nightfishing", 1955). Experience and the experiencing self are always changing, and language changes things in fixing things: "Language swings away/Before me as I go/With again the night rising/Up to accompany me/And that other fond/Metaphor, the sea." ("The Dark Dialogues", 1970). We "ride" experience as though it had a purpose beyond what we give it: "What is the language using us for?" is the opening poem of *Implements in their Places* (1977).

These concerns and procedures were explicitly discussed by Graham as early as 1946 in an essay "Notes on a Poetry of Release" in *Poetry Scotland:*

There is the involuntary war between me and that environment flowing in on me from all sides and there is the poetic outcome.

History continually arrives as differently as our most recent minute on earth.

A poem is made of words . . . All the poet's knowledge and experience . . . is contained in the language which is obstacle and vehicle at the same time.

He [the poet] has to explore the imagination by using the language as his pitch . . . It is no help to think of the purpose as being to "transfer collected emotion" or to "report significantly" or indeed to think of it as putting-across anything. The poem itself is dumb but has the power to release. Its purpose is that it can be used by the reader to find out something about himself.[5]

Such poetry might seem rarefied and monotonous. In fact, it can be very touching and powerfully elegiac in its rendering of the transience of experience. It offers an exploration of the "self" and its relationship to its world, experiential and linguistic, more subtle than is found in Thomas's early poetry. Though a lot of poetry in *The White Threshold* remains difficult to penetrate, there are a few pieces like "The Hill of Intrusion" that evince a control and awareness that are not merely artistically exemplary, but are geared to the exploration of experiences at once elusive and deeply affecting:

> The ear the answer
> Hears the wrecked cry
> Of the one-time
> Holiday boy who
> Feathered his oars
> On a calm firth
> Held still by hills.
> Now grey rock clenches
> Round the rower over—
> Taken by rough
> White-haired sea-troughs
> That ride the foam
> Of Time's bare back.
> Wrecked pile of past
> Events cindered
> Into a charcoal
> Of kindling power
> And constellations
> Of united hearts,
> These make reply
> To the flare flying
> Off from the endangered
> Watchman wornout.
> The winds from a hill
> Halfway Ben Narnain
> And halfway hill
> Of intrusion into

The silence between
My heart and those
Elements of nature
That are my food,
Sound out alarm
Over the baling
Prisoners of water
This night unsheltered.
The ear says more
Than any tongue.
The ear sings better
Than any sound
It hears on earth
Of waters perfect.
The ear the answer
Hears the caged cry
Of those prisoners
Crowded in a gesture
Of homesickness.
                    ("The Hill of Intrusion")

Such poems give an assurance that the whole volume aims at a controlled and serious exploration of experience. The submergence of
metaphor, the mingling of experiences, the way in which the sea is at
once a part of boyhood experience and also a metaphor for experience
in its fugitive aspect, fruitfully lead us into an apprehension of the
fleetingness of all experience, the elusiveness of what constitutes
human identity and all that a human being may attach himself to. This
is done with a sparseness that is at odds with the immediate impression
that most of the poems in the volume give. Already there is a hint of
the masterly handling of the extended short line paragraph that is crucial to the accomplished eloquence of *The Nightfishing*. In the last
lines quoted, the tension between the expected regularity of stress and
the attained conjunction of stresses contributes to the generation of a
distinctive "voice" that is to be the strength of Graham's later poetry.
The firm resilience of movement in his best passages is reinforced by
placing of words that produces a tension between line separation and
syntactic closeness.

While Graham's powerful successes in the forties were few, and
his real mark as a poet had yet to be made, he was very much a part
of the literary scene, remembered in Fitzrovia by Julian MacLaren-
Ross as "the most competitive poet I have ever met"—"just inordi-
nately prickly".[6] Starting from Dylan Thomas's earlier work, he produced something very different from Thomas, but nevertheless took
the conception of a poem as linguistic construct a step further—a step

too far, perhaps, for all except a poet of his unusual vision. His poetry is strikingly "rhetorical", in the sense that it departs, often grandiloquently, from normal usage; yet, unmistakably, its "meaning" is inseparable from the rhetorical distortions. The pressures to which he responds in his poetry took him beyond the concern with writing good honest poetry about human experience that was so much a feature of the period, and that is cultivated so creditably in the work of Alun Lewis, for example. In Graham's work of the forties we see the formation of one of the most fruitful poetic careers to have its beginning in that decade.

V

Another undisguisedly rhetorical poet was W.R. Rodgers, whose only two books of poetry, *Awake! and other poems* (1941) and *Europa and the Bull* (1952), were given lavish praise on their appearance. Rodgers was a late starter at poetry, being a contemporary of Auden and Vernon Watkins. On graduating from the University of Belfast, he studied for the ministry, and was ordained and installed as minister at Laughall in County Armagh in 1936. John Hewitt had introduced him to the work of Auden and his contemporaries, and he wrote his first poem when he was about 28. All the poems in his first volume were written between 1938 and 1940. His life in Armagh was torn by marital discord; and in 1946 he resigned from the ministry and was recruited by Louis MacNeice into the B.B.C. as a script writer.

Awake was an unusual first book in that it had such decided individuality of style. While there are one or two passages that betray the influence of MacNeice—"Punctually at Christmas the soft plush/Of sentiment snows down" ("White Christmas"), or Auden—"Side-step the strict keepers of paths/The pickets of prerogative; avoid/Confirming pass-word" ("Directions to a Rebel"), almost every poem has Rodgers' unmistakable manner:

> O these lakes and all gills that live in them,
> These acres and all legs that walk on them,
> These tall winds and all wings that cling to them,
> Are part and parcel of me, bit and bundle,
> Thumb and thimble.
> ("Ireland")

The last line and a half might at first sight seem an imitation of Dylan Thomas—the sort of rhetoric with which he bamboozled audiences, but the poem clearly anticipates Thomas's cultivation of this type of word play by several years. Alliteration, assonance and word play were Rodgers' favourite devices; and these were most variously deployed in *Europa and the Bull,* where a greater richness of texture is attained, and one is aware of the influence of Hopkins:

> Trees, grasses, wings—all
> On a hone of wind sluiced and sleeked one way,
> Smooth and close as the pile of a pony's coat,
> But in a moment, smoke-slewed, glared, squinted back
> And up like sticking bones shockingly unkinned.
>
> ("Autumn Day")

The relationship between rhetoric and theme was decidedly old fashioned, particularly in the first book: abstractions are often invoked directly, and the imagery has a complementing illustrative function.

There were pressures enough in Rodgers' life at the time, as one is aware in poems like "Paired Lives", "The Lovers" or "Beagles", with its picture of the poet tethered to the hunted hare. He was forced to leave his wife in a heartbreaking disintegration of their relationship; and, at the same time, he was leaving the church. The impetus for poetry no doubt came from these circumstances:

> When we are squeezed between two worlds and two flatly different loyalties—one of the flesh and one of the faith—what else can a poet say but 'a plague on both your houses', and what else can he do but cock a snook at both? How else do we get ease and issue except by projecting a newborn world of the imagination which will comprehend and inherit the old ones but will override both—the world of poetry.[7]

The outcome of these pressures can be seen in the poems that give a new treatment of Christian themes, such as "Christ Walking on Water", "Lent" and "Nativity", or the poems that take for their material classical myths of encounters of gods and mortals—"Europa and the Bull", "Pan and Syrinx" and "Apollo and Daphne". Rodgers favourite among his poems was "The Swan", which utilises the swan as an emblem of both earthly and spiritual beauty; but the swan finally resists flight (the customary image of spiritual or poetic inspiration) and becomes for the poet an image of reconciliation, as it rides the water serenely at dusk:

> Far from shore and free from foresight,
> Coiled in its own indifferent mood
> It held the heavens, shores, waters and all their brood.

"Europa and the Bull" is Rodgers' longest poem, and it treats the coupling of the Bull and Europa as a reconciliation of flesh and spirit, seeing it in terms of the Word becoming flesh, god becoming man. The poem has a surface felicity in its music and its handling of sensuous detail. Sunlight and ease, the richness and energy of physical impression, are what remain most memorable from its sometimes dazzlingly serene descriptions:

> Naked they came, a niggling core of girls
> Maggoting gaily in the curling wool
> Of morning mist, and careless as the lark
> That gargled overhead. They were the root
> Of all that writhing air, the frothing rock
> Of that grey sea in whose vacuity
> Footless they stood, nor knew if it or they
> Were moving now. Yet, even as they gazed,
> Cave after cave of light calved out of gloom,
> Roof rose on roof, laugh laddered into laugh
> As on they glided through the muddling veils
> Into the motionless meadow, clear as stone,
> Interminably domed.

The sensitivity to the surface of things and the amplitude of the rendering indeed combine to submerge the theme. The poem is spun out to the point of diffuseness, and yet this is no great criticism of it. Though Rodgers complained how abashing it was when "critics write about the technique and the craft of your writing, but never mention the ideas which you are trying"[8], it is the plenitude of the rhetoric that makes "Europa and the Bull" as engaging a poem as it is.

"I feel strongly," he said, "that poetry should be read aloud"[9]; and he admitted that "he cared more about *sound* sense than sound *sense*."[10] He relished the public nature that poetry could have in Ireland. "Nevertheless," as Howard Nemerov remarked, "it is disappointing that a poet so evidently interested in the sound of poetry should use, out of the enormous range of sympathetic resonance in the language, chiefly the blatant effects . . ."[11]: ". . . a niggling core of girls/Maggoting gaily in the curling wool" is coy and pretty in its contrivance of rather vulgar musical effects.

Throughout Rodgers' career, the relationship between theme and rhetorical device was very simplistic:

> To-day walk down the two-way street of words
> (Past empty shop-fronts of abstraction
> In which everyone views his own loved face) . . .

Frequently the poems seem overweighted by language deployed for its own sake. His best poems are often direct and boldly simple:

> Quick, woman, in your net
> Catch the silver I fling!
> O I am deep in your debt,
> Draw tight, skin-tight, the string,
> And rake the silver in.
> No fisher ever yet
> Drew such a cunning ring.
>
> ("The Net")

Set beside Barker, Rodgers seems obvious in his rhetoric; while comparison with Graham reveals how little complexity of vision there is behind the linguistic development. That he was so highly regarded in his hey-day is again a measure of the prevalent taste in the forties for the obviously poetic—some "real poetry" after all that guarded irony, that ugly modern stuff.

Chapter 6

THE LOVELY GIFT OF THE GAB

Dylan Thomas

"My early days, dear God. I never thought that one day I might be here or anywhere filling up time . . . by talking about my early days as though I were a man of letters", Dylan Thomas said to an American audience in 1952.[1] In fact those "early days" were very much in the past by 1939. His first three books, *18 Poems* (1934), *Twenty-five Poems* (1936) and *The Map of Love* (1939) had contained 59 poems in all: 45 of them were written before October 1934, or were based on poems written before that date. Between the publication of *18 Poems* in December 1934 and the end of 1939, Thomas had published only twenty entirely new poems; and he was in fact to write only a further thirty poems in the remaining fourteen years of his life. His mode of composition had changed: poems came only with difficulty and were laboured over to the point of obscurity exemplified by the sonnet sequence "Altarwise by owl-light" in *Twenty-five Poems*. Thomas's mode of life had also changed: he had begun the pattern of living from hand to mouth and pub to pub that was, in the main, to characterize his life until his death in 1953.

The poetry of the "early days" had been almost exclusively about Thomas's sense of "self" and its relation to the external world. Under a welter of images, often cosmic in suggestion and highly elliptical in their relation to one another, Thomas gave expression to his "process philosophy"—that we are all part of a process that takes us back to the earth, the source of life. Death is immanent in the act of creation— or procreation. The force that drives this creation, while not merely sex, is associated with sex, and sex is associated with guilt. These simple feelings, common enough in themselves, are explored with considerable complexity of style in poems that, even to those who have studied them closely, remain obscure. Apart from the linguistic vigour and the virtuosity in handling imagery that leads to many startling successes, what is striking is the pressing nature of the concern with the presence of death in everything. What is also striking is the way in which the imagery of some poems, far from developing or conditioning attitudes to themes ostensibly explored, in fact suggests a static contemplation that permits the intrusion of disturbing and diffusing suggestions not "contained" by the economy of the poem.

87

In July, 1937, he married Caitlin Macnamara, and in January, 1939, their son Llewelyn was born. Several of the sixteen poems in *The Map of Love* seem like those from the earlier books: they are either reworkings of early poems, or, like "I make this in a warring absence" (1937), which took a year to complete, they are overladen with imagery to the point of obscurity. "If my head hurt a hair's foot" (1938) is spoken by a child in the womb and is replete with the sexual, body imagery characteristic of the early poems. Yet it marks a decided change. It is a dialogue between Thomas's unborn son and its mother, in which the child asks not to be born if the pangs of its birth will hurt the mother. The concern is not the old egocentric preoccupation with death, but with the suffering of human beings other than the poet. The old apprehension that the beginning of life is the beginning of death is there; but there is a tone of tenderness and acceptance that is new: "Rest beyond choice in the dust-appointed grain" has a movement and collocation of suggestion that marks a new orientation.

The most celebrated of these poems in its day was "After the funeral" (1938). It is a poem in which the outer world is dwelt on for its own sake and not as imagery for the exploration of the poet's inner concerns. There is a stronger emphasis on narrative than there had previously been. A similar change occurred in Thomas's prose writing, as Vernon Watkins noted: "He suddenly abandoned the highly charged, artificial yet impulsive symbolism of such stories as 'The Orchards', 'The Lemon' . . . Quite suddenly he began to write about people as they actually were and behaved. Through the exact memory he had of his childhood and an extraordinary power to re-create it he released a spring of comedy, both of character and situation, which had been hidden from himself because it was at first too close to his experience."[2] "I remember him saying at this time of an early story: 'I shall never write a story of that kind again'."[3]

The new stories were brought together in *Portrait of an Artist as a Young Dog* (1940). They are marked by an unusual sensitivity to the natural world and a use of language that is evocative and relaxed—in contrast to the strained quality of the early poems and stories. Notable is Thomas's perceptive feeling for details of lower-middle class provincial life, its joys and its discomforts:

> A friendly family stood waiting some way off, the tousled women with their dresses tucked in their knickers, the bare-footed men in shirtsleeves, a number of children in slips and cut-down underwear. He bowled bitterly to a father standing with a tray before the wicket of hats.
>
> ("One Warm Saturday")

One is reminded that Thomas was at that time a frequent reader of

Dickens, another poet of innocence and childhood and an even more masterly observer of genteel eccentricity.

It became Thomas's habit to send his completed poems to Watkins for comment; and, in their lengthy correspondence, they developed the humorous classification of Thomas's poems as "opuses" and "opossums"[4]. The "opuses" (or "exhausters", as Thomas called them)[5] were the highly worked over poems that Thomas wrote in the thirties— "I make this in a warring absence", "How shall my animal"; and the "opussums" were simpler poems, usually based on earlier versions in his notebooks. The "opuses" are among the most obscure poems in the language, and are as dense and idiosyncratic in their imagery as the poems of Thomas's friend William Empsom. There seems to be no debt to Empsom, but there is a parallel exploration of the oblique techniques of modernism. Far from being *symboliste* or surrealist in his use of imagery, Thomas seems to have taken his images as literally as did Empson in his "Notes". An example of this is the explanation of "Into her lying down head" that Thomas sent to Watkins with that poem: "Man is denying his partner man or woman and whores with the whole night, begetting a monstrous brood; one day the brood will not die when the day comes but will hang on to the breast and the parts and squeeze his partner out of bed."[6] There seems a more literal use of hyperbole in the explanation than in the poem, not out of incoherence but out of an unreadiness or an inability to find a simplifying statement that freed itself from the *imagistic* presentation.

In a letter to Pamela Hansford Johnson in 1934, Thomas had made the distinction between writers who work "in the *direction* of" words and those who work "*out of* words".[7] After the publication of his *Collected Poems* in 1952, he wrote to Spender, praising Spender's review of the book for having made that distinction.[8] The distinction is illustrated in the description John Malcolm Brinnin gave of Thomas's method of work:

> I had noticed that on many of his manuscripts Dylan would add a single word or phrase, or a new punctuation, then recopy the whole poem in longhand. When another addition or revision was made, no matter how minor or major, he would then copy the whole poem again . . . he showed me his drafts of 'Fern Hill'. There were more than two hundred separate and distinct versions of the poem . . . He began almost every poem merely with some phrase . . . If this phrase was right . . . if it were resonant or pregnant, it would suggest another phrase. In this way a poem would 'accumulate'. Once 'given' a word . . . or a phrase or a line . . . he could often envision it or 'locate' it within a pattern of other words or phrases or lines . . . so that sometimes it would be possible to surmise accurately that the 'given' unit would occur near the end of the poem or near the beginning . . .[9]

The accuracy of this description is born out by the work sheets of his later poems.

While this laborious method of composition, evolved by Thomas in the middle thirties, was to remain with him for the rest of his life, Vernon Watkins saw a change in orientation towards material and language:

> The point of balance in the letters is perhaps 1939, the year in which he abandoned the struggling, symbol-charged prose of the intensely subjective early stories . . . Dylan had already anticipated this change . . .:
>
>> Once it was the colour of saying
>> Soaked my table the uglier side of a hill.
>
> . . . Both in poetry and prose his work from this time forward moved in the direction of the living voice.[10]

The change is observable in the poems he wrote between 1939 and 1941—a steady creative period for his poetry. The emergence of a new clarity, a greater naturalness of rhythm and imagery can be seen in "There was a saviour" or "On a Wedding Anniversary". This development was undoubtedly connected with a stronger concern with the world around him and with the central sources of human joy and suffering, as manifested in his prose fiction. The movement is away from an imagistic grappling with philosophical concerns towards an acceptance of all aspects of the human condition—what he was to call "unjudging love".

An event that sets a landmark between the earlier and later period was the selling of his notebooks in the latter part of 1941. He had drawn on them not only for *18 Poems* in the days when they were still new, but for most of the poems in *Twenty-five Poems* and *The Map of Love* too. It had been the "opossums" the simpler poems, that had come from the Notebooks; and, characteristically, his last use of these books was a redrafting of an early poem to produce one of his finest and clearest poems, "The Hunchback in the Park". This was in July, 1941; but it was already to be seen from poems that have no predecessors in the Notebooks that he had come to recognise the potentialities of the simpler style. From 1939 to 1941 there is an attempt to marry the virtues of the simpler poems to the imagistic virtuosity of his more ambitious pieces: this prepared for the maturing of his achievement a few years later.

The coming of the war threw Thomas into rather unseemly consternation over the impending call-up. Among other things, Thomas considered registering as a conscientious objector, though he had little basis for this other than his desire not to be taken away from his writing. After his medical, he was classified unfit for military service. For most of the war he wrote film scripts for Strand Films, who worked for the Ministry of Information. With the coming of the air-raids, Thomas was deeply moved, as can be seen in "Among those Killed in the Dawn Raid was a Man Aged a Hundred" (though the more famous "A Refusal to Mourn" was written later). The film work, necessitating being in London and making long and frequent wartime journeys, took too much of his energy, and he produced no poems between 1941 and 1944. Then in a little over twelve months in Wales, from July 1944 to September 1945, he wrote a series of poems that included some of his finest: "Poem in October"; "Vision and Prayer"; "Holy Spring"; "A Winter's Tale"; "A Refusal to Mourn"; "Lie Still, Sleep Becalmed"; "This Side of the Truth"; "The Conversation of Prayer"; "Fern Hill"; "In My Craft or Sullen Art". The last seven were written after the manuscript of *Deaths and Entrances* (1946) had gone to the publisher and Thomas was waiting for the proofs.

"The Conversation of Prayer", which opens *Deaths and Entrances,* offers a new mode in which the lucidity of the early simple poems is combined with the imagistic intensity of his more ambitious poems of the thirties. The old preoccupation with the immanence of death in life is brought out strongly in the paradoxical conclusion, when the child discovers death, and the lover, expecting death, finds joy. The whole poem, in the assurance and serenity of its movement, asserts an acceptance that is the basis of that joy.

> The conversation of prayers about to be said
> Turns on the quick and the dead, and the man on the stairs
> To-night shall find no dying but alive and warm
>
> In the fire of his care his love in the high room.
> And the child not caring to whom he climbs his prayer
> Shall down in a grief as deep as his true grave,
> And mark the dark eyed wave, through the eyes of sleep,
> Dragging him up the stairs to one who lies dead.

It is the superb handling of the passage from one sound to another that takes one back to this poem. Nothing by Thomas better exemplifies this mastery of movement and texture than does the celebrated "Poem in October". Sending it to Vernon Watkins in August 1944, Thomas asked: "Will you read it aloud too? It's got, I think, a lovely slow lyrical movement."[11]

> It was my thirtieth year to heaven
> Woke to my hearing from harbour and neighbour wood
> And the mussel pooled and the heron

> Priested shore
> The morning beckon
> With water praying and call of seagull and rook
> And the knock of sailing boats on the net webbed wall
> Myself to set foot
> That second
> In the still sleeping town and set forth.

Babette Deutsch wrote of this:

> The poem proceeds so resonantly that one scarcely sees, for the sound of
> the calling gulls and knocking boats, the simple fisher scene with its flying
> birds, rocking masts, and quiet "net webbed wall". The echo in "har-
> bour" and "neighbour" is one of many . . . "Heaven" "heron" "bec-
> kon" "second" are woven on one warp of vowels and "wood" "rook"
> "foot" are woven on another . . . there are other repetitive sounds,
> "woke" alone having five alliterations, and echoing again in the vowels
> of "shore" and "forth", the consonants of "rook" and "knock".[12]

The passage demonstrates Thomas's own sense that "you must endeavour to feel and weigh the shape, sound, content of each word in
relation to the shape, sound, content etcetera of the words surrounding
it. It isn't only the *meaning* of the words that must develop harmoni-
cally . . . but it is that which also informs the words with their own
particular life: the noise . . . that they make in the air and the ear, the
contours in which they lie on the page and the mind, their colours and
density."[13] The deft placing of details and their overall orchestration
make clear what Vernon Watkins was talking about when he said:
"He usually had beforehand an exact conception of the poem's length,
and he would decide how many lines to allot to each part of its development."[14] The poem is in syllabic verse, as were many of this
period; and this enabled Thomas to develop the rhythm in a fluid and
natural way, moving without jar from the conversational to the highly
rhetorical. The sound pattern is worked in terms of the assonances
that Babette Deutsch remarked on, and this gives a muted effect that
allows a running over of line ends to pass unnoticed in the structure
of internal assonance, while the stanza form may be used in the usual
way, when needed, to clinch the sense.

The poem celebrates a dividing point in Thomas's life—his thirtieth
birthday. Characteristically, he turns back to his childhood for a sense
of what he was and what he must hold to. There is a suggestion that
contact with "the true/Joy of the long dead child" (a phrase replete
with contradictory and reinforcing suggestions of innocence, loss,
death, resurrection) gives a sanctification to his life. The town below
him is "leaved with October blood", suggesting the brutality of the

natural, fallen world, but also the blood of redemption. As he wrote
in "Ceremony After a Fire Raid", "I know the legend/Of Adam and
Eve is never for a second/Silent in my service/Over the dead in-
fants"; and again the legend of the fall and of the Garden of Eden is
clearly implicit. These suggestions are reinforced by the recurrence of
religious words and images, creating an atmosphere of innocence
beyond the human: "the heron/Priested shore"; "the parables/Of sun
light/And the legends of the green chapels"; "the mystery/Sang
alive".

It would be wrong to leave "Poem in October" without remarking
on the sensitivity of visual observation and the evocativeness of description. These qualities are shared by "Fern Hill", another celebration of innocence. Fern Hill was the farm described in the story "The
Peaches" and was the home of his aunt, Ann Jones, for whom he
wrote "After the Funeral". The connection with the legend of the
unfallen world is explicit:

> And then to awake, and the farm, like a wanderer white
> With the dew, come back, the cock on his shoulder; it was all
> Shining, it was Adam and maiden,
> The sky gathered again
> And the sun grew round that very day.
> So it must have been after the birth of the simple light
> In the first, spinning place, the spellbound horses walking warm
> Out of the whinnying green stable
> On to the fields of praise.

The poem, read by Thomas to numerous audiences, became his best
known and best liked. Yet, as with so much of his "simple" writing
concerning childhood and innocence, it is stylistically sophisticated in
a way that draws attention to the fact—and to a degree in places that
is disconcerting. He uses modified cliché appropriately and effectively
in "happy as the grass was green"; but, while the repetition of the
trick in "singing as the farm was home" and "happy as the heart was
long", may be regarded as part of the structure of echoes and assonances in the poem, it sounds glib. Referring to the child's unaware-
ness of the passage of time, he uses a phrase imported from another
of his poems, "once below a time". The fairy tale suggestions of
"once upon a time" are appropriate, but the tricky inversion sits ill in
this high-toned celebration of innocence.

More disturbing is "Vision and Prayer", a religious poem in two
sections, one in diamond shaped stanzas, the other in a pattern of
wings (though the original printing in *Deaths and Entrances* seems
mis-set and obscures the Herbertian pattern). Merging religious and

sexual suggestion, it exploits religious imagery and emotions rather
than exploring or expressing them. As Thomas wrote to Watkins:
"Yes, the Hound of Heaven is baying there in the last verse . . ."[15]
Its cry is throughout the poem, which seems, like Thompson's poem,
to savour desolation and self-pity.

In
The spin
Of the sun
In the spuming
Cyclone of his wing
For I was lost who am
Crying at the man drenched throne
In the first fury of his stream
And the lightnings of adoration
Back to black silence melt and mourn
For I was lost who have come
To dumbfounding haven
And the finding one
And the high noon
Of his wound
Blinds my
Cry.

More interesting is "A Winter's Tale". It tells of a man in winter
in a Welsh farm consumed with a burning love for the spiritual that is
finally consummated in a union with the heavenly in the form of a
she-bird—a union that is also his death. The poem is in three parts:
the longing and prayer of the man in the winter landscape, symbol of
his hunger and need; a vision of the returning of spring; and the con-
summation of the love and prayer in his death and ascent, folded in
the wings of the bird.

Thomas told Watkins that he felt that the poem didn't "come
off . . . It isn't really one piece . . ."[16]; yet it is hard to feel the force
of this concern when one reads (or hears *him* read) the poem. There is
a notable unity of tone, despite the echo of "East Coker" in the vision
of the spring. The winter setting, redolent of deprivation, is permeated
with suggestions of the experience that will remove that deprivation:
"the hand folded flakes", "the winged snow", "the drifting bread".
Indeed, the poem is outstanding in its orchestration of imagery and in
its control of pace and of musical movement.

The reservations one might have are of a kind that Thomas does
not seem to have suspected. A first reading can leave the impression
that the poem is a story of erotic love with religious overtones, though
it is clear that this is not the case. The association of profane and

sacred love is found in the greatest religious poetry; but it is not clear
that Thomas was concerned to utilize the erotic elements to focus the
religious theme. Indeed, it is not clear that Thomas would have seen
anything in this type of objection. As in a good deal of his poetry,
there is a tendency to develop a richness of resonance for its own
sake, as in "black birds died like priests in the cloaked hedge row"
where the "priests" are appropriate only to the tone. As with "Vision
and Prayer", there is an exploitation of religious feeling, an invocation
of religious experience without an acceptance of the demands, spiritual
and doctrinal, that go with that experience. One result is that the imagery, in the fairy tale setting, emerges as "pretty".

Some of Thomas's stories from the thirties—"A Prospect of the
Sea" (1935), "The Mouse and the Woman" (1932) and "The Orchards" (1935)—contain visionary or dream stories of women who
bring a sense of purity and ease and a relaxation of guilt, tension and
sexual need. They have the same atmosphere as "A Winter's Tale".
There is relaxation rather than resolution of emotional conflict, and
this is the feeling generated by the conclusion of the poem:

> For the bird lay bedded
> In a choir of wings, as though she slept or died,
> And the wings glided wide and he was hymned and wedded,
> And through the thighs of the engulfing bride,
> The woman breasted and the heaven headed
>
> Bird, he was brought low,
> Burning in the bride bed of love, in the whirl-
> Pool at the wanting centre, in the folds
> Of paradise, in the spun bud of the world.
> And she rose with him flowering in her melting snow.

"A Winter's Tale" is at once a delicate and overwhelming performance, and it is not difficult to set aside any embarrassment one may
feel concerning Thomas's relationship to his material. The embarrassment becomes more pressing, however, when one turns to the later
poems that make up the sequence "In Country Heaven". Introducing
these poems in a broadcast in 1950, Thomas said:

> The godhead, the author, the milky-way farmer, the first cause, architect,
> lamplighter, quintessence, the beginning Word, the anthropomorphic
> bowler-out and black-baller, the stuff of all men, scapegoat, martyr,
> maker, woe-bearer—He, on top of a hill in Heaven, weeps whenever, out-
> side that state of being called his country, one of his worlds drops dead,
> vanishes screaming, shrivels, explodes, murders itself. And when he
> weeps, Light and His tears glide down together, hand in hand. So, at the
> beginning of the projected poem, he weeps, and Country Heaven is sud-

denly dark. Bushes and owls blow out like candles. And the countrymen
of heaven crouch all together under the hedges . . .[17]

This amalgam of Hans Anderson and T.F. Powys appears in the un-
completed title poem, "In Country Heaven":

> Always when he, in country heaven,
> >   (Whom my heart hears),
> Crosses the breast of the praising East, and kneels,
> >   Humble in all his planets,
> And weeps on the abasing hill . . .
>
> Light and his tears glide down together
> >   (O hand in hand)
> From the country eyes, salt and sun, star and woe
> >   Down the cheek bones and whinnying
> >   Downs into the low browsing dark.

One is reminded of the domestication of the divine encountered in
Rossetti's "The Blessed Damozel". The godhead is belittled, and the
final effect is prettiness.

The best known of the poems from "In Country Heaven" is "Over
Sir John's Hill", a musical *tour de force* like "Poem in October", set
too on the Welsh coast:

> There
> Where the elegaic fisherbird stabs and paddles
> In the pebbly dab-filled
> Shallow and sedge, and 'dilly dilly', calls the loft hawk,
> 'Come and be killed',
> I open the leaves of the water at a passage
> Of psalms and shadows among the pincered sandcrab prancing
>
> And read, in a shell,
> Death clear as a buoy's bell:
> All praise of the hawk on fire in hawk-eyed dusk be sung . . .

As in "Poem in October", the "young Aesop fabling in the near
night" seeks a sense of holiness in the natural setting, a mode of
acceptance of the evils that mar the innocent vision, so that the innocence may be restored. Yet this "passage/Of psalms and shadows"
does not lead into an acceptance and understanding of how the natural
predation of Sir John's Hill is "just"; and the cry of "dilly dilly",
attributed to the small birds as they go to their deaths, is in danger of
sounding inane.

It may seem ungracious to deflate so masterly and winning a poem,
but "Over Sir John's Hill" is symptomatic of a central difficulty in
nearly all of Thomas's later poetry. As Linden Huddlestone pointed

out many years ago, religious imagery is used in the early poetry ''in a highly unorthodox way''[18], reinterpreting the legends and symbols to become illustrations of Thomas's own preoccupations with sex, sin, and death. In the later poems, these images are again made free of to the point that all that remains of them are their associations, but now no longer in the service of an original, idiosyncratic vision. They are deployed in the orchestration of effects that are supportive of a comparatively simple attitude that strives to present itself with as much orthodoxy as it can muster: ''These poems . . . are written for the love of Man and in praise of God, and I'd be a damn' fool if they weren't.''[19] As Daniel Jones put it: ''To him, Jericho might just as well have been a person as a place; but the addition of the Jericho ingredient to a poem . . . could, he knew, induce a religious impression, in the same way as a mustard sandwich without ham can be imagined to be a ham sandwich with mustard.''[20] There seems no commitment to the meaning of the images other than to the suggestions they retain from his Welsh lower-middle class upbringing. They are the top heavy flowering of comparatively simple impulses and engender an intricacy of shading but little exploration of the impulses.

The simplicity of impulse evinces itself in the structure of sound:

> And out of sleep
> Where the moon had raised him through the mountains in her eyes
> And by the strong, eyed arms that fall behind her, full of
> Tides and fingers, to the blown sea
> He wrestled over the edge of evening, took
> The beginning as a goose to the sky, and called
> His furies by their names from the wind-drawn index
> Of grave and waters.

This is not of course one of Thomas's poems, but a passage from the story ''In the Direction of the Beginning'', which first appeared in 1938. Its appearance of having a metrical structure when arranged as syllabic verse shows how much the structure of sound depends on assonance and alliteration. Daniel Jones recalled that ''even before his final adoption of the 'syllabic count' he acquired the habit of counting syllables on his fingers while composing poetry, and kept this habit throughout his life. He never established in his mind the obvious connection between word-stress and musical accent.''[21] Indeed, it is not merely the connection that may have been missed, but the rich possibilities of tension between sense stress and musical accent. The verse is singularly free from tension in the later poetry, moving rather to keep long surges of sound afloat, as in ''A Refusal to Mourn''.

The elaboration of sound and image in that poem illustrates the way in which the ostensible impulse of a poem can become submerged beneath its rhetoric—a rhetoric responsive to impulses that have a life of their own. The poem is simple in its central impulse: he will not mourn the death of the girl who has become again a part of the earth from which she came. To do so would destroy the dignity of her death; and he refuses any consolation in the abrupt last line: "After the first death, there is no other". The poem moves down musically to this terse closing statement from an opening sentence that is two and a half stanzas long. Between are two sentences of five lines each. The musical structure has been justly admired; and it is a commonplace of judgement that, through the magnificence of its religious imagery, the poem turns the refusal into an elegy for the child. Yet there is much more concern for the particular death in the musically less engaging "Ceremony After a Fire Raid". The opening of "A Refusal to Mourn" is devoted to a periphrastic reference to Thomas's own return to the earth from which he came—one of his longstanding themes; and it is the occasion for a characteristically vertiginous performance with favourite images—"darkness", "light", "water", "seed".

Much more effective in its self-effacing simplicity is the poem for his own son Llewelyn:

> This side of the truth,
> You may not see, my son,
> King of your blue eyes
> In the blinding country of youth,
> That all is undone,
> Under the unminding skies,
> Of innocence and guilt
> Before you move to make
> One gesture of the heart or head,
> Is gathered and spilt
> Into the winding dark
> Like the dust of the dead.

This opening stanza marks the furthest development of the "simple" style of his earliest poems; and, in its plain, declarative manner, explores the themes of innocence and experience free of rhetorical trickiness. Equally enduring in its power is a poem that works very much "*out of* words":

> Lie still, sleep becalmed, sufferer with the wound
> In the throat, burning and turning. All night afloat
> On the silent sea we have heard the sound
> That came from the wound wrapped in the salt sheet.

The texture is as consummately worked as in "The Conversation of

Prayers''; yet it is easy to pass over the poem because, in spite of the syntactic clarity, it remains difficult to see what the poem is about. In fact, it gives focus to more genuine feeling than does the less baffling ''Vision and Prayer'', generating a serenity free of the factitious manipulation of religious imagery.

Thomas was at one time seen in the role of a tortured genius brought to an early end by a corrupt society that forced him to a course of public suicide through drinking. A clearer awareness is now possible. The drinking was not of great characterological importance, though it absorbed far too much of his time. What emerges as staggering is the growing level of dishonesty manifested in the begging letters that make up an increasing part of his correspondence after the war. Some of these letters are studied literary compositions, and Constantine Fitzgibbon records that Thomas took several days to draft some of them.[22]

Thomas squandered all of the comparatively large sums of money he made on his American tours in the late forties; and, when Stephen Spender attempted to raise money to help Thomas, people retorted, correctly, that he was making more money than they were. According to Daniel Jones, Thomas had a near preference for lying in certain circumstances. Throughout his life, particularly in the face of literary enquiries, Thomas was truculently defensive. ''While remaining hidden'', Jones wrote, ''he sent into the world a counterfeit image of himself, a fetch.''[23] ''The only ideal he clung to was an ideal possible to achieve only in childhood: the child-life itself.''[24] It involves no strain of interpretation to see a connection between this pattern of behaviour and the unironical cultivation of innocence that had its whimsical decadence in *Under Milk Wood* (1954) and ''A Child's Christmas in Wales'', where the adult world, particularly in its sexual behaviour, is given the quaint oddity it has for children, who cannot imagine its motivations.

Through these last pieces, as Walford Davies remarked, ''the rebel ended off entertaining the enemy''[25]. These works, like a good deal of the later poetry, were sensuously captivating, ostentatious in their play with words, a little above their audiences' heads, and ''uplifting'' without offering any challenge to the sensibility or valuations of the listener. It was Thomas's influence on the poetry reading public that was most important in the late forties. His dramatic, rhetorical, over-rich style of reading—a ''gong over a sea of treacle''—reinforced this well-mannered image of what poetry should be. People who had never even seen him referred to him as Dylan, though Auden, MacNeice and Eliot went by their surnames. The adulation was a debilitating one for the development of English poetry. Thomas's later verse is conservative and his attainments are very personal rhetorical triumphs.

His faults, obvious enough today, were often part of what was admired. He was no model for the aspiring poet, as Philip Larkin, for instance, was to discover; and the admiration he commanded stood in the way of the reception of poetry of a simpler idiom.

This is not surprising, for both Thomas and British poetry had turned their backs on "modernism" in contrary ways. While much of the life of Thomas's later poetry is in its imagistic rhetoric, the movement of feeling is not inherent in the imagery, but is carried or illustrated by it: we can say what "Fern Hill" is about, independently of its imagery, in a way that we cannot for "In the beginning was the three-pointed star". The imagery itself had become more traditional, and more traditional in the associations it evoked, and this no doubt accounted for Thomas being seen as a "new romantic" poet; though he clearly did his best, after appearing in the first Apocalypse anthology, to dissociate himself from the attempts made to count him under that name. Danny Abse and Jon Silkin were among the few younger poets of any note to learn anything fruitful from him. British poetry was to find renewal in a plainness the reverse of Thomas's rhetoric, and Thomas's achievement and popularity only stood in the way.

The achievement was a notable one, though it did not constitute the return to the "real poetry" that his more shallow admirers felt to be taking place. There are poems of undoubted power in *Deaths and Entrances,* even if some of the more popular ones are the most suspect. It was and remains easy enough to take him at his face value, to see him as he saw himself at the age of nineteen in his letters to Pamela Hansford Johnson: "Art is praise and it is sane to praise, for, praising, we praise the godliness that gives us sanity . . . And if I can bring myself to know, not think, that nothing is uninteresting, I can . . . believe once more, as I so passionately believed and so passionately *want* to believe, in the magic of this burning and bewildering universe, in the meaning and the power of symbols, in the miracle of myself & of all mortals, in the divinity that is so near us and so longing to be nearer, in the staggering, bloody, starry wonder of the sky I can see above and the sky I can think of below."[26] Even then, the passionate, unqualified vision seemed willed rather than given, something not quite congenial to the knowing young creator of Warmley (the iconoclastic fantasy he shared with Daniel Jones). Yet, as the early concerns with identity retreated, this vision of "the staggering, bloody, starry wonder" seemed all that remained; and, despite the intricate verbal contrivance of the later poetry, it was increasingly true, as Karl Shapiro remarked: "The more you examine him as a stylist the less you find."[27] All the same, the technical mastery of his later poems, within the narrow range of effects that Thomas sought, was far above that shown in most of the poetry of the decade.

Chapter 7

APOCALYPSE AND AFTER

The Apocalypse Movement, *Seven,* the New Romanticism—Henry
Treece, J.F. Hendry, Nicholas Moore—Alex Comfort—*Poetry
Quarterly—Poetry London—Life and Letters Today*—Meryn Peake—
the New Romanticism in Painting

The movement that called itself Apocalypse has often been equated
with the "new romanticism", or even with the poetry of the forties as
a whole. In fact it began in the late thirties and can be said to have
lost any clear identity by 1943. Poets associated with it were vocal in
their criticism of what they saw as the poetry of "social realism" or
the cult of the "object image", yet the ideology of the Apocalypse
movement had its origins in modes of thought and feeling characteristic of the thirties. The name of the movement is clearly derived from
Lawrence, who, as prophet of social renewal through the renewal of
the individual, was much esteemed by W.H. Auden and Stephen Spender in their early days. The work of Freud, and its association with
notions of social amelioration, was an infuence on Auden's thinking,
as it was on that of the Apocalypse writers; and the apologists for the
movement dwelt considerably on its relationship to surrealism, which
had its greatest literary impact in England in the thirties.

The movement is said to have been founded in 1938, by J.F. Hendry and Henry Treece, who had met through contributing poems to the
periodical, *Seven*. With Dorian Cooke, they collaborated in developing
a manifesto of their aims. As cited by Francis Scarfe, these were:

(1)   That Man was in need of greater freedom, economic no less than
aesthetic, from machines and mechanistic thinking.

(2)   That no existent political system, Left or Right; no artistic ideology, Surrealism or the political school of Auden, was able to provide this freedom.

(3)   That the Machine Age had exerted too strong an influence on art,
and had prevented the individual development of Man.

(4)   That Myth, as a personal means of reintegrating the personality,
had been neglected and despised.[1]

The early work of the movement can be found in the periodical
Seven, which ran for eight issues from the summer of 1938 to the

101

spring of 1940, and was edited initially by John Garland and Nicholas Moore from Taunton, and later by Moore from Cambridge. Cooke, Treece, Hendry, Moore, Norman McCaig and G.S. Fraser contributed poems, some of which were included in *The New Apocalypse. Seven* contained no editorials or manifestos. There was work by other new poets, among them Anne Ridler, Gervase Stewart, D.S. Savage, Ruthven Todd, Keidrych Rhys, Julian Symons, Roy Fuller and J.C. Hall. More interestingly, it published work by Lawrence Durrell (including excerpts from *The Black Book*) and by Henry Miller, along with contributions from Alfred Perlès and Anaïs Nin, who had been associated with them in the periodical *Delta. Seven* also included work by Wallace Stevens and by the Greek poet, George Seferis, both of whom were little known in England at that time.

In 1939, Hendry and Treece produced an anthology, *The New Apocalypse,* containing contributions by Hendry, Treece, Cooke, Moore, McCaig, Dylan Thomas, Philip O'Connor and the painter, Robert Melville. Of these, Hendry, Treece, Cooke, Moore and McCaig constituted the "movement". Dylan Thomas, who contributed a poem and a previously published story and was the subject of an article by Treece, was a reluctant passenger. Treece was already working on the book he wrote about Thomas, two years his junior. From Thomas's letters to Treece at that time, it is quite clear how unwilling Thomas was to be hooked. His poor opinion of the movement is reflected in his rude remarks about Treece, such as "Poems are made by fools like me, but only God can make a Treece."[2]

In an introductory essay to the anthology, "Writers and Apocalypse", Hendry stated:

> The writers included in this book have in common the fact that they alone are seeking and finding the optimum living synthesis of man and exterior world; the fusion of man and object in philosophy through the collapse of the subject-object relation; the fusion of man and government through the collapse of totalitarianism and "state" as a superhuman concept; fusion of man and art, by bringing art to actual life. (p.15)

The tone of the poetry is that of prophetic surrealism, and there is a similarity in style between the contributions of Hendry, McCaig, Moore and Cooke, with their exaggerated, doom-haunted imagery and loose lyrical connection, as in Cooke's "Meditation":

> In season now the quiet famine raves; and life
> Is smouldering with the feet of unfathering drums.
> It is a time for treachery in the dragoned flowers.
> But to survive, to create where death created man's dreams
> Is a level trap. Destiny furls the rock-flung years.
> In the soil is heard a desolate face beaten stiff.

In 1941 a larger anthology, *The White Horseman*, appeared. It contained contributions by Hendry, Treece, McCaig, Moore and Melville, along with pieces by G.S. Fraser, Tom Scott and Vernon Watkins. Scott's poetry is in the manner of the poetry of *The New Apocalypse;* but Watkins, whose controlled and delicate poems are easily the best in this volume, is out of place, and appearance in *The White Horseman* seems to have been his only association with the movement. Equally out of place are the poems of G.S. Fraser, whom Treece called "considerably more valuable as a critic than as a poet, in which medium he was scarcely Apocalyptic".[3]

Fraser contributes an article "Apocalypse in Poetry", which, along with Hendry's "Myth and Social Integration", is the most important statement on the nature of the movement:

> The New Apocalypse, in a sense, derives from Surrealism, and one might even call it a dialectical development of it: the next stage forward. It embodies what is positive in Surrealism, "the effort", in Herbert Read's phrase, "to realize some of the dimensions and characteristics of man's submerged being". It denies what is negative—Surrealism's own denial of man's right to exercise conscious control, either of his political and social destinies, or of the material offered to him, as an artist, by his subconscious mind. It recognizes, that is, that the intellect and its activity in willed action is part of the living completeness of man, just as the formal element is part of the living completeness of art. (p.3)

He speaks of the "image, the element of poetry that the Apocalyptic works with"; and, by his discussion and quotations, portrays the movement as an inheritor of the Imagist poetic. He contrasts the "romantic" Apocalyptic movement with "Auden and his group [who] are classical". He sees in the movement "a rather ruthless scepticism about political thought", and finds "the ideal the group sets before itself is that of men developing towards completeness."

J.F. Hendry's "Myth and Social Integration" gives the fullest and most intelligent statement of the aims of the movement, at least as he saw them: ". . . whereas Freud sought to adapt the individual . . . to the desires of society, the Social Pathologist would seek to adapt society to the individual, realizing that in many cases the ills of the individual are directly to be attributed to social evils, which are in themselves aspects of disease, or "social neurosis" characterized by illusion . . ." (p.158) The mode of adaptation was by myth—a term that had wide circulation in the forties, in reaction to the rationalistic, manipulative approach to the individual and society favoured in the thirties. "By myth, we mean the idea an individual has of himself, the sum of his aspirations and inspirations, the *incentive* to the sublimation discussed by Freud." (p.165) In another essay from 1943, "The Art of History", Hendry elucidates this: " 'Myth' . . . the era and aura within which man grows and which he makes his own, the particular history which he lives within." "There *is* no history—except the history of self-realisation."[4]

In his essays in the Apocalyptic anthologies, Hendry makes a number of references to Freud and Marx, those heroes of the thirties, and to their attitudes to myth. His own thinking was evidently more particularly influenced by that of Herbert Read, of whom he remarked "the key word is 'organic' "[5]. "Organic" was also a key word for Hendry and the Apocalyptics, employed with an approving tone in contrast to terms like "mechanistic". Another important influence was the rightist George Sorel, who, in *Reflections on Violence* (1908) wrote of "the profounder region of our mental life; revolutionary myths have their place there equally with religion."[6]

The Apocalypse movement was in many respects a reaction to the dominant poetry of the thirties. However, this did not mean that the movement eschewed political concerns; not only did the programme envisage a mode of social amelioration through myth; there was also a decided leaning towards anarchism in Hendry's thought. The influence of Herbert Read must have counted strongly here; and an association with anarchism is found again in the later "new romanticism" in the work of Alex Comfort.

Art, with its generation of a personal myth, was for Hendry a means of attaining "social integration". As Henry Treece wrote, "J.F. Hendry . . . believes that the image, recording as it does the poet's conflicts and his hopes, shows in germinal form both the disease of society and the cure of that disease, and furthermore that poetry of the right type could lead men into the right way of life, could give them back the personality and spiritual health which the Age of Machines has taken from them."[7] Unhappily, the poetry of the Apocalypse movement did not measure up in quality to this ambition.

The third Apocalyptic anthology, *The Crown and the Sickle*, appeared in 1943, and marked the end of the movement. The "Preface" by Henry Treece commented: "This, the third Apocalyptic anthology, contains no manifesto and presents no editorial policy distinguishable from a general desire to collect and display these international examples of a new Romantic tendency, whose most obvious elements are love, death, an adherence to myth and an awareness of war." Only Hendry, Treece and Cooke remained of the contributors to the earlier anthologies. There were poems by Treece, Hendry, Cooke, Alex Comfort, Gervase Stewart, Wrey Gardiner, Robert Herring, Sean Jennett and others. The prose included a fantasy by Stephan Schimanski, "Knight and Devil", later published by Wrey Gardiner's Grey Walls

Press. The only piece of any distinction was a story by Alex Comfort, "The Martyrdom of the House".

The Crown and the Sickle had been put together at long range. Hendry had joined the army in 1941, and Treece, the Air Force. Treece remarked, "our Introduction was symptomatic less of our general tolerance than of our tiredness."[8] Indeed, he contends that as early as "towards the end of 1939, a sudden phase of disintegration set in"[9]. Cooke had already left for the Balkans before the first anthology was produced: neither Hendry nor Treece ever met Moore. It might be argued, indeed, as Treece was later to do, that the movement was a very loose one, reflecting a similarity of feeling about poetry among its members, and that the ideology was largely Hendry's own.

The partnership of Hendry and Treece was to be replaced by that of Treece and Schimanski, who became leading purveyors of the "New Romanticism". At the end of 1941, along with Alan Rook, they took over the editorship of John Waller's Oxford periodical, *Kingdom Come,* and its character changed considerably. In the second issue under the new editors, Treece indicated the change: "the poetry which seems the most admirable is that which has given itself the title *Apocalyptic,* but which I would prefer to call New Romantic". ("A Statement on Poetry Today," 3, 10, 22). The new term was to mark a much looser association, and even looser thinking. Poets represented in the new *Kingdom Come* included Hendry, Treece, McCaig, Comfort, George Woodcock and Sidney Keyes. There was, again, little poetry of any distinction in the latter day *Kingdom Come,* and Schimanski's editorials are full of commonplaces. The periodical closed in 1943: the last two issues were from Wrey Gardiner's Grey Walls Press.

Kingdom Come was succeeded by *Transformation,* a symposium edited by Treece and Schimanski. In the first issue, an article by Hendry, "The Art of History", in which he asserts many of the Apocalyptic positions concerning myth, history and surrealism, provided a link with the old movement, as did Herbert Read's "The Politics of the Unpolitical", a classic statement of the anarchist position that had influenced Hendry. However, the editorial is entitled "Towards a Personalist Attitude":

> The Apocalyptic Movement was . . . a reaction against the deadening hand of political literature . . . Apocalypticism expressed its faith in man's freedom, wholeness and the necessity for organic living . . . Personalism follows these main lines but its survey of personality is wider-reaching, broader rather than deep-cutting. Instead of tunnelling into the subterranean depths of each single individual, it stretches out its roots to embrace the widest sphere . . .

Acknowledgement is made to "Herbert Read, whose concept of Anarchism approaches more nearly to the perfect state of living than any other we can call to mind."

> Personalism, being a belief of action, demands a complete revaluation of all aspects of life, a complete reorientation, a complete change of heart, and because such a change of heart is so obviously a natural thing, so patently necessary to good living, there will always be critics who overlook its truth in attacking its apparent naivete.

The "naiveté" (hard to overlook) is what is most characteristic of *Transformation*—the blend of good will, eclecticism and hopes for rejuvenation characteristic of the later years of the war and those immediately after it. In the fourth issue, Treece offers "Towards a Personalist Literature", but his thinking does not go beyond the unsatisfactory and commonplace distinction between subjective and objective (with the bogeyman from the thirties "Reportage" in the background). A comparison with the essays in *The White Horseman* measures the deterioration.

Treece's essay is only three pages long, and is perhaps too short for much to be achieved. This is true of so many contributions to *Transformation,* some of which are by respected authors. Hendry and Fraser contribute brief pieces, as does D.S. Savage, whose recently published *The Personal Principle* (1943) offered the detailed, coherent and sustained discussion of literature absent in *Transformation.* Though *Transformation Two* is devoted to education and *Transformation Three* to psychology, both are in fact collections of writing with little focus of topic or viewpoint. *Transformation* did not contain a great deal of poetry by British poets: there were poems by Herbert Read, Treece, Fred Marnau and Brenda Chamberlain; and the best pieces were by writers who had nothing to do with Personalism or the New Romanticism. There was considerable distinction in publishing "Childhood" ("The Childhood of Luvers") by Boris Pasternak, then little known in England; and *Transformation* did a service with its extended sections of French and American poetry that included work by authors not published in England.

The anthology that signalled the new grouping of "Romantic" writers was *Lyra*, edited by Alex Comfort and Robert Greacan, and published in 1942 by Wrey Gardiner at Grey Walls. Although the editors claimed that "like all anthologies" theirs was "a completely arbitrary parade of the editors' taste in contemporary writing", they conceded "that the book becomes, of itself, a contribution to a new romanticism . . . We feel that the over-thirty classicism which still insists on calling itself 'younger' has ceased to represent the growing edge of poetry.'' Herbert Read begins his preface: ''This anthology appears in the third year of a war which every day reveals more clearly its apocalyptic character''; but it is clear that this is not a reference to the Apocalypse movement and that the contributors do not regard themselves as part of that movement. There are poems by John Bayliss, Alex Comfort, G.S. Fraser, Wrey Gardiner, John Hall, Emanuel Litvinoff, Nicholas Moore, Norman Nicholson, Anne Ridler, Francis Scarfe, Tambimuttu, Henry Treece and Vernon Watkins. No doubt most of these poets would have underwritten the contrast between their work and ''the over-thirty classicism'' (of Auden and MacNeice and their associates, one presumes). Yet a reading of the anthology unguided by literary history would produce an impression of writing that was for its time unadventurous and conventional—perhaps deliberately so. The following poem by Peter Wells (who also appeared in *The Crown and the Sickle*) exemplifies this:

> In this moment of sea brawl and angelic commandment
> the fiery wings have knit me about with tongues of tempest:
> I am chained by the wooden branches of wrecked ships,
> the fingers of octopus reach me across the hollow beach.
>
> Yet in despair, I sit and cogitate upon reasons
> for the madness in me;
> and from afar I hear the seasons singing,
> and a golden girl bringing fruit from her garden.

There is so much that is commonplace in this poem that one cannot believe that it was included by mere oversight in an anthology of only 54 pages of poetry: there must have been a readiness to identify the conventional with the traditional—one of the besetting misjudgements of the ''New Romanticism''.

II

The poetry of the Apocalypse movement fell far short of the expectations aroused by its programme. The closest that Henry Treece came to following the precept of constructing his own myth was in two early sequences, ''The Never Ending Rosary'' and ''Towards a Personal Armageddon''. Treece saw Dylan Thomas as exemplifying the stance appropriate to an Apocalyptic poet, and Thomas's influence is obvious.

> The dancing man with the dagger of lath
> Slashes the bubble growing out of grief,
> And drops the leaden hours through the loam.

However, it was clear from the beginning that modernism was uncongenial to Treece, and his models included Swinburne, the early Yeats and Housman.

> So sigh no more, my lady,
> Sweet sleep shall come again
> To kiss you in your bed, lass,
> With some peace-lucky man.
>
> ("Homage to A.E.H.")

By 1940 he had started to write another long sequence, "The Black Prince", reminiscent of the early Yeats in style, in which he attempts to create a "myth" in the sense that the word applies to the old stories that he was later to retell in his historical novels. His hankering for "dying worlds" is everywhere felt in *The Black Seasons* (1945), which contains three other sequences—"The Lost Ones", "Second Coming" and "To the Edge and Back".

> Proud as an ancient prayer-wheel, the Prince
> Stepped with a purple flutter from the tomb,
> Kissing the silver locks . . .

In these poems he turns to a medieval romanticism that, in its telling of old myths and stories, has little to do with the Apocalypse movement. It is hard to feel much differentiation of emotion in his poems of this period, which are diffuse and slip easily off the mind and tongue:

> The pod bursts open and the seed
> Is left for all to see;
> So from the mouth breaks forth the word
> To all eternity . . .
>
> Once uttered, sound falls like a germ
> Into the womb of life,
> To ferment and at last to form
> The progeny of grief.

There seems to be no reason why "life" and "grief" should be half rhymes, when full rhymes are used in the same position elsewhere; nor why it is a progeny of "grief" and not "joy" that "the mouth breaks forth".

Poem after poem in *Invitation and Warning* (1942) and *The Black Seasons* gives expression to trite and hackneyed feelings in contrived naive forms; and when Treece aims at a visionary note, his imagery is frequently lurid. Julian Symons, reviewing *The Black Seasons,* distinguished "Intoxicated Housman", "Village Blake", "Wilheminia Stick with a dash of Rupert Brooke" and "fairly pure Treece".[10] Although this ignores the talent that there is in the book, it is hard to feel sorry for the man who could praise the literary movement to which he belonged as "organic . . . with all the madness and sanity of a bowel movement".[11] Treece's publisher was T.S. Eliot's Faber and Faber.

In Treece's last books of poems, *The Haunted Garden* (1947) and *The Exiles* (1952), the mythologising is less prevalent and the writing tighter. For the rest of his life, Treece turned to writing historical novels and to the retelling of old tales, an activity more congenial to his talents.

J.F. Hendry's early poetry has none of the distinction of his prose and little of the subtlety of his thinking is reflected in his verse. Treece called him "a writer of tortured and tortuous imagery"[12]; and, both descriptively and pejoratively, this is true of much of his poetry.

> Titanic tumult, mastered in a breath,
> Melts the ice of bayonets. Formality withers,
> Shattering man's gigantic iceberg—death.
> Even earth and moon float in their wake
> As they spread invisible wings. Drowned in opacity
> We flee the winter and the midnight tent quick as the bold
> Colossal stride of light divinity. Stars and flowers shake.
>   ("Spring"—from "The Four Seasons of War")

He published two books with Routledge, in the series edited by Herbert Read: *The Bombed Happiness* (1942); and *The Orchestral Mountain* (1943), a sequence of poems occasioned by the death of Hendry's wife in an air-raid while he was in the army. *The Orchestral Mountain* makes use of the legend of Orpheus and Eurydice; and, in its attempt to build the author's loss into his own sense of his historical situation, it might be said to follow his own prescription concerning myth and history. In some of the shorter poems Hendry pays adequate tribute to his grief and suggests a fruitful talent:

> Our time is shorn. Days huddle sheaves.
> The wind is a broken sky of leaves.
>
> In the broken city, still in a gale,
> The broken heart is a broken jail,
>
> Breaking from dark subconscious earth
> A river of leaves whispering in the sun
>
> "Persephone! Persephone!"

His career as a poet petered out in the late forties, to be renewed in a different style in the seventies.

Nicholas Moore, the son of G.E. Moore, and the editor of *Seven,* appeared in both *The New Apocalypse* and *The White Horseman,* but shortly afterwards decided that his aims were not those of the Apocalypse movement. He did not appear in *The Crown and the Sickle.* A protean and facile poet, his early admirations included Conrad Aiken and Robert Frost. Some of his poems written at Cambridge suggest the vaguely surrealistic extension of Auden's manner that Kenneth Allott sometimes achieved. A very characteristic poem, from *The White Horseman,* is "The Double Yew":

> Oh, darling, today I am more sad than ever,
> To be away from you when the yew is weeping over France,
> The yew that has wept over Spain and Europe,
> And now at this hour may begin to shed its tears
> Over this country and you, too, my dear.

The model is George Barker. The relaxed, lyric tone is one that Moore attains with felicity, but too much facility. His urbanity shows a debt to Auden—a debt that sets him apart from the other Apocalypse poets. But Moore's poem does not develop the tension between the private and the public that one finds in superficially similar poems from the thirties. G.S. Fraser spoke of his "quiet acceptance of complete individual responsibility"[13]; but his work of the early forties can be glib— a succession of poems that roll off the tongue so that one is scarcely aware of what they are about. In 1941 and 1942, Moore published three books and one pamphlet of poems. Wrey Gardiner, with whom Moore was associated at the Grey Walls Press, noted: "Nicholas has taken to typing poems straight on to his typewriter now."[14]

Moore had considerable perceptiveness and originality. He was interested in jazz and popular songs, and attempted to integrate their effects into some of his poems. In 1943 he wrote one of the first books on Henry Miller; and it is clear from some notes in *Poetry London* in 1944 on "The Woman that had more babies than that", that he was one of the first people in England to understand Wallace Stevens's work. However, in poetry, for all his fluency and sensitivity in rendering personal experience, he sometimes appears not to know what to make of it, and his conclusions can be crude. Like many of his contemporaries, he too frequently succumbs to the sense that what sounds striking must be significant and that all experience that is important to the writer will automatically make important poetry.

After producing a selection of his poems up to 1943, *The Glass Tower* (1943), Moore wrote two books under pseudonyms in 1944 and

1945, and then did not produce another book of poetry until *Recollections of the Gala* (1950). Here the stance is anti-romantic, and there are obvious echoes of Auden. Many of the poems are diffuse, but the book was before its time in some respects and deserved more attention than it got: it contained a good deal that was memorable.

> How dark, how deep it is! How in the abandon-
> ment of reason the runners stumble who
> Run their race in ignorance, running a five-mile
> Circuit of despair, their faces blue
>
> With cold, their fingers crisp with frost . . .
> ("The Peculiar Night")

The combination of lyricism and fantasy with a deliberate abandonment of any obvious rhetorical devices in fact anticipated much work of the 1950's. Moore did not publish another book of poems until 1970.

In his hey-day Moore won the Contemporary Patron's Prize in 1945 (judged that year by W.H. Auden) and the *Poetry* (Chicago) Harriet Monroe Memorial Prize in 1947. These awards perhaps say as much about the literary atmosphere of the day as they do about Moore's achievement. He had a greater talent than Treece or Hendry; and his facile production of book after book might be seen as a symptom of that collapse of standards thought to be generally characteristic of the nineteen-forties and certainly prevalent among the "New Romantics".

III

Alex Comfort, one of the editor's of *Lyra,* was a contemporary of Nicholas Moore at Cambridge. Like the Apocalypse poets, he was influenced by Herbert Read, and became a pacifist and a militant anarchist; though J.F. Hendry took issue with what he saw as Comfort's "revolutionary and evolutionary defeatism".[15] Comfort was one of the most prolific writers of the forties, producing several novels and plays, as well as five volumes of poetry between 1940 and 1951. His novels *The Power House* (1944) and *On This Side Nothing* (1949) deserve to be remembered, though they are somewhat schematic in conception, reflecting preconceived philosophic notions, and are distant from the author's own experience: *On This Side Nothing* seems to owe a great deal to Camus' *The Plague* (1947). Comfort saw "the awareness of death"[16] as differentiating his generation from the left-wing poets of the thirties: "I believe in one ethical principle, the solidarity of man against death . . . and against the human allies of death—those who side with Power." He goes on to speak of the "emphasis on death in my 'Elegies' ",[17] his third volume (1944):

> I believe in winter, in the season of ends.
> Quiet the doomed leaf hangs at the bough's tip
> teaches the lessons of death in a dead season
> here in my brittle year a sober preacher.
>
> ("First Elegy")

The lesson of death is evidently one of acceptance, and a distrust of the belief that changes in society can bring the millenium. Yet Comfort, in his fourth volume, *The Signal to Engage* (1946)—dedicated to four anarchists, "Prisoners on Victory Day", who had refused to fight—gives expression to political attitudes of a crudity seldom encountered in the poetry of the thirties:

> Remember when you hear them beginning to say Freedom
> Look carefully—see who it is they want you to butcher.
>
> ("Notes for my Son")

Comfort's poetry usually has an air of sensitivity and profundity: as George Woodcock remarked of *Elegies,* there is "a meditative solemnity, reflected in the slow beat of the lines"[18]. However, the distinction of the verse is illusory. The elegies evidently take as their model Rilke's *Duino Elegies* (1922), as did Sidney Keyes's most ambitious poems. Rilke's *Elegies* are one of the triumphant attempts to come to terms with the fact of death in a world bereft of traditional religious explanations. While isolated passages of Comfort's poems seem impressive, the general effect is to diffuse rather than resolve any pressures behind the poetry:

> Love is not strong to fight with history
> and those who love are sometimes buried together
> sometimes apart, and move like shells
> slowly into the heart of the cloudy hills . . .
>
> ("Sixth Elegy")

The tone is controlled and sensitive; but, once the lines are isolated for inspection, the inanity of the proffered consolation becomes obvious. The second and third lines are characteristically tautologous and longwinded; while one is left asking what reason, other than the wish for the right "tone", there is for the comparison of lovers to "shells" or for their supposed movement after burial into the "heart" of the (clichéd) "cloudy hills".

Like Moore, Comfort wrote too much, possibly squandering a talent that could have matured in an atmosphere less receptive to the portentous. His essays, *Art and Social Responsibility* (1947), give characteristic expression to the romantic anarchism frequently encountered among pacifist intellectuals in the latter part of the war and its aftermath, and are of much greater permanent interest than his poetry.

IV

Lyra was published by Wrey Gardiner at the Grey Walls Press. A generation older than Comfort and the Apocalypse poets, Gardiner published *New Road,* a miscellany initially edited by Alex Comfort and John Bayliss, which appeared five times (annually) between 1943 and 1947. More importantly, he published *Poetry Quarterly,* which ran from 1939 to 1953. Its first issues were under the European editorship of E.M. Channing-Renton, with Gardiner as Assistant Editor: Gardiner became editor in 1940. *Poetry Quarterly* then had the appearance of being a periodical that existed to publish the poetry of its subscribers. The books it reviewed were evidently intended for the middlebrow "poetry lover":

"Wild Swans" by Theodore Nicholl (Duckworth,3/6)

Although Mr. Nicholl can find his inspiration in a slaughter house or a coal mine, in the fiery sword blade of music or the bitterness of the human heart, in the sulpherous molten heart of fire itself, it is in the memory of past summers in Ungathered Harvest . . . that it achieves its highest expression.

The style of the review is not only indicative of the tastes of a substantial part of the poetry buying public of the day, but must also say something about the reviewer, Wrey Gardiner. Editorials spoke of "the expression of immortal beauty and truth" (Spring, 1941), and advised readers that "No hand of man can prevent the rain from making the grass green." (Summer, 1941). These first issues have their odd surprises, such as an early poem by Denise Levertoff:

> The roses tremble; oh, the sunflower's eye
> Is opened in sad expectancy.
> Westward and back the circling swallows fly,
> The rooks' battalions dwindle near the hill.
> ("Listening to Distant Guns")

As Gardiner was later to remark: ". . . I was still suffering from the miasmic mellifluence of the Poetry Society, when I inherited the dim genius of its would-be authors burbling reminiscently in the metres of yesteryear with all Wardour Street appurtenances . . ."[19]

At the end of 1941, there is a radical change in the type of poem published by *Poetry Quarterly,* and it begins to build up the group of contributors who are to give it its style for the rest of its run. Among the early contributions there had been ones not Wardour Street in tone—including poems by Alex Comfort and Nicholas Moore, whom Gardiner was later to speak of as his first "discoveries"[20]. It was Comfort who converted Gardiner to the new poetry. The Apocalyptic anthology, *The White Horseman,* was picked as the "Book of the Quarter" in Autumn, 1941; while the editorial asked "If the neo-romanticism of the Apocalypticists marks the birth of as fruitful a period as the Elizabethan . . ." The issue contains contributions by Alex Comfort, Nicholas Moore, G.S. Fraser, Henry Treece and Stephan Schimanski; while the Summer, 1942 issue contains poems by J.F. Hendry, Comfort, Schimanski, Treece, Alan Rook, John Bayliss, George Woodcock, James Kirkup, Iain Fletcher, Sidney Keyes and John Heath-Stubbs. The editorial hails the periodical *Kingdom Come,* which Treece and Schimanski had just taken over. However, 1942 saw the end of the Apocalypse invasion; and afterwards *Poetry Quarterly* settled down, transformed, with its stud of second team "new romantics".

The editorial for Winter, 1946-1947, lists as "worthy of study": "Alex Comfort, Nicholas Moore, Henry Treece, John Heath-Stubbs, Sean Jennet, Ruthven Todd, W.S. Graham, David Wright, Howard Sergeant, Denise Levertoff". All of these contributed fairly often, and some regularly; but the writers who seem to epitomise what *Poetry Quarterly* stood for are Gardiner himself, Derek Stanford, his friend John Bayliss, and Howard Sergeant. Stanford was later to write a series of critiques of the new romanticism, *The Freedom of Poetry* (1947), and was a frequent reviewer for *Poetry Quarterly.* In 1944 Stanford and Bayliss got together a joint publication of their poems, *A Romantic Miscellany:* ". . . we do not intend, under the aspect of poet as Red unofficial law-giver, to churn out exact reproductions of all the inane realities before us . . . In so far as we have called this book 'a romantic miscellany' we must expect to be called and to answer to the description of 'romantic poets' ": those "who seek behind authority for a personal law that should serve them as home; poets who gainsay the spoken word, the 'herd' testament of the common hour; poets who record the age at its turn." The above remarks are typical of their authors, even in being somewhat old fashioned for their day. Their poetry is decidedly "literary", and their acceptance of anything modern is cautious.

> In the ecstasy of sense
> he can feel the skeleton

shaking at primeval sins
through the archway of the bone;
he can see stone letters form
on the wall above the bed
well can guess the date and name
of the soon-forgotten dead:
but no stone the carver shaped
nor chiselled verse, nor compliment
nor any magic of his own,
music, picture, monument,
can console him for her breath
his known trumpeter of death.
(John Bayliss, "Reflection"—*PQ,* IV,3 (Aut, 1942)

The lack of individuality in the use of conventional images, the portentousness that has no pressure of particularised awareness behind it,
the obvious choice of epithet and the lack of subtlety of rhythm, is
typical of so many poems in *Poetry Quarterly.* Howard Sergeant's
"The Sea Dwellers" has more variety and subtlety of movement, but
one is left wondering what the visionary expectancy is prelude to:

Have you not seen them rising from the waves
at midnight, when the gulls are silent and
the sea opens its doors and watery graves;
have you not seen them swirling on the sand
like corybants, their white malignant thighs
whispering from the mirrors of the moon;
whose phosphorescent eyes are never eyes
but knives to turn the flesh and strip the bone?

Gardiner himself published several volumes of his own poetry from
the Grey Walls Press. As in the case of Bayliss and Sergeant, one
cannot say that it is the work of someone who has no idea how to
write a poem. What is saddening is that a moderate amount of talent
is used to push round the conventional stage properties of the poetry
of the day:

Waves of sound, waves of pain
Flickering sorrow, sonata of the rain,

A harsh voice from the past
Like a stone in the dark, cast

Into the backward pool of thought
Behind the grey curtain of day, caught

Here and there by the spider's thread,
Wavering tendril of the mind, dead

> To the wandering beauty of the earth,
> The eternal snake renewed from birth to birth.
> ("Poem to be Forgotten")

This type of writing is shown up by the work of a contributor to *Poetry Quarterly* who, both in poetry and prose, is frequently bathetic or emotionally embarrassing, and who seems to have been regarded by many as epitomising the delusions of aspiration, Paul Potts. George Barker called him "that lost revolutionary with the sentiments of an Irish tenor," and said that his poems were "not poems at all, but liturgical humanitarianism which his lack of technique has only half baked."[21] Perhaps only in the forties could poetry like that of Potts have got into print; and his readiness to find everything a matter of conscience was also typical of the era. Potts was a commando, but his recollections, *Dante Called You Beatrice* (1960) would give no sense of this, if he did not mention the fact; while his unctuous sentimentality mars his earnestness of conscience. Barker's judgement is largely right; yet there is something freshly winning about Pott's stand for saying what you mean directly and at all costs that contrasts with the preciousness of much of the writing in *Poetry Quarterly:*

> I sat around listening to men
> Talking revolution
> All about free love and no private property.
> So I went out and lived the way they talked
> Now when I got done for ninety days
> Did they send in a cigarette
> Did they write me all the news
> On long white sheets of paper?

Poetry Quarterly published some poets of quality and potentiality, and with a certain regularity. However, hardly any of the poets who had established a reputation before 1939 contributed, and then very seldom. At the other extreme, it developed a sizeable team of poets low in talent and high in pretension, whose work was taken as seriously by the editor as it was by the writers themselves. A review of *Gates of Beauty and Death* by C. Busby Smith commented: "The work of Mr. Busby Smith is characterized by a vibrant sensitivity to experience . . ." (*PQ* 11,1 (Spring, 1949) 54). Busby Smith was a frequent contributor; his "Conversations with the Moon" was given eight pages:

> Hunter of souls, betrayer of mysteries,
> uncover no more, our anguish bleeds in the fields
> furrowed by war and murder and black with hate.

Let the seas cease, pull no more, let the slow tides lull,
Let the ruined islands hide in the fevered dark.
                    (*PQ*, 11,3 (Autumn, 1949) 150)

In the years after the war, *Poetry Quarterly* lost what vitality and character it had picked up during the war years. Work by new poets, some of whom had not come close to achieving a mature manner, continued to appear—Michael Hamburger, Danny Abse, Vernon Scannell, Bernard Bergonzi, Harold Pinta (later Pinter), Muriel Spark, Christopher Middleton: again, the best of these writers showed up the regular contributors. Gardiner maintained a certain adventurousness and some perspicacity in his choice of foreign contributions. When Cyril Connolly was rushing over to Paris in 1945, Gardiner remarked that work from Paris "seems to us wretchedly poor . . . Hart Crane, Robert Frost, John Crowe Ransom, Allen Tate, Wallace Stevens are avowed influences on and mean much more to the young English poet than the older generation of poets over here." (*PQ*, 7,2 (Summer, 1945)) Whatever may be said for Gardiner's opinions of French writing, he was out in front in recognising how influential American writing was to be. Like George Woodcock, he published work by American writers who were still far from achieving recognition in their own country—among them Kenneth Patchen, a selection of whose poems, *Outlaw of the Lowest Planet* (1945) he published from the Grey Walls Press. The Press was also to bring out work of F. Scott Fitzgerald and Nathaniel West, both little known in England at the time. Unhappily, it combined with Peter Baker's Falcon Press; and, when Baker in 1948 was convicted for a financial offence, it brought bankruptcy on the Grey Walls Press.

In 1948, Gardiner still believed that "The forties have seen the appearance of a great deal of very good poetry which will stamp it as important as any decade this century . . ." (*PQ*,10,4 (Winter, 1948)); and in 1949 he contended that "Some indication of the direction poetry is going to take during the new decade which is now upon us can be seen in the considerable renewal of attention to the great figures of the Romantic tradition from Wordsworth to Yeats." (*PQ* II, 4 (Winter, 1949)). But the editorials were getting shorter; and, in 1953, the last issue of *Poetry Quarterly* appeared:

Ten years ago there was a definite change in the accent of the younger poets then beginning to write, a different mood. It was exciting as the birth of new movements in every kind of art always are. There was a promise of greatness, a promise in very few cases fulfilled. Unlike the post-war period after the first war the spiritual climate of our own after war period has been deadening and unproductive . . . Poetry is still being

written, but in this country the work of the under thirties is certainly remarkable for what one well-known reviewer called "a glib flatness".

Gardiner closed with characteristically stale afflatus:

> We shall now depart to a "resonant silence" among our desert crags, but
> may still allow ourselves the disinterested stare of the ageing eagle looking
> down on the dusty plains where the termites interminably devour. (*PQ*,
> 15,5 (Spring-Summer, 1953)

The work of *Poetry Quarterly* was continued to some degree in
Harold Sergeant's *Outposts*. *Outposts* began as a very modest publication of eight pages in 1944; and modesty has been its mark throughout
its more than three decades of publication, and its great strength. Its
contributors in the 1940's were mainly the less well known contributors to *Poetry Quarterly,* along with others who may have wished
that they could get into *Poetry Quarterly*. Editorials, as always, were
brief and informational, though a refusal to take positions—especially
on the question "modern and traditional"—was the one position that
emerged. Over the years, contributors to *Outposts* were to include
Kathleen Raine, Vernon Watkins, Alex Comfort, Norman Nicholson,
Dannie Abse, Judith Wright, Muriel Spark and John Heath-Stubbs.
Kingsley Amis remembered it as "the magazine which was the first
to publish a poem of mine".[22]

One does not wish to disparage such an achievement. However,
For Those Who Are Alive, published by the Fortune Press in 1946,
was described by Sergeant as "The First 'Outposts' Anthology". It
contains work by John Bayliss, Paul Dehn, James Kirkup and Norman
Nicholson—but these are its heavies. Of the unpublished poets among
its fifty or more contributors, virtually none were to make a career in
poetry—a remark that almost goes for the published poets. Sergeant
sees a "search for a more satisfying faith, combined with a sense of
responsibility to future generations" as "a basic element in the work
of all the contributors to the volume". Such remarks have little differentiating power concerning poetry; and it would not be unfair to
say that Sergeant's catholicity, in the forties at least, allowed in work
of promise by taking in a lot that had none. In this his activities were
symptomatic of the decade's readiness for uncritical recognition that
has so often been criticised.

V

Poetry London, like the Apocalypse movement, was conceived in
the last years of the thirties, though it, too, came to be identified in
its policy with the outlook of the succeeding decade. It was started

early in 1939 by Anthony Dickins, then a student at the Royal
Academy of Music, and James Tambimuttu, the son of a Ceylonese
government officer. According to Dickins, the idea originated when
Dickins, Tambimuttu, Dylan Thomas and Keidrich Rhys were in a
cafe in 1938. As Dickins and Tambimuttu had little money, they
raised what they needed in a prospectus offering six issues by subscription: the response was good, and the first issue, appearing in February, 1939, sold well, in spite of the fact that, under the heading
"Tuttifrutti", the then influential *New Verse* greeted it as "loony and
eccentric".[23]

Only two issues appeared in 1939: the money raised by subscription
was exhausted. No issue appeared between April, 1939 and
November, 1940; but, thanks to a gift from James Dobie, *Poetry London* did become, as promised, a bi-monthly for the next four issues,
thus fulfilling the commitment of its original prospectus. It might be
said that this was the last time that *Poetry London* would appear regularly until Tambimuttu gave it up; and it represented one of the few
commitments that were met anything like on time. Issues 7 and 8
appeared, with a bi-monthly dating, at the end of 1942; issue 9 appeared some time in 1943; while issue 10 was book length and appeared in 1944. The imprint of Nicholson and Watson is on Numbers
9 and 10, and Tambimuttu was being supported in his ventures by
them at that time. He was evidently engrossed in running his new
publishing house, under the pretentiously French sounding title of Editions Poetry London, also funded by Nicholson and Watson. *Poetry
London* was not to appear again until the autumn of 1947. By then
Nicholson and Watson had found the association too expensive. Tambi
acquired a new backer, Richard March, and March, with Nicholas
Moore, appears as Associate Editor for issues 14 and 15. Early in
1949, March took control of the operation, and from issue 16, in September, 1949, to the final issue 23, in the Winter of 1951, *Poetry
London* was edited by March and Moore. Tambimuttu returned to
Ceylon in 1949.

The original prospectus had promised that the periodical would be
an "Enquiry in Modern Verse"; and the earlier issues were prefaced
by a series of "Letters", nearly all by Tambimuttu, in which he offers
such an "enquiry", consisting (characteristically) of dogmatic statements. The "Letters" were a plea for the type of poetry that subsequently came to be regarded as characteristic of the nineteen-forties.

Every man has poetry within him. Poetry is the awareness of the mind of
the universe. It embraces everything in the world (Letter I, February,
1939)

Sensitivity to the *universal unconscious* presumably results in incantatory

rhythms . . . poetry is, like music, founded on the erotic part of our nature . . . (Letter, Fourth, January, 1941)

The importance of poetry in our age . . . derives from the fact that we
should now view our culture through spontaneity and vitality . . . (Sixth
Letter, May-June, 1941)

The poetry does not lie in the rhythm and rhyme but in the way of thinking
and feeling . . . (Eighth Letter, Oct.-Nov., 1942)

These statements run directly contrary to statements to be found in
New Verse, and it is not surprising that what was found wrong with
English poetry was diagnosed as being the fault of that periodical.

Geoffrey Grigson [persuaded us] . . . that poetry in which objects replace
emotions . . . was the only poetry worth publishing. (Third Letter,
November, 1939)

Imagism, Objective Reporting etc. Dead words . . . (Eighth Letter, Oct.-
Nov., 1942)

Such positions were identified with Rationalism, "the deeper current
in European philosophy", which was contrasted with "Oriental culture . . . founded on tradition which is in turn a form of spontaneity."
(Sixth Letter, May-June, 1941). Certain established poets fitted Tambimuttu's bill: "Dylan Thomas is a great poet" (Letter I, February,
1939); ". . . the most imaginative of the pre-war poets, like Spender,
Dylan Thomas, Barker, David Gascoyne . . ." (Fourth Letter, January, 1941).

   Tambimuttu evidently received encouragement from T.S. Eliot from
the beginning (encouragement that was to be steadily maintained); and
the first issue contains work by a number of very well known poets,
including Walter de la Mare, Stephen Spender, Louis MacNeice,
Dylan Thomas, Laurence Whistler and Herbert Read. Indeed, it was,
if anything, too catholic a start to give an important critical impact.
However, *Poetry London* soon settled down with a decided tone (and
quality) that conformed to a degree with the attitudes expressed in the
"Letters", and yet showed an editorial openness to diverse new talent.
The principal contributors of poems during Tambimuttu's editorship
were: Dylan Thomas, Lawrence Durrell, Henry Treece, G.S. Fraser,
Laurence Clark, Kathleen Raine, David Gascoyne, Nicholas Moore,
Anne Ridler, J.C. Hall, Stephen Spender, Louis MacNeice, George
Barker, Dorian Cooke, J.F. Hendry, Alun Lewis, Vernon Watkins,
Stephen Coates, Norman Nicholson, Keith Douglas, Sidney Keyes,
Terence Tiller, Bernard Spencer, and Iain Fletcher.

   There was surprisingly little rubbish. Both W.S. Graham and David
Wright had their first publication in *Poetry London;* and Tambimuttu

was one of the first to recognise Keith Douglas's quality, devoting his "Letter" in the long 1944 issue to the work of Douglas, and bringing out many of his poems. He published the first books of Kathleen Raine, *Stone and Flower* (1943), David Wright, *Poems* (1949) and Bernard Spencer, *Aegean Islands* (1946). He also brought out David Gascoyne's *Poems, 1937-43* (1943), Lawrence Durrell's *Cefalu* (1948), and volumes by G.S. Fraser, Michael Hamburger, Anne Ridler, W.S. Graham, and Nicholas Moore. *The Cosmological Eye* (1946), *Sunday After the War* (1946) and *The Wisdom of the Heart* (1947) were the first selections of Henry Miller's work to appear in England (probably at the prompting of Nicholas Moore, who joined the *Poetry London* editorial staff in 1944). In 1942 Tambimuttu announced ". . . I will devote most of No. 10 to the work of poets who have never appeared in print . . ."; and, despite the contention of Julian Maclaren-Ross that the motive for the volume was to keep quiet supporters whose poems had been accepted but had never appeared[24], the volume did contain only poems by people new to *Poetry London*, and some of them surprisingly good and not much noticed elsewhere. There were drawings by Mervyn Peake and lithographs by Gerald Wilde (a talent loyally supported by Tambimuttu), together with poems by Patrick Kavanagh, Alan Ross, Stevie Smith and R.S. Thomas—the last virtually unknown then.

It is easy to make fun of Tambimuttu and to dismiss him as a conman of literature. Many of the outrageous stories told about him are true. His handling of business went beyond the outrageous. Only six regular issues of *Poetry London* appeared between 1942 and 1948, and in the last three of these (in 1947 and 1948) there is evidence of failing interest: he draws heavily on authors whose books he has published, and over one third of the space devoted to poetry is taken up by translation of Rilke's *Duino Elegies* by Ruth Spiers, which Tambimuttu must have come across in *Personal Landscape*, a selection from which he published in 1945. He accepted more books than he could bring out; and David Wright's *Poems* (published 1949), Iain Fletcher's *Orisons, Picaresque and Metaphysical* (published 1948) and John Waller's *The Merry Ghosts* (published 1946), had been awaiting publication for several years after acceptance (as is clear from the poems they contain). Kathleen Raine's *Faces of Day and Night* was set up, but did not appear until it was unearthed in the 1970's: it was evidently among a number of books that were halted when March took control. He gave too much space to the Apocalypse poets, while in Laurence Clark and Stephen Coates (whose *Second Poems* he published in 1947) he sponsored two writers whose work has not stood up well. It was the appearance of such work, along with the editorials, that gave *Poetry London* such a bad name in fifties. Tambimuttu's own poems, *Out of this War,* produced by the Fortune Press in 1940, with a drawing of the author by Augustus John (in rather unfortunate imitation of Dylan Thomas's *The Map of Love* (1939)) are clumsy, prosaic and portentous. Nevertheless, he did publish people who mattered. He brought out the first books of Kathleen Raine, G.S. Fraser and David Wright. He published W.S. Graham's *2nd Poems* (1945) and the work of Keith Douglas (after his death) in *Poetry London* and in book form. In this, he showed a flair above that of most other editors of his day; and his decided achievements deserve to be disengaged from the legends that have come to surround him. As Kathleen Raine remarked at the time, "Perhaps only one publication—*Poetry London*—really gives poets the opportunity that they need to write with the certainty that their work will be read intelligently and presented in a living way."[25]

Under March and Moore's editorship, *Poetry London* appeared more regularly, but with less style and quality. Few of the better known contributors from the old days appeared, and there was a lack-lustre succession of single poems by people like E.B. Chamkin, Jon Manchip White, W.J. Harvey and Ruth Tenney. Some of the new names were destined to be heard again: W.J. Smith, Charles Tomlinson, Harold Pinter, T.E.F. Blackburn and Donald Davie. In January, 1950, "Comment" warned that "POETRY (LONDON) when it was founded by Anthony Dickins and Tambimuttu, addressed itself to a particular situation in poetry . . . Poets should take stock of themselves, especially with a view to improving their technical equipment and sharpening their wits . . . In this post-war decade . . . the 'profound' stanzas full of high-flown, vague emotion and undigested philosophy are not likely to be the most successful ones." In his "Valedictory" in the final issue for Winter, 1951, Richard March sounded even more like *Poetry London's* old enemy, *New Verse:* "The emphasis . . . is on *things.* In composing poetry the author makes an object which acquires an existence in its own right . . . the poet must be a master of artifice. Many of our poets rely too much on vague subjectivity." This was the voice of the fifties, and virtually a refutation of the periodical's initial stance.

VI

Most of the major periodicals of the decade seldom printed poetry of the "new romanticism". John Lehmann's *Penguin New Writing* deliberately did not: Reginald Moore's *Modern Reading,* a much slighter paper-back miscellany, did. One periodical of standing welcomed the new romanticism: *Life and Letters Today,* edited by Robert Herring. It ran as a monthly from September, 1938 (incorporating *The London Mercury* from early 1939) and closed, as so many later periodicals did, in 1950.

Life and Letters was about the same size (in printed words) as *Horizon* (which it accused in 1941 of stealing its best writers). Herring's editorials did not sustain the comparison: they were uniformly platitudinous. *Life and Letters* must be judged by its contributors; and among its poets were Edith Sitwell, Dylan Thomas and Vernon Watkins. Herring was a Welshman, and this perhaps accounts for the support by Thomas—never one to be taken along by the lesser movements of the period. Herring started the practice of "Special Numbers", which was to continue until the periodical closed, and to cover everything from Venezualan to Estonian writing. The first of these, a "Welsh Number" in March, 1940, had poems by Thomas, Watkins, Alun Lewis and Keidrych Rhys. In October, 1941, there was an editorial favourable to the Apocalypse writers and a selection of their poetry, among which Herring included work by Thomas and Watkins. In December, 1943 there was a special number devoted to the "Scottish Renaissance", with poems by George Bruce, Maurice Lindsay and W.S. Graham. Welsh and Scottish writing both got further special numbers in 1947, and Irish writing, in April 1949. It was this continuous responsiveness to regional writing that gave an individuality to *Life and Letters.* It also helped to define a literary spectrum with its publication of Welsh, Scottish, Irish and Apocalypse writers. Henry Treece was fond of emphasising the Celtic roots of some of the Apocalypse writers; and the movement might be seen as one of many revolts against the metropolitanisation of culture after World War I.

Life and Letters had its triumphs: in 1948 and 1949, Herring published stories by the Swedish Stig Dagerman, whose *Nattens Lekar (Games of Night)* had recently appeared; and in November, 1949, Lionel Trilling's remarkable story, "The Other Margaret". There were also stories by Elizabeth Bowen, Eudora Welty, Dorothy Richardson, Paul Bowles, William Sansom, and L.P. Hartley; as well as poems by W.H. Auden, George Barker, Marianne Moore, and Richard Eberhart. Yet, after the first few issues, there were few contributions by any poets who had been associated with *New Writing* or *Twentieth Century Verse.* These absences were significant and showed a dividing of estimations. Throughout the remainder of the decade, Herring was the "*doyen* of the fringes" and the supporter of "New Romantic" and regionalist writing. Nonetheless, *Life and Letters Today* still remains readable and mildly impressive in a way in which most professed "New Romantic" publications do not.

VII

An interesting associate of the New Romanticism was Mervyn Peake. He was a graphic artist, painter, novelist and poet; and between these manifestations of his talent there existed a connection. In *Convoy 4* he contributed a short prose report, "The Glassblowers", along with a pictorial sketch. The experience became the basis of the title poem of his second collection, *The Glassblowers* (1950), and was also the starting point for a painting (now in the Birmingham Art Gallery). In an essay, "How a Romantic Novel was evolved", he describes the writing of his novel *Titus Groan* (1946) and how he "made drawings from time to time which helped me visualise the characters and to imagine what sort of things they would say."[26] The novel was written in snatches while he was in the army from 1940 to 1943; and he reproduces a page of his notebook in which the text runs round the sketches.

His graphic art and his novels give a feeling of a talent at home in the medium and in no sense at full stretch. His sketches for Coleridge's "The Ancient Mariner" in *Poetry London* No. 10, are immediately recognisable as his and no one else's. Yet, despite the sometimes intimate connection between his work in the literary and the visual arts—as instanced in the case of "The Glassblowers", his poetry is quite lacking in the colour and power and individuality of his drawings.

> Is there no thread to bind us—I and he
> Who is dying now, this instant as I write
> And may be cold before this line's complete?
>
> Is there no power to link us—I and she
> Across whose body the loud roof is falling?

This comes from one of the most perceptively felt poems of World War II; yet it would be difficult to recognise it as Peake's. It may well be that Peake showed the uneven distribution of talents between the various media that one would expect: Peake's wife recalled that "above all things he did he wished to be a painter, and I think it was perhaps the medium in which he was least sure."[27] Yet, however one may value Peake's novels, they use the language with ease in a poetic fashion such as would lead one to expect from Peake poetry whose faults were something other than conventionality of language and image. In addition, the comparison of his work as a poet and his work as a graphic artist presses one to questions concerning the disparity in power between the New Romanticism in poetry and the New Romanticism in the visual arts in the nineteen-forties.

VIII

The New Romanticism was a successful and well defined movement in the visual arts in England in the nineteen-forties; but it was by no means an exact correspondence to the New Romanticism in literature. It had its beginnings in the late thirties in a reaction to non-representational art largely French in inspiration. It could also be seen as a turning away from the domination of the ideas of Roger Fry, who, with his doctrine of "significant form", attempted to find for art an aesthetic valuation independent of imaginative and emotional responses to life. Fry's ideas might be paralleled in Virginia Woolf's insistence on the paramountcy of "treatment" rather than "subject" in literature; but nothing like the doctrinaire rejection of subject that characterised the work of Ben Nicholson was to be found in literature—or was even possible there.

The turning away from formalism, to be seen in the work of John Piper, Graham Sutherland, Henry Moore, Victor Pasmore and Paul Nash, began a little before the war, though it was given added impetus by wartime isolation and the awareness of being English that war produced. In the work of Piper, the change was associated with the rediscovery of the great English Romantic artists, such as Constable and Turner: Piper wrote a short book, *British Romantic Artists,* in 1942. In 1944, he spoke approvingly of an "English vision"[28]. While such an awareness may again be seen as a product of the war, it may also be seen as a reestablishment of native forms, such as is found in Auden's *Look Stranger* (1936) or in Benjamin Britten's discovery of the potentiality of Purcell as a model in such works of the forties as his Second String Quartet. The great Romantic painters have a centrality for British painting that the great Romantic poets do not have for British poetry, and it was natural that a visual artist like Piper should turn back to them in terms of an "English vision". The movement to traditional and native models in music, poetry and the visual arts, was found in the work of the generation that came to maturity in the thirties, and who contributed most largely to the wartime "renaissance" in music and the visual arts.

If we look for a parallel in the visual arts to the New Romanticism in literature, it must be found in the accent on the visionary and the lyrical associated with the revival of interest in the work of the Victorian visionary painter and print-maker, Samuel Palmer. Palmer's influence was felt strongly in the work of younger artists like John Craxton, John Minton, and Cecil Collins, with their cultivation of the visionary mode, particularly in landscape. Collins contributed to *Transformation 3,* and his book, *The Vision of a Fool* (1947), made explicit the Apocalyptic orientation of his series of paintings, *The Holy Fool*. It is when we compare the deliberate naiveté of Collins with what Henry Treece made of the notion of the "fool" that we come to a valid and immediately illuminating comparison between the arts—and one that is damaging to the literary element.

The revival of interest in Romanticism saw many surprising collocations. George Grigson, the seeming enemy of Romanticism in the thirties, brought out an anthology, *The Romantics*, in 1942, dedicating it to John Piper. He had much to do with the revival of interest in Samual Palmer, and his collection of essays, *The Harp of Aeolus* (1948), contained pieces on Romantic subjects like the Upas Tree, alongside a strong attack on the poetry of George Barker and Dylan Thomas. In *The Romantics*, Grigson's selections emphasised the work of minor Romantics, as John Heath-Stubbs was to do in his study *The Darkling Plain* (1950)—though Heath-Stubbs and Sidney Keyes had already exploited in their poetry the work of writers like Darley before Grigson's anthology appeared. Ruthven Todd, associated with *Twentieth Century Verse* and *Now*, wrote a largely forgotten but excellent book, *Tracks in the Snow* (1946), dedicated to John Piper and Geoffrey Grigson, and containing essays on Blake, Fuseli and John Martin.

Grigson's *The Romantics* consists largely of very short excerpts, giving the effect almost of an imagist compilation. There is certainly a distrust of the more ambitious poems of the great Romantics; and one suspects that was due to their tendency to philosophise—something that cannot be done so explicitly in the visual arts. In addition, the Romantic movement in English literature was reactionary and secondary in a way that it was not in the visual arts: the reaction to eighteenth century literature produced a sense of themes that were appropriate or inappropriate to poetry; and this resulted in a turning back to Shakespeare and the King James Bible as linguistic models, with a consequent imbedding of archaism in the language of nineteenth century poetry. These effects constituted barriers for the serious contemporary writer that did not exist for the visual artist; while, for those who had a lingering dislike of the "ugliness" of contemporary literature, admiration of the Romantics was an invitation to the conventional. Conventional writing is what the New Romanticism in English poetry frequently offered.

The New Romanticism has loomed large in memories of British poetry of the nineteen-forties. Its rejection has sometimes been seen as implying a rejection of the whole renewal of interest in Romanticism during that period. It is certainly true that, partly because the paper shortage made publishing a seller's market, the poets of the Apocalypse and the New Romanticism got themselves into print very frequently. In fact their work is in no way central to the poetic achievement of the decade. An admiration of Romantic poetry is certainly explicit on the part of George Barker, Vernon Watkins and Kathleen Raine; and it is hard to imagine Tambimuttu without his advocacy of Romanticism. Nevertheless, none of these showed a strong support for the majority of writers discussed in this chapter, and Tambimuttu's perceptive championing of Keith Douglas as well as of Kathleen Raine and David Gascoyne shows a feeling more for quality than for doctrine. A renewed availability of Romantic poetry as a model was not crucial to the poetry of the decade, where continuities with the thirties remained important.

Chapter 8

DEFENDING ANCIENT SPRINGS
Vernon Watkins—Kathleen Raine—David Gascoyne

There have always been those who could not accept a completely secular world, a world in which man was an evolutionary accident with no purposes beyond those he could find for himself. Eliot had been one who felt that way, and he had returned to Christianity in a highly orthodox, institutionalised form. Edwin Muir was a writer for whom "human life without immortality would be inconceivable . . . because if man is an animal by direct descent I can see human life only as a nightmare populated by animals wearing top-hats and kid gloves . . . rubbing their muzzles together in the moment of lust . . . learning to make and to listen to music . . . or to pray."[1] Muir found significance in unchanging patterns of human existence reflected in the individual life:

> . . . we extend far beyond any boundary line which we can set for ourselves in the past or the future . . . the life of every man is an endlessly repeated performance of the life of man . . . what we are not and can never be, our fable, seems to me inconceivably interesting. I should like to write that fable, but I cannot ever live it . . . One or two stages in it I can recognize: the age of innocence and the Fall and all the dramatic consequences which issue from the Fall. But these lie behind experience, not on its surface; they are not historical events; they are stages in the fable.[2]

Muir embodied this sense of the fabulous very successfully in many of his later poems, written during the forties, such as "The Labyrinth" or "The Horses". Muir is one of the writers discussed so eloquently by Kathleen Raine in *Defending Ancient Springs* (1967), a book in which she expounds a similar view of art and life to Muir's and in which she finds kindred visions in the work of Vernon Watkins and David Gascoyne. Like Raine, both these poets reacted to rationalism, seeking, in the exploration of inwardness and of unchanging patterns, a meaning for life in a world that they perceived as spiritually derelict. In the forties they wrote a poetry that is visionary and anti-ironic, and in strong contrast to the dominant writing of the previous decade

II

"Defending ancient springs"—the phrase is from Vernon Watkins, and it epitomises the Romantic reaction to modernism that we find in his work and that of Kathleen Raine. Both had been in Cambridge in the late twenties and had found the atmosphere uncongenial: Raine because of the positivism and scientific realism that set the intellectual climate of the day; Watkins because of the analytic and linguistic discussion of poetry that was a feature of his modern language studies. Neither was to publish a book of poems until the early forties.

Although Watkins was placed first in his college in his subject, he left Cambridge abruptly at the end of his first year, in June, 1925. This reaction to Cambridge was also a reaction to the modern poetry then gaining an ascendancy there. As Kathleen Raine was to write, "Irony and vulgarity, so often associated with modern realism . . . are never found in any poem of Vernon Watkins"[3]; and Watkins himself said "lyric poetry should be exalted, or else I don't think it's worth writing."[4] Introducing Dylan Thomas's letters to him, Watkins wrote "natural observation in poetry meant nothing to us without the support of metaphysical truth"[5]; and, concerning the use of "natural speech"—one of the tenets of modernism, he said, "Natural speech may be excellent, but who will remember it unless it is allied to something artificial, to a particular order of music?"[6]

These positions constitute a repudiation of the Anglo-American modernism that was beginning to take hold as the major formative influence for the new writers emerging at the end of the twenties. Vernon Watkins went home to Swansea and for ten years wrote and developed his medium without publishing anything. He became a friend of Dylan Thomas, whom he met a few months after the publication of Thomas's *18 Poems* in 1934. His main influence and admiration was Yeats, to whom he paid a visit recorded and celebrated in his poem "Yeats in Dublin" (1938).

The key to his work is in the remark "I could never write a poem dominated by time"[7]. "Constancy within change is the theme of so many of my poems, and until it enters a poem I can never find my imagination wholly engaged."[8] The implications of these remarks might seem Platonic, and a Platonic and mythic orientation is present in a great deal of Watkins's poetry, particularly his earlier work. The changing world becomes accepted and redeemed when it is seen as the constant and recurrent exemplification of patterns that do not change. Men are continually drawn to the myths of the past because these myths are forever rehearsed before their eyes. This rehearsal

gives a timeless meaning to experience, but the myths themselves are
also timelessly renewed. It is an orientation that gives rise to powerful
writing.

> There is a moment when Apollo's tree
> Is Daphne still. The Past is not the Past
> But wound within a ring
> So finely wrought,
> It knows each path and avenue of thought.
> Downward he looks, through heaven and earth, to see
> The sunlight and the dayspring
> Caught in her eyes, all uttered love surpassed
> By that first heaven that knows her timelessly.
>
> ("The Turning of the Stars")

This redemption of experience through pattern or myth predominates
in Watkins's earlier poetry; but an insistence on the Platonic element
would miss important and vivifying tensions, present indeed in the
passages quoted. Watkins had been by upbringing and inclination a
Christian, and the author to whom he had turned in his rejection of
Cambridge had been Blake. While one senses a controlling pressure
that is almost overwhelming to seek solace in a vision of the eternal
within the changing, the point of rest sought is not static. He finds
renewing joy in the changing beauties of the world, and there is an
acceptance of changefulness in Watkins's best poetry. The serenity is
a serenity of perception rather than of abstraction.

> I cannot sound the nature of that spray
> Lifted on wind, the blossoms falling away,
> A death, a birth, an earthy mystery,
> As though each petal stirring held the whole tree
> That grew, created on the Lord's day.
>
> ("Music of Colours: The Blossoms Scattered")

The emphasis on Christian redemption is strongest in Watkins's later
poetry, but the change, as he developed, was one of *emphasis* rather
than a shift in thinking or sensibility. Watkins from the beginning
works with the central Christian paradox "bringing its great reward/
By loss" ("Discoveries"). While for the Christian the world is redeemed in terms of an eternal purpose, this does not imply, in most
versions of the faith, a rejection of living. Indeed, the recognition that
everything will be found meaningful and nothing in vain gives a striking freedom from the concerns of time and the cares of tomorrow.
Paradoxically, the discovery of an unchanging meaning can lead the
Christian to a carefree and imprudent embracing of everything that is
fleeting, through joy and in the humility of acceptance.

This is the theme of "The Healing of the Leper" (in *The Lady with the Unicorn* (1948)):

> What Sandro Botticelli found
> Rose from the river where we bathe:
> Music the air, the stream, the ground;
> Music the dove, the rock, the faith:
>
> And all that music whirled upon
> The eyes' deep-sighted, burning rays,
> Where all the prayers of labours done
> Are resurrected into praise.
>
> But look: his face is like a mask
> Surrounded by the beat of wings.
> Because he knows that ancient task
> His true transfiguration springs.

Blindness is a frequent image for acceptance, with Watkins, in contrast to looking before and after. The poem concludes, "Be nothing first; and then, be love." It asserts the primacy of the moment over concerns with time.

There are many poems by Watkins about animals, and the treatment is ultimately one of just this kind of unquestioning acceptance, rather than of poetic or heraldic interpretation. This is particularly true of poems about birds or animals of prey:

> Sheer from wide air to the wilderness
> The victim fell, and lay;
> The starlike bone is fathomless,
> Lost among wind and spray.
> This lonely, isolated thing
> Trembles amid their sound.
> I set my finger on the string
> That spins the ages round.
>
> ("The Feather")

"Stars", "white", "lightness" are also recurrent images that Watkins explores in terms of change and transcendence. Two related poems that make such an exploration are "Music of Colours—White Blossom" and "Music of Colours: The Blossom Scattered". They come from succeeding books—*The Lady with the Unicorn* and *The Death Bell* (1954). They are examples of the constancy of Watkins's themes and of the way in which he returns to explore them. Their separation in different volumes is not, however, evidence that their composition was separate in time. *The Death Bell* contains "Ballad of the Rough Sea", first published in *Life and Letters Today* in 1939, and existing in a manuscript from 1936. It is testimony to Watkins's constancy of preoccupation that he could "work on different poems over the years"[9], allowing them to mature as they would.

The central image is of "whiteness", explored as an image of purity and godhead, and the source of all other colours of the spectrum, separated and displayed by the rainbow, itself the sign of god's covenant with men. Light is known by contrast with darkness; but perfect whiteness, the Platonic, prototypical whiteness that is the whiteness of perfection and of god, can never be known.

> The spray looked white until this snowfall.
> Now the foam is grey, the wave is dull.
> Call nothing white again, we were deceived.
> The flood of Noah dies, the rainbow is lived.
> Yet from the deluge of illusions an unknown colour is saved.
>
> White must die black, to be born white again
> From the womb of sounds, the inscrutable grain,
> From the crushed, dark fibre, breaking in pain.
>   ("Music of Colours—White Blossom")

Yet the example of whiteness is the blossom, an image of fragility, presented with no sadness but rather with exultance in its beauty and delicacy.

> I cannot sound the nature of that spray
> Lifted on wind, the blossoms falling away,
> A death, a birth, an earthy mystery,
> As though each petal stirring held the whole tree
> That grew, created on the Lord's day.
> There is no falling now. Yet for time's sake
> These blossoms are scattered. They fall. How still they are.
> They drop, they vanish, where all blossoms break.
> Who touches one dead blossom touches every star.
>   ("Music of Colours: The Blossom Scattered")

These last lines express again the paradox of security in "blind" acceptance, and the healing of the leper is referred to again—"If there is white, or has been white, it must have been/When His eyes looked down and made the leper clean": an example of the Yeatsian return to images for a new perspective in Watkins's poetry. Both poems take up the myth of Leda and the Swan:

> Leda remembers. The rush of wings cast wide.
> Sheer lightning, godhead, descending on the flood.
> Night, the late, hidden waters on the moon's dark side.
> Her virgin secrecy, doomed against time to run.
> Morning. The visitation. All colours hurled in one.

Struggling with night, with radiance! That smothering glory cried:
'Heavenborn am I. White-plumaged heart, you beat against the sun!'
All recollection sinking from the dazzled blood.
("Music of Colours: The Blossom Scattered")

The "virgin secrecy", a static perfection, is broken by the "smothering glory", and she awakes "blinding white" with "white's bewildering darkness".

The rhetoric again reflects the essentially Christian paradoxes of security in the acceptance of the transient and of the birth of perfection out of darkness and loss. The imagery of the opening of "Music of Colours—White Blossom", at once evocative and paradoxical, is redolent of Valéry, particularly in the transference of sense impression in the phrase "the music by which white is seen":

White blossom, white, white shell; the Nazarene
Walking in the ear; white touched by souls
Who know the music by which white is seen,
Blinding white, from strings and aureoles,
Until that is not white, seen at the two poles,
Nor white the Scythian hills, nor Marlowe's queen.

Watkins's first book, *The Ballad of the Mari Lwyd*, was published in 1941 when he was thirty-five. Before he had met Dylan Thomas in 1934, he had already written hundreds of poems: as he put it "I have a natural facility and my poetry has to battle with that."[10] Under encouragement from Thomas, he started to publish poems in *Wales* in 1937, and later in *Life and Letters Today*, edited by his fellow Welshman, Robert Herring. *The Ballad of the Mari Lwyd* is Watkins's outstanding book, and was one of the best books of poetry by a new author in the forties. The title poem is based on the Welsh tradition of the Mari Lwyd, in which a group of singers went from house to house on the last night of the year with a skull of a dead horse, seeking admission and food and drink by challenging the inmates to a rhyming contest. It becomes a poem of confrontation of the living and the dead, of the acceptance or rejection of the past. "I have attempted to bring together those who are separated," Watkins wrote in his note to the poem. "The last breath of the year is their threshold, the moment of supreme forgiveness, confusion and understanding, the profane and sacred moment impossible to realise while the clock hands divide the Living from the Dead." It is a poem of remarkable pace, with its refrain "Midnight. Midnight. Midnight. Midnight./Hark at the hands of the clock." The book as a whole is marked by a delicacy of skill in the handling of rhythms. Many of Watkins's best poems are here: "The Collier"; "Elegy on the Heroine of Childhood"; "From my

Loitering"; "The Mummy"; "Thames Forest"; "Discoveries". There
is a notable serenity of vision in "The Sunbather" and "Two Deci-
sions" that he was seldom to attain again. Most of these poems were
in fact from the thirties.

His second book, *The Lamp and the Veil* (1945), was disappointing.
It consists of three long poems, "Yeats in Dublin", "Sea-Music For
My Sister Travelling" and "The Broken Sea". "Yeats in Dublin" is
a pre-war poem, understandably much influenced by Yeats, and a de-
monstration that Yeats's magnificent and rhetorical simplicity was not
Watkins's *forte*. The other two poems are even less satisfying. They
are meditations concerning his fears for this sister and godchild in time
of war. Both employ loose rhyming forms; both are diffuse and over-
developed.

> Beside the magnificent, quiet, sinister, terrible sea
> I hear the pebbles grieve, that eternal Genesis
> In the light and stupefaction of foam, where the great
>   white horses flee,
> Delirious clutches at sunbeams, delivered of life too soon,
> For which your mother does penance, caught in the tumult
>   of peace,
> Inhabiting, a rock-bird torn with cymbals, the silence
>   above the moon.
>   ("The Broken Sea", Section 10 [complete])

The Lady with the Unicorn (1948) is a better book, bringing together Watkins's short poems of the decade. Once again, there are
some fine poems: "Music of Colours—White Blossom"; "Sardine
Fishers at Daybreak"; "The Feather"; "The Healing of the Leper";
"The Song of the Good Samaritan". Yet, in its hundred or more
pages, the constant tone of exultance cloys, as it did in *The Lamp and
the Veil*. The craftsmanship is sustained and masterly, but the rhetoric
is too dense. Certain grammatical forms or certain figures of speech
will be repeated until they destroy their effectiveness, as at the beginning of "Zacchaeus in the Leaves", where a sequence of noun phrases
in apposition runs for almost a page. One at times has the sense of
pushing against a void: there is too little counter-pressure to the joyous
rhetoric of the poetry for the joy or the rhetoric to have much significance.

The rhetorical heaviness of some of the poems may derive from the
influence of Dylan Thomas. Most of the correspondence with Thomas
dates from this period, when Thomas was moving out of the clotted
rhetoric of the "Altar-wise by Owl-light" sonnets and the longer
poems in *The Map of Love* (1939). The influence of these poems is
felt in "Spoils of War" and "Papyrus":

I with papyrus fingers, bathed in myrrh,
Under the sad, laid stones where children play,
Taught by the syllable, for love of her,
Doomed to a spiral crypt, illumine day.

The very successful "Returning to Goleufryn", happily more rooted in particular experience than most of Watkins's poems of the period, has the feel of "Poem in October", and some of the lines could be mistaken as by Thomas: "picking a child's path in the turn of the Towy I meet the prodigal town"; "shut, like a book of Psalms,/On the leaves and pressed flowers of a journey." Watkins's poem seems in fact, to have been completed in 1943, a year before Thomas's.

It is certainly true that Watkins reattains the pellucid, delicate quality of his early poetry in the two books that follow *The Lady with the Unicorn—The Death Bell* (1954) and *Cypress and Acacia* (1959); but something more than the influence of Thomas is needed to explain the unsatisfactoriness of much of his poetry of the forties. When Watkins left Cambridge, it was not from boredom or disappointment alone. His departure marked the beginning of the major crisis of his life. Roland Mathias, who knew him, gives this account of it:

He described to friends later in life how, one Saturday evening in that autumn of 1927, he returned to his lodgings on the Taff Embankment in a state of high tension. He had been reading Blake again, and rushed hither and thither about his room shouting that he had conquered time and could control both his destiny and that of others. This penultimate stage was abruptly ended when he heard an enormous crash outside: on going to the window he saw a motor-cyclist dead on the ground and his pillion passenger staggering up the path towards him, his face covered in blood. Immediately—the underlying tenderness of his nature supervening—he was convinced that he had willed this and himself collapsed. But the ultimate stage of crisis was still to come. The following day, Sunday, he took train for Repton, visited such boys as still remembered him, attended chapel, and afterwards burst into Dr. Fisher's study, shouting that it was he, the uncomprehending Headmaster, who destroyed youth, that it had always been he. This tirade was followed by an ineffectual attempt to assault Dr. Fisher. Within less than a minute the young man was under restraint and the Headmaster, realising that he was in a state of mental collapse, arranged for his removal to a nursing home in Derby.[11]

Watkins's best poems from the thirties can be seen as arising out of his attempt to find spiritual equilibrium after that experience. In the work of the forties, one senses that this process has passed, and that a carefully protected serenity has supervened. The serenity was, one feels, so important to Watkins's emotional economy that any questioning or circumspection could never emerge. He had moved to Lloyds

Bank in Swansea after the crisis, and was to remain there until retirement, refusing promotion. No doubt the course presented itself—largely rightly—as the only one that would permit a full devotion to poetry; yet one can see it too as an uncompromising sequestration that was symptomatic as well as deliberate. Michael Hamburger recalled that "he would not write criticism himself and was deeply distrustful of analytical, as distinct from intuitive, processes of any kind". Watkins wrote, in 1951, that "any poet passing judgement on a living contemporary is damned." In another letter to Hamburger, he said, "In poetry of the soul what is fragmentary is completed by love, and the work of art is made fragmentary by love; both revolve around the same centre, and both create themselves continually in relation to their artist who was only a medium."[12] The pressures behind this deliberately uncritical and emphatic acceptance must have been immense. This is the "blind" acceptance of his poetry. The pressures must have been associated with a never recognised sense of how vulnerable his serenity might be if criticism ever crept in. It would then not be surprising that the poetry of the forties suffers from the absence of any countervailing disturbance in the face of which its joy is attained. The result is often diffuse exultance, a poetry that lacks shape because it lacks tension with a resistant experience that would give it shape.

As early as 1938 Dylan Thomas had remarked of some of Watkins's images: "They seem . . . to come out of the nostalgia of literature . . . A motive has been rarefied, it should be made common. I don't ask you for vulgarity, though I miss it; I think I ask you for a little creative destruction, destructive creation . . ."[13] These are valid criticisms, particularly of poems in which the emotional pressure is low; though at his best, Watkins wrote some lovely, tight, resonant poems that convey compellingly an individuality and purity of vision.

III

Kathleen Raine is the most eloquent exponent of her generation of the conception of poetry as a form of knowledge beyond the empirical and rational. She was one of the group of young writers that contributed to the magazine *Experiment* in Cambridge in the late twenties; but, while she was and remained a friend of William Empson, she found the positivistic, scientific atmosphere of Cambridge of that period completely uncongenial. In particular, she could not sympathise with the rejection of Romanticism that was part of the critical outlook of the time.

Her poems appeared in *New Verse, The Listener* and other periodicals during the thirties; and some of these early poems are included in her first collection, *Stone and Flower* (1943). They are recognisably hers; but many have a wraith-like quality compared with her better and later work. She did not find her identity as a poet until the first years of World War II. In a love affair that had the quality of a conversion or revelation, she started to write poetry again: ". . . I knew myself to be . . . no longer in Hades but in the holy world of life."[14] This feeling had less to do with the love affair, which came to an end, than with her escape from herself, from her upbringing in suburban Ilford, and from the ambience of her Cambridge associates. Through the friendship of Michael Roberts and his wife Janet Adam Smith, she went back to the Northumberland she had known as a child; and, in a house in Martindale in late 1939 and 1940, wrote the poems that made up her first book. It was published in 1943 by Tambimuttu, for whom she had a high regard, and who encouraged her in the sense of her worth.

There is in her writing a rejection of the notion that the poet should present reality as he sees it: "the artist is . . . concerned with the proper management of illusion . . . A reality that is only and always real; and an unreal, that is not there at all—how inadequately these categories cover the experiences of the human mind, the human heart, the human being . . . Culture is a quality of belief, the proper management of that illusion to which the human genius naturally tends."[15] Yet "illusion" is clearly not for her what most people would find "illusory": it has to do with something like the "truth of the heart" or the "truth of imagination", and is in fact a kind of knowledge. ". . . Jung's Collective Unconscious, Yeats's *Anima Mundi*, Blake's world of Imagination, or Plato's of Ideas. It is the test of the authentic poet at all times that his work should draw its inspiration from this source."[16] The images of the natural world are the language of this knowledge and meaning—rather as Emerson found them to be in his *Nature:* "The world-tree and its fruits, the birds of the soul, sun, moon, river, loom, dragon, gate and dark tower, may be likened to words of that language, whose meanings though not otherwise definable, are exact."[17]

Style as an end in itself was for her anathema: "Any writer who invents is an enemy of truth . . . whereas all true art comes from something within the self that is not the self at all."[18] Her attitude at first sight resembles the commonplace aesthetic of the early modernists: "A poem is the thing it states"[19] This is quickly qualified by what looks like a version of the doctrine of organic form: "discussions of the rules of poetry and its forms are meaningless . . . Every thought has its own living form . . ."[20] Her position is an extreme one: "The words of the poem lay bare the truth—that is, the poem."[21] "Lyric form is itself the supreme embodiment of archetypal order . . ."[22]

As the example of Yeats so eminently shows, a poet's ideas must be judged primarily in terms of what they do for his or her poetry; and for Kathleen Raine it was "naive indeed to suppose ourselves the victims of circumstances, who are continually weaving and fashioning according to our dreams the texture of the solid-seeming world, which reflects back . . . what in imagination we generate."[23] She evidently found great consolation in what Yeats saw in myth: "the perpetual return of the same thing"[24]—the recurrent flowering of the imaginatively true in the very embodiment of experience. This is the basis of the Edenic quality of her best poetry, with its sense of the density of experience, reaching back, unchanging.

> They walk towards us willingly and gently,
> Unblemished, the white kid, the calf,
> Their newborn coats scarcely dry from the natal waters.
> Each hair lies in its new place, ripple-marked
> By the rhythms of growth, the tides
> That washed them up onto the shores of time.
>
> ("The Victims")

Her belief in the imaginative relation between the inner and outer worlds is compellingly presented in the symbolism of reflection in "The Still Pool":

> Not to that under-world are the sky's stars native,
>   nor its birds,
> Nor the abundant trees, whose roots
> Stir in the water's depths an impulse to ascend
>
> Into those leaves and boughs, into those flowers
> Out of an element whose nature is to fall
> Yet, against nature, may in nature rise.

In the best of her books of the forties, *The Pythoness* (1947), there are poems of firmness, starkness and simplicity; and it is a great tribute to the concrete achievement of her vision in that book that it is so seldom maimed by reference to ideas conceived outside the experience of the eternal in the world of change. Yet, if as with Yeats, we seek the central wisdom of the poetry, for which the perhaps unacceptable world view is the basis, we find it very slight. The best of her poems achieve a serene celebration of the eternal order and beauty of things; but, beyond this—and here the comparison with Yeats is very telling—there is little else.

Willa Muir told Kathleen Raine that, in the first volume of her autobiography, *Farewell Happy Fields* (1973), she was "too much given to 'floating off into *anima mundi*'; bread and salt, she said, not honeydew, is the food of life."[25] There is an attenuated sameness about her best poetry, so that its qualities compel acknowledgement, but not the spontaneous acquiescence that the most powerful poetry commands.

> I see the blue, the green, the golden and the red,
> I have forgotten all the angel said.
>
> The flower, the leaf, the meadow and the tree,
> but of the words I have no memory.
>
> I hear the swift, the martin, and the wren,
> but what was told me, past all thought is gone.
>
> ("Angelus")

It is refreshing to come on a passage like the opening of "New Year 1943", where the "bread and salt" of the particular intrude:

> . . . the tear-wet streets, with cloud-torn moonlight shining,
> Ways underground are open, and the trains are running
> Oh to what end, in this dream-entangled city?

The outstanding quality of her best poetry in its economy, noticeable in the absence of adjectives and figurative effects:

> There is a fish, that quivers in the pool,
> itself a shadow, but its shadow, clear.
> Catch it again and again, it is still there.
>
> Against the flowing stream, its life keeps pace
> with death—the impulse and the flash of grace
> hiding in its stillness, moves, to be motionless.
>
> ("In the Beck")

Its worst faults are prosiness and a proclivity for poetic cliché:

> Waiting for the longed-for voice to speak
> through the mute telephone, my body grew weak
> with the well-known and mortal death, heartbreak . . .
>
> Then I saw every visible substance turn
> into immortal, every cell new born
> burned with the holy fire of passion.
>
> ("Passion")

The poem arises from experiences immediate and strongly felt, as her autobiography shows. Perhaps, indeed, it is the ultimate uncongeniality of the actual to her inspiration that accounts for its translation into phrases such as "the longed-for voice", "the holy fire of passion"; or for the awkwardness of the third line.

Reviewing her third book, *The Pythoness,* when it first appeared in

1947, Norman Nicholson remarked that "her position shifts from that of orthodox Catholicism to that of a Blakean Christianity or . . . quasi-Gnosticism." In the same review he noted "a controlled ambiguity of intention . . . that embraces the factual and the scientific."[26] The poems in *The Pythoness* were written not too long after her temporary conversion to Catholicism, so that, as in her previous volume, *Living in Time* (1946), one is aware of an attempt to acclimatise Christianity to traditional poetic stances. Nevertheless, her work as a whole leaves one with a decided uncertainty as to what she was committed to at various stages of her life—an uncertainty perhaps shared by her. In the second volume of her autobiography, *The Land Unknown,* published in 1975 but written in the early sixties, she not only comments on her discomfort with Christian mythology, but says of it: "it would never for a moment have occurred to me to believe in the factual historical truth of this marvellous and inexhaustibly rich mythological narrative, neither would it have occurred to me to doubt it . . . it was so clearly a symbolic allegory, not of the order of historical fact, but of the truth of the imagination, expressed figuratively."[27] Similarly she states: "If I use the Platonic (and Christian) word, 'the soul', that is because for all practical purposes I regard the total view of things implied by this word to be truer, at all events more humanly rewarding, than the alternatives".[28] This disclaimer is in keeping with a tone of evasion of explicit ideology recurrent in her writing: "that the assumption of any ideology should replace the perennial task and quest of the soul—should take from us the possibility of damnation or beatitude no social order can confer or take away—is, to me, still unimaginable."[29]

When her poetry embodies the perceived archetypal order with the economy that her theory of poetry suggests, it has an austerity, a clarity and a dignity that sets it apart from the rhetorical poetry of many like minded poets of her day. It speaks immediately in what she calls "the pre-verbal poetic language of which myths are made"[30]; and it has a lucidity that gives us a sense of seeing—as she said of Blake's drawings—"the forms of spiritual beings".[31] Her poetry is, of course, a poetry of celebration of her sense of things, not a poetry of tension; yet the serenity attained in her best poetry, for all her philosophical protestations, "contains" very little. It does not communicate a resolution of profound and experienced emotional conflicts, as does *Four Quartets*. Human agony abides in the particular, and it is the particular that we hence ask to see transformed. That the particular so seldom enters her poetry, she evidently sees as its strength: that it seems to exert so little pressure must appear as a shortcoming, particularly to those who cannot, apart from the experience of her poetry, share her vision of things.

IV

A writer who began by submerging himself in what Kathleen Raine called "the phantasmogoria of the Modern Movement", and then subsumed it to a visionary, religious poetry was David Gascoyne. By 1940 he had been through one career as a writer: his first book of poems, *Roman Balcony*, which appeared in 1932 when he was sixteen; an autobiographical novel, *Opening Day* in 1933; *A Short Survey of Surrealism* (1935); and *Man's Life is This Meat* (1936)—poems that established him at the age of twenty as the leading writer of surrealist poetry in England, and one of the few who had wholeheartedly taken up the mode. His poems appeared infrequently in periodicals after the end of 1936; and he seems to have become distrustful of surrealism, partly in the face of pressing practical demands of Left-wing ideology. In 1937 he was in Spain, broadcasting on the Republican side; while 1938 was spent in Paris, where, in a period of spiritual crisis, he was befriended by the French poet Pierre Jean Jouve and his wife.

Jouve's influence is strong in Gascoyne's *Hölderlin's Madness* (1938), which consists mainly of poems based on translations of Hölderlin by Jouve; and the influence is still felt in *Poems 1937-1942*—a volume of deeply religious cast, in a way that much of the poetry of the decade that took its hat off to religion was not. In its sombreness it contrasts with *Man's Life is This Meat*, though the agonised introspection of the early poems leads into the later work.

It is this agonised sensibility that emerges in *Poems 1937-1942*: ". . . to find in the poetic act a *religious* perspective—the only answer to the void of time" Jouve had written; and the remark epitomises the attempt of Gascoyne's volume.[32]

> "*It is finished.*" The last nail
> Has consummated the inhuman pattern, and the veil
> Is torn. God's wounds are numbered.
> All is now withdrawn: void yawns
> The rock-hewn tomb. There is no more
> Regeneration in the stricken sun,
> The hope of faith no more,
> No height no depth no sign
> And no more history.
> ("Tenebrae")

"Miserere", the opening section of *Poems 1937-1942*, offers, through a series of poems—"Pieta", "Kyrie", "Sanctus"—that echo the Catholic liturgy and recreate the horror of the first Easter, what Gascoyne called "The revelation of despair" ("Ex Nihilo"). As Gascoyne wrote in 1946: "The Void itself cannot be apprehended except by means of

a symbolic expression (self-contradictory representation). By realizing
such a term of reference we can free ourselves from the terrible non-
existence implicit in the negation of the Spirit.''[33] It is of this spiritual
condition that the poems make us aware.

Easily the most successful of these poems is "Ecce Homo", with
its once celebrated phrase, "Christ of Revolution and of Poetry"; and
one can see in it a transformation of Gascoyne's earlier left-wing in-
dignation into a religious despair at the violence of the times.

> Black shirts and badges and peaked caps,
> Greet one another with raised-arm salutes;
> They have cold eyes, unsmiling lips;
> Yet these His brothers know not what they do . . .
>
> He who wept for Jerusalem
> Now sees His prophecy extend
> Across the greatest cities of the world,
> A guilty panic reason cannot stem
> Rising to raze them all as He foretold . . .

The poem turns on a passage of great orthodoxy, which serves to connect it with the sequence that precedes it, and to bring the sequence
into contemporary focus:

> He is suspended on the cross-tree now
> And we are onlookers at the crime,
> Callous contemporaries of the slow
> Torture of God.

"Miserere" is followed by a section headed "Metaphysical" (or
"metapsychological", as Gascoyne's prefatory "Note" has it). The
term "metapsychological" is from Jouve: "Incalculable is the extension of our sense of the tragic that is brought us by metapsychology,
and even more incalculable the extension of the knowledge gained by
that eye which gazes into our secret parts—which eye is none other
than our own." That inner searching eye is a presence in Gascoyne's
poetry of the forties. Jouve's statement comes from a piece dated
"1933" that Gascoyne translated and published in the early forties as
"The Unconscious: Spirituality: Catastrophe"[34]. Jouve, who used the
phrase "the bloody sweat of sublimation", made a connection between
Freudianism and Christianity that was evidently a valuable example to
Gascoyne in the crisis that followed his abandonment of surrealism in
the thirties. As Kathleen Raine remarked, "It was the Messainic aspect
of surrealism (and also of Marxism) which has most strongly appealed
to David Gascoyne . . ."[35]

Jouve's influence was crucial for Gascoyne at the time. In his diary of August 23rd, 1939, Gascoyne wrote: "The essential nature of experience being *Negation. The Void, das Nichts, Nada, le Neant.* Practically the only image that presents itself at all strongly to me is *a black vacuum in (or through) which two eyes are fixedly staring.* Can find no simile strong enough to convey the utter *blindness of desperation* at the core of all this."[36] Jouve had written ". . . the Nada theme. It has run through the whole of my work and sustained three quarters of it."[37] In January, 1939, Gascoyne had received a copy of Jouve's recently published *Kyrie,* which seems to have been an important inspiration for the early part of *Poems 1937-1942.* In a "Note" to that book, he said: "The poems in this collection were originally planned as two separate ensembles: "The Open Tomb" (1937-39), and "The Conquest of Despair" (1939-42)." In a manuscript notebook, he made a list of contents for "The Open Tomb"[38], which included most of the poems that made up the first two sections of *Poems 1937-1942,* "Miserere" and "Metaphysical"; and in his diary he recorded: *"April to the end of June* [1939] Period of creative activity: poetry. Collection of poems completed and revised."[39] This was evidently "The Open Tomb". Jouve's *Kyrie* may have triggered for Gascoyne the conception of a body of visionary poems with a traditional religious centre. Certainly, poems from *Kyrie,* translated without the filter of Gascoyne's sensibility, could well be mistaken for pieces from *Poems 1937-1942:*

> We have amazed by our great sufferings
> The inclination of the indifferent stars
> We have stared at the blood of the wound
> With an outsider's eye, in secret we
> Have coupled through the false back door,
> We have become these iron systems
> Which wander directionless, caterpillar horsemen
> Of the last judgement, a vast, dismal boredom
> Bears us to your hoofs of consummation
> Red Horse black Horse yellow Horse white Horse.[40]

The energy was alien to Gascoyne's poetry, but the rhetoric seems to have been influential.

Gascoyne was already interested in Kierkegaard, Dostoevsky and existentialism—writing that had little currency in England until after the war.[41] He wrote of "stressing the importance of the 'magical' theory of poetry . . ." (as he had in *Hölderlin's Madness* (1938)); and spoke of "the surrender of English poetry to rationalism"[42]. "The tradition of modern English poetry is something quite different from the tradition of Hölderlin, Rimbaud, Rilke, Lorca, Jouve . . ."[43]. In *Hölderlin's Madness,* as in "The Open Tomb", he appeared to be cultivating a somewhat archaic diction, derived from English Romantic poetry, as appropriate to the new tone of his poetry. At its weakest it is conventional and trite:

> Its force like violins in pure lament
> Persists, sending ascending stairs
> Across the far wastes of the firmament
> To carry starwards all our weight of tears.
>
> ("Cavatina")

It might be argued, however, that he was merely trying to reproduce the rhetoric of Jouve's poetry, and that the violent, often conventional, and decidedly unresonant diction was that of his model. Indeed, it is the over-ripe, archaic diction of *Poems 1937-1942* that Gascoyne uses in translating Jouve:

> The rocky path is sown with sombre cries
> Archangels keeping guard over the gorges' weight
> The naked stones beneath the twilight waves . . .
>
> ("Gravida", in *New Road* 4, 1946)

Certainly the "Open Tomb" poems are not the best in *Poems 1937-1942,* and display a portentousness and a tendency to self-pity that are among Gascoyne's worst faults. Much finer are the poems in which he draws on the resources of contemporary English, and in which the diction is sometimes close to that of the dominant poetry of the thirties. These poems are found in Sections IV and V of *Poems 1937-1942*—"Personal" and "Time and Place": many were written in 1940 or 1941 ("The Conquest of Despair")[44]. They are the only poems from the forties in the book. (Section III, "Strophes Elégaiques à la Mémoire d'Alban Berg" were written in English in 1936, and again in French in 1939.) In the poems of "Time and Place", Gascoyne attains his most distinctive and perfect manner.

"A Wartime Dawn", "Walking at Whitsun" and "The Gravel-pit Field" are far from being purely descriptive of time and place, though they do in fact evoke the actual with a particularity that is a notable strength. As Kathleen Raine remarked, "it was David Gascoyne who finally realised and perfected a kind of poetry . . . in which an imagery of precise realism, gathered from the daily human . . . scene . . . is informed with a content not only supremely imaginative but infused with the imagination of the collective mind of which it is an eloquent, if unconscious expression . . ."[45] The notion of the "collective mind" is not one to which Gascoyne's poetry would naturally lead one, but her characterisation is very apt, particularly of the finest of these poems, "The Gravel-pit Field". It moves from the ordinary, to a vision of the ordinary transformed, so that this becomes an emblem of what is beyond the ordinary.

> As I stand musing, overhead
> The zenith's stark light thrusts a ray
> Down through the dusk's rolling vapours, casts
> A last lucidity of day
>
> Across the scene: and in a flash
> Of insight I behold the field's
> Apotheosis: No-man's-land
> Between this world and the beyond,
> Remote from men and yet more real
> Than any human dwelling-place:
> A tabernacle where one stands
> As though within the empty space
> Round which revolves the Sage's Wheel.

It is quite literally a *vision* of the ordinary, of what is potential in it for those who bring the redeeming vision. The bleak light of the March evening becomes the light of transformation, and a spiritual resonance that goes beyond the play of incidental metaphor is given to the picture.

"When Reason banishes the Spirit . . . Man immediately begins to lose his ancient sense of mission and purpose on earth. The increasingly apparent futility of his existence . . ."[46]—this is the theme of the best poems in Gascoyne's second volume from the forties, *A Vagrant* (1950).

> They're much the same in most ways, these great cities. Of them all,
> Speaking of those I've seen, this one's still far the best
> Big densely built-up area for a man to wander in
> Should he have ceased to find shelter, relief,
> Or dream in sanatorium bed . . .
>
> Blessèd are they, it might be said, who are not of this race
> Of settled average citizens secure in their *état*
> *Civil* of snowy guiltlessness and showy high ideals
> Permitting them achieve an inexpensive lifelong peace
> Of mind, through dogged persistence, frequent aspirin, and bile . . .
>
> Awkward enough, awake, yet although anxious still just sane,
> I stand still in my quasi-dereliction, or but stray
> Slowly along the quais towards the ends of afternoons
> That lead to evenings empty of engagements, or at night
> Lying resigned in cosy-corner crow's-nest, listen long
> To sounds of the surrounding city desultorily
> Seeking in loud distraction some relief from what its nerves

Are gnawed by: I mean knowledge of its lack of *raison d'être*.
The city's lack and mine are much the same. What, oh what can
A vagrant hope to find to take the place of what was once
Our expectation of the Human City, in which each man might
Morning and evening, every day, lead his own life, and Man's?
                                                    ("A Vagrant")

The poem, with its subdued yet carefully controlled rhythm, creating
so decidedly the tone of self-questioning protest that is its philosophical ambience, accepts Paris; and, despite its sense that the modern
city is the home of the spiritual emptiness and alienation that is the
source of the poet's despair, it sustains from time to time a note of
deep compliment to the city. The relaxed and unhysterical movement
mirrors the poet's acceptance that "The City's lack and mine are much
the same"—an acceptance that makes palatable his rejection (despite
the closing plea) of the lives of millions of others.

In an essay on the Russian existentialist philosopher Leon Chestov,
Gascoyne wrote in 1949: ". . . a man may suddenly have to admit
that the ordinary, reassuring truths and assumptions upon which we
all base our everyday life and which it might well seem outrageous
even to question publicly . . . seem . . . to have been simply
the . . . conventionally legitimized means whereby men commonly
stupify themselves so as to continue to be able to remain fast asleep . . ."[47] The attitude, both here and in the poetry, is similar to
that in sections of *Four Quartets,* though the pressure is towards
change (even though Gascoyne despairs of it) rather than towards acceptance. Both poets exemplify an alienation that involves a modification of the Romantic conception of the poet as visionary: despair at
the unredeemed quality of life is the beginning of wisdom, and only
the elect are capable of that despair, because only they see the need
for life, as lived, to be redeemed. For Gascoyne, as for all who are
concerned with the spiritual, redemption is a thing for the individual.
The aim is "personal authenticity".[48]

Though alienation is the powerful underlying feeling in Gascoyne's
poetry, a countervailing vision of life made acceptable in its authenticity also emerges. "The Sacred Hearth" (dedicated to George Barker)
follows "The Vagrant" in the collection of that name. Gascoyne looks
back on Barker's house through the trees of the orchard into which he
has wandered at night:

        . . . I stood
There staring back at the dark white nocturnal house,
And saw gleam through the lattices a light more pure than gold
Made sanguine with crushed roses, from the firelight that all night
Stayed flickering about the sacred hearth. As long as dawn

Hung fire behind the branch-hid sky, the strong
Magic of rustic slumber held unbroken; yet a song
Sprang wordless from inertia in my heart, to see how near
A neighbour strangeness ever stands to home. George, in the wood
Of wandering among the wood-hiding trees, where poets' art
Is how to whistle in the dark, where pockets all have holes,
All roofs for refugees have rents, we ought to know
That there can be for us no place quite alien and unknown,
No situation wholly hostile, if somewhere there burn
The faithful fire of vision still awaiting our return.

Gascoyne's poetry, at its best, speaks with a power that is a measure of its seriousness. Indeed, without that seriousness, it would be vulnerable to its very obvious unevenness. Despite the fact that Gascoyne continually exposed *avant garde* movements with a characteristic depth of commitment—surrealism, Marxism, existentialism—and with an understanding beyond that of many contemporaries, his writing contains numerous examples of the ineptly old fashioned. Even the startlingly good poems contain clumsy writing and trip us up with cliché. In "The Gravel-pit Field", as the poet "stand[s]/musing" he has "a flash/Of insight". These are not cliches of poetry, but cliches of everyday speech, and Gascoyne's poems too frequently fall into an inert prosiness. An anthologised poem, "September Sun: 1947", begins:

Magnificent strong sun! in these last days
So prodigally generous of pristine light
That's wasted only by men's sight who will not see
And by self-darkened spirits from whose night
Can rise no longer orison or praise . . .

The poem has undoubted power—though not as much as its currency would suggest; yet it contains an inversion and decidedly "poetic" words and phrases. The opening apostrophe is close to cliché, and what is most notable is the way in which the individual words "Magnificent strong sun" achieve no enhancement by interaction. In so far as the stanza succeeds, it does so in spite of the writing, riding on the sense of authenticity it communicates.

This sense of authenticity is in general supported by the fact that Gascoyne does not write highly figurative or imagistic poetry. Things, scenes, incidents are given their own metaphoric or symbolic connotation. In "Note on Symbolism" he saw the poet as sometimes being "given the power with which to extract a symbol from the incoherent welter of existence . . . The symbol is a bridge between the subjective reality of personal experience and the objective reality of the Spirit."[49]

"Apologia" would suggest that he saw the linguistic aspect of the poem as ideally the pellucid medium through which the symbol is seen:

> Before I fall
> Down silent finally, I want to make
> One last attempt at utterance, and tell
> How my absurd desire was to compose
> A single poem with my mental eyes
> Wide open, and without even one lapse
> From that most scrupulous Truth which I pursue
> When not pursuing Poetry.—Perhaps
> Only the poem I can never write is *true*.

Against this one must set the image of Gascoyne's career: the beginning in surrealism, followed by the stylistic changes, under the influence of Jouve, to the religious poetry of *Poems 1937-1942*, and thence to the increasingly plain and often flat poetry of *A Vagrant* and the portentous *Night Thoughts* (1956). The precocious facility of *Roman Balcony* and *Man's Life is This Meat* gives way to an uncertainty of touch in the forties, seemingly admitted by the poet in his designation "Make-Weight Verse" for the last quarter of *A Vagrant*. There seem to have been periods of silence and agonising in which writing was almost abandoned. In July 1937 he recorded: "I have stopped writing poetry since more than a year . . . because the writing of poetry seems to me to be a dishonest occupation . . ."[50]; and in 1939 (after writing "The Open Tomb") he said "I have at last left literature behind."[51] This confict between art and truth is of course a recurrent embarrassment in the history of twentieth century poetry. It is Gascoyne's readiness on the one hand to be completely radical and thoroughgoing in his conception of art, and on the other hand to concern himself unwaveringly with the recording of what he sees to be the truth, that constitutes the character of his art and for which we value it. Ideally though for him, one feels (in a phrase from Carlyle's *Characteristics* that he quotes with recommendation) "Literature is but a branch of Religion . . ."[52]

Chapter 9

REGIONAL AND TRADITIONAL

Regional differences—Welsh poetry—R.S. Thomas—
Scottish poetry—Irish poetry—Patrick Kavanagh—
Laurie Lee—Norman Nicholson—Jack Clemo—
The Wind and the Rain, Here and Now, Patric Dickinson—
Anne Ridler

The nineteen-forties saw an upsurge of regional awareness and of regional writing. Manifesting itself in Wales and Scotland as cultural nationalism, it was partly the result of the focus on fundamental issues induced by the war, and partly the outcome of an increasing metropolitanisation of culture, due to improved communications, and to an expanded educational system, whose character was inevitably dictated from London. In Ireland, regional awareness was a part of the nationalism that remains so central to Irish life. The increased availability, after World War I, of secondary and higher education was no doubt decisive in creating a situation favourable to the emergence of some of the writers discussed in this chapter—even if they never personally benefited from such education. In addition, the interest in regional cultures, like the cultivation of more traditional styles of poetry, can be seen as part of the wartime reaction to the cosmopolitan modernism that had transformed poetry at the beginning of the century. A regional tone was not confined to the work of poets from areas distinct by nationality from England: the writing of English poets like Norman Nicholson took its character from the culture of the locality from which they came.

The discussion of regionalism and regional poetry and culture requires a tactful discrimination between conflicting perspectives. In 1947, Howard Sergeant brought out *An Anthology of Northern Poetry.* It included contributions by writers as various as Lilian Bowes-Lyon, Leonard Clark, Roy Fuller and James Kirkup. It would be easy to dismiss it as a piece of factitious bookmaking, contrived by means of a favourite regionalist trick, literary kidnapping. In retrospect, it is impossible not to see it in terms of the distinctive contribution writers from the north were to be making ten years later. On the other hand, the type of correction that is called for is illustrated by Geoffrey Taylor's introduction to his anthology *Irish Poems of Today* (1946), chosen from a leading Dublin periodical, *The Bell:* "To make an Irish anthology *fully* representative one should, I think, include work by three other Irish poets whose poems would lend lustre to any pages, I mean Robert Graves, Louis MacNeice and Austin Clarke."[1] Poems by Graves in fact appeared in *Wales,* accompanied by similar claims[2]; while the work of Louis MacNeice, whatever it owes to his Irish background, belongs distinctively in the London in which he made his literary life.

The problem is most embarrassing when one turns to Welsh writing, and one is confronted by the valid complaint of Welsh nationalists that the Englishness of many of their writers is a mark of the fact that the English, through an English language educational system whose curriculum was decided in London, forced on Wales alien and denatured cultural patterns. The most famous Anglo-Welsh poet of his day, Dylan Thomas, was a product of that system: his education went no further than the English language grammar school, and his broad, eclectic knowledge of English poetry was derived largely from his school years. He spoke no Welsh, and attempts to demonstrate his peculiarly Celtic quality seem misguided. As he himself wrote: "I've never understood this racial talk, 'his Irish talent', 'undoubtedly Scotch inspiration', apart from whiskey."[3] He belonged where he quickly went, in the literary London of David Archer, Geoffrey Grigson, the Soho pubs and the B.B.C. Yet it would seem perverse to fault his appearance in collections of Welsh poetry.

Welsh cultural nationalism was a force in the forties, as it is today, and as undeniable as Scottish cultural nationalism. The problems that it raises are best understood in linguistic terms. In 1939, Celtic languages were certainly spoken much more widely than they are today. It was still possible to meet people on Snaefell whose first language was Manx. Today there are no native Manx speakers. Nevertheless, neither Eirse nor Gaelic was the first language of any large group in the main populated areas of Ireland and Scotland. Indeed, the use of Gaelic had for centuries distinguished the Scottish highlands from the lowlands. Welsh alone was a widespread first language. On the other hand, Scots was a well identified version of English, with a literary tradition going back beyond Dunbar and Henryson; but the same cannot be said for the English of Wales or Ulster. Scots could be, and was, revived alongside Gaelic as a literary language: it was a version of the contemporary speech of the Scottish lowlands, whereas Gaelic was a surviving antiquity. In Wales there was no such version of English, and the grammar schools were not only ousting Welsh but imposing standard English.

When we compare two anthologies, *Modern Scottish Poetry* (1946) and *Modern Welsh Poetry* (1944), it is difficult not to feel that, while the Welsh anthology has the better poets, the Scottish anthology has the more decided character. The English of the Welsh anthology is metropolitan educated English; and a number of contributors, like the editor, Keidrych Rhys, were educated at one of England's older universities. This is not so much the case with the majority of the poets in *Modern Scottish Poetry:* the poetry of Hugh MacDiarmid, William Soutar, George Bruce, Douglas Young and Sidney Goodsir Smith is linguistically and culturally Scottish poetry.

II

The poems brought together in *Modern Welsh Poetry* or published in Keidrych Rhy's periodical, *Wales,* are impressive as a group, but it is hard to see what literary identity they have, apart from the recurrence of Welsh subject matter. The anthology is, of course, a plea for seeing its poets as a group, with the hope that some sense of Welsh cultural identity might arise from this. Roland Mathias was a steady contributor to *Wales* and a supporter of its ideological positions, yet there is little to identify his poetry as specifically Welsh:

> We had gone down to Tabor, to the door
> My corduroy a green
> Tug at the ministerial spleen, a tweak
> At the white scarfe-knot, peak in pocket seen
> Capping the diaconate,
> In time to scalp the noise
> And scamper made by boys, evacuees
> With paper aeroplanes the teasing wind
> Forced down behind the chapel rails.
>
> ("Balloon over Rhondda")

The mannered style, unnecessary complexity of syntax, the lack of firmness of rhythm, and the over-development of visual elements, were characteristic of a great deal of English poetry in the forties. The work of the better poets in the anthology—Dylan Thomas, Vernon Watkins, Alun Lewis, R.S. Thomas—has been widely discussed, and, except in the case of R.S. Thomas, the few attempts to present these poets as "Welsh" writers have rung false.

The embarrassment concerning the identity of Welsh writing in English is encountered in a book by a leading Anglo-Welsh writer, Glyn Jones—*The Dragon Has Two Tongues* (1968): "who are the Anglo-Welsh? I defined them first simply as Welshmen who write in English. Later I qualified this, and I ought to qualify the definition further by confining the term to those Welshmen who write in English about

Wales."[4] He sees the twentieth century Anglo-Welsh writer as coming typically from a family in industrial South Wales that has a background of Welsh-speaking non-conformity but is in fact in its first generation of speaking English. Dylan Thomas's family had something of this character; but, as Jones observes, "One can call Yeats or Joyce an Irish writer . . . in a way one could not call Dylan Thomas a Welsh writer."[5] Jones contends that the "minority of Anglo-Welsh poets to whom Welsh is not literally a closed book . . . show in their English verse no traces, or rather very few traces, of having read Welsh poetry"[6]; and he states that the cross-fertilisation between Ango-Welsh literature and modern literature in Welsh is "nil".[6A] He rejects, however, "all . . . attempts to impose homogeneity on these writers on a basis of race or style or identity of vision or philosophy"[7].

The contributors to *Modern Welsh Poetry* were largely made up of writers who had appeared in *Wales,* also edited by Keidrich Rhys. In pre-war days, *Wales* had been a magazine of experimental writing published from No. 4 Parton Street, the home of David Archer's Left-wing and *avant garde* bookshop. In 1940, after eleven issues, it closed down. It started again in July, 1943, after Rhys had come out of the army, and ran for thirty-one issues until October, 1949. (It was later revived for eighteen months at the end of the fifties.)

Rhys, in his first editorial, recognised the change in character that would come over his periodical: "our public will enjoy this *transition* experimentation and originality best when it is interspersed between something more solid . . . The pioneer work of the old happy-go-lucky pre-war *Wales* is done" . . . "the war has made the Welsh realise that they are a nation with a country, a people, a culture and a tradition *different* from England's to fight for" and the "policy of *Wales* . . . will be a serious one *towards* Wales." ". . . *Wales,* at least, should aim at being the rallying-point of all those creative elements in our midst with some sense of nationhood." (*Wales* I (July, 1943) 4-5)

In Autumn, 1946, he published the " 'Wales' Questionnaire":

1.   Do you consider yourself an Anglo-Welsh writer?

2.   For whom do you write?

3.   What is your opinion of the relationship between Literature and Society?

4.   Should "Anglo-Welsh literature" express a Welsh attitude to life and affairs, or should it merely be literature about Welsh things?

5.   Do you believe that a sense of Welsh Nationhood is more consistent with one particular attitude to life and affairs than any other?

Those responding were: R.S. Thomas; Vernon Watkins; Sir Idris Bell; B.L. Coombes; David Aberpennar; Wyn Griffith; Glyn Jones; Emyr Humphreys; and David Jones. With the exception of R.S. Thomas, who took a very Welsh stance, the respondents seemed embarrassed by the questions or offered philosophical discussions of them. In his third issue, Rhys announced: "We . . . cannot ignore practical politics any longer." Political concerns became more pronounced as the decade progressed, and *Wales* moved away from being a mainly literary review.

Wales evidently achieved a considerable distribution, and did a great deal to sensitize its readers to the Welshness of their culture, though developments in communications would soon begin the obliteration of regional character that we have seen in the last quarter of a century. It published work by David Jones, Dylan Thomas, Vernon Watkins, Alun Lewis and many others. However, Rhys's great editorial achievement was the publication of R.S. Thomas, both in *Wales* and through the Druid Press, which brought out Thomas's first book, *The Stones of the Field* in 1946. Thomas, indeed, was the only militantly Welsh poet of any distinction to appear in *Wales*.

III

R.S. Thomas is often thought of as a poet of the fifties, and he was included alongside Larkin, Amis and Enright in the Penguin anthology *The New Poetry* in 1962. He first became well known, it is true, with *Song at a Year's Turning* in 1955, but this volume reprinted three early collections. He was in fact a year older than his namesake, Dylan Thomas, and a poem by him "Homo Sapiens 1941" had appeared in *Horizon* as early as October, 1941. His work appeared not only in *Wales,* but also in *Life and Letters Today* and *Poetry London*. *The Stones of the Field* was published in 1946, to be followed by *An Acre of Land* (1952) and *The Minister* (1953). The first of these was published in Carmarthon, and the others by the Montgomery Printing Company in Newton. No doubt this had a lot to do with Thomas's work not getting known, because even the first book contains poems that seem destined to be among those by which he is remembered.

Publication by a Welsh press is likely to have been Thomas's choice rather than a last resort. He contributed a number of significant articles to *Wales* that dealt with cultural nationalism: "The Depopulation of the Welsh Hill Country" (1945); "Some Contemporary Scottish Writing" (1946); and "A Welsh View of the Scottish Renaissance" (1948). In reply to the question, "Do you consider yourself an Anglo-Welsh writer?" in the *Wales* questionnaire in 1946, he said "No! A

Welsh writer." and, in response to "For whom do you write?" he quoted Yeats—"All day I'd looked in the face/What I had hoped 'twould be/To write for my own race/And the reality".[8] He attacked the notion "that art must be contemporary . . . meaning . . . that it must deal with the English urban and mechanised civilisation"[9]; and he spoke derogatively of the prospect of certain Scots writers as "like too many of our writers . . . limping along in the rear of Eliot, Auden, and company limited."[10] He felt a Yeatsian disgust for "that large body of Welsh people . . . who have willingly surrendered their age-old customs and traditions for the bric a brac of a bourgeois existence in houses indistinguishable from English suburbia."[11] In contrast to them he set "the hilly district of central Montgomeryshire" where "the buildings remain . . . but the people have gone":

> Dotted here and there about these lovely moors, in a small defile beside a hurrying stream, or crouching for shelter beneath a few pines or firs, there are still a considerable number of small farms and crofts, whose occupants manage to win some kind of living from the grudging soil. These are the true Welsh peasantry and to know them is to feel a real affection for them.[12]

He writes of the disfigurement of this life in a way that makes it seem natural that it was John Betjeman who wrote the introduction to *Song at a Year's Turning:* "Instead of the rich cultural life of *yr hendre* [the vallies] we get whist-drives and dances the winter through".[13]

"One of the problems of an Anglo-Welsh poet," Thomas wrote in 1964, "in any part of Welsh-speaking Wales is that of having to try to transpose the raw material of his imagination and experience into the alien medium of English speech . . . I mention that as personally applicable."[14] It was from the imaginative experience of the Montgomeryshire hills, as Thomas's poems attest, that he drew the material of his poetry; and, it must have been out of the effort to adapt the experiences of that Welsh speaking *milieu* to an English expression that he developed his own firm and individual idiom. That idiom was not there from the beginning; and it is not a groping hesitancy but a too fluent "literary" quality that marks the poems that he later chose not to collect from his first volume:

> Thoughts in the mind's bare boughs sit dumb,
> Waiting for the spring to come:
> The green lispings, the gold shower,
> The white cataract of song,
> Pent up behind the stony tongue
> In stiff tribute to the frost's power.
>
> ("Frost")

This complete short poem is accomplished but conventional, and might be by anybody. There are a number of such poems in *The Stones of the Field,* some of them more decidedly literary. Reviewing *Break in Harvest* by Roland Mathias, Thomas said, "I would advise him in his search for individuality not to be afraid of clarity and simplicity, but to concentrate on a greater objectiveness. Let him give more play to his national consciousness and to his powers of observation."[15] He must have been speaking from his own experience:

> . . . I know, as I listen, that your speech has in it
> The source of all poetry, clear as a rill
> Bubbling from your lips; and what brushwork could equal
> The artistry of your dwelling on the bare hill?
> You will forgive, then, my initial hatred,
> My first intolerance of your uncouth ways,
> You who are indifferent to all that I can offer . . .
>
> ("A Priest to his People")

Thomas is drawn to the ordinary people of mid-Wales, not with the unctuousness of a religious duty, nor by an attraction that is freely responded to, but with a reluctance that is overcome by the discovery of poetry in what he finds most alien and repulsive. It is this that takes him from the literary style of his earliest poems to a "recurring ideal . . . that of simplicity"[16]. A recurring figure in his poetry is Iago Prytherch ("You served me well, Prytherch" he was to write in 1963); and the first of his poems of affection and repulsion appeared in *Poetry London* X in 1944:

> Iago Prytherch his name, though, be it allowed,
> Just an ordinary man of the bald Welsh hills,
> Who pens a few sheep in a gap of cloud.
> Docking mangels, chipping the green skin
> From the yellow bones with a half-witted grin
> Of satisfaction, or churning the crude earth
> To a stiff sea of clods that glint in the wind—
> So are his days spent, his spittled mirth
> Rarer than the sun that cracks the cheeks
> Of the gaunt sky perhaps once in a week.
> And then at night see him fixed in his chair
> Motionless, except when he leans to gob in the fire.
> There is something frightening in the vacancy of his mind.
> His clothes, sour with years of sweat
> And animal contact, shock the refined,
> But affected, sense with their stark naturalness . . .
>
> ("A Peasant")

The telling selection and evocation of detail show an inwardness with the subject that produces a knowledge and an understanding that makes sympathy irrelevant. "This is your prototype", the poem continues; but there scarcely seems need of the closing injunction "Remember him", so fully is he realised.

The starkness and objectivity of this art discomforts us yet moves us in almost all of these early poems.

> You remember Davies? He died, you know,
> With his face to the wall, as the manner is
> Of the poor peasant in his stone croft
> On the Welsh hills. I recall the room
> Under the slates, and the smirched snow
> Of the wide bed in which he lay,
> Lonely as an ewe that is sick to lamb
> In the hard weather of mid-March.
> I remember also the trapped wind
> Tearing the curtains, and the wild light's
> Frequent hysteria upon the floor,
> The bare floor without a rug
> Or mat to soften the loud tread
> Of neighbours crossing the uneasy boards
> To peer at Davies with gruff words
> Of meaningless comfort, before they turned
> Heartless away from the stale smell
> Of death in league with those dank walls.
>
> ("Death of a Peasant")

The power derives from the firmness of observation, but, above all, from the capacity to enter intensely into experience that stands at a distance from the poet's normal experience. We are faced, without ostentation, with a disconcerting sense of what we are, derived from a situation that would normally evoke for the affluent reader sympathy or disgust, but never the shock of self-recognition. We have also to recognise that the poem is not a naive transcription of experience: Thomas has contrived a poetry that is not predominantly of language and imagery, but one where language is subservient to the presentation of a pattern of experience. Thomas's simplicity was an attained simplicity that went counter to the general aesthetic preferences of the day: ". . . we pride ourselves on a rather common-place poem, if it has one or two unusual adjectives in it" he remarked in 1964.[17] Thomas's poetry is singularly unadjectival.

The pressure to develop this style came from the experiences that moved Thomas to poetry and the stance that he sought. Yeats no doubt gave an example of what it would be "To write for my own race";

but Yeats's declamatory simplicity is not Thomas's simplicity. It is hard not to suspect the influence of Edward Thomas, whose very direct poetry also got much of its force from the realisation of the metaphorical power of actual instances and experiences. There is a poem "On a Line in Sandburg", and one is left wondering how much American poetry of the mid-West may have meant to Thomas and whether he was at all affected by Edgar Lee Masters' small town characters in *Spoon River Anthology* (1915). An early poem, "Out of the Hills", with its central figure returning intoxicated at midnight from his visit to the valley town, has a slight resemblance to Edwin Arlington Robinson's much more rhetorical "Mr. Flood's Party".

Thomas's achievement was a triumph of style and a triumph of perception that went together in the creation of an idiom direct and often devastating, and much out of tune with the poetic preferences of the period.

IV

Modern Scottish poetry had, at least in the forties, a more focusable character than had modern Welsh poetry. While Gaelic was far less widely spoken than Welsh, Edinburgh had retained a minor metropolitan cultural life through the centuries; and Scots, a dialect version of English, had been the language of Henryson, Dunbar and Gavin Douglas in the fifteenth century, and of Alan Ramsay, Robert Ferguson and, above all, Burns, in the eighteenth century. To this tradition, C.M. Grieve or "Hugh MacDiarmid" turned in the nineteen-twenties. His work was the beginning of the "Lallans" ("lowlands") revival. The revival was the subject of controversy, not least because what constituted "pure Scots", as opposed to "English as spoken in Scotland", did not easily define itself, and the language of the revival could be criticised as an artificial construction. Nevertheless, the existence of a language or dialect that did not immediately suggest the inflexions of British literary English helped to make possible an indigenous movement with its own literary character.

The impetus was at once literary and nationalistic. As Sidney Goodsir Smith wrote of MacDiarmid: "when he said 'Not Burns—Dunbar', he was saying . . . that we must recover not only the wider poetic field of Dunbar which Burns restricted, but recover also the whole intellectual concept of Dunbar's Scotland—a Scotland that had belonged to the European comity of nations . . ."[18] The language in which "Lallans" poetry was written was, in MacDiarmid's own phrase, "Synthetic Scots". It involved drawing on not merely the various versions of spoken Scots, but also on the vocabulary from the whole tradition of Scots poetry, and particularly that of the great "Makars" of the fifteenth century, Henryson, Dunbar and Gavin Douglas. The need to go back to them was enforced by the wish to "forget the whole poverty-stricken 'dialect' tradition that Burns and his immediate predecessors had been unconsciously responsible for . . ."[19]

The earliest followers of MacDiarmid were William Soutar (1898-1943), William Jeffrey (1896-1946), A.D. Mackie (b.1904) and Robert Garioch (R.G. Sutherland) (b.1909). However, as Alexander Scott, a notable Scots poet himself, has explained:

> During the Second World War, the linguistic poetical movement inaugurated by MacDiarmid achieved a "new wave" when, as it seemed, a whole generation who had been stimulated by his work began the attempt to do likewise. The impulse behind the verse of the Lallans Makars, as the group came to be called, appears to have been an emotional Scottish nationalism, allied to an inferiority complex arising from the fact that scarcely one of them had any considerable command of spoken Scots—writers who blatantly declared . . . their dependence on the Scots dictionary—'frae Jamieson's muckle buik the words tak wing', wrote Douglas Young . . . blissfully unaware that the wing was broken.[20]

This new wave included Maurice Lindsay (b.1918), R. Crombie Saunders (b.1914), and, most notably, Sidney Goodsir Smith. Scott's remarks are particularly applicable to Smith, as he was born in New Zealand in 1915, and came to Scotland as a youth.

Goodsir Smith's first poems were in English, and would have fitted modestly into any literary periodical of the period.

> News tells of distant raids and unreal movements
> But in this North Sea harbour the bruit is far,
> From Leuchars the menacing shapes of planes
> Become picturesque against the important sky
> Whose tale is portending redness, day after night,
> Like the funnels of the idle trawlers lolling at berth . . .

From 1940 on he wrote only according to the MacDiarmid prescription: *The Deevil's Waltz* (1946) shows something of the extremity of a convert, with its five page glossary to forty pages of poetry. His language was, in the words of George Kitchin, "a strange blend of sixteenth-century literary Scots, with monstrous Latinisms floating to the surface, and local dialect with modern jargon."[21] The book-learning was not fully absorbed, and the language and tone were often awkwardly inappropriate to contemporary subjects:

> Tchaikovski man, I'm hearan yir Waltz o Flouers,
> A cry frae Russia fulls this autumn nicht;
> As gousty fell October's sabban in ma room
> As the frantic rammage Panzers brash on Moscow toun . . .
>
> ("October, 1941")

In later books the idiom is more natural, though throughout his career the most successful poems are lyrics in which the pressures of the contemporary scene are less noticeable. He was at his best as a poet of love. His most celebrated work is *Under the Eldon Tree* (1948), a sequence of lyrics described by Smith's contemporary, Alexander Scott, as "the greatest extended poem on passion in the whole Scots tradition."[22] At times, as the poet himself remarks, they seem "Rhetoric!/Just sheer damned/Rhetoric"; yet much of their individuality stems from this recognition and the deflationary effects that Goodsir Smith contrives:

> Here I ligg, Sidney Slugabed Godless Smith,
> The Smith, the Faber, $\pi o \iota \eta \tau \acute{\eta} s$ and Makar,
> And Oblomov has nocht to learn from me,
> Auld Oblomov has nocht on me
> Liggan my lane in bed at nune
> Gantan at gray December haar,
> A cauld, scummie, hauf-drunk cup o' tea
> > At my bed-side,
> > Luntan Virginian fags
> —The New World thus I haud in fief . . .
>
> (V. "Slugabed")

He himself wrote that "This easy-going, fickle attitude towards the muse . . . this easy transition from mood to mood is typical of Scottish poetry . . ."[23]

"The Makar macironical", Goodsir Smith is most successful in his straight lyrical poems:

> What mair is there ye wish?
> Luve's memorie dwynes, the prufe
> Is there for ye that watch
> The hevins muve.
>
> ("Credo")

Norman MacCaig spoke of "the beautifully controlled, level utterance" of this poem[24]; yet some of his less powerful lyrics sound trite put into standard English, and one wonders what sharpness they have for those used to spoken Scots. He is most engaging when he celebrates love in the milieu he knew best:

> I loo ma luve in a lamplit bar
> Braw on a wuiden stool,
> Her knees cocked up an her neb down
> Slorpan a pint o yill.

The problems of the Lallans writer were sympathetically summarised by G.S. Fraser in 1948.

> The difficulty . . . about "synthetic" Scots, as Mr. MacDiarmid once called it—the more fashionable term to-day is "Lallans"—is that the finest texts surviving are in Middle Scots, an archaic language, reflecting the ideas of a society . . . which . . . is gone for good . . . there is no vocabulary to express the interests of modern town life, or the complicated predicament of the modern intellectual.[25]

Fraser went on to comment that "The Scots idiom in the use of English is as distinctive as the Scots system of phonetics."[26]

This was the view of the most notable poet to come out of Scotland in this century, Edwin Muir:

> . . . a Scottish writer who wishes to achieve some approximation to completeness has no choice except to absorb the English tradition, and if he thoroughly does so his work belongs not merely to Scottish literature but to English literature as well. On the other hand, if he wishes to add to an indigenous Scottish literature, and roots himself deliberately in Scotland, he will find there, no matter how long he may search, neither an organic community to round off his conceptions, nor a major literary tradition to support him, nor even a faith among the people themselves that a Scottish literature is possible or desirable . . .[27]

Ruthven Todd, in his early poems of his native Orkney, and G.S. Fraser, in his wartime poems of nostalgia for Edinburgh and St. Andrews, exemplify this unforced Scotsness that Muir speaks for. Muir's view is reinforced by the fact that the resurgence of Scottish poetry during the forties, under the stimulus given to Scottish nationalism by World War II, was not confined to the "Lallans Makars". The decade saw the appearance of poets as various as W.S. Graham, George Bruce, J.F. Hendry and Norman McCaig.

Some of the linguistic directness of Lallans writing—its freedom from the need for sophistication felt in literary English—is found in the Imagistic English poems of George Bruce's *Sea Talk* (1944) that draw on experiences of the fishing villages of the East coast of Scotland.

> My house
> Is granite
> It fronts
> North,

Where the Firth flows,
East the sea.
My room
Holds the first

Blow from the North,
The first from the East,
Salt upon
The pane.

                    ("My House")

An interesting career is that of Norman McCaig (later MacCaig). McCaig was born in Edinburgh in 1910, but his poetry first came to attention with the Apocalypse movement. Poems by him appeared in *Seven, The New Apocalypse* (1939) and *The White Horseman* (1941). He produced two books of poetry in the nineteen-forties, *Far Cry* (1943) and *The Inward Eye* (1946). His next book, *Riding Lights* came nine years later in 1955. Since then he has had a sustained career as one of the leading poets of Scotland.

His poems in the Apocalypse anthologies are among those that show most strongly the links that the movement had with surrealism: "The wrinkled builders I see under the flocked sky/with ash sifting in their eyes and a stroke of darkness/coiled on their bones . . ." (*The White Horseman*) None of these poems is included in his books of the forties, in which the writing is much more controlled, though it is still overwroughtly imagistic: "Lovers who carry their midnight with them/grow in the withering of time, and the axle after/spinning the bulbed world through its own whirling . . ." (*Far Cry,* 8) There is evidence of the influence of the dense, imaged poetry of the young Dylan Thomas: "Who in his knocking blood hears the blunt hammer/that gives the seasons to the highest bidder,/time, the invisible winker . . ." (*Far Cry,* 16) There are a few poems that point towards McCaig's later concern with what has been called the "enigmatic relations between observer and observed"[28]: However, even at their best, the poems in *The Inward Eye* work in terms of the development of abstract positions through imagery:

The lion sings, the eagle has the sun
imprisoned like a god in his cage of bone.
Yet sand will drag the melodious lion down
and in the eagle's breast a cinder will dry
all the quick juices of his circling sky
and he'll be twigs bundled on a cold stone.

                    ("Soon or Late for Dying")

There is nothing very individual (or Scottish) about the imagery of

his early work; and even though he was published in Scottish periodicals and anthologies during the forties, his few poems that take their
start from particular events or places, such as "At the narrow neck of
the Loch" (*Far Cry,* 7), do not have a notably Scottish flavour. There
is a marked change in individuality and particularly when we turn to
Riding Lights:

> This wind from Fife has cruel fingers, scooping
> The heat from streets with salty-finger tips
> Crusted with frost; and all Midlothian,
> Stubborn against what heeled the sides of ships
> Off from the Isle of May, stiffens its drooping
> Branches to the south.

("Double Life")

McCaig did not include any of the poems from *Far Cry* or *The
Inward Eye* in later collections. For him the journey to finding a distinctive voice rooted in the language and life of his region had been a
circuitous one, though the body of mature work is no less Scottish
than that of Sidney Goodsir Smith. Nevertheless, it perhaps helps explain by its false starts the extreme lengths to which some regional
writers went to break with the metropolitan culture.

Maurice Lindsay's *Modern Scottish Poetry* (1946), the companion
to Rhys's Welsh anthology, showed that Scottish poetry was as awk-
ward to define as Welsh poetry. On the one hand it included translations from the Gaelic and work by the "Lallans Makars", while on
the other hand it contained work by poets identified with groupings
south of the border: Ruthven Todd, a regular contributor to Julian Symons's *Twentieth Century Verse;* and J.F. Hendry, Norman McCaig,
Tom Scott and G.S. Fraser, all of whom had first published in the
Apocalypse anthologies. Indeed, these last named poets comprise the
majority of poets of their generation in Lindsay's anthology.

The embarrassing problems involved in the characterisation of Scottish poetry are again illustrated in William MacLellan's "Poetry Scotland" series and its parent periodical, *Poetry Scotland.* The "Poetry
Scotland" series included volumes by Douglas Young, Hugh MacDiarmid, Sidney Goodsir Smith, George Bruce and Adam Drinnan, as well
as by Ruthven Todd and W.S. Graham. Similarly, the second number
of *Poetry Scotland* contains an article by Hendry on "The Apocalyptic
Element in Modern Poetry"; and the first issue, with poems by Henry
Treece, Nicholas Moore and Alex Comfort, looks like an Edinburgh
outing for the Apocalypse movement. The editor, Maurice Lindsay,
evidently sought to avoid provincialism; and, to judge from both title
and contents, took as his model *Poetry London.* Ironically the linguis-

tically modernist W.S. Graham is in fact one of the few younger poets of any quality in *Poetry Scotland* whose work in English has a noticeably Scots inflexion of rhythm and speech.

Three issues of *Poetry Scotland* appeared in 1944, 1945 and 1946; and the third issue announced that it hoped to appear bi-annually. However, a fourth and last issue, edited by Lindsay and MacDiarmid, did not appear until 1949. The small number of issues made it difficult for the periodcial to provide an important focus for Scottish poetry. The "Poetry Scotland" series probably provided a more influential centre, though it too seems to have run aground after the war, with some announced titles not appearing.

Scottish Art and Letters, edited by R. Crombie Saunders, faced, in its first editorial, the problem of giving a Scottish focus to contemporary Scottish writing:

> Considering the state of the arts in Scotland to-day one is immediately faced with the problem of assessing the work of individual craftsmen who are separated from each other, not only in a geographical sense, . . . but also in the sense that they have little or no intercourse as fellow nationals. They are more likely to be influenced by the contemporary work of other countries than by that of each other. They have little chance of maintaining a defence against the overwhelming impact of the work of an individual who is part of a living tradition and who has behind him the strength of a national culture.

A substantial miscellany of some fifty pages an issue, it first appeared in 1944, published (again) by William MacLellan. Its second issue, in 1946, announced that it would be a quarterly, but it ran for only five issues in all, the last being for the Edinburgh Festival of 1950. It emphasised the importance of Scots as a literary medium: "the vast majority of people in Scotland speak Scots, . . . and . . . it may be presumed that . . . they think in Scots also. They are . . . forced to write in English because there is no standard Scots . . ." Its first editorial concluded: "it is not surprising that most of the world's best artistic work proves on examination to be, not cosmopolitan, however international its appeal, but racial and national in the most uncompromising way." (I, 3-4) In later editorials it took up the issue of Scottish political and cultural nationalism. Its final editorial, for the 1950 "P.E.N. Conference" in Edinburgh, is evidently by the guest editor, Hugh MacDiarmid, and is a fairly straight exposition of the Communist Party's views on literary freedom.

A significant article by J.F. Hendry, "Dunbar the European", sees the "conflict between [the] pull towards Europe and the pull towards England . . . throughout the body of Dunbar's work, as indeed . . . in the writing of most Scottish poets", and expresses the hope that "the original romantic bent of Scottish poetry . . . may yet revive and give rise to a body of work more truly Scottish, and more truly European, than any produced with the purely 'English' outlook . . ." (5,21-29)

Scottish Art and Letters published poems by Adam Drinan, Maurice Lindsay, J.F. Hendry, Norman McCaig, W.S. Graham, G.S. Fraser, Sidney Goodsir Smith, Hugh MacDairmid and Edwin Muir, as well as poems in Gaelic by Somhaille Macghilleathair. It also included stories, and articles on the work of Lewis Grassic Gibbon and Hugh MacDiarmid and on Gaelic poetry.

MacDiarmid's own periodical, *The Voice of Scotland,* which appeared from 1938 to 1939, was much concerned to give a Communist slant to Scottish nationalism, a mission that gave it what true character it had. It added little to the objective discussion of the possibility of a modern Scottish literature, and many of the poets it published, such as Treece, Hendry and Cooke, made what mark they were to make comfortably enough in the English metropolitan scene.

The forties seemed to see the full flowering of what the French scholar Emil Legouis had called the "Scottish Renaissance". In fact, the historical forces of geographical mobility and economic and cultural centralisation were against it. By the end of the Second World War, more people in Nova Scotia spoke Gaelic as a first language than in Scotland. As Maurice Lindsay wrote, in a preface to a new edition of *Modern Scottish Poetry* in 1966:

> Few young writers of any consequence today employ Lallans. Every new census reveals a further decline in the number of those who speak, let alone read, Gaelic. Yet the work of the half-century or so which this anthology celebrates, reflects a variety of experience and an integrity of expression which enable it to stand comparison with the output of any period of Scottish literature. These qualities, and not the question of which of Scotland's three languages her writers chose to use, are what constitute the real Scottish Renaissance.[29]

V

For Irish poetry, the basis of cultural distinctiveness might have seemed clear enough in the forties in the separation of Eire. The Irish literary Revival had been a notable feature of the nationalist movement and had produced writers of the stature of Yeats, Synge and O'Casey. Yet the deterioration of the nationalist spirit and the poverty of the thirties had changed the perspective of Irish writers. As Douglas Dunn has pointed out: "Beckett, in his essay 'Recent Irish Poetry' (1934), damned what he called the 'accredited theme' of time and place. The celebratory exposure of Irishness it tended to produce was the result, he said, of a 'happily obliterated self', a 'flight from self-awareness'."[30] Beckett's exile from Ireland may be seen as a quest for a more cosmopolitan and less provincial cultural milieu, as may that of Joyce, whom he admired so much; though Joyce's exile was a lifelong involvement with Ireland. There was a need for a break with the orientation of the Irish Literary Revival, as is seen in the work of Austin Clarke. Patrick Kavanagh, who did so much to achieve such a reorientation, wrote: "When I came to Dublin the dregs of the old Literary Revival were still stirable."[31]

This rejection of the values of the Literary Revival is seen in the stance of two young Ulster poets of the forties, Robert Greacen and Roy McFadden. Greacen's work appeared in the third Apocalypse anthology, *The Crown and the Sickle* in 1943 and in the New Romantic anthology, *Lyra* in 1942. While a student at Queen's University, Belfast, he attempted as editor of the university magazine, to turn it into "a literary periodical for the whole of Ulster" and featured the work of the Apocalypse movement.[32] His position was reflected in the words of his friend Roy McFadden: "There is no mist on our bogs, but there have been bombs on our cities; and I think it natural that we should be more concerned with a society that produces and tolerates such enormities than with the silk of the kine."[33] There is a rejection of the view that the proper Irish subject is the life of the Irish soil. In spite of this, McFadden's early work, in books like *Flowers for a Lady* (1945), is increasingly permeated by his feeling for Ulster life and the Ulster landscape.

Neither Greacen nor McFadden were poets of a power that makes an influential movement. A more impressive search for an orientation to the Irish heritage is to be found in the work of a somewhat older Ulster poet, John Hewitt, who was born in 1907 in Belfast. An Ulsterman of English descent, Hewitt felt himself an outsider to the culture of rural Ireland; but, unlike two other Ulstermen of his generation, Rodgers and MacNeice, he did not become acclimatised to the metropolitan culture of England. In 1943 he printed privately a long poem "Conacre" in which he attempts to come to terms with his place in Ireland:

> No tweed-bright poet drunk in pastoral
> or morris-dancers in the Legion Hall,
> I know my farmer and my farmer's wife,
> the squalid focus of their huxter's life,
> the grime-veined fists, the thick rheumatic legs,
> the cracked voice gloating on the price of eggs . . .

His poetry is modest in tone and at times flat in its attempt at naturalness of diction and rhythm. Like the work of the Welsh R.S. Thomas,
it is notable at its best for the expression of an attachment to rural life
that is based on a truth to its real qualities.

Hewitt cultivated a deliberate provincialism in the belief that in "the
Region" we have "an area of a size and a significance that we could
hold in our hearts."[34] His poetry explores his relationship with nature
and the countryside as a part of his own quest to "belong", yet he
remains an outsider.

Irish poetry in the nineteen forties showed little rejuvenative vitality.
Contemporary Irish Poetry (1949), a belated companion to *Modern
Welsh Poetry* and *Modern Scottish Poetry,* edited by Robert Greacen
and Valentin Iremonger, set out "to present a cross-section of poetry
by Irishmen since the death of W.B. Yeats . . . the bias being toward
the young and less known". Most of its contributors have remained
among the "less known", the only ones remembered today being Austin Clarke, Denis Devlin, Padraic Fallon, Robert Graves, John
Hewitt, C. Day Lewis, Donagh MacDonagh, Louis MacNeice and
W.R. Rodgers—all older poets. The inclusion of Graves, Day Lewis
and MacNeice—easily the best contributors—does nothing to focus the
Irish quality of the anthology. Among the younger writers, only
Donagh MacDonagh shows any individuality. His collection *The Hungry Grass* (1947) was one of the bright events of an arid year. His
output was not of the kind to give a lead: he produced only two other
collections in his lifetime—*Veterans* (1941) and *A Warning to Conquerors* (1968). His later work included many poems "from the
Irish", while some of the most notable poems in *The Hungry Grass*
are reprinted from *Veterans.*

Contemporary Irish Poetry omits the poet whose powerful rejection
of the Literary Revival's idealisation of Irish rural life was to revitalise
Irish poetry—Patrick Kavanagh.

VI

The outstanding regional poem of the nineteen-forties is Patrick
Kavanagh's *The Great Hunger* (1942). Kavanagh was born in County
Monaghan in 1907, but his first book was not published until 1936
and he came into his own only in the forties. Having left school at
13, he worked a small farm into the nineteen-thirties; and it is from
his experience of those days that *The Great Hunger* derives its authenticity. Yet it is not a work of autobiography or self identification. Its
hero, Patrick Mcguire, makes the "great refusal":

> The drills slipped by and the days slipped by
> And he trembled his head away and ran free from the world's halter,
> And thought himself wiser than any man in the townland
> When he laughed over pints of porter
> Of how he came free from every net spread
> In the gaps of experience.

The narrow emptiness of his life is what is referred to in the poem's title—a phrase normally used of the great potatoe famine of the nineteenth century.

It was Kavanagh's fidelity to fact that made the poem so revolutionary in days when the idealisations of the Literary Revival still coloured attitudes to Irish rural life:

> Clay is the word and clay is the flesh
> Where the potatoe-gatherers like mechanised scarecrows move
> Along the side-fall of the hill . . .

Kavanagh's achievement is not merely one of superior realism: if it were, it would be of relatively trivial interest. It is an achievement of tone. As he himself later wrote—reflecting his continuing war with the Irish literary establishment: *"The Great Hunger* is tragedy and Tragedy is underdeveloped Comedy. Had I stuck to the tragic thing in *The Great Hunger* I would have found many powerful friends.''[35]

> Their intellectual life consisted in reading
> *Reynold's News* or the *Sunday Dispatch,*
> With sometimes an old almanac brought down from the ceiling
> Or a school reader brown with the droppings of thatch.
> The sporting results or the headlines or war
> Was a humbug as profound as the highbrow's Arcana . . .
> He got a straight tip from a man in a shop—
> A double for the Guineas it was and thought himself
> A master mathematician when one of them came up
> And he could explain how much he'd have drawn
> On the double if the second leg had followed the first.

Like so many longer modern poems, *The Great Hunger* is not a continuous narrative in one verse form, but a lyric sequence utilising a variety of forms and, hence, of tones. Bathetic rhythms are used for deflationary effect. The dominant tone is one associated with the colloquial rhythms, firm but never sustained, of which Kavanagh was a master throughout his life.

> Watch him, watch him, that man on a hill whose spirit
> Is a wet sack flapping about the knees of time.

> He lives that his little fields may stay fertile when his own body
> Is spread in the bottom of a ditch under two coulters crossed in
> Christ's Name.

It was in terms of tone that Kavanagh made his own criticisms of the poem: "There are some queer and terrible things in *The Great Hunger,* but it lacks the nobility and repose of poetry."[36] The remark may seem a surprising rejection of his acknowledged masterpiece, yet what he meant is easily seen in the readiness for sententious generalisations and sweeping dismissals.

> Men build their heavens as they build their circles
> Of friends. God is in the bits and pieces of Everyday . . .

Associated with this is a proclivity for near cliché at odds with the authenticity of the best writing. Nevertheless, the poem offers more than enough of what Kavanagh called "the slow humous of pity and terror which gives full satisfaction to the soul of man."[37]

Despite Kavanagh's close ties with the life of the countryside, it would be wrong to regard him (as he has been) as culturally deprived or culturally naive. There are several poems in his first book that might support that view, but there are also poems such as "Shancoduff" (written in 1934, though not collected in his first book) that he came to regard as among his best.[38] His brother Peter wrote a doctoral dissertation on the Abbey Theatre at Trinity College, Dublin; and such outstanding achievement from two members of a family points to some cultural richness in their background. Indeed, Kavanagh was at pains to emphasize that: "Far from the poet being a peasant . . . he is the last word in sophistication."[39] The peasants, on the other hand, he characterised as "all that mass of mankind which lives below a certain level of consciousness. They live in the dark cave of the unconscious and they scream when they see the light."[40] This is in keeping with those recognitions that are the strength of *The Great Hunger,* and contains no suggestion of a sentimentalisation of the poet as inspired primitive.

Kavanagh's views of the Irish literary tradition were very unflattering. Of Yeats he wrote that he "was the last great Victorian poet. His work was born within the safety of that large, smug, certain world where no one questioned how much was being taken for granted."[41] He saw the "so-called Irish Literary Movement" as "a thoroughgoing English-bred lie."[42] "For twenty years," he complained, "I wrote according to the dispensations of this Irish school. The appraisers of this school all agreed that I had my roots in the soil, was one of the people and that I was an authentic voice. I wrote . . . a terrible piece about—

> My soul was an old horse
> Offered for sale in twenty fairs;
> I offered him to the Church, the buyers
> Were little men who feared his unusual airs.

One can at once see the embarrassing impertinence and weakness of it, the dissolute character whining. But it was the perfect Irish formula and English publishers loved it.''[43] It is the poem from which the title of his third book of poetry, *A Soul for Sale* (1947) was taken. Kavanagh regarded his first autobiographical novel, *The Green Fool* (1938) as a "stage-Irish lie", but contended that his second such work, *Tarry Flynn* (1948) was "the only *authentic* account of life as lived in Ireland this century . . ."[44] Later in life, he seemed to reject a great deal of his work before *Tarry Flynn*. He came to value most the lyrical poems he wrote in Dublin in the 1950's and 1960's. "My hegira was to the Grand Canal bank where I again saw the beauty of water and green grass and the magic of light."[45] The most famous of these poems is "Lines written on a Seat on the Grand Canal":

> A swan goes by head low with many apologies,
> Fantastic light looks through the eyes of bridges—
> And look! a barge comes bringing from Athy
> And other far-flung towns mythologies.
> O commemorate me with no hero-courageous
> Tomb—just a canal-bank seat for the passer-by.

These lyrical poems that commemorate Kavanagh's love for Dublin are among the most individual poems of their day, with their carefully subdued rhythms and partial rhymes; and one can see how Kavanagh could have become disenchanted with the unqualified stances of *The Great Hunger*.

During the nineteen-fifties, Kavanagh's poetry received little attention; and it was only after his death in 1967 that he became widely celebrated. Yet his work was known in the forties. Though not in *Contemporary Irish Poetry* or Geoffrey Taylor's *Irish Poems of Today* (1948), he was included in Maurice Wollman's *Poems of the War Years,* published by Macmillan in 1950. His work had appeared in Irish periodicals, and a part of *The Great Hunger* was published in *Horizon* as "The Old Peasant" in January, 1942. There is no doubt as to the significance of his achievement, particularly in that poem. As Seamus Heaney has put it, "Much of his authority and oddity derives from the fact that he wrested his idiom bare handed out of a literary nowhere."[46]

VII

Regionalist writing in the forties was not confined to work from Scotland, Wales and Ireland. In England there appeared a number of poets whose work was rooted in non-metropolitan areas. Among them were John Short, whose poems of Westmoreland in *The Oak and the Ash* (1947) are impressive and firm; and Os Marron, a Lancashire poet whose best poem is perhaps "From the North Country". Marron, the son of a miner and a cotton worker, was one of the few poets of working class origin to appear in the forties. He died of tuberculosis in 1947, and his poems appear not to have been collected. The best known of these regional poets is Laurie Lee, whose childhood in the Cotswolds and whose youthful wanderings in England and Spain are recounted in his well known autobiographies, *Cider with Rosie* (1959) and *As I Walked Out One Midsummer Morning* (1969). Lee had written (though not published) poems in the late thirties, and some of these are collected in his first book, *The Sun My Monument* (1944). His poems first appeared in book form in John Lehmann's third series of *Poets of Tomorrow* in 1942. A short volume, *The Bloom of Candles,* celebrating the seasons of the year was published in 1947. Lee's last—and again short—book of new poems, *My Many Coated Man,* was published in 1955: his first book contains over half of the seventy or so poems by him that have been collected.

His autobiographies say very little about his development as a poet; but elsewhere Lee has emphasised the relationship of his writing to his background: "We were . . . inheritors, after centuries of darkness, of our country's first literate peasantry . . . We had no regular newspapers and of course no radio or television . . . We were the inheritors still of an oral tradition of language . . . I am made uneasy by any form of writing which cannot readily be spoken aloud."[47] Prefacing his first collections of poems, in *Poets of Tomorrow,* he said: "I find most modern poetry rather too bleak for my liking; it is smart, polished, epigrammatic and often searching, but it seems to lack the heat of a genuine emotion."[48]

In fact Lee's poetry owes a great deal to that of the previous generation. Tambimuttu thought he was an admirer of Stephen Spender, and he has Spender's fondness for bright, over-realised images that tend to mask the feelings that they endeavour to explore:

> I think at night my hands are mad,
> for they follow the irritant texture of darkness
> continually carving the sad leaf of your mouth
> in the thick black bark of sleep.

> ("At Night")

Elsewhere he uses the "war" metaphors of the thirties poets—"the hawk's reconnaissance", "Your lips are turreted with guns"—to emphasize the violence of the times. Indeed, before his autobiographies, Lee might have appeared a sophisticated urban poet.

Lee's best poems have a sharp brightness of imagery and a lightness of movement that are unmistakable:

> Thistle, blue bunch of daggers
> rattling upon the wind,
> saw-tooth that separates
> the lips of grasses.
>
> Your wound in childhood was
> a savage shock of joy
> that set the bees on fire
> and the loud larks singing.
>
> ("Thistle")

The simplification of metaphor in the first stanza produces a startling visual realisation; but the same simplification in the second stanza— "set the bees on fire"—seems ultimately insensitive and an attempt to render experience gratuitously colourful. This type of effect is associated with an exploration of childhood as a time of lost innocence.

> Village of winter carols
> and gawdy spinning tops,
> of green-handed walnuts
> and games in the moon.
>
> You were adventure's web,
> the flag of fear I flew
> riding black stallions
> through the rocky streets.

The tone is very characteristic of Lee, and it is a surprise to realise that this poem was collected in 1942, four years before "Fern Hill" was written. As with Thomas's poem, the simplification of experience, ostensibly a realisation of its intrinsic innocence, actually involves a prettification. This tendency is more strongly felt in Lee's second volume, *The Bloom of Candles*, while metaphor has a frequently decorative effect in his third book, *My Many Coated Man*, where rhetorical features that had been intrinsic to Lee's exploration of experience became a trick of style. Indeed, *Cider with Rosie*, although first hand, makes the countryside of his childhood quaint. In the poems quoted, the effect is accentuated by a sameness of rhythm together with a certain archness in the muting of the rhyme.

Lee's first volume was his best. There the talent is associated with a genuine if limited engagement with experience. As is so often the case, the limitations of that early writing proved to be limitations to which the talent could finally succumb. *The Firstborn* (1964) and *I Can't Stay Long* (1975), two of his later prose works, are unctuous and unpleasant in their celebration of innocence. Lee nevertheless wrote some poems of enduring charm that have the brightness of visual perception so valued in the forties, and his first book is accomplished and has a memorable individuality.

VIII

It would be easy to characterise the plain writing of a modern Cumberland poet as "Wordsworthian"; but, as Norman Nicholson put it, "when I was writing about the country I kept off Wordsworth." Though Nicholson's first book, *Five Rivers* (1946), leaves an immediate impression of sensitivity to natural detail, the permeating vision is religious. His earliest poems were rather like those of Herbert: "the first Nicholson poem, he recalled, was 'The Blackberry'."[49]

> Between the railway and the mine,
> Brambles are in fruit again.
>> Their little nigger fists they clench,
>> And hold the branches in a clinch.
> Waggons of ore are shunted past,
> And spray the berries with red dust,
>> Which dulls the bright mahogany
>> Like purple sawdust clogged and dry.
> But when the housewife, wind-and-rain,
> Rubs the berry spick and span,
>> Compound it gleams like a fly's eye,
>> And every ball reflects the sky.
> There the world's repeated like
> Coupons in a ration book;
>> There the tall curved chimneys spread
>> Purple smoke on purple cloud.
> Grant us to know that hours rushed by
> Are photographed upon God's eye;
>> That life and leaf are both preserved
>> In gelatine of Jesus' blood.
> And grant to us the sense to feel
> The large condensed within the small;
>> Wash clear our eyes that we may see
>> The sky within the blackberry.

Nicholson writes as something of a convert: he grew up a Wesleyan (though his father was Anglican), and the reading of Shaw in his youth came as a radical revelation of what industry had done to his part of Cumberland in exploiting it and abandoning it—a revelation to which Nicholson gave a religious quality.

"The Blackberry" is a poem of Anglican dogma (rather than of Wesleyan fervour). The notions of immanence, omniscience, and salvation and purification through grace are elicited from the image of the berries—images themselves of unredeemed nature—reflecting the world around them. The homely play on words in "preserved/In gelatine of Jesus' blood" is Herbertian, as is the witty use of the contemporary image "the world's repeated like/Coupons in a ration book". The relating of the firmly realised local landscape to this redemptive process, along with the sensitive but unostentatious observation of details of nature, is characteristic of Nicholson's poetry as a whole.

In *Man and Literature* (1943), which he describes as "an enquiry into the assumptions as to the nature and purpose of Man which underlie much of modern writing", Nicholson says: "Of the doctrines of Man which have developed largely since the Renaissance two are very common in modern literature—Liberal Man and Natural Man . . . against these two pagan and romantic doctrines, I see the classical and Christian conception of Man re-emerging in literature."[50] This latter conception he characterises as "Imperfect Man". "Materialism and poetry do not agree" he contends; and it is not surprising, after the conjunction of "classical" and "Christian", that he should find *Four Quartets* "the finest poetry written in our time".

In reading Eliot's poetry he found, for the first time, all the features of his world—meadow, slag heap, small town—rendered meaningful. This bringing together, in a pattern of meaning, of the everyday features of the world in which he grew up and chose to live, is a constant endeavour of Nicholson's poetry. He looks out on his surroundings with a firm piety that is summed up in the last words of his autobiography, *Wednesday Early Closing* (1975): "I thank God for a lifetime spent in that same town".[51]

> Beneath the soil the long shoots bore
> To limestone and to iron ore,
> Where through the rock the waters ooze
> Red as the sap in the live trees,
> And becks swill seaward, rich as wine,
> The haemorrhage of the spilt mine.
>
>   ("The Wood of the Self-Murdered")

Characteristic of Nicholson's poetry is the subdued tone and the low imaginative pressure. Indeed, so many of the topographical poems in *Five Rivers* seem prosey and circumstantial, in spite of the firm and sensitive rendering of observed detail. The effect can be exemplified in one of his better poems from *Rock Face* (1948) that is short enough to quote in full:

> We did not expect this; we were not ready for this;—
> To find the unpredicted spring
> Sprung open like a broken trap. The sky
> Unfolds like an arum leaf; the bare
> Trees unfurl like fronds of fern;
> The birds are scattered along the air;
> Celandines and cresses prick pinpoints white and yellow,
> And the snow is stripped from the fells.
> We were not prepared for this. We knew
> That the avalanche of war breaks boundaries like birches,
> That terror bursts round our roofs; we were aware
> Of the soft cough of death in the waiting lungs. But this
> Has caught us half-asleep. We had never thought of this.
>
> ("Early March")

Again, we encounter a sensitivity of observation that is not factitious, but springs from intimate knowledge and feeling. We know that "the soft cough of death in the waiting lungs" is not a poetic stage property but something experienced by the author, who had come close to death from tuberculosis. Yet, like the details of leaf and flower, it has no function but to be itself: it does not set up resonances within the poem, or connect with and illuminate other images. This inertness in even so good a poem is the recurrent fault of Nicholson's poetry, and it is made more noticeable by what is, at best, a virtue of his writing—the natural, unassuming rhythms. In fact, the rhythm too seldom serves to draw the poems together musically. Nicholson looks out on the world with a Christian vision that clearly imbues his world for him: that vision is not always felt as a unifying force in the poems, because their elements do not always pull together imaginatively.

The inertness is accentuated in *Rock Face* and the early poems in *The Pot Geranium* (1954). Nicholson, evidently under the influence of Kathleen Raine, attempted a visionary type of Christian poetry in which the accent is on the eternal as manifested in the particular. "The Seven Rocks", a group of poems on the "main types or groups of rocks" in the Lake District is impressive; but its message "To wait, accept . . . Is the one virtue" comes dead from its geological perspective. In *Five Rivers* he had found the Christian rituals of redemption, sacrifice, epiphany enacted in the natural details of the local scene that he knew with such loving intimacy. In the early fifties his writing suffered a break in inspiration; and it was only with a reading of Robert Lowell's *Life Studies* (1959) that he was brought back to his true subject, the life of the region in which he has always lived, in *A Local Habitation* (1972).

George Barker, reviewing *The Pot Geranium,* argued: "It is, surely, possible to put too much responsibility upon the facts in a poem . . . Norman Nicholson, I am quite sure, speaks the circumstantial . . . truth about all his subjects . . . But I am left wondering what to do with a book containing geological specimens, geraniums, clocks, Ravenglass Railway Station, fossils, etc., but very few poems. I wish Mr. Nicholson would report more often not on the things that any reasonably alert man can see for himself, but those matters that only the responsible poet can perceive."[52] Against this abrupt dismissal one might set Nicholson's own praise of William Cowper: ". . . he brought a new kind of directness into descriptive poetry, showing the English country scene as it really was and less as it was imagined to be . . . The word 'exciting' is perhaps the most over-used cliché in modern criticism, and it is refreshing to be able to say of Cowper's poetry that it did not set out to be exciting."[53] In expressing his admiration, Nicholson seems to epitomise what he himself does so well at his best.

IX

The Christianity of Jack Clemo is altogether fiercer and more forthright than that of Norman Nicholson or any other poet of his generation. Clemo was afflicted with periods of blindness from the age of twelve, and eventually became completely blind and deaf. His life and his faith are a triumph over these afflictions and over the attendant poverty and loneliness—a triumph that consorts with exultance rather than humility in Clemo's somewhat truculent autobiography, *Confessions of a Rebel* (1949).

> Throughout this book events and values are interpreted from the Calvinist-Barthian standpoint, i.e., on the premises that the human soul is darkened by original sin and needs a saving illumination of divine grace, distinct from the revelation of God's wisdom and power in Nature . . . the "natural religion" produced by art, poetry and idealism is not only inadequate but deadly apart from the grace revealed to the elect.[54]

An orphan in a poor Cornish family, he was prevented from taking what educational opportunities were open to him by his health. Indeed, his eyesight made it impossible or inadvisable for him to read for extensive periods of his youth. Nevertheless, with the assistance of his mother, he became acquainted with a great deal of literature, and composed novels from an early age. His first poem was written at the age of fourteen, but it was in February, 1945, at the age of eighteen, that he "wrote, quite effortlessly, some lines which I knew at once were the finest poetry I had ever penned . . . "Christ in the Clay-pit" . . . that set my mind to its mature, individual poetic rhythm".[55]

> I peer
> Upon His footsteps in this quarried mud;
> I see His blood
> In rusty stains on pit-props, waggon-frames
> Bristling with nails, not leaves. There were no leaves
> Upon His chosen Tree,
> No parasitic flowering over shames
> Of Eden's primal infidelity.

Clemo had lived all his life beside the clay pits and had witnessed the swallowing up of natural features by the encroachment of the pits and their tips. This encroachment is not seen in his poetry, as it is in so much contemporary literature, as a wanton human destruction of a divinely given and potentially healing or paradisal nature. Nature for Clemo is a spiritual trap without the redemption of grace: "God's image was washed out of Nature/By the flood of the Fall" ("Neutral Ground"). In "The Excavator", the bar of the machine becomes a cross "Like His Whose stooping tore/The vitals from our world's foul secrecy"; and the poem concludes with the speaker "Under the dripping clay with which I am baptized." In *The Invading Gospel* (1958) he commented, "in all my mature writings I have stressed the aspect of disturbance and even violence, in the impact of grace . . . In my poetry I have often made use of the imagery of Cornish clayworks with their constant blasting and excavating."[56]

Clemo's poetry is most successful when it can work by an unforced use of imagery from the landscape in which he grew up, as in "The Flooded Clay-pit" or in "A Calvinist in Love", which appeared in *Penguin New Writing* for Autumn 1946, and was one of his earliest poems to be published in a literary journal:

> I will not kiss you, country fashion,
> By hedgesides where
> Weasal and hare
> Claim kinship with our passion.
>
> I care no more for fickle moonlight:
> Would rather see
> Your face touch me
> Under a claywork dune-light . . .

We cannot fuse with fallen Nature's
    Our rhythmic tide:
    It is allied
With laws beyond the creatures . . .

Our love is full-grown Dogma's offspring,
    Election's child,
    Making the wild
Heats of our blood an offering.

The neat poise of movement and the delicacy with which it follows
the feeling is something that makes the poem stand out today as it did
when it was first published. These early poems offer a vision of an
unredeemed nature that asserts itself as an experienced thing and that
can be shared by a reader who cannot consent to Clemo's theological
positions. However, too many of his poems seem dominated by preconceived notions; and, in his later poetry, after the failure of his
sight, it is often difficult to discern what particular idiosyncratic
spiritual stance a poem is taking. This is in part a manifestation of the
bent of his art. He has written approvingly of "a Browning, a Donne
or a Vachel Lindsay—a man who uses his art, even violates it, in the
interests of theological tub-thumping."[57]

Clemo was in no sense a self-conscious modernist. His influences
were as much theological as literary, and the literary figures whom he
admired were ones whose vision was close to his. Browning, Barth,
C.H. Spurgeon, Oral Roberts, T.F. Powys are all mentioned with respect. The cultivation of a deliberately contemporary idiom does not
seem to have been something he attempted: the freshness and modernity spring from the individuality of the vision and from Clemo's disdain for orthodox education and religion. His poetry nevertheless goes
to the heart of the modern predicament in seeking an acceptable religious orientation to experience in the face of a vision of nature far
from benign.

X

By 1940, the clear cut antagonism between traditionalists and mod-
erns had begun to blur. What public there was for poetry displayed a
taste that was moderate or middle of the road. It would listen to Eliot's
"La Figlia Che Piange" side by side with a sonnet by Drayton on
Patric Dickinson's B.B.C. programme, "Time for Verse". Such listeners no doubt constituted the public for periodicals like *The Windmill*
or substantially produced symposia like *Orion*. There existed, too,
young writers who admired the celebrated modern poets of the day,
but who seemed, nevertheless, dedicated to the moderate. The extent

to which this turn of taste was widespread in England is evidenced by Cecil Day Lewis's *Word Over All*—perhaps his finest book—published in 1943. Not only in the imagery, form and diction, but also in attitude and poetic strategy, the conventional and meditative replace the modern and imagistic.

Two periodicals of moderate stance were the quarterly, *The Wind and the Rain,* and the symposium, *Here and Now.* Both were started by groups of young writers:

> In 1940 *The Wind and the Rain* was founded by a group of six schoolboys whose ambition was to produce a quarterly that would interpret the Christian Order in the light of current affairs, philosophy, literature and the arts.[58]

> . . . before the war, a group of young people met regularly to share their common interest in poetry, drama and music . . . Came the war . . . we kept in touch by a type-written quarterly passed among our members . . . HERE AND NOW is the best of all that appeared in that "periodical" in 1940.[59]

The Wind and the Rain, founded by Michael Allmand and edited by Neville Braybrook, ran throughout the decade, closing for "financial reasons" (as did so many periodicals in the late forties). Five issues of *Here and Now* appeared between 1940 and 1949: its editors were Peter Alberry and Sylvia Read. *The Wind and the Rain* contained the more distinguished contributions, coming to be an established review of some international character. It claimed to be the first periodical to publish work by Simone Weil in England; and the issue for Winter 1948-49, partly devoted to American writing, contained contributions by F.O. Matthiessen, Kenneth Patchen and Sidney Tremayne. It was the British contributors, however, who set the tone: they included writers like Richard Church, Henry Treece, James Kirkup and Francis King, and the tone was respectably advanced—but respectable.

Here and Now remained true to the subtitle of its second symposium: "A Group Production of Collected Verse and Prose". Contributors included Norman Nicholson, Patric Dickinson, Anne Ridler, Nicholas Moore, C. Day Lewis and Francis King (a schoolboy of eighteen when the first number appeared). The continued appearance of these periodicals throughout the decade testified to the steady interest of serious readers in the traditional poetry they published; it was also evidence of the existence of a body of younger writers dedicated to less *avant garde* writing.

Throughout the decade, and particularly in the first half, there appeared volumes of poetry by new writers that seem decidedly traditional in retrospect, but which formed at the time a part of the body of "new writing". Martyn Skinner's five part *Letters to Malaya* (1941-1947), highly praised by Desmond MacCarthy and awarded the Hawthornden Prize for 1944, is deservedly not remembered: there was some talent, but no distinction; and his books, still common on second-hand book stalls, are a symptom of what received praise from the literary establishment of the day. John Buxton's *Such Liberty* (1944), written in a prisoner of war camp, showed a more controlled and cultivated talent than did a great deal of "modern" poetry published at the time, and the same may be said to a lesser degree of the poems of Hal Summers. Congenial and typical is a poem from John Arlott's *Of Period and Place* (1944), the evocative "Cricket at Worcester, 1938":

> Dozing in deck-chair's gentle curve,
> Through half-closed eyes I watched the cricket,
> Knowing the sporting press would say
> 'Perks bowled well on a perfect wicket' . . .
>
> Closer, the bowler's arms swept down,
> The ball swung, swerved and darted,
> Stump and bail flashed and flew;
> The batsman pensively departed.
>
> Like rattle of dry seeds in pod
> The warm crowd faintly clapped,
> The boys who came to watch their gods,
> The tired old men who napped . . .

The poet who best exemplified this type of writing was Patric Dickinson, famous in the middle forties for his B.B.C. "Time for Verse", which featured classic poems alongside modern ones. Dickinson's work, in its firmness of diction, its economy and its finish, shows that the traditional idiom still had a great deal of life and that sentimental Georgianism was not the only alternative to doctrinaire modernism. Dickinson was an admirer of Eliot and Owen and Yeats. Yeats in particular was an important model for the meditative lyric that was a favoured form with Dickinson:

> Last night my mother died
> Again, in a dull dream.
> Some master I did not know
> Had set me to strange work,
> And then the message came.
> O God my grief broke
> From a lead-coffin-cloud
> Of inward snow
> In tears too cold to weep:
> For when my dream began

> I could have come to her
> And standing beside her bed
> Kissed her dear brow again.
> She felt so much more dead
> Dying there in my sleep
> And I not there.

("A Dream")

The poem's idiom is assured and well maintained: the very definite rhythm, in contrast to the broken rhythms of much modern poetry, is a symptom of the singleness of impulse and absence of pervading irony. The biting sense of loss through the passage of time—a pressing theme with Dickinson—is poignantly brought home. It is only in the whimsicality of "Some master I did not know/Had set me to strange work" that we see a depleting feature of Dickinson's poetry, where the rhetoric sometimes leads the thought and exemplifies the distortion that the "literary" bent of traditionalism could bring.

XI

An altogether firmer talent was Anne Ridler's, showing a creative adaptation of the traditional and the modern to generate an individual idiom. "It was Auden's use of stanza and stress which proved the easier for the novice to handle: the strict stanza form to contain his inchoate ideas . . . it was Eliot who first made me despair of becoming a poet: Auden (with, of course, dead poets, notably Sir Thomas Wyatt) who first made me think I saw how to become one."[60] The conjunction of Auden's use of traditional stanzas with the possibility of learning from Sir Thomas Wyatt indicates that the whole tradition of English poetry was still felt to be (perhaps for the last time) a source of models for the new poet. We see too the readiness with which Eliot's poetry could by then be accepted by those of decidedly traditional leanings. Anne Ridler had been Eliot's secretary, and for her that acceptance and admiration was no doubt enhanced by Eliot's Christianity, as indeed it must have been for many other writers and readers of the period. In becoming an Anglican, Eliot had become a supporter of tradition in a sense that had not seemed implied by his early poetry and by his essay "Tradition and the Individual Talent" (1919).

Ridler's *Poems* (1939) had been conventional, linguistically and in sentiment. *Nine Bright Shiners* (1943), which incorporated almost all the poems in her pamphlet *A Dream Observed* (1941), had a firmer and more individual idiom, which was sustained and developed in *The*

Golden Bird (1951). The first two poems of this last volume exemplify contrasting styles that Ridler developed. "Bathing in the Windrush" has the contemporary imagistic manner, marked by a visual sensitivity and a resolution that does not draw on everyday satisfactions.

> This wonder is only submarine:
> Drawn to the light
> Marble is stone and moons are eyes.
> These are like symbols, where half-seen
> The meaning swims, and drawn to the surface, dies.

"Beads from Blackpool" is very different in style and in orientation towards experience:

> In that town, nothing is sane but the sea.
> Thank God, the waves break all winter over the
> Ice-cream caves and fairy grottoes, over the
> Lavatory bricks, the scaffolds of flimsy fun,
> Ring contempt through rungs of the pier, fling
> Black sprays among the crowds, orphaned of summer,
> Who nose the shops and gaze at boards announcing
> Epstein's *Jacob,* erotic displays, and oysters.

The visual elements consist only of observed details, which are not drawn into a figurative perspective, but are utilised for their commonplace associations. There is a firmer sense of place than in "Bathing in the Windrush". More notably, the movement of the poem is utilised to suggest a particular tone of voice, and hence the poet's attitude. A great deal of the imagistic poetry of the forties lacks any feeling of individual voice, and it is the achievement of Ridler's poetry that the created "voice" can be manipulated so subtly.

In Ridler's best poetry, this subdued, controlled tone goes along with a tightness of argument and what G.S. Fraser called a "lovely and surprising precision of phrase"[61]; while Lawrence Durrell spoke of a "scrupulous clarity of statement"[62]. Her debt to the seventeenth century metaphysical poets is seen in this, and more obviously in lyrics such as "Parting" that consciously imitate the older manner. Unfortunately, her poems often disappoint, becoming diffuse after a tight beginning.

Her strength is her genuine and subtle feeling for ordinary things, to which the technique of the poetry sensitively responds. Her feeling for domestic relations and affections is deep yet self-effacing, though some of the poems about her baby in *Nine Bright Shiners* (which takes its title from the nine months of pregnancy) seem trivial to those who do not come with a readiness to respond to the subject. In *Some Time*

After (1972) she showed herself a powerful poet of death, transience and loss; and her poems of separation are quiet, yet among the most affecting of the war. In 1943 she wrote: "I vicariously prefer death to dishonour, yet at the same time my heart tells me that I would sooner we lost the war than he [her husband] were killed."[63] This unassuming honesty, that goes along with an unwillingness to press experience to a significance that it does not readily reveal, is what is so winning about her poetry. There is nothing bogus in her work.

XII

While many of the poets discussed in this chapter saw themselves as defenders or sustainers of endangered traditions, time has destroyed the patterns of reference to which they appealed. The work of Eliot and other writers of his generation is no longer seen as "modern" in contrast to less advanced or "traditional" contemporary writing, but has itself entered the heritage of past writing. On the other hand, improved communications and increased affluence have had a levelling effect on regional differences in speech. Phenomena like the Lallans movement seem the last stand of an old tradition rather than the renaissance of a suppressed culture, and the life of regional writing is seen to persist in a sense of place and of cultural individuality rather than in linguistic differences.

It might be argued that the resurgence of traditionalism and the vitality of regionalism in the forties were both reactions to the metropolitanisation of culture and to the metropolitan nature of modernism in the arts. There have been a number of notable regionalist movements in twentieth century writing, such as the renaissance of Southern writing in the work of writers like William Faulkner and Katherine Anne Porter. The regionalist bias did not emerge as a limitation in their work, but was the basis of its universality. Patrick Kavanagh drew a distinction: "Parochialism and provincialism are opposites. The provincial has no mind of his own; he does not trust what his eyes see until he has heard what the metropolis . . . has to say on the subject. The parochial mentality on the other hand is never in any doubt about the social and artistic validity of his parish. All great civilisations are based on parochialism . . ."[64]

Norman Nicholson uses "provincial" almost as Kavanagh uses "parochial": "By provincial I do not mean someone who merely happens to live in the provinces—I mean someone who lives in the place where he was born . . . Someone who has shared from childhood the culture of his native region . . ."[65] Both recognise the condition they describe as a strength; and it undoubtedly afforded a strength in the forties such as Fitzrovia could not offer.

The conjunction of regionalism, traditionalism and the religious can also be seen as a common one in the decade, and one that is illustrated in the work of Norman Nicholson, Jack Clemo, R.S. Thomas, and Anne Ridler. Modernism frequently went with a secular confidence, and a reaction against its metropolitan tendencies and its stylistic pre-scriptions went naturally with a rejection of secularity. Much of the bad poetry of the forties is rootlessly metropolitan. Nicholson however recognised that "Civilisation is becoming more and more centred on the metropolis and . . . we may expect that literature and art will continue to be mainly metropolitan."[66] The forties may in fact have been a final high point of regional writing before the almost complete suburbanisation of the British Isles.

Chapter 10

VERSE DRAMA

Drama and the Church—The *Mercury* plays, Ronald Duncan, Anne
Ridler, Norman Nicholson—Peter Yates, Laurie Lee, Lawrence
Durrell—Christopher Fry—Radio Drama, Dylan Thomas's *Under Milk
Wood*

During the forties the writing of verse drama, first given prominence
in a modern style by T.S. Eliot, and later by W.H. Auden, seemed
one of the most flourishing aspects of the poetry of the period. It
must then have been easy to see the development of verse drama in
England in terms of the work of three generations of writers and their
influence on one another. In fact, while the two fragments of *Sweeney
Agonistes* (1926-7) were important examples, they were the only
dramatic verse by Eliot to precede the composition of Auden and
Isherwood's *The Dog Beneath the Skin* (published in 1935, but written
before the performance of Eliot's *The Rock* in 1934); and all the plays
of Auden, Day Lewis and Spender preceded Eliot's second complete
play, *The Family Reunion* of 1939. In a like manner the writers who
turned to verse drama in the forties, found their models in an ambience
that had little to do with the political, expressionist drama of the thirties. Finally, when the success of Eliot's *The Cocktail Party* in 1949
inaugurated a minor vogue for plays in verse, most of the interesting
verse drama by writers of the forties had been written.

Eliot's *Murder in the Cathedral* in 1935 had a lasting influence,
but this is best understood in terms of the events that led up to its
being sponsored by the Friends of Canterbury Cathedral. At Whitsun,
1928, George Kennedy Bell, the Dean of Canterbury, arranged for a
nativity play to be performed in the nave of Canterbury Cathedral.
This seems to have been the first dramatic performance inside an Anglican church since the middle ages. The following year, Bell brought
Nugent Monck's Maddermarket players from Norwich to perform
Everyman at the west door of the cathedral and *Dr. Faustus* in the
Chapter House. This led to a regular Canterbury Festival under the
auspices of the newly formed Society of Friends of Canterbury Cathedral, with a play each year in the Chapter House. Tennyson's *Beckett*
was chosen as the first play, but a policy was soon inaugurated of
commissioning plays by modern authors. Among those commissioned
were Laurence Binyon's *The Young King* (1934), T.S. Eliot's *Murder*

in the Cathedral (1935), Charles Williams's *Thomas Cranmer of Canterbury* (1936), Dorothy Sayers' *The Zeal of the House* (1937), Christopher Hassall's *Christ's Comet* (1938) and Sayers' *Devil to Pay* (1939). There were no festivals during the war, but Laurie Lee's *Peasants' Priest* was the play for 1947 and Christopher Fry's *Thor with Angels,* the play for 1948. Performance in the Chapter House involved the use of an open stage, more revolutionary in its day than the use of verse. The resulting innovations were brought to prominence by the unusual success of *Murder in the Cathedral,* which, after production in Canterbury, ran for 800 performances in London between November, 1935 and March, 1938.

Before the commissioning of *Murder in the Cathedral,* George Bell had become Bishop of Chichester. At Chichester he made the first appointment of a drama director for an Anglican diocese, that of E. Martin Browne. Browne worked with Eliot on *The Rock* and *Murder in the Cathedral,* and ran a travelling group, The Pilgrim Players, during the early part of the war. Browne's work linked the church drama with the secular production of verse plays. In 1945 he produced a season of plays at a small London theatre devoted to verse drama, *The Mercury.* The plays were Norman Nicholson's *Old Man of the Mountains,* Anne Ridler's *The Shadow Factory* and Ronald Duncan's *This Way to the Tomb.* Once again, there was an unexpected success: *This Way to the Tomb* moved to the West End and ran for 300 performances, as well as having a special season at *Studio des Champs Elysées* in Paris. Under the patronage of Ashley Dukes, and with the support of the Arts Council, a poet's workshop was inaugurated by the Pilgrim Players at *The Mercury.* Among the plays produced there were Patric Dickinson's *The Stone in the Midst* (April, 1949) and Christopher Fry's *A Phoenix too Frequent* (April, 1946).

In 1948, Fry's *The Lady's Not For Burning* opened at the *Arts Theatre* with John Gielgud in the leading role. It toured for eight weeks, had an eight month run at *The Globe,* and was produced at the *Royale Theatre* in New York. It was awarded the Shaw prize for the best play of the year. In conjunction with the success of Eliot's *The Cocktail Party* at the Edinburgh Festival in 1949, it made verse drama popular for a time with the sophisticated theatre audience, and Lawrence Olivier commissioned Fry's *Venus Observed,* which was produced at the *St. James* theatre in 1950. However, the minor resurgence of poetic drama that began in the middle of the decade had already run its course. It had a last burst in the Festival of Britain in 1951 with productions like Duncan's *Our Lady's Tumbler,* written for performance in Salisbury Cathedral.

The conjunction of literature and religion—one congenial to the decade—had been crucial in the development of verse drama. The opportunity and impulse had come together for writers of abiding religious vision like Norman Nicholson and Anne Ridler, through the example of Eliot's work and through the existence of *The Mercury* theatre, both of which stemmed from the original Canterbury initiative. It is fitting that the period was rounded out by the production, in April, 1951 at Oxford in the University Church, of Christopher Fry's *A Sleep of Prisoners,* commissioned for the Festival of Britain by E. Martin Browne.

II

The three new verse plays that made up Martin Browne's season at *The Mercury,* Norman Nicholson's *The Old Man of the Mountains,* Anne Ridler's *The Shadow Factory,* and Ronald Duncan's *This Way to the Tomb,* were all religious dramas, and all owed a great deal to the example of the Canterbury productions and to Eliot's development of the poetic drama and his writings about it.

Eliot had always been concerned with the possibility of an acceptable poetic drama. There had, in fact, been no lack of poetic dramas in the nineteenth and early twentieth centuries, but few were suitable for acting and many were spoiled by archaism of subject and treatment. The problem was to find a form of drama and a concomitant form of verse suited to the presentation of a modern scene where the poetry was neither out of place nor a mere decoration, but was felt as intrinsic to the realisation of a poetic quality inherent in the vision of the play. Whether the problem was ever satisfactorily solved is arguable.

Murder in the Cathedral had seemed triumphantly to create a drama in which the speech was poetry in a modern idiom, and where there was a perfect union of that idiom with theme and setting. Yet Eliot himself came to see that "I had not solved any general problem; but that from my point of view the play was a dead end"; and that "in so far as it solved the problem of speech in verse for writing to-day, it solved it for this play only".[1] The play was set in the past, concerned itself with the temptations of a saint and was performed in a cathedral. It was hence suitably liturgical, accommodating easily a poetry that declared itself to be poetry, while, as religious drama, it had no problem concerning the obtrusiveness of the religious dimension, as this was the explicit concern of its main character.

In *The Family Reunion* (1939), Eliot gave a spiritual theme a modern setting in a play whose pattern is based on a classical tragedy. There is no chorus, except for the choric grouping of characters, the form being that of the drawing room play. The poetry found its justification in the projection of the inner life of the main characters. Formally it marked Eliot's first attempt to write a verse that could modulate from the matter of fact to the highest poetry, obviating the need for prose, and thus creating a seamless idiom.

Eliot's solutions to the formal problems of modern verse drama were not the only possible ones, and his solutions had decided limitations. While drawing on Eliot's example, Nicholson, Ridler and Duncan each made a different attempt to solve the formal problem of creating a contemporary verse drama for the modern theatre and the modern audience.

Ronald Duncan's *This Way to the Tomb* (1946) owes a great deal to *Murder in the Cathedral*. It is in the form of a masque with anti-masque. The masque presents the temptation of St. Anthony on the island of Zante in the fourteenth century. Anthony is alone with three novices who come to represent three aspects of himself that embody his temptations. Duncan had "felt intuitively that spiritual awareness was inseparable from physical vitality".[2] Anthony's final temptation is the sin of spiritual pride—pride in being a saint. It is only when he recognises this and calls for mercy that his body, in the shape of one of his novices, revives: with this comes an acceptance of the body and its unsaintly limitations. The theme of pride and the acceptance of self is recurrent with Duncan: the balancing theme of the anti-masque is the spiritual indifference of the modern world. In parody of the masque, the anti-masque shows the "Astral group" investigating the truth of the legend of the reappearance of St. Anthony. Unknown to them, he does appear to modern characters who are the repersonifications of his novice companions, and the play closes in a recognition of the need for redemption.

The anti-masque shows a debt to Auden and Isherwood's *The Dog Beneath the Skin;* but Duncan's hatred of the modern world is so violent that the satire is quite hollow. Duncan's sense of things is asserted rather than dramatised in the anti-masque, so that here is an imbalance between the two halves of the play.

The masque is indebted to *Murder in the Cathedral* in its static treatment of the temptation; and, as such, it offers the opportunity for extended verse speeches. Duncan has written:

I was nauseated with the flood of so-called 'free verse' . . . I therefore decided in writing this masque to use various verse forms with strict limitations. A year or so previously Ezra Pound had read me his translation of Guido Cavalcanti's *Canzone, Donna me Pregha.* I chose this form for St. Anthony's Meditations because of its complicated structure, its division into five strophes, each divided into three stanzas with sixteen internal rhymes . . . I found that the form did not inhibit what I wanted to say.

On the contrary, it drove me to concision and an intensity which I certainly would not have achieved otherwise.[3]

While Duncan's canzoni have a fluency and a lightness that is immediately impressive, concision and intensity are not their most noticeable qualities. Literary echoes of manner and attitude are frequent (as of Hopkins, in this passage):

> The prune trunks stand ugly
> > > sometimes they appear
> To shake a fist; Thine
> > > Hand Divine?
> > > > Raised in wrath?
> Then held for a brief
> > > moment which was merciful.

Much of the verse shows the facility that was Duncan's besetting shortcoming: he claimed to have dictated a scene of his play *The Eagle Has Two Heads* in the back of a taxi.[4] Much of the verse is superficially brilliant and self-admiring, focussing attention on itself rather than bringing feeling into focus:

> The red fox, the sun,
> tears the throat of evening;
> makes the light of day
> bleed into the ocean.

This type of lyric, clotted with visual imagery, is the idiom for the sublime in the libretto he wrote for Benjamin Britten's chamber opera, *The Rape of Lucretia* (1946). Britten was an old friend and collaborator, and wrote the music for *This Way to the Tomb*. An oratorio, "Mea Culpa", for Britten, makes up a considerable portion of Duncan's second collection of poems, *The Mongrel* (1960).

This collection, while more finished and controlled than his first, *Postcards to Pulcinella* (1941), in fact confirms the impression of diffuse facility given by *This Way to the Tomb* and *The Rape of Lucretia*. It opens with two canzoni in which the sentiments are more commonplace than the complexity of form at first suggests, and in which the imagery is not integral to the expression. The book is filled out by "A Short History of Texas" in *terza rima*, a translation of the Anglo-Saxon poem "Widsith", and poems from the Provencal and other Medieval and Renaissance sources. The imagery is characteristically bright and striking, but often vulgar: "the fat hips of the ocean / Swing into the harbour" ("Motto Perpetuo").

Looking back on *This Way to the Tomb*, Duncan wrote:

. . . in spite of the success of *This Way to the Tomb*, if success is measured by the number of performances, I came quickly to regard the play as a failure. Eliot thought of *Murder in the Cathedral* in a similar way. We both saw that by writing plays about saints in a remote period we had evaded the essential challenge, which was to find a flexible verse form to express the age we lived in, on the stage . . . we applied ourselves, he to *The Cocktail Party*, I to *Stratton*.[5]

In *Stratton* (1950), Duncan turns to a modern subject and a new idiom. Once again, a major theme is pride, though this rather long play involves a number of preoccupations not easy to sort out. A good deal of *Stratton* is in prose, which modulates into low toned verse. Though Duncan evidently felt that this change of idiom paralleled Eliot's developments in *The Cocktail Party*, it is hard to see how the play would have suffered from being in prose entirely. Very many of Duncan's subsequent plays were.

In 1947 Anne Ridler wrote: "We owe it to W.B. Yeats and to Eliot that it is possible to attempt poetic drama again, although we are still far from having a tradition secure enough to lift the burden of perpetual choice of style from the poet's shoulders . . . Eliot achieved a style which could do without prose in *The Family Reunion*, and it is in that direction that playwrights will follow."[6]

The Shadow Factory takes that achievement as its starting point. It is set a year or two after the war in a "modern" factory that has cultural projects that are intended to contribute to the smooth running of the factory. One such project is the commissioning of a mural for the canteen. When the mural is unveiled, as part of the Christmas celebrations, it is found to be satirical, with the director depicted as god, the chess player. The director, incensed, is nevertheless persuaded to take part in a nativity play that is part of the Christmas celebrations. He is converted. The baby in the crib is a child of an employee, and the pressure is to see the Christmas story as a recurrent and contemporary event, sanctifying the empty modern life of the factory. As with Eliot and Duncan, there is an evident distaste for modern secular life, unacceptable in its own right.

The crucial nativity scene is obtrusive, and, in presuming too much on Christian sentiment and belief in the audience, reveals the weakness of the play, which realises much more strongly its negative than its positive vision. The scene is not built up to or justified by other events in the play. Yet, in itself and in its intended illuminative function, it is the only poetic scene in a play, which, as has often been remarked, is naturalistic in treatment and structure. The verse is low toned, perhaps following the example of *The Family Reunion;* and it would

not be surprising if an uninitiated audience were unaware that the play
was not in prose.

This prosiness is the fault of Ridler's other plays of the period,
including the non-naturalistic *Cain* (1943) (not intended for production), and *Henry Bly* (1950), where she draws on folk material. Her
work is best where emotion can shine through this flatness, and none
of her plays of the forties succeeds like her stark one-act opera *The
Departure* (1972).

Norman Nicholson felt that "if the modern poetic drama addresses
itself solely to that public which reads poetry, then it will become
weak and etiolated": the "poet . . . is almost bound to address himself to those who do not particularly want to hear him". While "the
time is now past when poetry should dissociate itself entirely from the
'realist' drama" it had to be remembered that "the audience is used
to the convention of the picture-frame stage and of a fairly reasonable
imitation of the appearance of life". The modern poet had "no accepted form or standard to follow . . . no convention of language":
Nicholson chose a mixture of prose and verse, which, he felt "need
not disturb the unity of the play if both poetry and prose have a common diction and idiom". He rejected the "suburban English" of the
contemporary stage and recalled:

> In my own town, in the drab slate houses, behind the plots of soil where
> the royal fern grows dusty with summer, beneath the smoke and the iron,
> there are men to whom the psalms are banners, the great myths that trum-
> peted for Byron and Milton are like the sound of a brass band coming
> faintly, but still distinctly, across distant roofs.

Nicholson believed that his Cumberland speech could "be used as the
basis of a verse which shall be close enough to contemporary speech
to maintain the illusion of realism, yet can be heightened and reinforced with the full power and pride of poetry."[7]

For *The Old Man of the Mountains,* his contribution to the *Mercury*
season, Nicholson used the form of a folk play. The story of Elijah is
given a modern Cumberland setting, just as biblical stories were given
a contemporary setting in medieval plays. The choice of this form
may have been suggested by S.L. Bethel's *Shakespeare and the Popular Dramatic Tradition,* which was published in 1944 by the Staples
Press that had first brought out Nicholson's poetry in book form.
Nicholson was certainly influenced by *Murder in the Cathedral,* and
his debt to Eliot shows in the speeches of the Raven, the voice of god:

> But when you hear my voice there is no need to read it in words;
> You know what it means without interpretation.
> Down in that hidden gully of your soul,

Where words never trickle and eyes never probe,
You know what my voice means, And those
Who pretend they never hear it, or deceive themselves into deafness,
They perhaps better than any, know truly what it means.
It is not often that you hear my voice but it is time you heard it
again.

For the rest of the play, Nicholson moves from prose to verse, which
he gives, as prescribed, "a common diction and idiom".

Elijah is a Cumberland farmer none too sure of his prophetic gifts.
He is opposed to Obadiah, the embodiment of the modern secular belief in progress, who ignores the traditional life of the fells. Elijah
triumphs over him eventually, prophesying rain that will bring an end
to a drouth. Associated with Elijah is a boy, David, whom he reput-
edly brings back from the dead, and who embodies the unquestioning
wisdom that abides in "babes and sucklings". Elijah himself has eventually to face a disturbing revelation—that he too must return to the
farm and perhaps accept the works of progress when the life of the
world has been sanctified by the acceptance of the true god.

The rationale of the play is a convincing one, but the result is very
conventional, as were Nicholson's later plays *Prophecy to the Wind*
(1947), *A Match for the Devil* (1955) and *Birth by Drowning* (1960).
The action is conceived largely in terms of the realistic depiction of
the interplay of character. The prose and the verse have a unity of
idiom, but there is too little that differentiates one from the other. The
play is not poetic in structure and it does not project the inner lives of
the characters through its poetry. Its pressures are pietist, traditionalist
and somewhat commonplace. The aim of the action is to lead to a
recognition of a need for a faith that will sanctify everyday life.

This same pressure is there in *The Shadow Factory*. In all three of
the *Mercury* plays there is a highly conservative dislike of modern,
urbanised and industrialised life, and this is not set aside by the acts
of sanctification in which *The Old Man of the Mountains* and *The
Shadow Factory* culminate. The dislike is so strong in *This Way to
the Tomb*, that it unbalances the play with the shallowness of its second half. What remains with one most forcefully is the contrast between the modern and the traditional; but the distrust of the modern
world is of a kind that can only be termed commonplace. The development of this contrast is not such as to demand, except in a few places,
the use of verse. It could be argued that it was largely because these
writers were Christians, poets, and admirers of Eliot that they wrote
verse drama, and that their careers in the theatre were a search for
material suitable to poetry. Duncan, Ridler and Nicholson each attempts to solve the problem of idiom that Eliot had faced: each, like

Eliot, gives great prominence to the choice of language in solving that problem. Duncan moves from the rather clotted idiom of *This Way to the Tomb* and *The Rape of Lucretia* to the more naturalistic *Stratton*. Ridler and Nicholson lean from the beginning to a more naturalistic idiom. In the case of all three poets, we are left with the question of how far this naturalistic leaning is compatible with calling their dramas "poetic".

III

Verse drama was essayed in the 1940's by more poets than is now remembered. *Transformation* published a series of plays by Robert Herring, Cyril Saunders, Gervase Stewart and R.H. Bowden. Patric Dickinson wrote for the stage as well as for the radio. Two almost forgotten plays are *The Assassin* (1945) and *The Burning Mask* (1948) be Peter Yates. Yates published three volumes of poetry in addition to his two verse plays: *The Expanding Mirror* (1942); *The Motionless Dancer* (1943); and *Light and Dark* (1951). John Lehmann was virtually the only editor to publish his work.

He works in terms of abstractions that in their interplay reflect the tensions that are at the root of his frequently tortured impulse to write: "We think, and thought corrupts love's image of the world." ("Thought and the Poet") There is a vision of a world shattered and made unclean through a loss of unreflective innocence. In his first two books there is already a distinctive individuality, a fluency of style and a suggestive interplay of words that are the mark of poetic vocation. His poems are fiercely intellectual and "wrestle with that spectral crime/Whose human sentence is: to be?" ("How many Times") At their best, they are carefully worked in traditional form and seem subtle and agile attempts to grapple with intense inner pressures:

> Yet we are scratched forever by that thorn,
> Infected by a dark unrest
> That saturates the golden corn
> And bread-white body like a stain
> Taxing the blue and bulging vein
> For more than being has expressed.
>   ("The Thorn")

Unhappily, Yates seldom attained this tightness, reminiscent of seventeenth century poetry. There is a monotony of rhythm that signals a simplicity of impulse. While his work stands out from much of the writing of the decade in its self-questioning and discipline, one has the sense of a manner not fully achieved, and a tendency to abstraction that went beyond the writer's power philosophically and poetically. There seem to have been no books between 1951 and 1983, when he brought out a selection, *Petal and Thorn,* his most rewarding book. He met with a nearly fatal motor-cycle accident in the fifties.

Alan Ross, in *Poetry, 1945-1950,* singled out Yates's *The Assassin* as "an extremely interesting poetic drama"[8]; yet the plays seem more rewarding as plays than for their poetry. In *The Burning Mask,* concerning the actor Edmund Kean, Kean is virtually the only character to speak in verse. In *The Assasin,* about John Wilkes Booth, the actor who assassinated Lincoln, verse is used more widely, and there are masked choric figures. Yates was described by Graham Greene as a dramatist of great promise; and *The Assassin* was successfully produced at the *Lyric* Hammersmith. Nonetheless, his plays are essentially naturalistic dramas of character, in which the effect of the verse is largely felt in a local heightening of emotional level.

Another little known play, Laurie Lee's *Peasants' Priest,* the Canterbury play for 1947, shows a contrasting pitfall for verse drama. With a story "based on the Serfs' Rebellion of 1381", its verse fits easily to its medieval plot. However, action, characterisation and verse are too reminiscent of Shakespeare's history plays, and the poetry is not out of place solely because it contributes to an overall archaism of vision:

> Your majesty, in grief I come to you,
> Forced hard against my will
> To bear the word of riot

In the case neither of Yates nor Lee can it be said that the use of verse produces a desirable or significant modification of the medium.

One remaining drama that calls for notice is Lawrence Durrell's *Sappho,* which Durrell described as "a play which is never destined to be published or played."[9] It was in fact completed in 1947, published and broadcast in 1950, but not produced until 1959 in Hamburg and 1961 at the Edinburgh Festival, by which time the Alexandrian novels had given Durrell a reputation.

Durrell does not have to face the problems of adapting poetry to a modern medium and a modern subject, as his play is set in Lesbos about 650 B.C. The theme of the play seems to be embodied in the contrast between two brothers who are lovers of Sappho: Pittakos, a soldier; and Phaon, a diver who has withdrawn to be a hermit on a lonely island. Pittakos, the man of action, is rejected by Sappho; while, in a brief encounter with Phaon, she finds sympathy for her sense of the unsatisfactory nature of action (and even words) compared with the peace that is found in the silence that lies beyond words. Pittakos, after being voted tyrant, is eventually toppled, and takes refuge with his younger brother.

The theme of withdrawal, congenial to Durrell, is reinforced imagisticly when Phaon dives into the sunken city of Eresos destroyed by earthquake:

> Sappho
>
> Beyond the capes and headlands of the wish,
> Beyond the menhirs of desire premediated,
> Most awkward and timid with those who most require
> One subtle and beautiful and quite at ease,
> We move and founder on tides of illusion,
> Fumbling outside immortality's immobile doors.
>
> Phaon
>
> Lucky the founders of the buried city,
> Transparent their acts, their wishes and their laws,
> Undivided as we have been divided.

For Phaon

> Knowledge to knowledge gives only hard fact . . .
> There remains some other thing, some other way
> To make them all related to the whole . . .
> A factor, like some colourless precipitate,
> Unlike time, yet of it, that is the clue,
> The great clue to the world of unseen forms.

The speech echoes Durrell's conception of an "heraldic universe" associated with a mode of understanding available to the poet in which perceived relations between events are not those established by logic. These reflections are related to the theme of action in Phaon's remark that "we have a world upon our hands/To make or unmake as our natures lead us."

The tensions set up in the early part of the play are not adequately resolved in the second half. The rise and fall of Pittakos stands as a commentary on the impurity of action; and the characters each discuss at great length their attitudes to action and its pitfalls. The conclusion of the play is precipitated by Sappho: it was she who, as oracle, had sent Pittakos on the expedition that brought him to power; and, in doing so, she had omitted to drug herself and had imposed her own conscious will as the voice of the oracle. Later it is surmised from tablets brought up by Phaon from the sunken city that she had accidently married her own father Kreon. For this she is exiled to Corinth, while Pittakos cruelly keeps her children as hostages. From Corinth she devises the overthrow of Pittakos. It might be argued that, in all this, she is working out the ambiguities of her own action in sending Pittakos to war. Yet it is through action, and not through its rejection, that she triumphs. There is bitterness in the conclusion; but it seems to reflect a sense of a hollowness behind all experience—a feeling recurrent in Durrell's writing, but one that cannot stand as a resolution of the tensions of the play:

> Listen to the silence, child, do you hear it?
> It contains everything, drinks up everything,
> The oceans of our silence where such words
> As mothers and daughters use in meeting
> Can only make islands or peninsulas of meaning,
> Surrounded by the waters of our history,
> Contracted into little spots of time
> By the briefness of kisses given the innocent:
> Or wrongs done to the guiltless in their sleep.

The play, as Durrell recognised in a "postscript", "suffers . . . from the defect of excessive length". He suggested that it could be made actable by eliminating the sub-plot concerning the poet Diomedes. T.S. Eliot, before publishing the play, had remarked: "I am sure that the surgical operation by a good producer would be so beneficial that I had rather print the play after than before".[10] The play required more than shortening. The fourth scene, thematically crucial, between Pittakos and Phaon and Sappho and Phaon, is not merely far too long: the tensions in the arguments between the characters do not emerge in the form of imagery or imagistic action. Durrell's "object" (as stated in the "postscript") of "marrying up pace, plot and poetry" seems not to be attained here and elsewhere, and the scene is largely an occasion for the characters to express their views.

The texture of the verse is the most successful feature of the play, though Durrell did not have to accommodate recalcitrant aspects of contemporary life and speech: the setting is one that the audience is accustomed to hearing about in verse. Durrell himself remarked (concerning Sappho): "I can never understand this distinction between poetry and prose"[11]: and the verse passes seamlessly from the prosaic to the lyrical. There is no prose. In fact, just because the play has few passages of emotional power, the verse is not heavily taxed expressively. Indeed, some of the most characteristic triumphs are lyrical interpolations:

> Shut up from pleasure in a holy fountain,
> A nymph lies, hearing the woollen water,
> Softly on the cones of the ear uncurling.

A static beauty, the beauty of the Aegean landscape and its past, so eloquently as so frequently evoked by Durrell, is what remains endearing about the play, which still has a freshness that most other verse plays of the period have lost. But it is not the triumph of integration of poetry and action that Durrell may have imagined it was, and that the playwrights of the decade so earnestly sought.

IV

It was the success of Christopher Fry that gave the appearance of a renaissance of verse drama in the later forties. In 1946 *A Phoenix Too Frequent* was produced at *The Mercury* theatre and then moved to the *Arts Theatre* for a longer run. Fry's next play, *The Lady's Not For Burning* was taken up by John Gielgud in 1948, and had a long season in London and a New York production. At the end of that season, in 1950, *Venus Observed,* commissioned by Laurence Olivier, was produced, an earlier play, *Boy with a Cart* was revived, and Fry's translation of Anouilh's *Ring Round the Moon* opened. Fry's explanation of the vogue was that "poetry provides something people lack and wish for: a richness and reaffirmation."[12] The remark captures very well the type of experience his plays offer.

Fry's early career was in the theatre, in 1934 as director of the Tunbridge Wells Repertory Players, and in 1940 as director of the Oxford *Playhouse.* In 1944 he was resident playwright at the *Arts Theatre* in London. Fry also had an intermittent association with the revival of religious drama. His first surviving play, *Boy with a Cart,* was written at the request of the vicar of Coleman's Heath in Surrey. *The Firstborn* (1946), a play about Moses in Egypt on which Fry had been working since 1940, was performed outside Tewkesbury Abbey; and *Thor with Angels,* a religious play of the early Saxon period, was the Canterbury Festival play of 1948. Fry wrote *A Sleep of Prisoners* as a play for performance inside a church for the Festival of Britain in 1951.

All of Fry's plays present themselves as religious: this is notably true of *The Lady's Not For Burning;* and it was this play and Fry's two related comedies, *A Phoenix too Frequent* and *Venus Observed* that made Fry's success. The earliest of these, *A Phoenix too Frequent,* is the best and most characteristic. It is set in the tomb of Virilius near Ephesus. The wife of Virilius, Dynamene, has vowed to fast there until death in the company of her servant, Doto. A soldier, Tegeus-Chronis, wanders into the tomb and rearouses Dynamene's interest in life. While he is away, one of a group of corpses of executed men is stolen. To save Tegeus from death, Dynamene suggests substituting her husband's body for the missing corpse.

To an audience innocent of awareness that this was "verse drama", the play must have seemed to belong to the genre of *Androcles and the Lion*. Fry's comedies owe a lot to Shaw in the use of false argument that rides on the figurative features of the dialogue. The form of the play, as often with Shaw, is anarchronistic drawing-room drama, with an unusual setting, and most of the "action" is in the form of conversation. The attitudes of the characters are entirely mid-twentieth-century British middle class; and a great deal of the comedy comes from the dissonance between these attitudes and the setting.

Dynamene: How can they hang you for simply not being somewhere?
     How can they hang you for losing a dead man?
     They must have wanted to lose him, or they wouldn't
     Have hanged him. No, you're scaring yourself for nothing
     And making me frantic.

Tegeus: It's section six, paragraph
     Three in the Regulations. That's my doom.
     I've read it myself. And, by my doom,
     Since I have to die, let me die here, in love,
     Promoted by your kiss to tower, in dying,
     High above my birth. For god's sake let me die
     On a wave of life, Dynamene, with an action
     I can take some pride in. How could I settle to death
     Knowing that you last saw me stripped and strangled
     On a holly tree? Demoted first and hanged!

The comic writing is more genuinely "poetic" than the poetry it is set beside. As with Shaw, there are constant changes of tone, frequently from the trivial to the sublime, that distract the audience's sense of the play's framework of values. Frequently the poetic is punctured by the bathetic, seeming to qualify the afflatus of the poetry.

       . . . the sun itself
     Trails an evening hand in the sultry river
     Far away down by Acheron. I am lonely,
     Virilius. Where is the punctual eye
     And where is the cautious voice which made
     Balance-sheets sound like Homer and Homer sound
     Like balance-sheets?

In fact, the tone of the play is fundamentally unironic, and the ironies that are exploited turn on whimsical oddities of human nature.

Fry's own conception of comedy is "that there is an angle of experience where the dark is distilled into light: either here or hereafter, in or out of time: where our tragic fate finds itself with perfect pitch, and goes straight to the key which creation was composed in. And

comedy senses and reaches out to this experience. It says, in effect,
that, groaning as we may be, we move in a figure of a dance, and, so
moving, we trace the outline of the mystery." His characters have to
"unmortify themselves: to affirm life and assimilate death and perse-
vere in joy."[13] Which is to say no more than his plays say: that life is
a miracle and we should learn to see this and rejoice.

These attitudes, undeveloped as they are, are simplistic; and Fry's
plays do not *develop* or *demonstrate* attitudes. Through a froth of
paradox and word play, the characters *state* their attitudes, and the
poetry is static and lyric rather than dramatic. We find this in his
non-comic play of the period, *A Sleep of Prisoners*, where a group of
prisoners of war, imprisoned in a church, enact their natures in a series
of scenes that mirror the history of man as told in the old testament.
The verse is more sobre, but its local effects call attention to themselves and do little to develop a resonance of insight in the play.

> God, have mercy
> On our sick shoals, darting and dying.
> We're strange fish to you.

Its version of "straight" sublime is simple, but not as impressive in
its simplicity as it intends.

> The human heart can go to lengths of God.
> Dark and cold we may be, but this
> Is no winter now. The frozen misery
> Of centuries breaks, cracks, begins to move;
> The thunder is the thunder of the floes,
> The thaw, the flood, the upstart Spring.
> Thank God our time is now when wrong
> Comes up to face us everywhere,
> Never to leave us till we take
> The longest stride of soul men ever took.
> Affairs are now soul size.
> The enterprise
> Is exploration into God.

Fry's characters, at their most "poetic", sound like the older Dylan
Thomas's public pronouncements on poetry:

> . . . the shape and shade and size and noise of the words as they hummed,
> strummed, jugged and galloped along. That was the time of innocence;
> words burst upon me, unencumbered by trivial or portentous association;
> words were their spring-like selves, fresh with Eden's dew, as they flew
> out of the air.[14]

Thomas's writing has, as ever, here and in *Under Milk Wood*, a better
underlying movement of sense than that of Fry; but that the two most

popular writers of verse of their generation should feel that something so tricky was the mode of the poetically impressive gives a discomforting measure of the taste of the late forties. Their audiences, and the critics who admonished them, also found such writing congenially impressive. In the case of Fry, perhaps this was because his plays offered the appearance of challenge and poetry on the surface, while in every respect reinforcing conventional attitudes concerning the good and the beautiful.

IV

The thirties and forties were the golden age of radio. The loudspeaker radio made its appearance in the late twenties, putting an end to the need for earphones. Television did not become an overbearing competitor until the fifties. The finest of these radio years were those of the BBC Third Programme, inaugurated in October, 1946 to broadcast high-brow material. Transmissions were mainly in the evening; and, for those who wanted to hear the complete works of Buxtehude, with repeats, it was a boon in the days before the long-playing record. It would be nice to think that the Third's achievement in bringing music from all over Europe to British listeners was paralleled in its exploitation of the radio as a medium for poetry and the poetic drama. In fact, this does not seem to have been the case. According to Patric Dickinson (writing in 1965) his programme, "Time for Verse" for the BBC Home Service, "was the only 'regular' programme of poetry the B.B.C. has ever allowed itself."[15]

Radio drama was in those days a largely ephemeral art. The B.B.C. Home Service and Light Programme both insisted on live transmissions, though the Third Programme did allow itself some pre-recording and recorded repeats. All that appears to survive are those scripts that writers and publishers chose to bring out in book form (though some recordings and manuscripts exist in archives or private hands). Henry Reed's adaptation of *Moby Dick,* which contains a little verse to set the mood and perform a narrative function, was published in 1947, but his long *Pytheus,* all in verse, does not seem to have survived in print. In addition, there seems ground for Rayner Heppenstall's contention that the Drama department of the B.B.C. made no attempt to get scripts from outside writers "but simply added Greek tragedies and Restoration comedies to their existing repertoire."[16] The Third Programme, according to Heppenstall, "never had its own producers . . . It bought programmes from Features, Drama, Talks, Music . . . "[17], none of which, presumably, had a special interest in commissioning programmes in verse. Those that did appear were written mainly by poets on the B.B.C. staff—Louis MacNeice, Patric Dickinson, Henry Reed, Terence Tiller and W.R. Rodgers. Louis Mac-

Neice's famous published scripts, *Christopher Columbus* (produced 1942, published 1944) and *The Dark Tower* (published 1947) were all written before the Third Programme appeared. The most adventurous productions for the Third seem to have come from Features, which had a good deal to do with the airing of Dylan Thomas's *Under Milk Wood*.

Other verse drama scripts from the period that have survived in published form are: Patric Dickinson's "Theseus and the Minotaur" (produced 1945, published 1946) and "The Stone in the Midst" (produced and published 1948); Laurie Lee's *The Voyage of Magellan* (produced 1946, published 1947); Henry Reed's *The Unblest* and *The Monument* (produced 1949, published 1971); Henry Treece's "The Tragedy of Tristran" (produced 1950, published 1952); and Dylan Thomas's *Under Milk Wood* (produced and published 1954, though in part written earlier). Works in verse for a variety of voices by W.R. Rodgers, Anne Ridler and R.S. Thomas are among those broadcast and later published.

It is difficult to judge a radio drama from a script. As Louis Mac-Neice remarked "a script is not necessarily a piece of 'good writing' " and "the radio dramatist must think in terms of sound rather than of words alone".[18] MacNeice's own "The Dark Tower" was an impressive experience, with its music by Benjamin Britten; and the role music played cannot be fully determined from reading. Nevertheless, it is clear that, apart from these scripts of MacNeice, a poet of an older generation, radio drama in verse from the forties has left very little of permanent value. Patric Dickinson's plays are professional but conventional adaptations of naturalistic drama to poetry and the radio; Laurie Lee's *The Voyage of Megallan* is slightly more experimental: "a form of speech has been sought that would be simple, concentrated, intelligible, yet heightened towards poetry; aiming first to capture the eye before attempting to move the other senses." ("Introductory Note")

Henry Reed's *The Unblest* and *The Monument* are based on episodes in the life of the Italian poet, Leopardi. Both are completely in verse— in a sprung pentameter, which Reed handles with a delicate formality. The conception of dramatic verse is that advocated by T.S. Eliot and demonstrated in *The Cocktail Party*: one which can accommodate the most mundane conversation and the highest reaches of poetry. In fact, no great emotional strains are put on the verse, even at its most poetic:

> Will it ever be certainly there, my house of peace?
> The servants docile and good, a beloved view from the window.
> A cypress-walk, the sun on the balustrade,
> The distant sea, and a daily boat-sail plying . . .
>
> (*The Monument*)

The action has its tensions and its resolutions, which are sensitively rendered. The plays derive their form from what they are—dramatised biography. They utilise the power of radio to move the listener rapidly forward in time by means of short scenes in a manner not possible in the theatre, where actor and action are seen.

However, the mode is that encountered in so many plays since Ibsen, and adapted by Eliot himself: a drama of conversation in which the inner life of the characters is revealed and explored through the dialogue. The poetry functions merely as a heightening or intensification of this process, and one is reminded of plays like *Stratton* or *The Shadow Factory,* where the conventions of the naturalistic drama are adapted to the use of verse. In his next published play, *The Streets of Pompeii* (from 1955), Reed used verse only for the more poetic moments; and, after that, he appears to have written his radio plays in prose.

The one work for radio that makes a claim to be of permanent interest is Dylan Thomas's *Under Milk Wood* (1954). Like so much of Thomas's later work, it was a long time coming. It had its origins in a radio talk given in 1945, "Quite Early One Morning". It had its first performance in 1953 at the Young Men's Hebrew Association in New York during Thomas's third visit to America, but it was undoubtedly intended for radio and was first broadcast on 25th January, 1954.

Thomas's "Play for Voices" presents a night and a day in the life of a small Welsh town, Llareggub ("Bugger all" (or "Nothing") spelled backwards). The voices, in the first half, project the dream life of the inhabitants, and the tension of the play is between that dream life and actuality. The use of voices in this way owes a good deal to James Joyce's *Ulysses,* and specific passages from Joyce seem to be echoed. But it is equally true that the use of voices in the play reflects possibilities inherent in radio drama. As Louis MacNeice wrote, "You can make a point with a scene consisting of three lines and no one need fiddle with a curtain or black out the lights."[19] Thomas exploits and expands this potentiality of radio, switching from voice to voice, to create a panorama of the inner and outer lives of the town. The use of a narrative voice that merges with the dramatic voices is also a device characteristic of radio drama.

First Voice

Mrs. Organ Morgan, groceress, coiled grey like a doormouse, her paws to her ears, conjures

Mrs Organ Morgan

Silence.

The combination of extensive passages of verbally complex impressionistic narrative with simple realistic dramatic speech is another possibility of radio drama, where there is no requirement for interesting and realistic movement on the part of the speakers, who are invisible. Thomas was also able to give songs or spoken lyrics to his speakers, as there is no problem of dramatic convention for the disembodied voice in moving in and out of formal set pieces, once the over-all non-realistic convention is accepted. Throughout Thomas exemplifies the force of a maxim of MacNeice for the radio dramatist: "He must 'envisage'' what kinds of voices will be heard together on the air and he must apportion the lines in such a way as to help any necessary contrast."[20]

In these respects, *Under Milk Wood* marked a valuable advance in poetic drama. Thomas had put his experience in writing film scripts and in working for radio to good use. The very rapid cutting from character to character is more usual in film than in drama; and, if any cavil were made concerning the dramatic form of *Under Milk Wood,* it might be that there are many *voices* but not much *play. Under Milk Wood* is almost a poetic documentary, with only a loose core of action to carry its intent, and it has been suggested that, as the work developed, Thomas moved increasingly towards the form of the radio feature rather than the radio drama.[21]

Criticism of the work would not be of its form, which is a triumph when one compares it with the unadventurous use of radio elsewhere. One's reservations concern those features that most endeared the play to Thomas's public: the colourful eccentricity of the characters; the stream of verbal surprises. Thomas was an inveterate reader of Dickens, and his writing is capable of a Dickensian feeling for personal oddity:

> The Reverend Eli Jenkins, in Bethseda House, gropes out of bed into his preacher's black, combs back his bard's white hair, forgets to wash, pads barefoot downstairs, opens the front door, stands in the doorway and, looking out at the day and up at the eternal hill, and hearing the sea break and the gab of birds, remembers his own verses and tells them softly to empty Coronation Street that is rising and raising its blinds.

There is a very acute feeling for lower class speech and attitudes: Second Neighbour/"Using language"/First Neighbour/"Singing in the w" However, Thomas's work in this vein almost always involves whimsical exploitation of the quaintness of character.

> From Manchester House, Llaregyb. Sole Prop: Mr. Mog Edwards (late of Twll), Linendraper, Haberdasher, Master Tailor, Costumier. For West End Negligee, Lingerie, Teagowns, Evening Dress, Trousseaux, Layettes. Also Ready to Wear for All Occasions . . . Beloved Myfanwy Price my Bride in Heaven . . .

This type of sentimentality is "protected" by ostentatiously aggressive touches of realism.

> And they thank God, and gob at a gull for good luck, and moss-slow and silent make their way uphill, from the still still sea, towards the Sailors Arms . . .

The writing in the first passage is related to one of Thomas's favourite figurations—piled oxymorons and hyperboles that suggest abashed wonder at the miraculous and stupefying variety of a universe that can only be accepted open mouthed. With just such an arch effect the play closes.

> The Wood, whose every tree-foot's cloven in the black glad sight of the hunters of lovers, that is a God-built garden to Mary Ann Sailors who knows there is Heaven on earth and the chosen people of His kind fire in Llaregyb's land, that is the fairday farmhands' wantoning ignorant chapel of bridesbeds . . .

The effect is strikingly like that engendered by Fry's more "daring" passages in *The Lady's Not For Burning*. The rhetoric is a self-admiring rhetoric, something to be savoured for its own sake. This is disturbingly true of the would-be impressive writing with which Thomas sets the opening scene:

> It is spring, moonless night in the small town, starless and bible-black, the cobblestreets silent and hunched, courters'-and-rabbits' wood limping invisible down to the sloeback, slow, black, crowblack, fishing boat-bobbing sea.

It is to be relished as a performance and it asserts how wonderful life is, without involving any disturbance of understanding or acceptance. It left its admiring middle class audience cosyly and patronisingly happy with the world.

V

The nineteen-forties were a period of remarkable acting in the British theatre; and, at the time, it seemed that a part of the rich theatrical life was the revival of verse drama. The success of plays by Eliot, Fry and Duncan contributed to this impression; but today there is little to look back on. In spite of the apparently impressive achievement, the verse drama of the forties seems now a misdirection rather than a new start.

Throughout his career Eliot was, quite rightly, concerned with questions of language as basic to the business of poetry; and he came to see the problem of poetic drama as one of language. His solution to this problem was influenced by his general concern to write poetry with a diction grounded in ordinary speech; and it is not surprising that this concern should lead him, in contrast to Yeats, to conclude that verse should adapt itself to a theatre where action simulates ordinary behaviour. For the theatre he sought a verse that could encompass the most ordinary remark and the most intense poetic expression. Such a verse he sought to adapt, from *The Family Reunion* on, to the current form of naturalistic drama, the drawing room play. This attempt to graft poetry on to the naturalistic drama was influential in the forties, and the limitations one might expect are to be found in *The Shadow Factory*, and also in *The Old Man of the Mountains*, despite its supposed "folk" basis. The drama of character, written in verse, is, in the modern theatre, merely a heightened or decorated version of the naturalistic play. It is perhaps preferable to the pseudo-medievalism of Lee's *Peasants' Priest* or Fry's *The Lady's Not For Burning*. Nevertheless, it constitutes nothing more than a muting of the Shakespearian tradition from which it sought to disengage itself. The drama of Shakespeare was a distortive medium in a manner akin to opera. The notion that verse could profitably be adapted to the non-distortive naturalistic drama lead to the relegation of verse to a minor function or to its association with formal elements that ran counter to its effect. For drama to be truly poetic, there needed to be the acceptance of distortion that ran through the whole medium and that was the product of a heightened non-naturalistic treatment of experience. Such an acceptance may be seen in *Murder in the Cathedral* and *This Way to the Tomb;* but the authors of both plays came to recognize them as special cases whose themes were harmonious with a ritualistic convention. Something much more radical was needed in the departure from naturalism, something that recognised that the life of the drama was in its action. The forties produced nothing so intrinsically or cohesively poetic as Samuel Beckett's *Endgame* (1958), a work of prose.

Chapter 11

POETRY AND THE WAR

War Poetry—Roy Fuller—Alun Lewis—Charles Causley—*Personal Landscape*

The second World War is, of course, the main event in British experience in the nineteen-forties. Indeed, it almost *is* the nineteen-forties in Britain, taking up over half of the decade in actual fighting and a major portion of the remainder before those who had fought had returned. Yet what one can characterise as the poetry of the war—or as "war poetry"—does not dominate the poetry of the period. It has been lovingly anthologised and critically examined; yet only Alun Lewis stands out as a poet whose chief material was the experience of war and who found himself through the war. There are others—Roy Fuller, Charles Causley, Alan Ross, Vernon Scannell—for whom the experience of war and writing about it was an important and formative part of their careers as poets. There are also those who are most remembered for a few poems based on wartime experiences—Henry Reed, F.T. Prince, Bernard Gutteridge; and finally there is a sizable list of very young poets of promise, of whom Keith Douglas and Sidney Keyes are the best known, who died, in most cases, before they had had time to write any body of notable poetry or see much action.

The war of 1939 to 1945 has never entered the popular imagination in the way in which the war of 1914 to 1918 did. No doubt this has much to do with the absence of a body of poetry that epitomises an awareness of historical catastrophe. The second World War did not come as so great a shock as did the first one: it was for long expected, feared and warned against. It is not remembered for devastation in battle and the prolonged horrors of trench warfare, but rather for the laying waste of whole countries and the callous destruction of the lives of millions of non-combatants. It is not recorded as the graveyard of a British generation.

All this seems born out in the poetry of the two wars and in the lives of those who wrote it. There is little poetry of combat from the second World War, because few of the poets who were in the services actually saw combat. Of the two best known, Alun Lewis and Sidney Keyes, Keyes was killed in his first action and Lewis did not see action at all. Keith Douglas's poems are an outstanding exception. There was not the contrast between life in the trenches and life at home, because, for many in the services, life was a good deal safer and more leisured than life under aerial bombardment in London or Plymouth or Hull. There were few battles with the systematic butchery of tens of thousands of men—at least, not in British fighting. Indeed there were extensive periods when fighting on land was confined to a few remote areas. Yet certain statistics concerning the poets in the services give qualification to this picture. Brian Gardner's anthology, *The Terrible Rain,* culls with noticeable tenderness examples from the work of almost every writer who might be considered a part of the second World War. He includes work by 87 poets who served in the forces: twenty died in active service. Of these, fifteen were 26 or younger and eleven were 22 or younger. Of the 29 poets in Gardner's anthology born after 1918, fifteen died on active service, all before their twenty-fifth birthdays. More than half of these young men lost their lives with the Air Force or Fleet Air Arm—services where life was often comfortable enough, but where one found oneself periodically exposed in an ariel shooting gallery. The young infantry officer was the prototype of lost promise in the first World War; but only three poets of any note lost their lives with infantry regiments in the second one: Alun Lewis, Sidney Keyes and Drummond Allison. Yet there is in fact little poetry of ariel combat or of flying from World War II: Hugh Popham's *Against the Lightning* (1944) and *The Journey and the Dream* (1945) are the only books of any quality where we find it.

"Nearly all the poets of the 'thirties were acutely aware of the impending catastrophe . . . When it came . . . the circle was completed and it was too final for them to be able to speak."[1] These words of John Lehmann applied in good measure to the younger writers as well, who, in Alex Comfort's phrase, belonged "to a generation brought up in the certainty that it would be killed in action on behalf of an unreality against an insanity."[2] Left-wing hopes had been set on the possibility of avoiding the seemingly inevitable war by timely resistance to fascism; and, when the war came, along with the Hitler-Stalin pact, there was widespread disillusionment with radical solutions. After all, the war that had arrived now presented the only way to defeat fascism. To many, like Roy Fuller, however, "it seemed . . . impossible that the capitalist powers would really carry through a war that would destroy the fascist régimes . . . "[3]; and, especially before the entry of Russia into the war, criticism of the war and resistance to it was widespread and often active, particularly among communists and anarchists. 50,000 conscripts registered as conscientious objectors, and 43,000 exemptions from combatant service were granted. Patriotism of the kind found at the beginning of World War I, and expressed in the poetry of Rupert Brooke and Julien Grenfell, was not to be expected.

The war came to be seen in terms at once of a struggle for survival and a fight for freedom and a better world, with a consequent amount of unctuousness. Denys Val Baker's literary quarterly *Opus* announced typically: "OPUS is dedicated to the propagation of the ideals of love and brotherhood, freedom of thought and action, and especially to the maintenance and strengthening of the individual way of life."[4]

As the war progressed, there was a growing sense of what apparently civilised human beings were capable of doing to one another News of atrocities became frequent, yet it would be hard to find a wartime poem that mentions them. R.N. Currey, in introducing *Poems from India*, mentions the Bengal Famine, which killed one and a half million people in 1943, as "a disaster which impressed every British soldier who witnessed anything of it, but appears among British writers to have numbered rather than inspired expression."[5] There are no poems about the British thousand bomber raids on German cities, and the atom bomb and the gas chambers had virtually to wait until the late fifties and sixties for the poetic expression of the horror they evoked.

There was an inevitable public tendency to see World War II in terms of World War I, and one of the cries of the first year of the war was "Where are the War Poets?". Ironically, Cecil Day Lewis's reply became one of the best known poems of the war:

> They who in folly and mere greed
> Enslaved religion, markets, laws,
> Borrow our language now and bid
> Us to speak up in freedom's cause.
>
> It is the logic of our times,
> No subject for immortal verse—
> That we who lived by honest dreams
> Defend the bad against the worse.

World War II in fact saw the publication of far more poetry than the years preceding it or the years succeeding it; but, as Julian Symons pointed out in 1942, "War poetry is not a specialised department of poetry: it is . . . quite simply the poetry . . . of people affected by the reality of war."[6]

The type of poetry the war produced is well epitomised by Roy Fuller:

> The poets who *were* called up felt by and large that the war was necessary to destroy fascism, but they had no enthusiasm or confidence about the governments that were to be the instrument for this. Patriotism was absent, but so too was indignation about horrors. Pacifism was an untenable position: equally so was a crusading spirit . . . The virtue arising from the erotic affairs of two people—sometimes this seems to be all the poet is

able to set against the disasters of a world . . . the only widespread, non-private assertion in the poetry of the Second World War [was] the idea that the soldier, the human unit, is worth more than the war, and that the unit has become inescapably involved in an inevitable conclusion.[7]

He saw as ". . . the essential message of this poetry . . . that the killing of one human by another is an evil incapable of justification or expiation."[8]

Such a poetry was not, in fact, out of the tradition of the best war writing of the modern world, which has been anti-heroic and soberly realistic—a tradition that goes back to the first major war in democratic society, to Whitman's great prose diary of the American Civil War in *Speciman Days*. Such poetry shows us war as it strikes the ordinary, non-professional soldier. Its ultimate hero is the Unknown Soldier. In the hands of Sassoon and Owen, such poetry was deeply radical; and what strikes one in retrospect about the poetry of World War II is not the absence of the heroic, the epic or the patriotic, which could, in the perspective of our society, only be fulsome or false, but the very low key quality of the writing, the way in which it moves quietly towards acceptance. That this was not a necessary outcome of the experience of World War II can be exemplified by contrast through Vaino Linna's *The Unknown Soldier* (1954)—a novel of the second Russo-Finnish war, strongly disillusioned, yet confronting the horror and bravery of war in a powerful and disturbing way.

Typical of British poetry is a poem, seemingly uncollected, by Geoffrey Parsons, "Airgraph I" (*Orion* IV, 1947). The poem assumes the most modest of forms, the epistle, in the guise of the war-time microfilmed letter, the "airgraph", which the poet is writing in his tent in Burma. After mentioning "Torn Toungoo, and Rangoon wrecked and ransacked/ . . . the countless, nameless villages,/Their brittle bashas splayed, splintered and charred . . .", the poet turns his back on the war to find consolation in the sensed presence of a woman he loves:

> Remembrance of you is my refuge; and yet, not remembrance,
> Rather say consciousness: memory buries the dead
> But you are my present prop . . .
> So that to-night in my tent, as at all times,
> In every particular place, I am not entirely alone;
> Nor am I from you in your flat, in absolute absence.
> And as I observe now, on my crude table,
> The marvellous mantis, green like a growing grass,
> Chafing his delicate knees, praying in profile;
> And, as the frogs' lament lingers and lengthens
> While the eternal rain seeps through the seams,

> I feel this a shared, not singular, experience,
> Which we, together again in time and place,
> Together shall recall, not I recount.

The disruption of personal relations is a recurring theme of World War II poetry:

> My hand waving from the window
> Felt still the touch of your fingers:
> Sorrow that made me dumb
> Becomes pride in your love: and now,
> As you turn the key in the door,
> Or enter the room where our lives
> Are still touched by the cushions and cards,
> The tea gone cold in the cups,
> My train takes me as though through sleep
> To an empty room and the night.
> ("Platform Goodbye"—H.B. Mallalieu)

The war emerges as something to be got through. Kingsley Amis recalled: "My feelings about the war as such were and are highly conventional, that it was very unpleasant, but altogether necessary; because the Germans had to be put down."[9] It is the quality of off-duty meditation, in which the poet turns his back on the war, that is so characteristic of British poetry of World War II, and that can still make some readers feel that this war really produced no "war poetry".

A fact that contributed to the production of this type of poetry was that the war created a situation conducive to philosophical speculation and gave many people a lot of opportunity for it. In addition, more time was spent by more people in waiting or in boring occupations than was spent in actual fighting. This boredom could be accompanied by brutalising treatment and circumstances, as expressed in "What I Never Saw" by Timothy Corsellis, killed at the age of twenty:

> We sat together as we sat at peace
> Bound by no ideal of service
> But by a common interest in pornography and
>   a desire to outdrink one another . . .
> Then came the queueing, the recurrent line of pungent men
> Dressed in dirt with mud eating their trousers legs,
> The collar that is cleaner than the shirt
> And the inevitable adjectives.

"Lessons of War" by Henry Reed, perhaps the most anthologised poems of the war, express this bored alienation. The three poems take their titles from topics of infantry training, "Naming of Parts", "Judging Distances" and "Unarmed Combat". (Reed was much later to add two other sections.) They work by the ironic contrast between the voice of the instructor and the inner voice of the poet, whose mind, bored, wanders off into an aesthetic contemplation of his surroundings. As in all of Reed's poetry, there is a deftness in the handling of verse movement, and there is a virtuosity in projecting the voice of the instructor. The ironies of the poetry are enhanced, in the best of the poems, "Naming of Parts", by the sexual suggestion that underlies the lesson on the parts of the rifle.

> And this you can see is the bolt. The purpose of this
> Is to open the breech, as you see. We can slide it
> Rapidly backwards and forwards: we call this
> Easing the spring. And rapidly backwards and forwards
> The early bees are assaulting and fumbling the flowers:
>   They call it easing the Spring.
>
> They call it easing the Spring: it is perfectly easy
> If you have any strength in your thumb: like the bolt,
> And the breech, and the cocking-piece, and the point of balance,
> Which in our case we have not got; and the almond-blossom
> Silent in all the gardens and the bees going backwards and forwards,
>   For to-day we have naming of parts.

The ironies are paraded before the reader; but, as in much of Reed's poetry, one senses a certain emptiness behind the virtuosity. The life of the poems is in the imitation of the instructor, while the counterpoised poetic response seems, in contrast, a little precious.

A similar unease might be felt in places concerning another celebrated anthology piece of the war, "Soldiers Bathing" by F.T. Prince. The poem exists in several versions: this one is from the mid-forties. Prince, the infantry officer, is watching his platoon bathe and "forget the fear of war":

>   I see
> The idea of Michaelangelo's cartoon
> Of soldiers bathing, interrupted before they were half done
> By some sortie of the enemy, an episode
> Of the Pisan wars with Florence. I remember how he showed
> Their powerful limbs that clambered from the water,
> Heads turned across their muscular shoulders, burning for the
>   slaughter,
> Forgetful of their bodies that are bare,
> And eager but to buckle on their weapons lying there.
>
> And I think then of the theme another found
> When, shadowing men's bodies on a sinister red ground,

A Florentine, Uccello or Pollaiuolo,
Painted a naked battle. Warriors, straddled, hacked the foe,
Dug their fierce toes into the soil and slew
The brother-naked man who lay between their feet and drew
His lips back from his teeth in a grimace.
They were Italians who know war's sorrow and disgrace
And showed the thing suspended, stripped . . .

The passage, like the whole poem, is impressive in the fullness of its movement, its sureness of tone and its clear visual quality. It shows a deep sympathy for both the vulnerability and the innocence of human beings: but the memory of Pollaiuolo's celebrated engraving brings him back not merely to the violence of the war from which his soldiers have turned aside, but to the root of that violence. He sees his own men as ones who might spring from the water "burning for the slaughter". However the poet later reflects

That some great love is over all we do,
And that is what has driven us to this fury, since so few
Can suffer all the terror of that love:
The terror of that love has set us spinning in this groove
Greased with our blood.

Whether or not this is meant to be an orthodox Christian reflection is hard to say; and the suspicion that it is literary posturing is heightened by the ease with which the poem earlier accommodates the Shakespearian reference to man as "Poor bare forked animal". Nevertheless, except for its conclusion, "Soldiers Bathing" remains a justly celebrated memorial of the war—mature and, in its initial apprehensions, undeceived.

An "off duty" poem that is congenial because of its frank and relaxed enjoyment of the hiatus in war is Julian Brooke's "Abruzzi":

The woman spins in the doorway, her kerchiefed head
Demanding a nimbus . . . Love in this formal land
Is sculpture, and Faith is a function of flesh, like Birth;
Life here is sliced at need, like the stacked clover,
And Death is the Autumn, the waited, welcome return
Of the rainy season, and thunder over the mountains.

As Roland Blythe remarked: "The war demanded a temporary suspension of personal identity but . . . offered a great profusion of those experiences by which identity is fed: foreign travel, sexual freedom, bereavement, pain, separation, companionship."[10] There was also a heightened experience of life in the imminence of death.

One of the few poets to write about actual fighting was Bernard Gutteridge. He contributed to *New Verse* before the war, and his war poems give that clear rendering of the contemporary scene that the thirties would have called "reporting". His poems seldom move to a tight resolution of the responses they record: he recalled that it was "like keeping a diary. I wrote them . . . because I felt I ought to." Finding that his war "was not like the one Owen and Sorley wrote about", he wrote "about my brother officers and their girls"—but discarded most such poetry when his only book of the period, *The Traveller's Eye,* appeared in 1947. The sequence, "Burma Diary", has considerable power, but Gutteridge belittles it, finding that it shows "signs of someone saying: you are a poet and occasionally in action."[11]

> We found the colonel in the smoking gully,
> His body looted, his face blown out. His servant
> Was sobbing, holding a tree as if his wife,
>   Femoral artery pumping
>
> His life into the thorns.
>   ("Burma Diary:2. Mogaung")

The clarity and the drawing back from the portentous recommend these poems.

It must not be forgotten that World War II was only the second time since the seventeenth century that civilians in Britain faced bombardment. The air-raids were particularly shocking and pitiful, in that they resulted in the random and pointless death of children and others who could contribute nothing to the war. Writers who, like Dylan Thomas, felt no commitment to the war and avoided active engagement in it, wrote compassionately of this suffering. Edith Sitwell, whose writing of the twenties seemed to affront any suggestion of the profound, found a new idiom in poems about the raids such as "Still Falls the Rain":

> Still falls the Rain—
> Dark as the world of man, black as our loss—
> Blind as the nineteen hundred and forty nails
> Upon the Cross.
>
> Still falls the Rain
> With a sound like the pulse of the heart that is
>   changed to the hammer-beat
> In the Potter's Field, and the sound of the impious feet
>
> On the Tomb . . .

It is difficult to see the willed simplicity of this poetry, with its deliberate repetition of archetypal imagery, as the simplicity of great poetry. It has the air of an utterance occasioned by the sense that great events demand grand gestures. The tone is less moving than that of Mervyn Peake's "Is there no Love can Link Us" with its modest facing of a sense of pained bafflement:

Is there no thread to bind us—I and he
Who is dying now, this instant as I write
And may be cold before this line's complete?

Is there no power to link us—I and she
Across whose body the loud roof is falling?

The poetry of World War II is typically, and, at its best, humanistic rather than apocalyptic. In its use of natural speech rhythms and diction and ironic juxtaposition, and in its exploitation of the everyday and the personal, it continues the idiom of the poetry of the thirties. The predicament created by the contrary demands of the personal and the public was the theme of many of the central poems of the earlier decade. As Ian Hamilton wrote, in introducing *The Poetry of War: 1939-1945* "in direct descent from Eliot and Auden, [it] attempted to confront a disintegrating world in personal terms that could make poetic sense out of it." Its distrust of any patriotic stance is an obvious inheritance from the thirties, as is its strong valuation of personal sensitivity. Death provides a humbling perspective in which experience is viewed, though death itself is seldom grandly centre canvas. How many of the attitudes and poetic strategies of the thirties recur in the war poetry can be seen from this poem of 1943, "Assault Convoy" by Norman Hampson, an Oxford contemporary of Sidney Keyes and Philip Larkin:

How quietly they push the flat sea from them,
Shadows against the night, that grow to meet us
And fade back slowly to our zig-zag rhythm—
The silent pattern dim destroyers weave . . .
Only at intervals the truth breaks on us
Like catspaws, ruffling these quiet waters.
Our future is unreal, a thing to be read of
Later; a chapter in a history book.
We cannot see the beaches where the dead
Must fall before this waxing moon is full . . .
Bound, as we are, by humanity's traces of sorrow
To anxious women, alone in the menacing night,
Where the rhythm of Europe is lost in their private fear
And El Dorado cannot staunch their grief.

Not only is there the tension between the historical perspective and the private grief found in Auden's poetry, but also the sense of the individual fate being shaped by violent and indifferent forces beyond the individual's control. There is the sense, frequently encountered in the poetry of the thirties, that the appearances of the present are false and hide a menacing situation. The individual is trapped in the present, awaiting the end of the war to live his life: "Our future is unreal"—a characteristically "thirties" expression. The accompanying strategies are also typical of the preceding decade: the detailed presentation of a particular scene that leads to a meditation that reveals what lies behind or beneath the scene. The mode is inevitably realist rather than symbolic, though the sense of menace and other pressures of the poem are reinforced through the imagery.

II

A poet whose work was brought into focus by the war and whose poetry has subsequently seemed to epitomise what was best in the British reaction to it is Roy Fuller. Two years older than Dylan Thomas, five years younger than Auden, Fuller belonged with the group of poets associated with Julian Symons's *Twentieth Century Verse* in the late thirties. Coming to maturity in the depression and after the emergence of Hitler, Fuller took politics as a natural and abiding ambience in a way it was not for Auden and some of the upper-middle class poets who gave the poetry of the thirties its tone. Through the war Fuller's radicalism was modified and deepened, but it remained an essential part of his reaction to events.

His first book, *Poems* (1939), shows decidedly—and often separately—two important influences: that of Auden; and that of Robert Graves, mediated through the poetry of Norman Cameron. Auden's poetry, with its industrial imagery, its tensions between the liberal ideals of the personal life and radical demands of public commitment, its accommodation of contemporary speech in traditional forms, was the sustaining basis for the poetry of Fuller and his friends in the thirties, and remained, as he has said, "a continuing influence".[12] "Cameron's verse was an antidote to the rhetoric of the left and to the imitations of Auden".[13] Cameron is the source of the "brief mythologic-anecdotal poems"[14], and Auden that of the meditative, political poems.

Auden is still too noticeable an influence in *The Middle of a War* (1942)—the book with which Fuller established himself; and one can see that he was still not "a manageable influence"[15]. Even in a poem as well developed and controlled in structure as "Soliloquy in an Air Raid", the rhetoric of *Look Stranger* and *Another Time* obtrudes to create an effect of poetic posturing rather than resolution:

> I am the old life, which promises even less
> In the future, and guarantees your loss.

It is not merely in the portentous stance of such comments, but in the very web of rhetoric that Auden is echoed: "melancholy/And madness in the isolation of its writers"; "the play/Unfolds spontaneous as the human wish". Such permeating rhetoric is inseparable from the attitudes of the poetry from which it is borrowed; and, indeed, the poem is a structure of borrowed strategies and second-hand perspectives. No doubt the feeling was authentic, but the style is not yet developed to the point of rendering the individuality that is a mark of authenticity.

Conscription into the Navy in 1941 brought changes: "war service exercised several evils that might have gone on constricting me as a poet." He found that

> . . . nothing, except the non-war experience of Africa, affected me as much as the proletariatization resulting from service on the "lower deck". I had got to know something of working-class life in left-wing politics during my early twenties: the first part of my war service confirmed in a practical way the necessity for social revolution, not least for the middle-class intellectual. It extricated me from the great problem of the thirties—how to live and write for a class to which one didn't belong. Such extrication was obviously mainly subjective, but there is certainly a simplification and greater concreteness in the first poems I wrote after calling-up, and I think the Marxist conception of things underlies them in a less strained and dragged-in way than hitherto.[16]

The poetry becomes cleared of its earlier rhetoric and concerned with the particularity of experience:

> A honeycomb of cabins, boxes, cells,
> To which each man retires alone.
> A snatch of singing, like a groan,
> Broken off quickly. Sour, damp smells.
>> ("Saturday Night in a Sailors' Home")

The historical significance flows naturally from his own fate:

> My photograph already looks historic.
> The promising youthful face, the matelot's collar,
> Say "This one is remembered for a lyric.
> His place and period—nothing could be duller."
>
> Its position is already indicated—
> The son or brother in the album; pained
> The expression and the garments dated,
> His fate so obviously preordained.
>> ("The Middle of a War")

One of the best known of these poems, "Spring 1942", shows how the stylistic simplification went along with a deepening of attitude and understanding:

> Once as we were sitting by
> The falling sun, the thickening air,
> The chaplain came against the sky
> And quietly took a vacant chair.
>
> And under the tobacco smoke:
> "Freedom," he said, and "Good" and "Duty".
> We stared as though a savage spoke.
> The scene took on a singular beauty.
>
> And we made no reply to that
> Obscure, remote communication,
> But only stared at where the flat
> Meadow dissolved in vegetation.
>
> And thought: O sick, insatiable
> And constant lust; O death, our future;
> O revolution in the whole
> Of human use of man and nature!

There is a crudity in the conclusion, with its invocations, that suggests that the poet did not know how to end after the powerful simplicity with which the scene is presented in the first two stanzas. The telling comment is "We stared as though a savage spoke": it makes a connection between the historical failure and an inveterate flaw in human nature.

Such an awareness becomes explicit in Fuller's third book, *A Lost Season* (1944). He had two "prolific periods—waiting to be drafted after a long radar course, and almost the whole of my time in Africa"[17]; and most of his wartime poetry belongs to these two periods. It was the experience of Africa that modified Fuller's attitude to human nature and the catastrophe of war. In some of the poems Africa is seen "politically" in terms of the degradation of the native culture by white "civilisation":

> The murder done by infinitesimal doses,
> The victim weaker and weaker but uncomplaining.
> Soon they will only dance for money, they'll
> Discover more and more things can be sold.
> ("The Green Hills of Africa")

". . . in the white men's towns the tribes are gathered/Among the corrugated iron and/The refuse bins" ("The Tribes"); but it is the vision of man and animal side by side as inhabitants of the primitive landscape that was evidently most telling for Fuller.

In "The Giraffes", he sees the animals as "creatures walking without pain or love"—a vision that is recognised implicitly as a reflection of the human longing to walk without the constant awareness of pain and love. It is easy then to see "The Plains" as achieving an acceptance of a natural world in which beauty and death are events occurring "in dimensions/Impertinent for us to use or watch at all" ("October 1942"), in which "The animals gallop, spring, are beautiful,/ And at the end of every day is night." These closing lines of "The Plains" come close to being trite—and are trite if we see them purely as a comment on the natural world; but he asks "Have I discovered all the plains can show me?"

> This awful ceremony of the doomed, unknown
> And innocent victim has its replicas
> Embedded in our memories and in
> Our history. The archetypal myths
> Stirred in my mind.

This vision of an inveterate, meaningless cruelty stirs in him the realisation that history may not offer the opportunity of amelioration or the discovery of purpose. He finds a disturbing affinity with animal life in contemplating the lop-sided crabs of "Crustaceans" and the monkeys in "The Petty Officers' Mess":

> Most sad and tender,
> They clasp each other and look round with eyes
> Like ours at what their strange captivities
> Invisibly engender.

The vision of what human beings have brought themselves to through the war comes to him in a biological not a political image:

> It half convinces me that some great faculty,
> Like hands, has been eternally lost and all
> Our virtues now are the high and horrible
> Ones of a streaming wound which heals in evil.
> ("October 1942")

This vision finds its most direct expression in "What Is Terrible".

The vision is the culmination of being "moved across two oceans . . . Bored, systematically and sickeningly . . . threatened with . . . Peril and death":

> To blame our fathers, to attribute vengeance
> To the pursuing chorus, and to live
> In a good and tenuous world of private values,
> Is simply to lie when only the truth can give
> Continuation in time to bread and love.

> For what is terrible is the obvious
> Organization of life: the oiled black gun,
> And what it cost, the destruction of Europe by
> Its councils; the unending justification
> Of that which cannot be justified, what is done.
>
> The year, the month, the day, the minute, at war
> Is terrible and my participation
> And that of all the world is terrible.
> My living now must bear the laceration
> Of the herd, and always will. What's done
>
> To me is done to many. I can see
> No ghosts, but only the fearful actual
> Lives of my comrades. If the empty whitish
> Horror is ever to be flushed and real,
> It must be for them and changed by them all.

The historical explanation that frees the participating individual of some of his guilt is rejected, but passing images combine to give the poem a frightening, non-intellectual impact—the sense of some disorienting disaster beyond the power of rational explanation. "The innocent scene, the innocent walls and light/And hills for me are like the cavities/Of surgery or dreams." ". . . the furious/Inner existence of objects and even/Ourselves is largely a myth".

This "intense/Dissociation from the act/Of living"—"nightmarish/Slippings down the abyss of time/Backwards"—is the subject of "Night", where objects of vision themselves seem strange:

> Emotionless, the forms of nature
> Confront the upright system of cells,
> That ailing and inadequate
> Machine, that nerve and flesh-racked creature,
> Who from his spirit's endless hells
> Made his reality and fate.

"Night" is one of Fuller's most perfectly achieved poems, where the experience seems to offer its own meaning in direct physical terms. It connects with "Sadness, Glass, Theory" where "The present is/A lucid but distorting medium,/As though the cunning of perspective had/Been lost by nature and all was flat and savage/And terribly more truthful." This sense of experience isolated in a setting where the normal reassuring web of association has vanished is there in an earlier poem of loss and departure, "End of a Leave":

> Suddenly our relation
> Is terrifyingly simple
> Against our wretched times,

Like a hand which mimes
Love in this anguished station
Against a whole world's pull.

Vulnerability and impotence are both suggested in the image of the
isolated hand that "mimes" love. This devastating contemplation of
isolation, in a world rendered unrecognisable by the destructive consequences of evil that is seen to permeate all experience, is one of the
most powerful visions offered in the poetry of World War II.

If the vision is a powerful one, the force of these images suggests a
limitation in Fuller's poetry as a whole: the number of such memorable
images is small. His own description of the poetic process characterises his poetry well: "the poem, starting from its compelling donnée
or image, usually makes its further discoveries, sustains its narration,
finds its form, by a process of refinement rather than extension, a
process of interior working, of technical difficulties avoided or overcome, a process more likely to throw up generalizations than observations."[18] The journey, often circuitous, from observation to abstraction
by way of meditation and argument, is the one usually taken by Fuller's poems. In an interview in 1969, he spoke respectfully of his
favourite abstractions: "I don't think much has changed in the way
I've used these abstractions or the associations I've made round them—
for instance, History as a process which proves one's prognostications;
Society as meliorable; Art as a human activity admitting of no duplic-
ity."[19] These Audenesque abstractions too frequently provide a frame
of reference for his poems where others might have chosen to proceed
imagistically. A wartime poem, "Good-bye for a Long Time", begins
in a farewell scene, and develops and contemplates the feelings associated with departure. It produces a reversal through the image of
"the small/Body of a bird, startling against the gravel". The image
irradiates the whole poem, focussing the feelings of vulnerability and
loss, pointing forward to his own feared death. It also brings the poem
back into reality, and both the situation of the poem and the image of
the bird are seen in a variety of perspectives through their interplay.

Such an interplay occurs too seldom in Fuller's poetry. He has said
that "the total meaning of the poem often resides in its details"[20]; but
he has also suggested that "The value of poetry should always be
checked, away from its noise, by a consideration of its logic and
technique."[21] His remark that "the poet's overwhelming sense is that
if he gets his conception down beauty will take care of itself"[22] seems
a just epitome of what many writers must feel: but in these things it is
a matter of bent and emphasis; and the ratiocinative tendency, in union
with Fuller's exemplary concern with honesty, can take over his
poems. One senses a distrust of his poetic impulses; and Ian Hamil-

ton's remark is not an isolated one: "there is always [the] suspicion that he feels not only rhyme but all the taxing stanzaic patterns he sets himself to be 'useless', in the sense that they have no central expressive or synthesizing function in the modern world."[23]

Yet Fuller's self-mistrust is one of his strengths and is in tune with the age in which he writes. "January 1940" summarises the attributes of the great English poets and concludes:

> I envy not only their talents
> And fertile lack of balance
> But the appearance of choice
> In their sad and fatal voice.

Balance seems too ready a condition for Fuller, one associated with restraint; whereas choice, in what one feels compelled to speak of or in the poetic stance one might take, seems to him, as a twentieth century writer, restricted—and restricted by the rational. Nonetheless, his poetry is among the finest produced by the war, in its unusual sanity in the face of deeply disturbing apprehensions.

III

Alun Lewis perhaps qualifies best as the "war poet" of World War II. He found himself as a writer through the war, and some of his poems give classic expression to the experience of it. Characteristically, though Lewis died on active service, he did not see action.

"Thinking back on my own writing, it all seemed to mature of a sudden between the winter of 1939 and the following autumn . . . Was it Gweno and the Army?"[24] By that time he was 24. His early poetry had shown little promise of the development that was to follow. Although almost all the poems in his first book, *Raiders' Dawn* (1942), had been written since 1939, there are a surprising number of them that are old-fashioned and literary for their day and that have little individuality. From the time of his sudden maturing, Lewis had four years to live—a prolific four years for a soldier. *Raiders' Dawn* went through three impressions in 1942. *The Last Inspection and other stories* appeared the same year. While in India, Lewis prepared for press his second collection of poems, *Ha!Ha! Among the Trumpets* (1945), but did not live to see its publication. A collection of letters, *Letters from India*, was published in 1946, and was republished in 1948 with some new stories as *In the Green Tree*.

It is easy to see Lewis as the decent, lower-middle class Welsh boy responding to the experiences of war. It is certainly true that his feeling for the touching details of everyday life is one of his great strengths. "Private Jones", the story of the joining up of an illiterate man from the Welsh countryside, is a powerful piece of imaginative identification. Several of his earliest admirers, such as John Lehmann, felt that his future was as a writer of fiction. Yet, despite the seeming ordinariness of Lewis's outlook, it would be wrong to see his moralistic, simple decency as a limitation. Like his stories, his best poems are concerned with "the rootless life of soldiers having no enemy"[25], and their strength comes from Lewis's sensitive, observant and almost guileless reaction to circumstances shared by so many.

"All Day It Has Rained"—Lewis's most celebrated poem and perhaps the most enduring poem of army experience in World War II—arises from what Vernon Scanell called "the slow, remorseless strangling of individuality, the crushing of the spirit and imagination that almost every wartime soldier in the ranks had to endure."[26]

> All day it has rained, and we on the edge of the moors
> Have sprawled in our bell-tents, moody and dull as boors,
> Groundsheets and blankets spread on the muddy ground
> And from the first grey wakening we have found
> No refuge from the skirmishing fine rain
> And the wind that made the canvas heave and flap
> And the taut wet guy-ropes ravel out and snap . . .
> And we stretched out, unbuttoning our braces,
> Smoking a Woodbine, darning dirty socks,
> Reading the Sunday papers—I saw a fox
> And mentioned it in the note I scribbled home . . .

Lewis, when an officer on board a troop ship to India, was vocal in his disgust for the conditions in which "other ranks" were forced to live, but this poem is clearly not a poem of protest. It is, as Lewis remarked of his first collection, "so quiet. But really it's the quietness I seek—the adagio, the touch, the grace."[27] Even the menacing purpose behind the inactivity of the soldiers is muffled and implied in the last line, about Edward Thomas—"till a bullet stopped his song". The poem seems strongly moral in tone and very ready for overt statements of position, yet it impresses as undistortive of the experience in which it is rooted.

The poem is a triumph of tone. It exploits, without being explicit, a variety of feelings associated with the falling rain. There is the contrast between the sense of being trapped with oneself (and with others) in circumstances that are depersonalising, and the tranquility and melancholy induced by the rain. The poem's ambiguous attitude to this melancholy is redolent of Edward Thomas, whose poem "Rain" Lewis must have known, and to whom Lewis owed a conscious debt at the time. He spoke of "the Edward Thomas country which inspired so much of the poetry"[28]. "All Day It Has Rained" shows a debt to Thomas in the movement and the subdued meditative tone:

> Yet thought softly, morosely of them, and as indifferently
> As of ourselves or those whom we
> For years have loved, and will again
> To-morrow maybe love; but now it is the rain
> Possesses us entirely, the twilight and the rain.

Lewis also shares Thomas's ability to bring out the metaphoric elements implicit in an actual scene.

In "To Edward Thomas", the tone again shows an indebtedness, though one that has resulted in the attainment of a secure personal voice. Lewis speaks of "the placid afternoon enfolding/The dangerous future", and this introduces a passage that is one of the triumphs of his poetry.

> I sat and watched the dusky berried ridge
> Of yew-trees, deepened by oblique dark shafts,
> Throw back the flame of red and gold and russet
> That leapt from beech and ash to birch and chestnut
> Along the downward arc of the hill's shoulder,
> And sunlight with discerning fingers
> Softly explore the distant wooded acres,
> Touching the farmsteads one by one with lightness
> Until it reached the Downs, whose soft green pastures
> Went slanting sea—and skywards to the limits
> Where sight surrenders and the mind alone
> Can find the sheeps' tracks and the grazing.

It is not merely the sensitivity and particularity of observation that compel admiration: the sense of a rich yet elusive meaning implicit in experience is rendered in the teasing spectacle where "sight surrenders and the mind alone/Can find the sheeps' tracks". The succeeding lines "And for that moment Life appeared/As gentle as the view I gazed upon" make a richly and subtly qualified statement.

The congeniality of Thomas as a model undoubtedly had a great deal to do with the melancholy Lewis shared with Thomas.

> Divining this, I knew the voice that called you
> Was soft and neutral as the sky
> Breathing on the grey horizon, stronger
> Than night's immediate grasp, the limbs of mercy
> Oblivious as the blood; and growing clearer,
> More urgent as all else dissolved away . . .
> Till suddenly, at Arras, you possessed that hinted land.

In a review of a selection of Thomas's poems, Lewis spoke of "Death, the ultimate response"[29]. In a letter from India to his wife, he protests "death doesn't fascinate me half as powerfully as life: you half hinted so . . . but you know really . . . how I turn insatiably to more and more life . . . Death is the great mystery, who can ignore him? But I don't *seek* him."[30] Yet he seems drawn by the illusion of some ultimate resolution of impulses beyond death. Concerning his operation in a hospital in Poona, Lewis wrote "I surrendered to what Edward Thomas foresaw—the land he must enter and leave alone"[31]. Several poems, such as "The Sentry" and "Dawn on the East Coast", while ostensibly about the war, are suffused with a melancholy, the exploration of which is their real subject.

Against this melancholy must be set a longing for fullness of experience. When offered a choice of a staff job rather than a return to his regiment, Lewis said of his men: "They seem to have some secret knowledge that I want and will never find until I go into action with them and war really happens to them."[32] As the time of going into action came nearer, he had the sense that he was "still waiting for my big moment, my big word."[33]

> And although I'm more and more engrossed with the single poetic theme of Life and Death, for there doesn't seem to be any question more directly relevant than this one of what survives of all the beloved, I find myself quite unable to express at once the passion of Love, the coldness of Death (Death is cold) and the fire that beats against resignation, acceptance. Acceptance seems so spiritless, protest so vain.[34]

What is being said here is not quite clear (and seems coloured by reminiscence of Rilke in the phrase "what survives of all the beloved"). Like any sensitive man in his position, Lewis was concerned with the significance of life that might suddenly be cut off, and with the problem that the aim of all his action was that some day he would kill someone. "The Jungle", an ambitious lengthy poem written in India when he knew that he would soon see action, seeks an inner meaning for experience:

> In the mole-blue indolence the sun
> Plays idly on the stagnant pool
> In whose grey bed black swollen leaf
> Holds Autumn rotting like an unfrocked priest.
> The crocodile slides from the ochre sand
> And drives the great translucent fish
> Under the boughs across the running gravel.
> Windfalls of brittle mast crunch as we come
> To quench more than our thirst—our selves—
> Beneath this bamboo bridge, this mantled pool

> Where sleep exudes a sinister content
> As though all strength of mind and limb must pass
> And all fidelities and doubts dissolve . . .

In "Karanje Village" he wrote of "A little Vishnu of stone,/Silently and eternally Being,/Bidding me come alone". Yet, for all their intent to be impressive and find impressive meanings, these poems do not offer an achieved coherence. Perhaps, like Sidney Keyes and so many young writers living under the threat of sudden death, Lewis felt an urgent need for a "big statement". The one point of resolution in "The Jungle" is the image of "the instinctive rightness of the poised/ Pied kingfisher deep darting for a fish", preferred to "all the banal rectitude of states". The passage is disturbingly detachable, not growing imagistically or by argument out of its context. It is a familiar image of the rightness of the natural world, not poisoned or made devious by an awareness of purpose. It is strikingly similar to an image in an earlier poem, "The Soldier":

> I who am agonized by thought
> And war and love
> Grow calm again
> With watching
> The flash and play of finches . . .

The explicit treatment of "large themes" was in fact no enhancement of Lewis's work: "if I get too far away from the *thing,* the *thought* becomes flabby and invalid . . ."[35] Lewis responded to India earnestly and adventurously, yet he could never attain the inwardness he had with his Welsh experiences. His letters seem to show a recognition of this. A poem such as "Holi" ("The bankrupt peasant feels the wheat/Spring green within his stony loins") could have been written by any of several expatriate British poets of the day. Lewis realised that his early poetry was excessively adjectival and over-written, and he tried for greater simplicity. Of the poems he wrote while recuperating from an operation in April 1943 he said: "I've cut out nearly every rich adjective and high metaphor"[36]. The result is not a telling simplicity: the language has a desirable plainness, but little resonance of suggestion. The rhythms are frequently monotonous and the sense invariably ends with the line. The suppleness of the best poems written in England has gone. Symptomatic is "Song (On seeing dead bodies floating off the Cape)": what is realised most intensely are the details of home rather than the scene of the experience.

Lewis's best poems are at once the touchstones of his weaknesses and the attestations of his importance. "Goodbye", with its relaxed, unassuming tone, its humility before the details of the scene, is a poem that needs no grand meaning to give it significance. Lewis, between a deeply touching beginning and a finely handled conclusion, attempts to modulate into generalisation, only to deflate the poem with vacuous sentiments:

> So we must say Goodbye, my darling,
> And go, as lovers go, for ever;
> Tonight remains, to pack and fix on labels
> And make an end of lying down together.
>
> I put a final shilling in the gas,
> And watch you slip your dress below your knees
> And lie so still I hear your rustling comb
> Modulate the autumn in the trees . . .
>
> We made the universe to be our home,
> Our nostrils took the wind to be our breath,
> Our hearts are massive towers of delight,
> We stride across the seven seas of death.
>
> Yet when all's done you'll keep the emerald
> I placed upon your finger in the street;
> And I will keep the patches that you sewed
> On my old battledress tonight, my sweet.

The title poem of the first book epitomises in its sixteen lines the main features of Lewis's poetry:

> Softly the civilized
> Centuries fall,
> Paper by paper,
> Peter by Paul.
>
> And lovers waking
> From the night—
> Eternity's masters,
> Slaves of Time—
> Recognize only
> The drifting white
> Fall of small faces
> In pits of lime.
>
> Blue necklace left
> On a charred chair
> Tells that Beauty
> Was startled there.
>   ("Raiders' Dawn")

There is a lyric intensity behind the muted movement, and a direct handling of emotion without protective irony. The first four lines have a felt particularity, despite the general nature of the first statement. It is with "lovers" that the authenticity of the poem begins to be shaken, and "Eternity's masters/Slaves of Time" shows the proclivity for poetic cliché that was a characteristic failure for Lewis. A much sharper and more powerful resolution is attained in the suggestiveness of the final detail, which in fact shows up the taste for the "literary" behind the superficially impressive "drifting white/Fall of small faces".

It is easy to outline Lewis's apparent limitations: the almost trite moral positions that seem to be substituted for poetic resolution in some poems; his uncircumspect decency; his tendency to immature "poeticising" about love. Concerning the censoring of his men's letters, Lewis wrote of "all of us cherishing the same simplicities, afraid to lose the same things"[37]. Lewis's honesty in admitting to this shared simplicity is an aspect of his centrality as a poet of wartime experience. The absence of irony concerning the simple and everyday is related to this centrality and to his attainments.

Lewis was only too well aware of the distance between himself as an intellectual and the ordinary soldier. Indeed, there is a sense of mission in his attitude towards himself and his work that is disturbingly at odds with his proclaimed humility. Someone told him "You're the most selfish man I've ever met, Lewis. You think the war exists for you to write books about."[38] But, after reading *Brighton Rock*, Lewis wrote: "I feel a sort of horror at the gusto with which so many writers portray the detailed disintegration and instability and bewilderment of modern humanity."[39] Elsewhere he complained that "the poets today, they break up, they analyse, then they leave it."[40] His decency and his straightforwardness were considered things, and were behind the individuality of tone of his best poetry.

> And we stretched out, unbottoning our braces,
> Smoking a Woodbine, darning dirty socks.
> Reading the Sunday papers—I saw a fox
> And mentioned it in a note I scribbled home;—
> And we talked of girls, and dropping bombs on Rome,
> And thought of the quiet dead and the loud celebrities
> Exhorting us to slaughter, and the herded refugees . . .
>
> ("All Day It Has Rained")

The adapting of the everyday to poetry without the protective denigration of irony and without sentimentality was an attainment not common in the poetry of the day. It was to become an important component, years later, of the tone of Philip Larkin's poetry. This tone is a mark of the centrality of Lewis's poetry, which gives authentic and classic voice to what so many poems by young soldiers tried to capture. Lewis, like many who fought in World War II, had considered being a pacifist. It seemed to him better to be killed than to kill; and, as he approached the action he never encountered, he spoke of "the foulest day"—the day in which he would be part of the killing. His unspoiled sense of the human dimension of the war makes him the poet whose work speaks most typically and powerfully of the experience of those years.

IV

Another writer who found poetry through the war was Charles Causley. Causley was born in Launceston in Cornwall in 1917, and before the war had published some plays. In 1940 he was called up and chose the Navy, where he served as a coder until his release in 1946. "It was Hitler who pushed a subject under my nose; and the fact that poetry could be put together in one's head—when working at other jobs, lying half-asleep in a hammock, sitting in a bar—and written down complete, on a bit of paper the way a play or novel or short-story couldn't, gave me a form."[41]

Causley did not publish any books of poems until *Farewell Aggie Weston* (1951) and *Survivor's Leave* (1953). These early books contain some of his most memorable work. His poems from the war years appear to have been mainly realistic. "Chief Petty Officer" gives a brilliant and acid treatment of its subject that depends on the juxtaposition and sharp rendering of detail:

> He writes on your draft-chit,
> Tobacco-permit or request-form
> In a huge antique Borstal hand,
> And pins notices on the board in the Chiefs' Mess
> Requesting his messmates not to
> Lay on the billiard table . . .
>
> Or when you return
> Browner than Alexander, from Malta,
> Where you have leaned over the side, in harbour,
> And seen in the clear water
> The salmon-tins, wrecks and tiny explosions of crystal fish,
>
> A whole war later
> He will still be sitting under a pussar's clock
> Waiting for tot-time,
> His narrow forehead ruffled by the Jutland wind.

Causley was one of the few poets to see the war continuously from the point of view of the lower ranks.

These realistic poems are low-toned and offer no comment or philosophical reflection. Nevertheless, they give a greater sense of the vulnerability of human life and aspiration in wartime than do many poems that present horror full-face:

> We sit here, talking of Barea and Lorca,
> Meeting the iron eye of the Spanish clock.
> We have cut, with steel bows, the jungle of salt-water,
> Sustaining the variable sea-fevers of home and women,
> To walk the blazing ravine
> Of the profitable Rock . . .
>
> Rain's vague infantry, the Levant, parachutes on the stone lion
> And soon, soon, under our feet and the thin steel deck
> We shall be conscious of miles of perpendicular sea,
> And Admiralty weather.
>
> ("Conversation in Gibraltar")

Menace is suggested in the vocabulary—"Cut, with steel bows" or "Sustaining the variable sea-fevers"; and nowhere more than in the understated phrase "conscious of miles of perpendicular sea", where the juxtaposition of "perpendicular" and the measurement of depth in "miles" is strongly vertiginous.

There is a quite explicit debt to Louis MacNeice in these poems, as in "Homage to Louis MacNeice"; while "HMS Glory" simulates the movement and echoes the opening of MacNeice's "Carrickfergus":

> I was born on an Irish sea of eggs and porter,
> I was born in Belfast, in the Macneice country,
> A child of Harland & Wolff in the iron forest,
> My childbed a steel cradle slung from a gantry.

There is also a considerable debt to John Betjeman's rendering of everyday detail in traditional verse forms. A poem from the fifties is "Betjeman, 1984", and the title of another, "On Seeing a Poet of the First World War on the Station at Abbeville" is clearly meant to recall Betjeman's "On Seeing an Old Poet in the Café Royal". This influence of Betjeman is felt in the opening of a very characteristic and powerful early poem, "A Ballad for Katherine of Aragon":

> As I walked down by the river
> Down by the frozen fen
> I saw the grey cathedral
> With the eyes of a child of ten.
> O the railway arch is smoky
> As the Flying Scot goes by
> And but for the Education Act
> Go Jumper Cross and I.

However, the Betjeman manner is then acclimatised to a style redolent
of the folk ballad:

> The olive tree in winter
> Casts her banner down
> And the priest in white and scarlet
> Comes up from the muddy town.
> O never more will Jumper
> Watch the Flying Scot go by
> His funeral knell was a six-inch shell
> Singing across the sky.

Causley related:

> I think the event that affected me more than anything else in those years
> was the fact that the companion who had left my home-town with me for
> the navy in 1940 was later lost in a convoy to Russia. From the moment I
> heard this news, I found myself haunted by the words in the twenty-fourth
> chapter of St. Matthew: "Then shall two be in the field; and one shall be
> taken, and the other left." If my poetry is "about" anything, it is this.[42]

The death of his friend, the death of Henry VIII's dismissed queen,
and Causley's experience of watching Spanish girls swimming during
the war, are brought together in the ballad-like framework to give a
timeless but powerfully bitter aspect to the poet's sense of loss:

> O the Queen of Castile has a daughter
> Torn out by the roots
> Her lovely breast in a cold stone chest
> Under the farmers' boots.
>
> Now I like a Spanish party
> And many O many the day
> I have watched them swim as the night came dim
> In Algeciras Bay . . .
>
> O shall I leap in the river
> And knock upon paradise door
> For a gunner of twenty-seven and a half
> And a queen of twenty-four?
> From the almond tree by the river
> I watch the sky with a groan
> For Jumper and Kate are always out late
> And I lie here alone.

The use of the ballad and other older forms supports the casting back
of contemporary emotion into an archetypal framework—often into a
dream or fantasy setting, where the emotion, though particularised in
sensuous detail and still contemporary in reference, is isolated in naked

directness. At times Causley's modern ballads are reminiscent of Kipling, with their combination of Naval slang, contemporary detail and archaic manner; but Causley early gave the form a quality entirely original:

> Oh mother my mouth is full of stars
> As cartridges in the tray
> My blood is a twin-branched scarlet tree
> And it runs all runs away.
>
> Oh *Cooks to the Galley* is sounded off
> And the lads are down in the mess
> but I lie by the forrard gun
> With a bullet in my breast.
>
> ("Song of the Dying Gunner A.A. 1")

The firmness and individuality of the idiom is attested to by the way in which it carries "lads" as a working class term with no suggestion, so frequent in modern balladry, of Housman's sentimentality. Indeed, Causley's simple forms imply and permit naively pure attitudes against which experience is judged. The diction is contemporary, as, within the traditional forms, are the rhythms. The stance is anti-romantic; and a distinct poetic persona is created from the interplay of the traditional forms and the modern experience.

This manner was to be the most frequent in Causley's later poetry; and, as he himself suggests, he revisits his theme, deepening it with new (or old) associations:

> I am that man who asked no hate, nor pity.
> I am that man, five-wounded, on the tree.
> I am that man, walking his native city,
> Hears his dead comrade cry, Remember me!
>
> ("For an ex-Far East Prisoner of War")

V

Many British writers found themselves, like Roy Fuller and Alun Lewis, separated from England for long periods by the war. Indeed, all the land fighting between Dunkirk and the Normandy was far away, so that no home leave was possible. The feelings of exile became a frequent subject of war poetry. Nowhere was this more pronounced than in North Africa, where the armies faced one another from 1940 to 1943. When Italy entered the war in 1940, the Middle East became shut off; and, with the occupation of Greece by the Germans in 1941, many British civilians found themselves faced with the prospect of spending the rest of the war in Egypt. Among these were Olivia Manning, Robert Liddell, Bernard Spencer, Robin Fedden and Lawrence Durrell. Fedden had known Durrell and Spencer in Athens; and, with manuscripts likely to take three months to reach England, they decided, in the summer of 1941, to start a poetry periodical, *Personal Landscape*. The first issue, in January, 1942, contained contributions by the three friends, together with a piece by Terence Tiller, who taught along with Spencer and Fedden at Fuad al Awal University in Cairo.

"The title expressed our wish to emphasize the importance of personal life and values when the current of all thought and feeling around us set strongly in the channels of war . . ."[43]. It was the sense of being exiles that brought the contributors together—though ". . . not . . . the tragedy of exile . . . but rather . . . its *stagnation*."[44] Many things conspired to make the exiles feel not only cut off from England, but locked into a confining and unhappy situation. The climate, with its extremely hot periods and its absence of well defined seasons, did not suit the British, and they felt isolated in an Islamic civilisation whose underlying assumptions they were not familiar with. Linguistically they were cut off from the real Egypt, and their contacts were largely with the Europeanised upper classes and their pseudo-French culture. Finally, there was the appalling physical experience that a city like Cairo offered: "Such a country," Lawrence Durrell wrote to Anne Ridler,"—cripples, deformities, ophalmia, goitre, amputations, lice, flies. In the street you see horses cut in half by careless drivers . . . One writes nothing but short and febrile like jets by this corrupt and slow Nile . . ."[45]

Robbin Fedden's "The White Country", in the first issue of *Personal Landscape*, captures the nostalgia and listlessness of exile:

> Time, like snow, blurs the clear shape of things;
> And drifting even on our hands
> Obscures the gesture and intent.
> We do not know the landmarks any more,
> Cannot tell what people we once were.
> Like ghosts we wander in our tracks,
> Carrying dimmed intentions
> Through the still white country.
> If it were possible
> To take a bearing and be gone
> We should have found a way to go;
> We should have left long since.
> But Time, like snow, drifts everywhere,
> Mantles the beating heart;

> You see there's nothing here,
> Nothing but the white fields;
> And we can never leave.
>
> *(PL* I, 1 (Jan., 1942) 7)

The same issue contains "Aegean Islands" and "Delos" by Bernard Spencer and "To Argos" by Lawrence Durrell and a letter from the Greek poet George Seferis (then in Pretoria). Their sense of exile was as much from the Greek world as from Britain—a world that they were constantly reminded of in Cairo and in Alexandria, the one time home of the great modern Greek poet Cavafy, who is the subject of two short articles in *Personal Landscape*. Modern Greek poems were among the most important pieces published in the periodical: Elite Papadimitriou's own translation of parts of her long poem *Anatolia;* and the first English version of George Seferis's "The King of Asine"—one of the great poems of the twentieth century, then ony recently written.

The impact of Greek civilisation and the Greek landscape is strongly felt in the poems of Bernard Spencer published in *Personal Landscape*. During the nineteen-thirties, Spencer had been associated with *New Verse,* and his poetry had shown not only the respect for intelligence and the honesty of observation that was characteristic of that periodical, but also a poised, mature humanity that was something unusual in an era of much displayed ideological concern for the oppressed. It was in this decade that his style was formed; though his career as a poet was one of slow and intermittent flowering: the original *Collected Poems* of 1965 was little longer than many single volumes of poetry. His years in Cairo were one of his productive periods and saw important changes in his work. They culminated in the publication of his first book of poetry, *Aegean Islands,* in 1946.

The title poem of that volume seems to show, in its sharpness of observation, what Spencer called his "very strong visual sense"[46]; while the movement of this and other poems in the book is suggestive of the relaxed tone of Cavafy or Seferis:

> . . . To sun one's bones beside the
> Explosive, crushed-blue, nostril-opening sea
> (The weaving sea, splintered with sails and foam,
> Familiar of famous and deserted harbours,
> Of coins with dolphins on and fallen pillars.) . . .
>
> The dark bread
> The island wine and the sweet dishes;
> All these are elements in a happiness

More distant now than any date like '40,
A.D. or B.C., ever can express.

(PL I, 1 (Jan., 1942) 3)

Seferis provided an important formative friendship for Spencer in those years, when, from 1942, he was Press Officer in Cairo for the Greek government in exile: Spencer saw a great deal of him and frequently showed him poems, manuscripts of which have survived among Seferis's papers. In a contribution to *Personal Landscape* (2,3) Seferis wrote "All poems written or unwritten exist . . . The special ability of the poet is to see them . . . The faculty of seeing them makes the poet . . ."; and Spencer, in a note he wrote shortly before his death for the *Poetry Book Society Bulletin* to accompany *With Luck Lasting* in 1963, remembered how he "learnt . . . from . . . Seferis, to think of poems as sometimes waiting around to be written . . ."[47] Such an approach to poetry would no doubt have been congenial to Spencer, whose work very largely mirrors the events of his life; while the accent on "seeing", reinforced by the powerful visual impact of the Greek landscape and modern Greek poetry, must have had a great deal to do with expanding Spencer's sensibility into areas untouched by his poetry of the thirties.

"On the Road", which appeared in *Penguin New Writing* in 1947, is very much a Seferis poem, despite the setting of the central memory in France:

Our roof was grapes, and the broad hands of vine
as we two drank in the vine-chinky shade
of harvest France;
and wherever the white road led we could not care,
it had brought us there
to the arbour built on a valley side where Time,
if Time any more existed, was that river
of so profound a current, it at once
both flowed and stayed.

This celebration of a moment when time "both flowed and stayed" in a place that "for a lifetime glows with noon" recalls the tension in Seferis's poetry between the burning immediacy of experience and its temporal elusiveness. Spencer brings the poem home in his own way "making/words to say 'grapes' and 'her skin'."—asserting, as always, with this conclusion, the primacy of the particular, and turning away from any clinching generalisation. He must, at the time the poem was published, have been working with Lawrence Durrell and Nanos Valaoritis on their cooperative translation of Seferis's poetry, *The King of*

Asine and Other Poems (1948). He also collaborated in translations of poems by Odysseus Elytis that appeared about the same time. Spencer shared Seferis's preoccupation with time and the strange and sad perspectives its passage brings—something both had in common with one of Spencer's earliest and decisive models, Edward Thomas. "The Building of the House" pays homage to Thomas's poem "The New House".

Spencer was to say of his poetry, in an interview in 1962, that ". . . being in some sort of continuity with earlier civilisations does have an exciting effect on me . . . It is the only recurrent theme, if there is one, that I can think of." He saw himself as ". . . interested . . . in people in a landscape, with some dramatic situation. But very much . . . in the landscape with them, because . . . the landscape is involved in their feeling."[48]

> All day they had worshipped at the Virgin's picture
> and now they camped, their families and their beasts,
> with harness and piled fruit and mothers suckling
> around the little mountain church, or moved
> among the stalls, where tradesmen cried.
> The petrol flares lit light and dark; and starlight
> and the blind peaks and resin bleeding forests
> cupped them above the plain.
>
> What brought them riding here were not our customs,
> and yet it was good to share their food with them
> —wine from the village and white cheese—and know them
> across some hundred years with their high boots
> and great moustaches. And their songs,
> love songs and bawdy songs at fall of night,
> said after-things which rang like that cold air
> as, one voice sang
> under the dark trees; "If I entered Heaven
> and did not find you there and your little breasts
> I should understand nothing."
>
> ("Peasant Festival")

Though the poem is meditative, like "On the Road", it is not rounded out by a comment, but by an observed detail: the significance of the experience is felt through the accumulated observations of people and their setting. This deliberate resting in the particular and the reluctance to extrapolate from it is seen in poem after poem, and very notably in "On the Carved Axle-Piece of a Sicilian Cart" (1947) which recalls an early admiration, Louis MacNeice:

> The village craftsman stirred his bravest yellow
> and (all the carpentry and carving done)

put the last touches to his newest cart,
until no playing-card had brighter panels;
with crested knights in armour, king and crown,
Crusaders slaughtering infidels, and crimson
where the blood laves . . .

Though Spencer's poetry is marked by a poise that is a manifestation of a civilised acceptance of experience, he said, in a note in *Personal Landscape,* that poetry "has also to be rooted in the uncivilised layers of the mind, where what is ugly and what is beautiful can both be contemplated and do not exclude each other." (*PL* 1,4(1942)2) The sense of powerful experiences lurking forgotten or hidden beneath the everyday surface is there in many of his poems, especially in "Greek Excavations" or "In an Auction Room":

the terrible settee
with worn red flowers, the table de nuit,
the picture with the little man
walking the infinite road
to a West of gold:
these have all been (and are to be)
loves truer than our human mould,
or desperate walls
flung up against the shock of things,
what has no name; or growing old.

The mundane and the objects of ecstasy jostle in his poems, with an effect that is at once humbling and enhancing. In his poems of the Middle East, he is drawn by the ever present reminder of the generations of the dead whose achievements are forgotten, and of the millions of poor for whom acceptance without achievement is the only spiritual lot. Yet he is not drawn to pity or disgust: "Pity and disgust . . . are . . . attitudes of separation, not of joining . . . True poetry is a dance in which you take part and enjoy yourself." (*PL* 1,4(1942) 2)

Aegean Islands was published by Poetry London in 1946 at the end of the wartime interest in poetry. It brought together sixteen poems from the thirties and twenty-two from the forties—a small gathering, but one that should have established an unmistakable and important poetic voice. Yet it passed largely unnoticed in an atmosphere unpropitious for the recognition of its virtues of tact, understatement and precise observation. The same may be said of *The King of Asine and Other Poems,* the volume of translations of Seferis's poetry that Spencer produced in 1948 with Durrell and Nanos Valaoritis: the first collection of Seferis's poetry to appear in English, its original edition was still available when John Lehmann's publishing house closed four years later. During the period between the end of the war and Spencer's illness in 1948, his poems appeared in *Penguin New Writing, Poetry London* and other periodicals; but it was only with his death in 1963 and the revival of interest in the poetry of the thirties that his work got any considerable attention.

Besides the work of its three founders and their friend Terence Tiller, *Personal Landscape* included contributions from Olivia Manning, Robert Liddell, Hugh Gordon Porteus and a few other English writers. There were translation from Rilke by Ruth Spiers, the wife of John Spiers, who was then at Fuad al Awal University; and Keith Douglas left poems with them when he went back to the Western Desert. The magazine ran for eight issues, rising from 16 pages at its beginning to 20 pages in later issues. It closed in 1945. "For three years it has provided a vehicle, the only one available in English, for serious poets and critics in the Middle East. It has also, at a time when propaganda colours all perspectives, emphasized those 'personal landscapes', which lie obstinately outside national and political frontiers. Today with the end of the European war almost in sight . . . there is no longer literary isolation . . . the present number of *Personal Landscape* is to be the last. We prefer to die at meridian." (*PL* 2,4 (1945)) *Personal Landscape* may not be particularly rewarding to return to, because so many of its poems are familiar from the collections of Lawrence Durrell, Bernard Spencer, Terence Tiller aand Keith Douglas; yet, in spite of its small size and small number of issues, it remains one of the most impressive verse periodicals of the decade.

Personal Landscape was not the only literary periodical of war-time Cairo. An international group that included the poet John Waller constituted itself the Salamander Club and produced *Salamander. Salamander* included poetry by Waller, G.S. Fraser and Hamish Henderson, but most of the contributions were decidedly (and deliberately) traditional. From the Anglo-Egyptian Institute *Citadel* was edited by David Hicks: it published work by Keith Douglas.[49] There was also *Orientations*, which Douglas regarded as a "shocker",[50] and which was evidently jeered at by civilian poets like Bernard Spencer. It was put out by the Victory Club "to give the common soldier a chance to express himself"; though G.S. Fraser, who had a strong hand in it, felt that it was unsuccessful in this, in addition to not being a literary success.[51] That there was a need for expression is attested to by the two anthologies of poems from the Eighth Army—*Poems from the Desert* (1944) and *Poems from Italy* (1945); though nobody of the least literary reputation contributed to either.

VI

Interest in poetry that concerned itself with war collapsed within a year of the conclusion of hostilities. Books that had run through more than one edition during the war were to remain, in some cases for decades, on publisher's shelves. The war left no literary heroes whose work was to influence a new generation of writers, as had the work of Owen after the first World War. The poetry of World War II does not loom large in the history of English poetry in the twentieth century. Nor does the poetry of World War I, despite the reverant mythology that surrounds it. Yet the writing that came out of the first war has entered the consciousness of the nation as an emblem and a focus of awareness for a catastrophe that delivered an unforgettable shock to our conception of what existence might hold. There was more in World War II to afront our conception of civilised humanity: the gas chambers; 20 million Russian dead; the Japanese treatment of prisoners of war; the thousand bomber raids; the atom bomb. They were not, on the whole, part of immediate British experience; and much of the horror became known only after the war. In any case, after the first world war, nothing could ever shock in quite the same way.

Chapter 12

THE O.C.T.U. GENERATION

The wartime generation—Cambridge poetry—John Heath-Stubbs—
Sidney Keyes—David Wright, William Bell—Drummond Allison—
Keith Douglas—Alan Ross—other poets

It might be argued that the poets who should have been remembered
as the poets of the forties were those who came of age early in the
decade. As will be seen, in the main the talent of their generation was
either aborted by war or flowered late.

These were the writers who, in Alex Comfort's phrase, had grown
"from early adolescence in the almost complete certainty that we
should be killed in action"[1]. They were called by Sidney Keyes "the
O.C.T.U generation", after the Officer Cadet Training Units to which
many of them belonged, often while at the university. With few exceptions, they did not view the war politically—in contrast with the generation before them, who had tried, by political means, to avert a war
with fascism.

The most celebrated book in its day by a member of this generation—and one deserving of continued memory—was Richard Hillary's
The Last Enemy (1942). Hillary was shot down and severely burned
in the Battle of Britain; but, after repeated surgery, he insisted on
returning to active service, only to be killed shortly afterwards. The
autobiographical *The Last Enemy* made him the first literary hero of
the war.

His attitude to the war at its outset was far from heroic:

> We were depressed by a sense of its inevitability, but we were not patriot-
> ic . . . we were convinced that we had been needlessly led into the pre-
> sent world crisis, not by unscrupulous rogues, but worse, by the bungling
> of a crowd of incompetent old fools. We hoped merely that when war
> came it might be fought with a maximum of individuality and a minimum
> of discipline. (14)

He recalled too that

> the seed of self-destruction among the more intellectual members of the
> University was even more evident. Despising the middle-class society to
> which they owed their education and position, they attacked it, not with
> vigour but with adolescent petulance. They were encouraged in this by
> their literary idols, by their unquestioning allegiance to Auden, Isherwood,
> Spender, and Day Lewis. (15)

238

This tallies with the impression that John Lehmann had of the young men at Cambridge at the time "as being without any faith or spiritual impulse . . . an emptiness that reminded me of the Germans of the same generation I had known before the war broke out."[2] A characteristically supercilious tone is found in John Waller's editorial in his new Oxford periodical, *Kingdom Come:* "The hedonist in the early days of war has a faith only a little below that of the pacifist. For in war time it is not so much that pleasure is the chief good, it is the only good." (I,2 (Dec-Jan, 1939-40) 35)

Yet what emerges from *The Last Enemy* is unwavering decency and courage. "Twenty-four of us flew south that tenth day of August 1940: of those twenty-four, eight were to fly back." (100)[3] The fact that of his group of friends only he was left alive by early 1941 was what drove Hillary back to active service. The experience of living and fighting with a group that was slowly obliterated was more common in World War II than popular memory allows, particularly for the young.

Those who came to maturity after the war began seem to have questioned it less and to have had little cynicism concerning it. Two anthologies introduced new poets of the day, *Poets of Tomorrow: Cambridge Poetry 1940* and *Eight Oxford Poets* (1941), and they revealed a developing attitude. The introductory note to the Cambridge volume states:

> These poets are oppressed by a general feeling of disgust at the world as it is, and are less certain than the poets of the 'thirties of finding an obvious way out; the political note is less insistent, and there is an increase in imaginative fantasy. At the same time they feel that their constant aim should be to write as simply and directly as possible, and this goes hand in hand with an interest in the ballad and all forms of popular art . . . they would all like to write some form of contemporary legend.

Introducing the Oxford volume a year or so later, Sidney Keyes wrote:

> We seem to share a horror at the world's predicament, together with the feeling that we cannot save ourselves without some kind of spiritual readjustment, though the nature of that readjustment may take widely differing forms . . . we are all . . . *Romantic* writers, though by that I mean little more than our greatest fault is a tendency to floridity; and that we have, on the whole, little sympathy with the Audenian school of poets.

II

Cambridge Poetry: 1940 included poems by Stephen Coates, Alex Comfort, Maurice James Craig, Nicholas Moore, George Scurfield, Gervase Stewart and Terence Tiller—to name only those who were to

publish books of poems during the decade. Some of them, such as
Terence Tiller, had been at Cambridge in the last years of the thirties;
and the work of the group does not constitute as great a reaction to
the poetry of the previous decade as was contended. Their interest in
"imaginative fantasy" is found in the work of Auden and of Kenneth
Allott; while their "interest in the ballad" had been evinced by both
Auden and *Contemporary Poetry and Prose*. The poetry of Nicholas
Moore, despite his later association with the Apocalypse movement,
had from the beginning an Audenesque stylishness:

> Do you see there the ugly twist
> In the one-eyed man or the face unkissed,
> > The unloved and unloving?
> > > ("Song II": *Cambridge Poetry* 1940)

The same may be said of the poetry of his friend Gervase Stewart.
Stewart was the only contributor to the Cambridge volume to be killed
in the war, and his poems were edited posthumously as *No Weed
Death* (1942) by Henry Treece. Posthumously too he was included in
The Crown and the Sickle (1943), the last of the Apocalypse anthologies. In fact his best poems have an urbane blend of "imaginative
fantasy" and a sensitive awareness of the everyday world that was
characteristic of the poetry of the thirties:

> He craved no weed death but a rose extinction,
> Gracefully by degrees, resolved his dying
> Should be more dignified, without compunction
> Upon the family four poster lying,
> All his relations standing by his side
> To hear some final words before he died.
> > ("Obituary Notice for the Squire")

His book contained few notable successes: there was nothing written
after the end of 1940, when he was twenty.

A Cambridge poet not included in Lehmann's collection was Brian
Allwood. While still at school, he had poems in *Twentieth Century
Verse*. He was one of the few poets before the fifties to show the
influence of the leading Cambridge modernist, William Empson.

> Who lives alone in cut-throat Europe,
> Where man grows permanent, but not to-day
> Will see wild horses at the gallop?
> Adam or man, his latest isotope?
> Trouble his veins but let him get away.
> > ("Getting the Best")

He attains at his best a sharp and mordant vision that depends on a stylishness derived from Empson and Auden:

> Now is the time when all the doubtful fables,
> Deeper than fish-shop violence, may uncurl
> And stretch between the polished fingers of that girl
> Playing so lightly along kitchen tables.
>
> ("Atmosphere")

Allwood was killed in action in Italy in 1944. One small pamphlet of his work was published, *Now or Never* (1943). The attainment is slight, but the orientations are interesting. In a letter to *The New Saxon Review,* he summed up an embarrassment of many aspiring poets of his age: "I think most people still feel Auden looking over their shoulder, and they don't know which way to run. In which direction will the new hegira be?" (I, 47).

The Cambridge poets showed little stylistic cohesiveness; and those, such as Comfort, Moore and Tiller, who were to make any impression were to do so independently of one another. Their work has already been discussed. Scurfield and Coates, like Moore, had volumes published by Tambimuttu—possibly at Moore's suggestion. They were not among Editions Poetry London's successes.

III

The "Eight Oxford Poets" were Keith Douglas, Gordon Swaine, John Heath-Stubbs, Michael Meyer, Roy Porter, Drummond Allison, J.A. Shaw and Sidney Keyes. In contrast to the Cambridge poets, most of them had come to maturity after the war began; though Douglas had left Oxford in 1940, and the characterisation of the group by Keyes as "Romantic writers" hardly seems to apply to him. In so far as the introductory remarks have any validity, they apply to a group of friends—Heath-Stubbs, Keyes and David Wright (not included in the collection), of whom the slightly older Heath-Stubbs was the literary mentor. At the close of the decade, Heath-Stubbs published a study, *The Darkling Plain* (1950), in which he praised largely forgotten minor Romantics—Darley, Beddoes, Clare and Doughty—along with the then maligned pre-Raphaelites. He published a volume of translations from Leopardi in 1947, and became a great admirer of Charles Williams, after hearing him lecture at Oxford in 1943. These admirations formed the literary ambience of his friendship with Keyes.

This orientation was highly original in the early nineteen-forties, when "Romantic" was, in many circles, an unfavourable critical term.

Heath-Stubbs remarked: "The modern poet who deliberately rejects the Romantic tradition, rejects an experience through which the European consciousness has passed, and which has affected it profoundly."[4] The poets to whom he gave attention illustrate, however, the unavailability at the time of Wordsworth and the other great Romantics as a basis for creative reaction to modernism. The "romanticism" of Keyes and Heath-Stubbs and their friends owes little to other movements of the period: and Heath-Stubbs made this clear in an early article "Tradition or Anarchy?" in *Cherwell* in 1941, where he calls Tambimuttu's stance "the *reductio ad absurdum* of the Romantic method, with its emphasis on the importance of the writer's personality and his private emotions". He goes on to call for "the return to the classical tradition of English poetry". Important for Heath-Stubbs were minor Augustan poets, such as Lady Winchilsea and John Gay. Indeed, an article "The Poetry of John Gay" in *Cherwell* in February, 1941, seems to mark a turning point for him. His earliest undergraduate poetry had been ironical and slightly Audenesque: the first poem in the true Stubbsian manner seems to be "Pavanne Pour Une Infante Defunte", which appeared in March, 1941. From then on we see the emergence of his characteristic early style, with its background of the lesser Romantics, the minor Augustans and the pastoral tradition.

Heath-Stubbs's first collection of poetry, *Wounded Thammuz* (1942), takes as its theme "the resurrection of God in and controlling history".[5] Its structural myth is the death and rebirth of the Babylonian Thammuz, to which Heath-Stubbs gives Fraserian and allegorical undertones. A long poem, divided into parts and sub-sections, the book is striking in its combination of the fresh and the archaic to achieve a stylish pastoral quality. The movement of the verse and the flow and interplay of vowel and consonant are unusually deft for a first collection.

> Southward, O wind, seeking the trellised vine,
> Long has the fickle-pinioned swallow flown,
> To amethystine clusters; but your breath,
> Though nursing next year's seeds, rudely shall pine
> Those birds who salt with song your bitter teeth . . .

It has a Tennysonian mellifluousness, and the book is strongly literary in inspiration, recalling self-consciously the minor Milton and the classical pastoral tradition; though it was original in combining these influences to bring a new tone to poetry. Heath-Stubbs's contributions to *Eight Oxford Poets* included a dramatic monologue, "Leporello", concerning the old servant of Don Juan:

Do you see that old man over there?—He was once a
    gentleman's gentleman;
His skull is bald and wrinkled like a leathery snake's egg;
His forehead is not high, but his eyes, though horny, are cunning.
Like an old jackdaw's beginning to moult a few grey feathers;
His nose is sharp like a weasel's, and his lips always a little smiling,
His narrow shoulders crouched forward, hinting a half-finished bow . . .
    He can remember his master well—those were the days!—
Feast days, Carnival days—fans and flowers and bright silk shawls
Tossing like a poppy-patched cornfield the wind dishevels,
And then the milky moonlight flowing over close-kept courtyards;
And while his master climbed the balcony, he would keep watch,
Whistle and rub his hands and gaze at the stars—
His co-panders . . .

The theme of Don Juan and his relationship to fear and death was evidently one that had haunted Heath-Stubbs for a long time. In the "Preface" to *Selected Poems* in 1965, he recalls that "Leporello" was "conceived when I was eighteen years old, though it was not written till about four years later". The movement of the voice is captured well, in the manner of the model, Browning. The stance is typical for Heath-Stubbs at the time: the outsider remembering lost experience or experience only vicariously attained. His second collection, *Beauty and the Beast* (1943), contains a number of pieces about exiled and departed heroes—"Stone-Age Woman", and "Edward the Confessor", with its thematic phrase "Some say this world is dying, being done with". In an early article on "The Poetic Achievement of Charles Williams", Heath-Stubbs wrote: "the Europe of the Dark Ages . . . presented a picture perhaps closer to our time than that of any intervening period—the civilisation of Europe threatened by the forces of barbarism, the rise of new phases of faith and patterns of society."[6] Such a view seems to have remained an abiding vision of things for Heath-Stubbs. However, as Alan Ross remarked, when *The Divided Ways,* Heath-Stubbs's third collection, appeared in 1946: ". . . 'The Old King' . . . may indeed symbolize a personal sense of frustration and exist validly as a direct expression of that sense of never being quite at the centre of life . . ."[7] The early poems are frequently a vehicle for the evocation of nostalgia for a world of tenderness now shattered.

Writing later on the influence of Charles Williams, Heath-Stubbs said: "Younger poets became interested in mythological and religious symbolism, as means of expressing areas of experience inaccessible to the intellect alone."[8] Of Leopardi he wrote: "Since the traditional forms of religious belief seemed largely to have lost their significance, the poets constructed their own systems, taking their symbols from revived mythologies, or from the experience of erotic passion or of natural beauty.''[9] These remarks (redolent of Yeats's retrospective view of his career) have a bearing on Heath-Stubbs's own poetry. In *The Divided Ways* and its successor, *The Swarming of the Bees* (1950), there are translations from the French symbolist poets Gerard de Nerval and Mallarmé, and a sonnet on Hart Crane, who sometimes used language in their suggestive manner. Their influence is felt in the language of the symbolic sonnet sequence that concludes *Beauty and the Beast,* "The Heart's Forest''; while one senses the presence of Mallarmé in some elusive but evocative handling of language in *The Divided Ways:*

> In the time of the unbearable tenderness of roses,
> And the small speaking bird among the quick-set thorn,
> The slow significance of swans, procession borne
> On dark but lucid streams, where softest air reposes . . .

Heath-Stubbs's early poetry is, paradoxically, freshest and most successful when it draws on literature or history for its inspiration, as in "An Heroic Epistle (From William Congreve to Anne Bracegirdle. Circa 1729)'':

> Now it has all gone black, you are more than ever
> The cadence of a voice to me, the turn of a prose phrase;
> For my words in your mouth were a movement in time,
> Like your hand's movement suddenly spreading the white
> Fan, your turned wrist twisting the air;
> Or the curve of your white neck, caught in a slant-light,
> The tilt of your chin, and your smile mocking, mocking—
> And then your laughter—and so your voice again.

The movement of the voice is captured well in the fluent variation within the long lines that Heath-Stubbs favoured.

In contrast to much modern poetry in English up to that time, Heath-Stubbs's early poetry is unironic—or tinged with a nostalgic, romantic irony. It was a mark of originality to turn his back, as he did after a few youthful (but uncollected) poems, on a tone that was still so highly favoured. Even though some of his first books may seem rather precious in style and subject matter, they had the distinction of offering a new tone—ethereal, wistful, accomplished:

> The winter moon that clambers through the pine-trees,
> Nor stirs the beaded rime upon their boughs,
> That haunts the forest with a pelt of ermine,
> Printing no trace upon the fallen leaves,

And breeds a silver blossom in my heart,
Finds the dew dry, the stream that cannot weep.
("Sestina")

In 1946 Heath-Stubbs brought out his volume of translations, *Poems
from Giacomo Leopardi*. It is easy to see the attraction of Leopardi.
Heath-Stubbs said of him "He is . . . at once a Romantic and a Classicist"[10]; and "Leopardi's language is highly literary and allusive. His
poems contain many echoes of the Greek and Latin classics, and turns
of phrase inherited from the Arcadians of the late seventeenth or
eighteenth centuries in Italy".[11] The remarks might be applied to
Heath-Stubbs's own poetry, particularly if "Augustans" were substituted for "Arcadians". Leopardi wrote in *endecasillabi*, the equivalent
of English blank verse, and in *canzone libera*, a form akin to the
freely rhyming verse of Milton's "Lycidas". Heath-Stubbs uses the
corresponding English forms widely in his earlier poetry, as well as
the poem in dialogue, also favoured by Leopardi. It is with Leopardi's
poetic stance, however, that Heath-Stubbs has the most in common:
Leopardi and Heath-Stubbs look on events from the outside. In
Leopardi this is associated with the sense of being excluded from experience—a feeling present in less extreme form in the poetry of
Heath-Stubbs.

As the decade came to a close, the historical and literary subjects
seemed to evoke a less vital response, and *The Swarming of the Bees*
(1950) is not so attractive, with its translations from the French and
the Provencal, and the long historical narrative of "Alexandria". In
the fifties, there came a change of style, marked by the ironic
"Epitaph" in the next collection, *A Charm Against the Toothache*
(1954). Nonetheless, there is a perceivable continuity to his work; and
he has been one of the few outstanding poets to come out of the brilliant Oxford of the early forties whose work shows such a continuity
with his beginnings.

IV

The most famous in his day of the eight Oxford poets was Sidney
Keyes, whose death in 1943 finally gave England the war poet it had
been looking for. At The Queen's College, he became friends with
Heath-Stubbs, who encouraged him to concentrate on poetry: Keyes
had already written two plays and a number of stories by his
eighteenth birthday. In an unpublished letter to David Wright, Keyes
spoke of "J.H.S., the fountain-head of my skill wherever I show
any."[12] Like Heath-Stubbs, Keyes was strongly drawn to literary sub-

jects, and his models, too, were the Romantic poets. It was his poem on William Wordsworth that so impressed Herbert Read, who, at Routledge, arranged the publication of *Eight Oxford Poets:* "One poem, 'William Wordsworth', immediately convinced me that Keyes was a poet in the absolute sense, and I can think of no English poet who has produced a comparable poem at the age of nineteen."[13]

> No room for mourning: he's gone out
> Into the noisy glen, or stands between the stones
> Of the gaunt ridge, or you'll hear his shout
> Rolling among the screes, he being a boy again.
> He'll never fail nor die
> And if they laid his bones
> In the wet vaults or iron sarcophagi
> Of fame, he'd rise at the first summer rain
> And stride across the hills to seek
> His rest among the broken lands and clouds.
> He was a stormy day, a granite peak
> Spearing the sky; and look, about its base
> Words flower like crocuses in the hanging woods,
> Blank though the dalehead and the bony face.

The poem achieves a distinctive, if rather bland tone, largely through the fluency of movement characteristic of Keyes. It is evocative, yet little is brought into focus, and even this rather plain poem is diffuse and whimsical. Its whimsicality is part of its charm, but also part of its attempt to be poetic. Whimsicality, diffuseness and poetic posturing are recurrent faults of Keyes's poetry. Typical is "War Poet":

> I am the man who looked for peace and found
> My own eyes barbed.
> I am the man who groped for words and found
> An arrow in my hand.

His proclivity for the literary rather than the actual extended to a tendency to pitch everything in a "poetic" key, with a constant avoidance of direct reference to experience. In the literary nature of his inspiration he had much in common with Heath-Stubbs, as also in the absence of irony from his poetry.

Keyes saw for himself an important role, though one pictured again in terms that are literary in a limiting sense: "I believe the greatest and most influential poets in the last 100 years or so to be Yeats and Rilke. There two brought back reports from a kind of Ultima Thule of Romanticism, which suggest that there is even more—much more—to be discovered there: and the starting point of my quest is therefore an attempt to synthesize this information."[14] He saw the twentieth cen-

tury as dominated by a death wish because there had been a failure to
accommodate death poetically: "that is why there had to be a "Poet
of Death" in C.20; and why Rilke is the most important European
poet since Goethe and Wordsworth", he wrote in his Notebook shortly
before he died.[15] His two longer poems, "The Foreign Gate" and
"The Wilderness", are clearly attempts to write the grand poem on
these lines, and both echo very obviously Yeats's later poems, the
Duino Elegies and *The Waste Land*.

> Were I to mount beyond the field
> Of battle and the lovers' wood to that high-pillared house
> Where the great sit, in stone unmoved yet knowing
> The world's minute catastrophes;
> . . . were I to speak out clear
> In that high house, a voice of light might answer.
>
> ("The Foreign Gate")

There is in fact no development in these sectioned poems, and much
reference to "drums" and "flags" and "bones" and "lovers", but
none to any aspect of the modern war in which Keyes was about to
fight. David Wright summed him up: "The references are not to life,
but literature; not to human beings, but cut-out figures from history
and legend . . . the fatally tempting romantic/literary high-falutin' that
disturbs so many of his poems." Wright went on to remark "how
consumingly ambitious Keyes was to be a poet."[16] That ambition
seems to have been a main impulse to his poetry. When we compare
him with another poet of precocious attainment, John Cornford, who
died in the Spanish Civil War—also near his twenty-first birthday, we
see how vacuous was Keyes's writing about death: "Young men walking the open streets/Of death's republic, remember your lovers" compares poorly with Cornford's "Heart of the heartless world,/Dear
heart, the thought of you/Is the pain at my side,/The shadow that
chills my view." Keyes's own poetry, in off-duty moments, reveals
by contrast his usual failings. The following poem, written at the age
of sixteen in memory of his grandfather, who brought him up, shows,
in its movement and imagery, a responsiveness to the resolution of
disturbing feeling too infrequent in Keyes's later work.

> It is a year again since they poured
> The dumb ground into your mouth;
> And yet we know, by some recurring word
> Or look caught unawares, that you still drive
> Our thoughts like the smart cobs of your youth—
> When you and the world were alive.
>
> ("Elegy")

Though Keyes owed a great deal to Heath-Stubbs stylistically, his work frequently resembles that of Alex Comfort, his contemporary at Cambridge. Both saw themselves as poets of "death", which they sought through their art to transcend; both had a proclivity for large, pseudo-Rilkean gestures. Comfort was an avowed anarchist; Keyes showed little partisan interest in politics: yet, despite Comfort's political fervency, they both give the feeling that all specificity has gone from ideology, leaving merely the manipulation of tokens of grander aspirations.

How did Keyes become the legend he became? His first book, *The Iron Laurel* (1942), did not gain much attention. His death in 1943 preceded the appearance of his second book, *The Cruel Solstice* (1944), and it was this that gave rise to the adulatory reviews on which his posthumous reputation was launched. Victoria Sackville-West wrote: "The astonishing maturity of his mind, the intense seriousness of his outlook, and his innate pre-occupation with major things, suggests that here potentially was the war-poet for whom England had been waiting."[17] *The Cruel Solstice* went through three printings in the first half of 1944, and Keyes became a part of the story of the war.

V

A friend of Heath-Stubbs and Keyes who did not appear in *Eight Oxford Poets* was David Wright. He took rooms at 52a High Street, an "inauspicious address as it turned out; nearly all the Oxford poets who took digs there in the forties were allotted early and violent deaths."[18] Keyes moved into the room beneath him, and Drummond Allison, also killed in the war, lived there. "Keyes' poetry," Wright recalled, ". . . was extraordinarily assured and polished; it hypnotized his contemporaries. Sooner or later everyone, including me, found himself writing Keyesian poems whose chief characteristic was a kind of romanticism one associates with the paintings of Fuseli."[19] Wright's first book, *Poems,* predominantly showed this influence, though this was in no way his true bent as a poet.

> Cloud and rain
> swell the black root, and bring
> the green lance of the alder and gold flowers;
> and the blind bird remembers Proserpine
> in whose cold womb the iron fruit remain
> that wait the sequence of the sliding hours . . .
>   ("Libra")

Poems gives a false impression, as it was one of the casualties of Tambimuttu's publishing antics. It appeared in 1949 (dated 1947); but, as Wright recalled, "The poems had been in the hands of the publisher since 1943 . . . The young man who wrote them had died around 1947."[20] A few of the poems, such as "Atlantic Eclogue", show the influence of George Barker; and, partly through his friendship with Barker, Wright came to a firmer and sparer rhetoric in his second collection, *Moral Stories* (1952). Even the expanded version of that book in 1954 was small, but its directness of engagement and the absence of any parade of polite sensitivity makes one feel that it would have been salutory had some of its poems been better known in the decade in which they were written.

> I walk beneath a powerless moon
> Where a sea creases like a face
> Turned upwards in the morning sun;
> A murderer from the barren park
> Where the self-wounded grips his breast,
> Waiting for the police. Who come
> Into the daylight from the dark?
> Four followers, and each 'I am'
> I shed at the septennium;
> They hold the knife into my back,
> And bend the neck I kneel upon.
> My blood must follow from my thrust,
> And this the hand that dealt the wound
> Write 'O assassin!' in the dust
> ("Images for a Fourth Septenary")

This change of style (recognised in the celebrated "A Funeral Oration" of 1951) is some measure of the limitations of the earlier Stubbsian manner, which Heath-Stubbs himself moved away from at about the same time.

52a High Street had a third victim. "Some time after Allison's death his room was taken by William Bell, a poet whose potentiality may have been greater than that of either [Keyes or Allison]", Wright remembered. "Bell died at twenty-four, killed while climbing the Matterhorn."[21] Wright's estimate is reinforced by Heath-Stubbs in his introduction to the posthumous collection, *Mountains Beneath the Horizon* (1950). Heath-Stubbs reported that Bell "distrusted the 'Romantic' formlessness which was beginning to be fashionable among undergraduate poets at Oxford"; but his love of images "drawn from the quasi-Pythagorean world of Ovid's *Metamorphoses*" and the fact that he "tended to see all mythical images as expressive of truth" puts his outlook in tune with that of Heath-Stubbs and Keyes.[22]

His admirations were Yeats and Pound, but he wrote frequently in older, highly rhetorical forms. His first book, *Elegies* (1946) (entirely distinct from the "Twelve Rhetorical Elegies" of *Mountains Beneath the Horizon*) shows, in its pastoral dialogues and complex Italianate forms, an affinity with the work of Heath-Stubbs, to whom the first poem is dedicated. There is, however, a firmness of diction not then cultivated by Heath-Stubbs, and a remarkably controlled amplitude of movement for a first book:

> Now I have come at evening all alone
> for the last time into this darkening valley,
> and now my heart is racing as I climb
> little by little to those ribs of stone
> and rippling heart of water.
>
> ("Elegy VI")

This facility is again evinced in the posthumous volume (parts of which may have been written before *Elegies*). However, there is a monotony of rhythm, and the penchant for mythological imagery leads to a mannered avoidance of direct reference to experience, such as marred the work of Keyes. Though Bell's potentiality may have been great, he left scarcely any poems that can be valued for the insights and perceptions that they offer.

The work of Heath-Stubbs, Keyes, Wright and Bell forms a romantic, "literary" backwater in the poetry of the forties. A product of literary friendships, it showed the influence of Heath-Stubbs's interest in minor writers of the eighteenth and nineteenth centuries, and had little in common with the "New Romanticism" of Treece and Schimanski. Its artificiality is attested to by the fact that Wright and Heath-Stubbs had to turn away from their early styles in order to find themselves again as poets in the fifties.

VI

More impressive in retrospect than Keyes is Drummond Allison. His posthumous collection, *The Yellow Night* (1944) contains far fewer achieved poems than Keyes's *Collected Poems,* but it is consistently vital and startling in its use of language. There is a compression of syntax and a tightness of argument reminiscent of Auden; and, like the young Auden, Allison is often in consequence obscure. However contorted the line of a poem—and Allison makes surprising changes of metaphor—one feels that this is in response to the patterns of feeling behind the poem.

So sorrow casts out sorrow, minus times
Minus makes plus. The truthful tapes are running
Across the minefields of my fear, and I
Can trace and follow them to-night.

("The Cold Thoughts")

Allison's poetry does not belong with that of Heath-Stubbs and Keyes stylistically. The vision is predominantly ironic, the language colloquial, and understatement and juxtaposition are frequent devices. "Wade", with similarities to Kingsley Amis's "Beowulf", could have found a place in *New Lines:*

Expunged from song the hero of the Churls,
Mentioned by Malory when absent-minded,
And no lies left about his grief amended
Who died refused by henwives and goosegirls.

The violence of his poetry is a reflection of his sense of the violence of the times, in face of which he finds no easy explanatory schema:

If soon by violence and political police, if soon our class
Is to be flung through doors it opened with such care,
If the cream telephones are to be answered
By black slouchcaps and oilstained dungarees
. . . if under similar standards
I too go down with some self-conscious laugh
Like one too late
Discovering the examiners were serious;

We shall have company who haunt that highway's ghost . . .
We shall ride out on quaggers, on mastodon and mammoth . . .

("We Shall Have Company")

Triumphs of tone are not to be expected from a poet who had so little time to form his style; yet there are passages where diction, imagery and movement are sensitively harmonised with the modulation he seeks:

Run up again, as gravely smile as ever,
Veer without fear your left unlucky arm
In His so dark direction, but no length
However lovely can disturb the harm
That is His style, defer the winning drive
Or shake the crowd from their uproarious calm.

("Verity", *Poetry from Oxford in Wartime*)

Most of his poems date from his time as undergraduate. He was killed on December 2nd, aged twenty-two.

VII

Keith Douglas was the only one of the "eight Oxford poets" who was killed in the war and who lived long enough to write poems about the experience of action and to begin to mature his style. He died a year younger than Wilfred Owen; and, as with Owen, an extended sick leave in the year before his death gave him the opportunity to write some of his best poems. Nevertheless, about half of the hundred or so pieces that make up his *Collected Poems* were written before he joined the army in 1940. He was killed in France in 1944, but was in action mainly in the Western Desert in the three months following the Battle of El Alamein in October, 1942.

Douglas, like Richard Hillary and John Waller, came to Oxford before the war; and, as with them, there is a tinge of disillusioned hedonism in his outlook. However, at his best, even in poems written before he saw action, Douglas is moving and impressive:

> Today, Cheng, I touched your face
> with two fingers, as a gesture of love;
> for I can never prove enough
> by sight or sense your strange grace,
>
> but mothwise my hands return
> to your fair cheek, as luminous
> as a lamp in a paper house,
> and touch, to teach love and learn.
>
> I think a hundred hours are gone
> that so, like gods, we'd occupy.
> But alas, Cheng, I cannot tell why,
> today I touched a mask stretched on the stone
>
> person of death. There was the urge
> to break the bright flesh and emerge
> of the ambitious cruel bone.
>   ("The Prisoner")

In this poem of reconciliation to the loss of love, the vulnerability and uncertainty that were so much a part of Douglas's experience and that of his generation coexist with a poise and acceptance that is achieved in the movement of the poem. The imagery evinces Douglas's customary vituosity, but here every element combines in the groping forward of experience to its resolution. The contrast of touch with hearing—the fingers tentative, the longing for the palpable that extends to the whole of his experience: this is perfectly married to the shifts of movement in the first three stanzas. This movement is finally broken as the threatening image of the bone asserts the possibility of death to which the love had been a hoped for but fragile counterpoise.

Douglas achieves a similar success in a poem in which he contemplates the oncoming offensive:

> this month will see Time fashion
>
> the action we begin
> and Time will cage again
> the devils we let run
> whether we lose or win:
>
> in the month's dregs will
> a month hence some descry
> the too late prophecy
> of what the month lets fall.
>
> ("The Offensive")

The repetition of "month", with the shift in perspective from puzzled and tense apprehension to prophecy after the event, reinforces the sense of the minds bafflement and its doubt concerning the issue or its value. The poem returns on itself with just that amount of resolution, elucidation and acceptance that the situation and its exploration will allow.

Douglas's poems derived from action do not achieve this type of success. The imagery has often the same brilliance and the same power to focus a particular experience or feeling, and the argument shows a similar tightness and suppleness in its ironic juxtaposition of perceptions; but the poet seems at a loss to find a resolution:

> Under the parabola of a ball,
> a child turning into man,
> I looked into the air too long.
> The ball fell in my hand, it sang
> in the closed fist: *Open Open*
> *Behold a gift designed to kill.*
>
> Now in my dial of glass appears
> the soldier who is going to die.
> He smiles, and moves about in ways
> his mother knows, habits of his.
> The wires touch his face: I cry
> NOW. Death, like a familiar, hears
>
> and look, has made a man of dust
> of a man of flesh.

One wonders whether the poem should not have ended here. It continues:

> This sorcery
> I do. Being damned, I am amused

> to see the centre of love diffused
> and the waves of love travel into vacancy.
> How easy it is to make a ghost.

One feels that Douglas himself is trying to find a way for the poem to continue—trying to find a centre for it. He concludes with another suggestive and delicately controlled image:

> The weightless mosquito touches
> her tiny shadow on the stone,
> and with how like, how infinite
> a lightness, man and shadow meet.
> They fuse. A shadow is a man
> when the mosquito death approaches.
>
> ("How to Kill")

Neither progression of argument nor progression of image brings the poem to a resolution, and in its explicit third stanza, with the rather playful and forced reference to witchcraft and damnation, it takes us away from the experience rather than into a resolving focus.

The poem went through "fourteen sheets of drafts and revisions".[23] In the development of this ironic style, in which his lyricism is deliberately broken up, Douglas was quite clear about what he was doing, as he protested to John Hall, who did not like his new poems:

> my object . . . is to write true things, significant things in words each of which works for its place in line. My rhythms, which you find enervated, are carefully chosen to enable the poems to be *read* as significant speech: I see no reason to be either musical or sonorous about things at present.

It was part of his attempt to be true to his experiences of the desert:

> I never tried to write about war . . . until I had experienced it. Now I will write of it, and perhaps one day cynic and lyric will meet and make me a balanced style.[24]

Yet, if we ask what truth, other than the purely factual, Douglas offers, we would stumble on the embarrassment that he himself seems to encounter at crucial points in some poems. There are local successes where the landscape and experience of war are tellingly evoked:

> dead tanks, gun barrels split like celery . . .
> . . . a man with no head
> has a packet of chocolate and a souvenir of Tripoli.
>
> ("Cairo Jag")

Douglas has a sharp eye for the conjunction of disparate things, often woven, with irony and levity, into an argument with Donnean syntax. Yet, too often, he is brought up short, as in "Negative Information":

> To this, there's no sum I can find—
> The hungry omens of calamity
> mixed with good signs and all received with levity,
> or indifference, by the amazed mind.

Here, as elsewhere, there is a coolness that seems to be suppressing all too immediate pressures—experience that ages too soon ("women old and young at once"), beauty conjoined with horror ("the fantastic moon/in the Atlantic—we descried the prisoner laden/with the thornbush and the lantern"). It is only in one poem, "Dead Men", that he seems able to move his argument through an exploration of experiences of love and violent death to a resolution in terms of images first encountered in the evocation of those experiences:

> And the wise man is the lover
> who in his planetary love revolves
> without the traction of reason or time's control
> and the wild dog finding meat in a hole
> is a philosopher. The prudent mind resolves
> on the lover's or the dog's attitude forever.

There is great strain in the verbs, and the language pulls together disparaties that earlier in the poem made reality seem the landscape of fantasy: "dead men, whom the wind/powders till they are like dolls". It is through the fantasy that we sense the pressures contained by Douglas's customary reticence.

More usually, however, as in the highly effective "Behaviour of Fish in an Egyptian Garden", the irony of the conclusion seems inadequate to the imagistic fertility of the poem, and both imagery and subject seem as though relinquished, however urbanely:

> Now the ice-cream is finished, is
> paid for. The fish swim off on business
> and she sits alone at the table, a white stone
> useless except to a collector, a rich man.

Ian Hamilton spoke of Douglas's "reticence stiffening into the tight-lipped insensitivity of the officer's mess".[25] His insecure childhood had left him with a brittle and fulminatively defensive personality that he found hard to control. Towards the end of his life he attempted to write a poem "Bête Noire" about the beast on his back, that was to be the theme poem of a volume of that title. He said of it, with some truth "it is the poem I begin to write in a lot of other poems".[26] A protective distancing may have been involved in the irresolution of some of Douglas's ironies. Equally, though, there is an ambivalence in his attitude to war itself.

His most assured writing about war is in his prose account of his experiences from the battle of El Alamein, in 1942, to the end of the Tunisian campaign, in 1943. Douglas wrote this work in a desk diary during the latter part of 1943, and it was published posthumously as *Alamein to Zem Zem* in 1946, with poems and drawings by Douglas. During most of the period covered by the account, Douglas was recovering from minor wounds in Palestine, and it was then that he wrote most of his war poems.

It is an artfully seamless narrative, apparently following the events that controlled Douglas's existence from its beginning to its end, without anticipation or distortion. In fact, within that framework, it achieves a very deft handling of scene and character, and of pace and climax. Its great virtue is its honesty to what Douglas did or did not feel and his completely untheatrical presentation of the rather dramatic events he encountered. Its mat surface goes along with a power to move one that is a function of its honesty.

> We repeated over and over again in our thoughts and conversation that the battle was over. The continual halting and moving, the departure at first light, the shell-fire, the interminable wireless conversations—and the strain, the uncertainty of tomorrow, the fear of death: it was all over. We had made it. We stood here on the safe side of it, like swimmers. And Guy, lying under the flowers in Enfidaville cemetary, Piccadilly Jim, buried miles behind us, Tom, and all the others, back to the first casualties, during Rommel's attempt to break through to Alexandria; they didn't make it, but it's over for them, too.
>
> And tomorrow, we said, we'll get every vehicle we can find, and go out over the whole ground we beat them on, and bring in more loot than we've ever seen. (p.167, *Penguin* ed.)

Douglas's honesty, his dislike of "bullshit", did not endear him to the "county" people who made up his regiment, the Sherwood Rangers. Yet Douglas brings out strongly the sense of companionship in the regiment, the bravery behind the hunting jargon employed on the intercom—a bravery whose dimensions emerge from the narrative, only to be fully clear when Douglas returns to the regiment to find many of its former members dead. The most touching moment is Douglas's incredulity as he reads, in a pavement cafe in Palestine, of the death of "Piccadilly Jim", the colonel.

Douglas was in fact an odd war poet. As he says at the beginning of his narrative: "I never lost the certainty that experience of battle was something I must have." (p.5) He had been a very keen member of the O.T.C. at Christ's Hospital, and his approach to war has an undoubted zest to it. If his honesty and sanity are important virtues that in their quality set him apart from the other officers of the regiment, he seems to share too unreflectively their stiff-upper-lip attitudes in battle; and he is rather far from Sassoon and Owen when he writes

> . . . it is exciting and amazing to see thousands of men, very few of whom have much idea why they are fighting, all enduring hardships, living in an unnatural, dangerous, but not wholly terrible world, having to kill and be killed, and yet at intervals moved by a feeling of comradeship with the men who kill them and whom they kill, because they are enduring and experiencing the same things. (p.6)

His encounters with the dead, for all their truth to his reaction, are described in a distanced, literary manner, with a heavy emphasis on aesthetic qualities. "There were no signs of violence. As I looked at him, a fly crawled up his cheek and across the dry pupil of his unblinking right eye. I saw that a pocket of dust had collected in the trough of the lower lid." (p.32)

His most famous poem, "Vergissmeinicht", is built round such a figure. Its images and narrative are striking, but its language is blemished and its rhythms lose their subtlety as the poem concludes in somewhat contrived and obvious irony. It is as though Douglas cannot find the poem in the experience, and the last lines seem forced:

> For here the lover and killer are mingled
> who had one body and one heart.
> And death who had the soldier singled
> has done the lover mortal hurt.

Its gestures feel contrived beside a prose description of an experience very like that in the poem:

> He had tried to cover his wounds with towels against the flies. His haversack lay open, from which he had taken towels and dressings. His waterbottle lay tilted with the cork out. Towels and haversack were dark with dried blood, darker still with a great concourse of flies. This picture, as they say, told a story. It filled me with useless pity.
>
> (*Alamein to Zem Zem,* 47)

The last sentence has an honesty and unsought for irony that quite eclipses the poem.

VIII

Mention should be made of the periodicals, *Kingdom Come* and *Fords and Bridges* in which some of Douglas's early poems appeared, if for no other reason than to illustrate the renascent Georgianism prevalent in Oxford in the early forties. *Fords and Bridges* ("The Oxford and Cambridge Magazine") began as a news magazine, but developed into a literary periodical under editors that included John Waller and Nicholas Moore. It ran from 1936 to 1939. It included contributions from both inside and outside the University. "Lightness" was its most frequent tone. *Kingdom Come,* started at Oxford by John Waller in 1939, may be seen as a successor to *Fords and Bridges.* Its early editorials, already quoted, had a tone of cynical superiority on behalf of those who were about to be thrust into a war in which they had no belief. Like *Fords and Bridges,* it included contributors from outside the university, among them writers as various as Herbert Read, Lawrence Durrell, Marie Stopes and the Duke of Bedford. The voice of undergraduate poetry, it obviously favoured a return to "tradition" in reaction to the acerbic modernity of Auden and *New Verse.* Laurence Whistler's "On the Present State of English Verse" (*Kingdom Come* 2,1) attacked the poets of the thirties as "too cerebral" and sought to restore the lost qualities of "delight" and "sensuousness"—a position angrily rebutted by Geoffrey Grigson in the next issue. Nicholas Moore's diagnosis in the following number—"It is simple to agree that something is wrong with poetry in its present state, but not so simple to recognize the causes"—put the periodical's position in a clearer perspective than he perhaps realised.

The first two issues contained poems by J.C. Hall, John Short, Alan Rook, Norman Nicholson, Nicholas Moore, Gervase Stewart and John Waller, the editor. Waller published several volumes of poetry during the decade, but his poems, despite some successes, are too frequently versified autobiography. The only Oxford poet to make anything out of the traditionalist reaction was J.C. Hall (a one time editor of *Fords and Bridges*) who was instrumental in getting Douglas's poems published in book form, as *Selected Poems* by J.C. Hall, K.C. Douglas and Norman Nicholson in 1943. Hall has been a sparse poet, and his contributions to this 1943 volume still constitute a sizeable portion of his published poetry. Of strong Quaker sympathies, he was exempted from military service; and his work has a carefulness that makes one ready to accept his small output as a mark of spiritual and poetic integrity.

> In a darker age I surveyed that green domain
> And thought how the living always come too late.
> The house lies empty, even the mice are gone,
> Only a dusty sunlight haunts the rooms.
> We knock. Eternity echoes back upon
> Our hearts, and a terrible loss consumes.
>
> ("Alfoxton")

At its best, his poetry has an attained simplicity that lets the experience through with a directness we find in the later poetry of Edwin
Muir—one of Hall's admirations. Yet coming on phrases like "Time's
oldest question" or "our future meaning", one senses a shortcoming
more than linguistic: the rhetoric begs the philosophical questions it
addresses, and one realises how rare is the attainment of a poetry of
simple wisdom.

Waller relinquished *Kingdom Come* when he left for the middle-east
in 1941. The issue for Summer of that year contained three poems:
one was a sonnet by Lord Alfred Douglas on "Winston Churchill";
and a second was a poem by Marie Stopes on the same subject. With
the next issue, the editorship changed. Alan Rook, Stephan
Schimanski and Henry Treece took over *Kingdom Come,* which was
removed from Oxford, to become, until it closed in 1943, another
organ of the "New Romanticism".

IX

One poet from the Oxford and Cambridge of the 1940's who saw
action and survived was Alan Ross. A contemporary of Keyes at Oxford, he seems not to have known Keyes and his friends. He joined
the Navy in 1942 on his twentieth birthday, and left it in 1947: he did
not return to Oxford. Constantly in action, in Arctic and North Sea
convoys, he found it "exciting rather than frightening". "The issues
of the war seemed to me clear beyond all ambiguity, therefore one
could concentrate on recording a kind of existence as accurately as
possible." "I felt a week was wasted that produced no poem. Out of
a hundred or so I've kept a dozen . . ."[27]

> The bulkhead sweating, and under naked bulbs
> Men writing letters, playing ludo. The light
> Cuts their arms off at the wrist, only the dice
> Lives. Hammocks swing, nuzzling-in tight
> Like foals into flanks of mares. Bare shoulders
> Glisten with oil, tattoo-marks rippling their scales on
> Mermaids or girls' thighs as dice are shaken, cards played.
> We reach for sleep like a gas, randy for oblivion.
> But, laid out on lockers, some get waylaid;
> And lie stiff, running off films in the mind's dark-room.
> The air soupy, yet still cold; a beam sea rattles
> Cups smelling of stale tea, knocks over a broom.
> The light is watery, like the lights of the sea-bed;
> Marooned in it, stealthy as fishes, we may even be dead.
> ("Messdeck")

In this characteristic poem, we are given the everyday setting of war-time action—the dirt, confinement, boredom—built up through a finely observed sequence of details. The figurative elements are subdued—"We reach for sleep like a gas, randy for oblivion", yet suggestive here of tedium and danger, and of isolation from the normally human in the incongruous "randy".

A blemish in this poem, easily passed over (or even noted and savoured) is the image of "nuzzling-in tight/Like foals into flanks of mares", which suggests welcomed and sustaining closeness at odds with the distasteful absence of privacy that the poem evokes. The image seems chosen for its visual appropriateness, and this attention to visual evocation is the noticeable and surprising feature of Ross's war poems. One of the earliest to be published, "Night Patrol", de-scribes a night in "E boat alley" off the East coast:

> Night and towards midnight, the stars high
> over Europe, cold and frozen, nailed to the sky,
> like tinsel above the white flickering lights
> of Holland, the flashes of gunfire
>
> Licking out over the silent coastline, betraying
> the stillness.

No doubt this is how it felt—the stillness and beauty of the wartime night at sea overpowering the menace of the situation, with the hyper-aesthesia associated with action or excitement. The absence of any event in the poem is deliberate and again true to experience. Yet, by making this type of writing a largely unvaried mode, Ross's war poems give the impression of an over-cultivation of the visual and the aesthetic. This was true of a great deal of poetry in the forties—the final legacy of the Imagist heritage of modernism. It was also a feature of much of the brilliant work of British war artists, pictures by many of whom were reproduced in *Penguin New Writing,* where "Night Pat-rol" first appeared.

This concentration on the surface is an accomplished version of what was called in the thirties "reporting"; and Ross's poetry has a closer relationship to the writing of the thirties than that of most of his contemporaries.

> For the first eighteen years of my life, I scarcely read anything but rub-bish. Those years were single-mindedly devoted to sport of one kind or another. When I went to Oxford . . . I started to read Eliot, Auden, Spen-der, MacNeice . . . I came to them not having read previous poetry very much . . . They fulfilled some need which I scarcely knew existed until they were suddenly there in front of me.[28]

Reviewing MacNeice's *Holes in the Sky* in 1948, Ross spoke of "a bringing to the surface of the anonymous X qualities that lurk under the behaviourisms of society and which in the end characterize it."[29] This gives a very apt characterisation of his own writing. However, the visual element in Ross's writing is located less in similes and other figurative features than is the case with MacNeice's poetry: for Ross the visual involves the objective presentation of the actual, and it achieves an extension of the particular through the collocation of details in the poem. In this and in other respects, his poems recall those of Geoffrey Grigson:

> Your body is under water flowers
> where your face holds the afternoon
> hours under cellophane, and your fingers
> stretch out midnight and midday. . .
> ("Sand and Water")

There is metaphor in the verbs here, but the passage illustrates a handling of word position and rhythm that is reminiscent of Grigson: "hours" is separated from "afternoon" by the line end, so that the voice must move over the break to make the conjunction "afternoon hours"; and this looping over muffles the emergence of any caesura in the second line, producing a quiet, conversational pacing.

Ross's most ambitious war poem, and one that transcends the limitations of his others, is "J.W. 51 B", a narrative of an attack on a convoy bearing that code number *en route* for Murmansk. The power of its subdued and varied language and of its overall movement is not easily illustrated by quotation.

> Not dawn, for dawn means light,
> And from this light sun was withdrawn,
> But eventually it was not night
> Any more, and a sardine-coloured sea
> Tipped into clouds torn
> Here and there, the dull grey
> Glinting, as it turned to metal.
>
> And Hyderbad sighted them first,
> On a bearing of 180 . . .

Distanced and unhistrionic, it gives no sense that the author was involved in the most dangerous part of the action. It is one of the most powerful poems of action in English from World War II.

Ross's first volume, *The Derelict Day* (1947), did not contain any war poems, being confined to poems about the occupation of Germany. The best, through their choice and depiction of detail, evoke the desolation and indirection, the lassitude in the face of destruction and waste:

> The blown bridge leans towards the dykes, one end
> suspended in a hand floating on the dirty scum
> of water. A green tunic huddles like a trodden cloth;
> nearby, two wrists grope beneath a petrol drum.
>
> ("German Gun Site")

However, too many poems in this volume are diffuse and slack. The seventy-four pages of poetry were the product of twelve months of writing; and Ross rejected them when he collected his poems in 1967, keeping a few titles, but writing virtually new poems around the experiences.

Ross described his wartime poems as "perhaps the most important things that have happened to me"[30]; and he has frequently returned to his wartime experiences and their consequences. "Cricket at Brighton" (1948), one of his most assured poems, congenial to his gift, seems to speak of the gap made in experience by the war. In 1975, the idea of a collection of poems "on and around the experience of war", *The Open Sea*, "was given impetus by discovering an early journal containing pages of notes and a number of half-developed ideas." One of his most powerful pieces is "One of those Hot Days" (written in 1961) where, awakened out of doors by a plane diving, he finds himself back in a wartime attack:

>   this has been always
> How it happened, nobody looking
> Or thinking or doing anything
> In particular, one of those hot days . . .
> When IT happens, and the bubble
> Bursts, and we are not asleep,
> But what happens, happens for keeps.

Yet it is not for poems so decisively clinching that we remember him:

> The shadow falls on table, desk;
> the room assumes a different bearing,
> posing to greet each stranger; as if
> conscious of what his mind is wearing.
>
> So that when, at last, the conversation
> lags, the room itself takes charge:
> puts on an intellectual face, or becomes
> virulent and moody, and grows more large.
>
> ("Furniture in a Room")

The poem is modest—though not with the aggressive modesty of "Movement" poetry, which Ross described as "timidly skilful . . . a modest poetry by modest men, with their eyes pretty much on their boots . . ."[31]. Ross's poem might be styled "urbanely skilful", a triumph of tact and arrangement—but with its "eyes pretty much on" . . . what? It is the sensed absence of substantial pressures given articulation by the brilliant surface that arouses reservations concerning some of Ross's poetry, though his best poems take us tellingly into the experiences they evoke, and there is always a fine balance between tone and experience. In poems like "J.W. 51 B", where the subject is powerful and disturbing, he achieves a realisation of that power.

X

A volume of war poetry that appeared after the war—and after interest in war poetry was past—was *Elegies for the Dead in Cyrenaica* (1947) by Hamish Henderson, who had been at Cambridge when war broke out. Written between 1943 and 1947, it is intended as a cycle of poems that would reflect Henderson's sense that the "conflict seemed rather to be between 'the dead, the innocent' . . . and ourselves, the living, who cannot hope to expiate our survival but by 'spanning history's apollyon chasm' . . ." They are, as he later pointed out, "poems of passive suffering . . . of stoicism"[32]; those who die will be forgotten by those who survive:

> the queue forming up to see Rangers play Celtic
> forms up without thought to those dead. O, to right them
> what requiem can I sing in the ears of the living.

The consolation must be a human one—"the words that I have looked for . . . are words of whole love" ("Sixth Elegy"). The poems juxtapose recollections of the desert campaign with memories of wars real and legendary, especially those of the Scottish Highlands, and suggest the unity of all those dead in war. The literary inspiration is the traditional Scots literature and the Cantos of Ezra Pound; though there are echoes of the modern Greek poet of Alexandria, Cavafy, and of several other writers and literatures. Nonetheless, the poems are more impressive locally than as a whole; and the most individual moments involve the evocation of the experiences of war in the desert.

It is for these that one returns to the book affectionately. Its qualities can be seen from the "Ninth Elegy", published in 1946 as a separate poem, "Fort Capuzzo":

> *For there will come a day*
> *When the Lord will say—Close Order!*
> One evening, breaking a jeep journey at Capuzzo,
> I noticed a soldier as he entered the cemetary
> And stood looking at the grave of a fallen enemy.
> Then I understood the meaning of the hard word 'pietas'
> (a word unfamiliar to the newsreel commentator
> as well as the pimp, the informer and the traitor)
>
> His thought was like this. Here's another 'Good Jerry'.
> Poor mucker. Just eighteen. Must be hard up for manpower
> or else he volunteered, silly bastard. That's the fatal
> *the—fatal*—mistake. Never volunteer for nothing.
> I wonder how he died? Just as well it was him though
> and not one of our chaps—Yes, the only good Jerry
> as they say, is your sort, chum. Cheerio, you poor bastard.
> Don't be late on parade when the Lord Calls 'Close Order'.
> Keep waiting for the angels. Keep listening for reveille.
> ("Fort Capuzzo": *New Road* 4, 1946)

The feeling for detail and voice, never forced up into "poetry", is engaging and rare enough. However, the conclusion one feels has little hope of carrying ironies beyond those the dramatised speaker was capable of, though it was apparently intended that it should; while the "pimp, the informer" seem to have no place in the poem, unless for some ideological reason not established. This forcing of the implications of the poetry is a fault of Henderson's book, the one ambitious and compelling attempt to write an extended poem on World War II.

Less than wholly successful in a similar way are the war poems in J.M. Russell's *The Grinning Face* (1947). The "grinning face" is the mask, a replacement for a state of grace or sensitivity, that is assumed by men to keep them from the madness that would come if they saw killing for what it is. Several of the poems are unusual in that they deal with the act of killing full front; but the impact of their realism is muted by the diffuseness of the ambitious attempts to elucidate the experiences. Far more telling is an uncollected poem published at Oxford in 1949, in which the act of killing is brought into focus obliquely:

> The single nature of the beast
> Lies half-concealed.
> But all kenspeckle coverings
> Of colour, curve or prayer change least
> The pattern of the blood congealed.
>
> The peacock has no time to ask
> If teeth disguise

Some hunger, hate or malady,
Some need or lust behind need's mask.
It only feels the way it dies.

           ("The Single Nature of the Beast" in 5 (1949))

Here the experiences of war finds its place in poetry at a distance, as it does in Geoffrey Household's *Rhine Jump*—a first book by a poet of this generation that appeared as late as 1974. The same is true of some of the later writing of Vernon Scanell, whose first book, *Graves and Resurrections* (1948), is very conventional and gives no sense of the power that was to come.

XI

There remain to be mentioned some young writers who died in the war, the publishing of whose poems seems in retrospect an act of patriotism or piety: Richard Spender, David Bourne, Keith Footit, T.R. Hodgson, David Raikes and James Farrar. Farrar's perceptive and honest diaries were brought together as *The Unreturning Spring* (1950) with an introduction by Henry Williamson describing him as "a poet and prose-writer of the rare first-class". Farrar conveys very well how it felt to be just out of grammar school in the R.A.F., but the only interest of his writing is its representative decency. The writings of many of these young men fit Roy Fuller's recollection of "the reiteration by so many poets, often scarcely out of their boyhood, of the essential brotherhood of mankind."[33] In many cases, the poetry has nothing to do with the war: it is the juvenilia of young men killed shortly after they entered the services.

Yet it would be wrong to leave these writers without reflecting that their early deaths, along with the deaths of Keyes, Douglas, Allison and Stewart, must make us qualify the picture of World War II as far less costly in youthful talent than World War I. As David Wright recalled of those he met in his first days in Oxford in 1939: "Nearly all were waiting to join the air force, and nearly all, it seemed, were to be killed in the Battle of Britain or shortly after . . ."[34] Keyes, Allison and Stewart were not "war poets" in the sense that they wrote out of the direct experience of fighting: they had no chance to do so. Neither did they have the opportunity to mature away from war: Keyes and Stewart were dead before they were 21, and Allison died aged 22. All we have in each case, is, as John Heath-Stubbs said of William Bell, "the fragmentary and unequal work of a very young man."[35] This is almost true of Keith Douglas, half of whose *Collected Poems* are brilliant undergraduate writing. If we look for a fully articulated reaction to war from writers of this generation, we must turn to Hillary's *The Last Enemy* and Douglas's *Alamein and Zem Zem*. Here we do not find ourselves wishing that death had given them time to do it better.

Yet death and war were not the only stiflers of talent for this generation of poets. Of those discussed in this chapter, only Heath-Stubbs, Wright, Ross and Hall were to have extended careers as poets; and only Ross and Hall built throughout their careers on the style of their earliest poetry. Both Heath-Stubbs and Wright were to find that they had to turn away from their early styles. The wartime situation, so receptive to new talent, in fact saw few good starts. The humbling effect of the defeats that culminated in the evacuation from Dunkirk in 1940 and the widespread devastation and brutality of war put radicalism and irony in abeyance. This, and the associated reaction against the poetry of Auden and his generation, set the tone for the poetry of many younger writers. Yet the reaction towards "romanticism" and an unironic seriousness led to writing that was often grandiose and vacuous, as in the work of Sidney Keyes or the radical Alex Comfort; while the early writing of Wright was "literary" in a defeating sense. The best wartime work of the generation—of Douglas, Ross and Allison—has an ironic, realist stance that in fact owes a good deal to writing of a similar stance from the thirties.

Chapter 13

THE AGE OF AUSTERITY

Philip Larkin, Kingsley Amis—Michael Hamburger, Christopher
Middleton, Danny Abse, Denise Levertov—*Mandrake, Nine, Focus,
The Critic, Politics and Letters*

Oxford Poetry had been published by Basil Blackwell since the early
part of the century, bringing together each year a collection of undergraduate poems. During World War II, its production was curtailed to
a single issue for 1942/43. In it appeared Allison, Bell, Heath-Stubbs,
Keyes, Porter and Wright. The same group, except for Keyes, appeared in an anthology assembled by Bell for the Fortune Press in
1945 (though probably solicited earlier)—*Poetry from Oxford in Wartime*. What is startling about these volumes is that *Oxford Poetry* also
contains poems by Philip Larkin and Michael Hamburger, while the
Fortune Press anthology contains poems by Larkin and Christopher
Middleton. Larkin was a contemporary of Keyes at Oxford, both being
born in 1922; and Michael Meyer had wanted to include his work in
Eight Oxford Poets (1941) but Keyes had decided against it. Keyes's
posthumously celebrated *Collected Poems* was published in 1944,
while Larkin's first book of poems to gain any attention, *The Less Deceived*, appeared in 1955. Keyes and his friends are regarded as poets
of the forties: Larkin, Hamburger and Middleton are associated with
the succeeding decade.

   Among Larkin's friends at Oxford was Kingsley Amis. Amis in turn
was a friend of John Wain, who in 1945 started *Mandrake* as a university periodical. In a Cambridge companion to the Fortune anthology
from Oxford, *Poetry from Cambridge in Wartime* (1946), we find
poems by Donald Davie alongside those of Stephen Coates, Nicholas
Moore and George Scurfield, all of whom had appeared in *Cambridge
Poetry 1940*. Larkin, Amis, Wain and Davie became widely known
only through the anthology *New Lines* in 1956, as did its editor Robert
Conquest, a poem by whom had appeared in 1939 in the last issue of
Twentieth Century Verse. Hamburger's first book of poems (other than
translations) appeared in 1950; while Middleton did not produce a mature collection until 1957. All these poets were writing steadily
throughout the decade. What happened that they received so little attention?

Books by Larkin, Middleton and Amis were in fact published by
the Fortune Press, whose owner evidently canvassed each contributor
to *Poetry from Oxford in Wartime*.[1] It is customary today to treat Larkin's first book, *The North Ship* (1945), with great respect, because
of the later achievement of its author; but, if any of the poems in it
were submitted to editors of national literary periodicals, it would have
been understandable if they were turned down: Larkin himself recognised "a general immaturity".[2] Poems by Middleton appeared in
Poetry Quarterly: they do not seem out of place, and are not among
the most distinguished pieces in even that periodical. The critical
question becomes how, in a decade where Heath-Stubbs and Keyes—
and Alan Ross—could achieve a personal style with considerable
fluency, these writers were so long in finding themselves.

II

If Philip Larkin had died in 1950 at the age of twenty-eight (having
lived seven years longer than Keyes and four years longer than Douglas) he would be regarded as a minor novelist of the forties who wrote
less successful poems. His first book with a major publisher was *A
Girl in Winter*, published by Faber in 1947, preceded in 1946 by *Jill*.
Both novels are tellingly evocative of the dreariness of England in
wartime. They show a feeling for the nuances of everyday life quite
absent from his early poetry. *Jill* was begun when he was 21, in 1943,
and took a year to write; while *A Girl in Winter* was completed in
1945. During that period Larkin recorded "I wrote continuously as
never before or since":[3] His gift for capturing the particularlity of experience (so much a strength of his mature poetry) was canalised into
prose at this time.

In contrast, the poetry is lacking in individuality of either language
or experience, as seen in this Oxford poem later included in *The North
Ship*.

> I dreamed of an outstretched arm of land
> Where gulls blew over a wave
> That fell along miles of sand,
> And a wind climbed up the caves
> To tear at a dark-faced garden
> Whose black flowers were dead,
> And broke round the house we slept in,
> A drawn blind and a bed.
>
> (*Oxford Poetry*, 1942-43)

Larkin got to know Vernon Watkins when he visited the English Club at Oxford, and "his likes became my likes, his methods my methods". As a result, Larkin spent "three years trying to write like Yeats".[4] "I wrote a great many sedulous and worthless Yeats-y poems, and later on far inferior Dylan Thomas poems . . . It wasn't until about 1948 or 9 that I began writing differently . . . There was a whole period between *The North Ship* and *The Less Deceived* which produced a book with the portentous title of *In The Grip of Light,* which went round the publishers in the middle and late forties, but thank God nobody accepted it."[5] The following uncollected poem from *Mandrake* for May, 1946 was to have been in that collection (many poems for which survive in a manuscript in the British Library):

> Her hands intend no harm:
> Her hands devote themselves
> To sheltering a flame;
> Winds are her enemies
> And everything that strives
> To bring her cold and darkness.
>
>   ("Portrait")[6]

The change came with the reading of Hardy in 1946: "When I came to Hardy it was with a sense of relief that I didn't have to try and jack myself up to a concept of poetry that lay outside of my own life—this is perhaps what I felt that Yeats was trying to make me do. One could simply relapse back into one's own life and write from it."[7] With that recognition, the sensibility of *Jill* and *A Girl in Winter* was free to enter the poetry; and the Yeatsian romantic rhetoric could be discarded. Most of the poems from his next two collections, *XX Poems* (1951) and *Philip Larkin: Fantasy Poets No. 21* are carried forward into *The Less Deceived*. Nonetheless, Larkin brought together many Yeatsian poems in the unpublished *In the Grip of Light* in 1947, showing perhaps that a recognition of the misdirection it represented was slow to come. The transition from a mode that was in tune with the dominant poetry of the forties was a hard one—"the unhappiest time in my life creatively".[8]

Indeed, *XX Poems* shows a much more deliberate cultivation of the conventionally poetic than does *The Less Deceived*. There is only the occasional touch of the colloquial, anti-poetic, deflationary manner of the later book. Alongside powerful, assured pieces like "At Grass", in 1950 Larkin is still writing poems like "Arrival", where the style seems to collapse, to deliquesce just where it aims most for the ethereal or the poetic:

Let me breathe till then
Its milk-aired Eden
Till my own life impound it—
Slow-falling; grey-veil hung; a theft,
A style of dying only.

("Arrival")

The longing for the transcendent, the ineffable is not always contained by the sense of the actual. The recognition that one can use a demotic tone to evoke an important experience and be true to it, not merely deflate it, is still a little way off. It was for this realisation of the possibility of pitching poetry in a new key that Larkin's work—and English poetry too—had to wait. In his work of these years, we see him extricating himself from the idioms of the forties.

The work of Larkin's friend Kingsley Amis showed a similar uncertainty. His first book, *Bright November* (1947), like *The North Ship*, was published by the Fortune Press. The majority of the poems had been "written since October, 1943" and the general impression is of a manner not yet formed. A poem entitled "27 January 1946" begins "Oh gentler than time's touch on angel's cheek", and appears to be unironic. In contrast, "Berkhamstead" has

Follow the tall green bus to the High Street
Past teas of cress and Marmite, rooms that face
Unnoticed sadness and blank playing-fields

where the capacity of the thirties idiom to accommodate everyday experience is given a contemporary development. Irony is a much more frequent tone in *Bright November* than in *The North Ship*. One of the two poems carried over to *A Case of Samples* (1956) was the deflationary "Beowulf"; and the number of such poems in his second book, *A Frame of Mind* (1953), seems to indicate that the only way forward for him was by a guarded rejection of poetic pretentions. He was one of the first to espouse an anti-romanticism in reaction to the dominant taste of the period. With James Michie he edited *Oxford Poetry* for 1949, and found that the poems he received increased his respect for Auden and showed how harmful the influence of Dylan Thomas could be. As he said, in introducing his poems in D.J. Enright's *Poets of the 1950's (1955)* "Their great deficiency is meagreness and triviality of subject-matter: nobody wants more poems about philosophers or paintings or novelists or art galleries or mythology or foreign cities or other poems." Amis, the same age as Larkin and Sidney Keyes, and a year younger than Drummond Allison, spent three and a half years in the army. His one collected poem about the war, "Belgian

Winter'', shows that he saw possibilities in Auden's work beyond the anti-romantic.

> From my window stretches the earth, containing wrecks:
> The burrowing tank, the flat grave, the
> Lorry with its underside showing, like a dead rabbit.
> The trees that smear all light into a mess;
> World of one tone, stolid with falling snow.
> Here is the opaque ice, the humdrum winter,
> The splintered houses suddenly come upon
> Left over from wounds that pierced a different people.

Bright November is not a book to go back to, except for the occasional poem of moving directness, such as "Letter to Elizabeth"; but it shows an attempt to get free from the enervating poetic expectations that beggared so much poetry of the forties.

Larkin and Amis were not the only poets of their generation who found it difficult to see a way to a new and more direct style. Similarities are to be found in the development of their friend, John Wain, or of Donald Davie, their contemporary at Cambridge. Davie's poetry appeared in the mid-forties alongside that of Nicholas Moore; but before Davie's first pamphlet appeared from the Fantasy Press in 1954, Moore had published his last book for many years. Larkin, Amis, Wain and Davie all contributed to *New Lines,* the anthology that marked a change of tone in British poetry in the mid-fifties.

III

It is interesting to consider the emergence during the decade of some poets who did not become identified with the "Movement" in the fifties—Michael Hamburger, Christopher Middleton and Dannie Abse.

Hamburger's career shows the ready reception of new talent that was a feature of the forties. In his autobiography, *A Mug's Game* (1973) he describes the encouragement of Herbert Read and T.S. Eliot, his friendships with Dylan Thomas, David Gascoyne, Sidney Keyes, John Heath-Stubbs, David Wright and Philip Larkin, and calls the Soho pubs his second university. His *Poems of Hölderlin* (1943), to be followed by *20 Prose Poems of Baudelaire* (1946), established him in his early twenties as a published poet; yet it was not until 1950 that a collection of his original poems, *Flowering Cactus*, appeared. It contains early poems, such as "Holderlin" (*Oxford and Cambridge Writing,* 1942) or "Charles Baudelaire" (*Oxford Poetry*, 1942-43), that are characteristic in their muted lyricism and subdued irony; but the much later appearance of this first published collection attests to indirections on the way.

> My religious preoccupations made me look for transcendental hints where I should have been trusting my senses. In the poem 'London Night' (published . . . as 'Later Hogarth') what I suppose was a buzz-bomb became 'the metal humming bird whose breath is fire/Whose beak is our undoing' . . . A few shorter lyrics written in 1942, and published in *Oxford Poetry*, were at least felt, if somewhat vaguely . . . I was seized by a veritable frenzy of what I took to be not only inspiration but revelation . . . When the paper currency ran out, there was no petty cash of simple observation to fall back on.[9]

In a sequence of poems, "Profane Dying" (*Poetry London,* X) he takes up the "Apocalyptic" rhetoric of the period:

> Soon the night is like a drum,
> More gravid than Jove's thunder,
> And vast as Nemesis.
> Houses are torn asunder
> By explosive thunderbolts.
> Is it Death's own festival?

By the middle of the decade, experiences in Austria led to a questioning of his moral code and "a revulsion against the romanticism and idealism of my early verse" in a sequence "From the Note-Book of a European Tramp". "The reaction was too extreme. In my endeavour to be direct, unliterary and true to life, I fell into triteness and flatness."[10] Only at the end of the decade was balance restored.

Christopher Middleton was 24 in 1950, but had already published two volumes of poetry, *Poems* (1944) and *Nocturne In Eden* (1945)—both from the Fortune Press. By that time, as his poems in *Oxford Poetry,* 1950 show, this episode of precocious publishing was in the past. He was not to produce another volume until *torse 3* in 1962. *Nocturne in Eden* shows an interest in non-rational sequences that he was to utilise in his later work, but the general impression is of a fluent command of the rhetoric of the "new romanticism":

> Yet soon and sooner that tomorrow is
> her love on miles of trees, greater than
> space, on matrimonial doors of tears and sun,
> comes in softer than silk or a vein of snow.
>   ("Eden")

A penchant for hyperbole is still evident in the poems he contributed to *Oxford Poetry* for 1950 and 1951. As Middleton has related, "From about 1947-8 I wrote absolutely nothing . . . it took me a very long time before I discovered what I wanted to do or what I could. I wrote . . . about 150 poems between the years 1948 and 1955 and then it wasn't until about 1955 that I began to discover what I could write."[11]

Dannie Abse was one of the few poets to take his bearings from writing current in the forties and to build from this a mature career as a poet. He was a friend of Alex Comfort and Emanuel Litvinoff. He was born in Cardiff in 1923, and his first book, *After Every Green Thing*, was accepted for publication in 1946, though it did not appear until 1949. As Abse put it, "that first book of mine contained for the most part linguistically florid and faulty poems".[12] Its manner shows the influence of the poet for whom Abse was to write one of his more celebrated later poems, "Elegy for Dylan Thomas".

> Pain is a pattern of pebbles in his face,
> but his harp of sabbaths to a sleeping girl
> forgets the dream floating through the blood,
> and all his planets of tears are still,
> and all that is forgotten is understood.
>
> ("Portrait of an Older Poet")

In 1949, Abse started *Poetry and Poverty*—a duplicated periodical that sold 1000 copies. In looking back on it, he seemed to recognize that the direction he had taken did not have the potentiality for regeneration that the reorientations of the Movement had.

> I did not want to publish civilized, neat poems that ignored the psychotic savagery of twentieth-century life . . . At odds with the prevailing critical climate of opinion *Poetry and Poverty* changed from an eclectic magazine into a crusading, dynamic one that finally found expression in the controversial anthology, *Mavericks,* which I edited with Howard Sargeant, and which was intended to rival the fashionable *New Lines* anthology . . . Yet, editorially we failed . . . the best poets in the opposing camp had a genuine, even an exciting talent . . . too few poems written during the 1950's . . . lived up to my editorial ideal of being written out of the heat of personal predicament . . . It was not until 1962 that A. Alvarez published *The New Poetry* and echoed more directly, more succintly, the sentiments I had been vocal about eight years earlier.[13]

Finally, it is only appropriate to mention here the work of a poet who was an acquaintance of Abse, who was published, like him, in *Poetry Quarterly,* and whose first book, *The Double Image,* appeared in 1946, when she was twenty-one: Denise Levertoff. Her book is very much a book of the period—sensitive, diffuse, self-consciously "poetic"—and shows how unpromising a time it was even for a talent that had notable power of self-development. In the poems written immediately after the acceptance of her book, there begins to emerge a voice assured in tone and rhythm, offering a sense of the fulfilment that was to come in her work after she settled in the United States in 1948:

> Folding a shirt, a woman stands
> still for a moment, to recall
> warmth of flesh; her careful hands
>
> heavy on a sleeve, recall
> a gesture, or the touch of love;
> she leans against the kitchen wall,
>
> listening for a word of love,
> but only finds a sound like fear
> running through the rooms above.

All these poets had remarkable talent. None was to find a personal idiom in the ironic poetry of *New Lines,* with its preference for a poetry of statement. For each, a quite different mode was to be the destination. Nonetheless, with the exception of Abse, none was to find in the "new romantic" idiom (in which all achieved minor success) a basis for the development of a mature style. For Hamburger and Middleton there was later to be the explicit recognition that their work in the forties constituted false starts—a recognition paralleled in the career of Larkin.

IV

The periodical that might have been expected to herald new things was *Mandrake,* started by John Wain in Oxford in May, 1945. It appeared five times up to the end of 1947, after which it was published intermittently (following a gap of nearly two years) from London by Arthur Boyars. The early issues are mainly of historical rather than intrinsic interest, and perhaps a certain indefiniteness of character in *Mandrake* is an indicator of the indirections and uncertainties of the period.

There is no editorial statement of any kind until the third issue, which contains a declaration in favour of "all those writers whose prime motive is the fulfillment of artistic aims" (3, p.2). The fourth issue promises to "oppose sham and cant . . . and to stand as testimony against the fraud and fear of the days we live in". (I, 4, p.3). Only in Wain's short piece "Scrutiny on the Bounty" in the fifth issue do we find any particularised critical stance, when he says that Leavis's writings "contain the only body of responsible and concerted literary criticism . . . that we have." (I, 5, p.84)

A similar uncertainty of character and direction is shown in the poetry, despite now famous names. No.2 contains poems by William Bell and by Arthur Boyars; No.3, by Larkin and Wain; and No.5 by Kingsley Amis and James Kirkup. Wain's own "Against Taking Thought" (*Mandrake* 3) gives no hint of his later style, except in its title:

> Asking brought never happiness, no chart
> Can trace, can guide uncasual feet towards
> That laughing pool of sun: therefore
> Leave searching, only travel clueless on,
> Relax the puckered brow, the questioning.

One has the sense of writers adrift in the lee of the overpowering but completed experimentation of the great poets of the early twentieth century, cut off by ideology from their immediate and admired predecessors in the thirties, concerned not to handle the inflated currency of the "new romanticism", yet unable to formulate a stance of their own. That new stance was to be found eventually, but not in the pages of *Mandrake,* though it continued with very sporadic publication into the mid-fifties, and published work by many young and later influential critics such as A. Alvarez, George Steiner, W.W. Robson and Frank Kermode. Boyars aimed to turn *Mandrake* into an international literary periodical, with a double "Italian Arts Number" and special features on new poetry from Australia and from America. The cover came more and more to resemble that of *Horizon,* and the editorial comments reflected a pessimism similar to Connolly's—one very understandable in a period apparently so unfavourable to new periodicals: "any magazine which struggles for existence in these times must expect intrigue, financial losses and derision" (I, 5, p.5); "we do not seriously believe that in England 140,000 original and stimulating words are being put on paper in the course of a year" (II, 7, p.1). It spoke of "writers harried out of their ambition by the facts of poverty and unsuitable employment" (II, 8, p.119). By the time this last phrase was written in 1952, this generation of writers was beginning to find (in novels like Wain's *Hurry On Down* (1953)) that the situation of poverty and unsuitable employment might indeed be the subject matter in terms of which they could find themselves.

Cultural despair was also the note struck by *Nine* in its opening editorial: "Within the enormous apparently-dead stump of civilization there are still trickles of sap . . . Perhaps the old stump is going to die. We cannot tell—long, long after our time it may burst forth again IF we keep the almost blocked channels free." (I, 1, p.5) It claimed that it "asserted the need to replot the traditions of European literature" (II, 4, p.269); and, despite its protests that it would not deal heavily in translations and in critiques of past or foreign authors, it did. Against a poetry of "romantic bewilderment and symbolist self-consciousness" it set "poetry that shows the poet responding to a living tradition of custom and sensibility" (II, 1, p.8). It was seen by those who identified themselves with the "new romanticism" as an exponent of "neo-classicism".[14] Edited by Peter Russell, it included poems by G.S. Fraser and Iain Fletcher, who were also on the editorial board. It appeared first in Autumn, 1949 and ran until the mid-fifties. Its stance and its predicaments were nevertheless symptomatic of the immediate post-war period.

At Cambridge in 1945 there appeared the first of what was intended to be a series of collections, *Focus One,* edited by B. Rajan. Rajan himself was to emerge a little later as an exponent of the new scholarship in *Paradise Lost and the Seventeenth Century Reader* (1947), a discommoding book that argued that one should read Milton's poem in the light of the predispositions of his contemporary readers. However, *Focus* brought together some of the younger Cambridge writers (who had appeared in *Scrutiny*) such as D.J. Enright, with contributors who had been associated with *Now*—Julian Symons, D.S. Savage, George Woodcock, Louis Adeane. The bulk of the first issue was given over to a "Symposium on Kafka and Rex Warner", though there was a substantial poetry section. Contributors included Vernon Watkins, George Barker, and John Heath-Stubbs. The "Editorial" contained the usual protestation against any "manifesto"; though the contribution of R.G. Leinhardt, for instance, displays the rigid positions by then to be associated with *Scrutiny*. The catholicity of poetic contributions, together with the meeting of writers who had been influenced by Leavis and others whose association was with Orwell and the wartime Left, might have suggested that *Focus* would have a lively and valuable influence. *Focus Two* retained some of the character of the original issue, with a symposium on the novel in the thirties that included contributions by Orwell, Savage, Woodcock and Enright; but the third volume, *Focus Three,* is remembered for what it was—one of the earliest collections of critical essays on T.S. Eliot: the symposium had taken over, and it gave the form to the remaining two issues.

The Critic, started in Cambridge in 1947 by Wolf Mankowitz, Clifford Collins and Raymond Williams, is also only of marginal interest to the study of English poetry of the period. Its editorial and its contributions pronounce it a junior *Scrutiny:* "Standards in the Cinema"; "Themes and Conventions in *Wuthering Heights*"; "F.R. Leavis and *Scrutiny*" (by H.A. Mason). The editorial, "The Reading Public and the Critical Reader" states: "If the purpose of criticism is to cultivate an intelligent reading public then the function of THE CRITIC may be understood without strong underlining from a manifesto . . . if we are interested in the standards which many works of art embody, and if we wish to see these standards preserved and extended, and if we do not wish to dictate terms to the individual artist, we had better concentrate our powers upon the cultivation of public taste; we had better concern ourselves with the problem of creating again an intelligent reading public." (I, 2, p.5) D.J. Enright's "The Significance of *Poetry London*" (I, 1) applies these recommendations in studying the symptoms of contemporary poetic ill health: "Since 1939 (in February of which year the magazine *Poetry London* was inaugurated) something, it would seem, has happened to poetry. To suggest another aspect of the problem we might vary the proposition and say that since 1939 very little of any permanent value has happened *in* poetry. Never before have poets sprung up so thickly, never before has publication (given the right contacts) been so easy—but hardly ever before has accepted and recognized work shown such a striking uniformity of weakness. The question before us now is: Has the latter fact any connexion with the former facts? Can it, even, be a case of effect and causes?" The diagnosis suggested is of course shown to be the right one. The interest of the article is in what it shows of how the situation appeared at the time to a young critic and poet beginning a career. Indeed, the interest of *The Critic* as a periodical is of the same kind. We see the great influence that *Scrutiny* already had among certain aspiring writers—an influence that was to prove at once so fruitful and so constricting in the fifties. The wholesale dismissal of the poetry of the forties had begun.

The Critic ran for two numbers, when it was amalgamated with another new periodical, *Politics and Letters,* produced by the same editors. After the first dual issue, there was one other. *Politics and Letters* had an impressive list of contributors that included F.R. Leavis, A.J. Ayer, J.P. Sartre, Harold Laski, D.W. Harding, the editors and Colin Macinnes. It concerned itself very little with poetry.

The chief interest of these periodicals in the history of British poetry in the nineteen-forties is that they all give voice to the feeling that the period is one inhospitable to the development of new talent—a feeling emphasised by the small amount of original poetry they contained. Yet, apart from periodicals like the Oxford *Gambit* (1949-1950) that had little circulation outside undergraduate circles, they are all that these years can show for a "growing edge".

V

The "age of austerity" that succeeded the war was clearly most inhospitable to those who were trying to find themselves poetically. With Hitler gone, full employment and the welfare state at home, and the early modernists established as the great poets of the time, it seemed to many younger writers that they had been born too late, after the days of the Great Causes. The constrictions that war had brought were not all eased: rationing and shortages continued, foreign travel was restricted, and the middle classes found themselves relatively impoverished. People slowly became aware that England was no longer the world power that it had been, and that British experience no longer had the centrality it had had. Europe was destroyed, the atom bomb had been dropped, and many older writers turned to lament the evil in the heart of man: Kierkegaard and Rilke were widely read and acclaimed.

It was the lassitude at home, as *Hurry On Down* (1953), *Lucky Jim* (1954) and *Look Back in Anger* (1956) were eventually to show, that most affected the new generation of writers. Beside the strong writing that was coming out of France, Italy and the United States, British writing of the post-war period, with its stock of decency and sensitivity, seemed timid. There were scarcely any interesting first books of poetry between 1946 and 1950. 1948 and 1949 brought only five books by new poets of any consequence: Maurice James Craig's *Some Way for Reason;* Hamish Henderson's *Elegies for the Dead in Cyrenaica;* Vernon Scanell's *Graves and Resurrections;* Danny Abse's *After Every Green Thing;* and Paul Dehn's *The Day's Alarms.* More distressing still was the near absence in the post-war years of books from major publishers by poets born after 1923—writers who were in their mid- or early twenties by the end of the decade: J.M. Russell's *The Grinning Face* of 1947 was the only one. This was partly due to the decline in sales of poetry after the war, the effect of which was made worse by rising costs of publication. Literary periodicals, which had sold so well in the period of wartime shortages and enforced but restricted leisure, now closed down one after another, until there were almost none left at the end of the decade.

Reviewing *Oxford Poetry* for 1948, John Wain wrote: "I have combed the book for evidences of what used to be called 'contemporary sensibility', but there are almost none. Pylons, nylons, pistons, cisterns, all are banished . . . hardly a single poem is about *ugliness* . . . Nature . . . supplies about two-thirds of the imagery in the book . . . the lesson . . . is that English poetry has now thoroughly learned the lessons of modernism . . . so thoroughly that a new return to beauty and melody is possible within the framework."[15] Experience did not bear out this conclusion. Current tastes generated a debilitating milieu for writing. The one widely admired book was Dylan Thomas's *Deaths and Entrances* (1946), though few attempted to imitate the technically difficult poems it contained. At times one had the sense that the state of affairs predicted by Henry Reed in 1943 had finally come about—"we may confidently expect that in 1953 young writers will be reading only each other."[16] The poetic climate at Oxford was well represented by a symposium, "5", an uneven collection of largely faceless poems. Talent of promise showed itself from time to time:

> Behind her public gestures lay the bare
> statement of death; the strips
> of orange peel, and children on whose eyes
> the flies walked casually.
> > (Michell Raper, "In the South", *Gambit,* May, 1949)

It was not surprising if, in such a situation, it failed to develop or was lost. In this "worst doldrums English verse has known", as Philip Hobsbaum put it,[17] the problem was one of finding a direction. The depressingly lifeless books produced by older poets gave little inspiration or hope: Vernon Watkins's *The Lamp and the Veil* (1945); W.H. Auden's *The Age of Anxiety* (1948); C. Day Lewis's *Poems, 1943-47* (1948); Stephen Spender's *The Edge of Being* (1949). According to John Wain, "After the war there was a great deal of reconstruction to be done in the arts . . . It was rather like being confronted with a smashed-up tangle of railway lines and wondering which one to repair first . . . The 'thirties were no use, at any rate as far as the main line was concerned, the Auden line; it was worn out even before it got smashed, and what smashed it decisively was not the war but Auden's renunciation of English nationality . . . My own answer . . . was that the Empson track was the best one . . ."[18] Wain's essay on Empson, "Ambiguous Gifts", in the final issue of *Penguin New Writing* (1950), was one of the signs of the times. Two writers who had stood outside the main stream of Anglo-American modernism and who had continued to write with a reverence for the traditional sources and forms of poetry were Robert Graves and Edwin Muir. Both seemed to write with added power in the forties, and to offer a viable example. We can see the force of that example in some of the early poems of Elizabeth Jennings in *Oxford Poetry* and *Oxford Viewpoint*.

Years later, D.J. Enright, in an address entitled "Robert Graves and the Decline of Modernism" (1960), was to say "To be contemporary now, whatever it may be positively, is pretty obviously *not* to be modernist.";[19] and Robert Conquest, in interview in 1963 that echoed earlier attitudes, criticised the oblique mode of much twentieth century poetry: "The feeling that if you say something in an oblique fashion, it is better than saying it straight, is a definite highly-established fad . . ."[20] This recognition of the decadence of the Imagist impulse was forming in the late forties. In a review of *Poets of the*

Pacific in *Poetry London* in 1950, Donald Davie wrote, "For the young English poet resentful of the tyranny of the "image" in the restricted sense of "metaphor" . . . this American anthology points in a direction which may provide a wholesome alternative, i.e. it points to a renewed poetry of statement, openly didactic but saved by a sedulously noble diction, from prosiness."[21]

The frequently vatic, imagistic poetry of the forties, with its concern for sensory impact and sensitivity of sensory observation, was to be replaced by a poetry that favoured directness, accepted statement and eschewed metaphor, was moral and ironic. This was to be the type of poetry found in *New Lines,* with its odd mixture of conservatism and radicalism that consorted with the influences of F.R. Leavis and George Orwell. In the final lengthening shadow of the predominantly American achievement of the great modernists, the formation and acceptance of the new style took a long time. Almost all the poets who appeared in *New Lines* had begun to publish poetry by the mid-forties, and many of them were contemporaries of poets posthumously celebrated before the decade had ended; yet their work was not to attain maturity or acceptance until the mid-fifties.

The difficulty these writers had in being poets in the forties illuminates the poetic situation of the decade. The "neo-romantic" manner chosen by Keyes led to an early fluency and a definite if limited achievement. Keyes's manner was consonant with the milieu in which he started writing—a milieu that marked the decadence of the modernist impulse in Britain. For those who did not find the milieu congenial or fruitful, it was difficult to find an alternative direction. Experiment seemed to have been carried already beyond profitable bounds, and every radical possibility of the medium seemed preempted. It required considerable critical imagination to see poetry free of the modernist aesthetic, with its insistence on image, metaphor, sensory impact, oblique presentation. On the other hand, ideologically, the "doldrums" of the late forties were in part the result of the stunned self-recognition that the new Britain after the war had to undergo. Most importantly, they were the flagging period between the death of one impulse and the growth of another.

CONCLUSION

Undoubtedly the events that most influenced the course of English poetry during the nineteen-forties were the coming of war and the attendant collapse of the left-wing literary movement of the thirties. The thirties saw themselves as an era of "enlightenment": ignorance was to be replaced by a new awareness. Freud and Marx, the prophets of the period, each presented a path to the amelioration of the human condition by a manipulation of the human situation. The optimism bred by that outlook was stunned by the war. There remained those who saw the war as a classic error of bourgeois society, one of the upheavals predicted by Marx; though the most common feeling about the war was one of resignation. What was new was the appearance at the other extreme of those who saw the war as a manifestation of evil in the hearts of men—a species of original sin.

There was a consequent turning away from new ideas to "ancient wisdom"; though it would be truest to say that a tension between the two is to be found in much work of the decade. The first half of the forties saw a growing humility concerning the human ability to order the fate of humanity, and an end to debunking and to the enlightened superiority that was a frequent tone in both Bloomsbury and thirties writing. In T. S. Eliot's *Four Quartets,* in Edith Sitwell's "The Song of the Cold", in the work of the Anglican poets Anne Ridler and Norman Nicholson, and in the revival of a Christian verse drama, the attitudes are explicitly religious. For others, such as Edwin Muir, the notion of myth was crucial—of an art that embodied a mode of feeling that reached back into the sources of the most basic human feeling and the deepest human wisdom. This was the mode of Vernon Watkins and Kathleen Raine. It produced a symptomatic work in Robert Graves's *The White Goddess* (1947). A related tendency is seen in the large number of works that explore the world of childhood as an earnest of an innocence that humanity is capable of, or as a mysterious source of a rightness of feeling that experience and sophistication have destroyed: Joyce Cary's *A House of Children* (1941), L.P. Hartley's *The Shrimp and the Anemone* (1944), Dylan Thomas's "Fern Hill" and his many childhood stories, and C. Day Lewis's *Word Over All* (1943) are among such works.

The demise of the left-wing literary movement gave opportunities for the writers who had come to maturity in the mid- or late thirties. Some, like Lawrence Durrell or the young Dylan Thomas, carried forward the modernist conception of poetry as an autonomous form.

Others, like Julian Symons and Roy Fuller, continued the poetry of social realism begun in the nineteen-thirties; while, in contrast, the writers of the Apocalypse movement attempted a reaction to the poetry associated with Auden, *New Verse* and *New Writing*.

The writers who continued the line of the thirties, Julian Symons, D.S. Savage, H.B. Mallalieu, George Woodcock and Roy Fuller, had all, except for Fuller, stopped writing poetry before the end of the decade. On the other hand, the decline of the alienated, ironic vision of the thirties made for the dominance of poetry of the kind written by Dylan Thomas, George Barker and David Gascoyne. There was no "movement" on the part of these writers, and the character of their work had been largely set long before the war. All had published books of poetry by 1934. Thomas's second book had been greeted by Edith Sitwell as constituting a return to the great subjects of poetry—in contrast to the work of the "Pylon Poets" of the thirties. Thomas had little interest in politics, though Barker wrote political poems in the late thirties in a visionary mode owing much to Shelley and Blake, while David Gascoyne had been sufficiently committed to the Left-wing cause to go to Spain to work for the Government cause. Their work arose from an excited engagement with modern developments in poetry, and its bent was not social-realist or ironic.

Their poetry was characterised earlier as a type of visionary modern-ism—heavily imagistic, oblique, obscure, given to distorted or frag-mented syntax, but not ironic. The distrust of the new and the turning to the traditional that came with the war, produced a situation very receptive to their type of poetry, despite its inveterate modernity. Thomas became (unwillingly) the mascot of the Apocalypse move-ment. His early work was the starting point for W.S. Graham's intros-pective and highly linguistic poetry. The work of Thomas, Barker and Gascoyne was in tune with the aims of Tambimuttu's *Poetry London,* and Thomas and Barker became literary heroes of Fitzrovia.

They became identified, in the jargon of the day, with the New Romanticism, though there is nothing to show that they had anything to do with fostering such a movement. The New Romanticism, in one of its manifestations, was an outgrowth of the Apocalypse movement—a development that was associated with increasingly conventional writ-ing, particularly in the pages of *Poetry Quarterly*. The resurgence of traditional forms was frequently accompanied by a resurgence of tradi-tional sentiment, and it is clear that many lesser writers felt that mod-ernism had gone too far.

This resurgence of traditional forms was, indeed, a notable feature of British poetry in the nineteen-forties. It is seen in the work of Dylan Thomas himself, where there is not merely a return to rhyming forms, but also to narrative, and, despite the heavy overlay of imagery, to a more direct statement of theme, which is no longer inseparable from an oblique use of imagery, as it was in his earlier work. In the poetry of Vernon Watkins, the traditional forms were associated with a return to what he felt were the traditional sources of poetry in myth and the sacred role of the poet, in a poetry of visionary traditionalism. A similar return is found in the work of Kathleen Raine, and both were in conscious revolt against the rationalism and secularism of modern humanist thought as they had encountered it a generation before in Cambridge. Kathleen Raine writes eloquently in defense of her conception of poetry, but this eloquence is not shared by her poetry. For all her talk of tradition, her work—and that of Watkins—lacks the sturdiness of a well rooted mode. Jack Clemo, whose visionary quality is much more literal and whose art is less sophisticated, gets a sturdiness in his early work that they lack.

This visionary traditionalism is related to the style of poetry attempted by Sidney Keyes. Yet, despite a largeness of ambition, Keyes's poetry is very minor, owing most to the writing of his friend, John Heath-Stubbs. Heath-Stubbs's style was distinctive, but involved the decidedly literary cultivation of writers like Lady Winchelsea or lesser Romantics such as Darley or Clare. It is noteworthy that, despite early successes, both Stubbs and his admirer of early days, David Wright, had to turn away from their early styles.

Associated with such work was the return to admiration of Yeats and a growing responsiveness to the work of Rilke—especially the *Duino Elegies* and the *Sonnets to Orpheus,* related monumental gestures of the acceptance of death; though Keyes and Alex Comfort— both writers who came to maturity *during* the war—are among the few poets of the decade whose work shows the influence of Rilke. The same may be said of the influence of existentialism and the work of Kierkegaard, much of which was published in English during the decade. Apart from David Gascoyne, it would be hard to point to any younger British poet in the least influenced by these writers whose works filled the shelves of Zwemmer's bookshop in Charing Cross Road. The cultivation of inwardness was not congenial to the British cultural scene.

Traditional forms and modes were found at their strongest in regional poetry, most notably in the work of R.S. Thomas and Patrick Kavanagh, where the actual stands forth with all the emotive power that everyday association can give it. Theirs is essentially a poetry of realism, in contrast with the mythic or visionary quality so often extolled in the decade. There is no reluctance concerning statement or narrative, and things are things, not images. This bent is seen in the work of two religious and essentially traditionalist writers, Norman Nicholson and Anne Ridler.

The resurgence of regionalist impulses was a reaction to the growing, and increasingly effete, metropolitanisation of culture. Reaction to this metropolitanisation was found in all quarters: in the Apocalypse movement, most of whose proponents were from provincial centres; in the criticism of *Scrutiny;* and in the emergence of writers like Laurie Lee and Norman Nicholson, whose early background was decidedly provincial, and whose education had been limited. Indeed, the bad writing of the period, apart from the vast amount of what may be called "amateur" poetry produced by the war, was metropolitan, stemming from the ethos of Fitzrovia, the B.B.C., the suburbs, and the proliferation of little magazines made possible by the shortage of reading material. It was frequently in what has here been termed the visionary modern or the visionary traditional mode. The work of the Apocalypse movement and of the self-styled New Romantics belongs to these modes, and it is this writing that has given the decade its bad reputation. Yet it is related to a dominant movement in taste and to work of quality, like that of Thomas, Barker, Gascoyne, Watkins and Graham, that did much to give the decade its particular character. It is worth remarking that there is an element of the bogus and pretentious in the work of Thomas and Barker (though not in that of Watkins and Graham) that corresponds to the faults of many of their followers in the forties.

Similarly, there is a shallowness in the religious writing of the decade and a preciousness in the cultivation of innocence. The mark of much bad poetry of the forties is portentousness or mock naivete; and it is for these tones that it is remembered. Despite the reasonableness of the call for an "emotional" poetry in an era where events touched human emotions at the profoundest level, the poetry of the period is at its worst when vatic and unreservedly emotional. "Fern Hill", the Apocalypse anthologies, *Poetry London, Poetry Quarterly,* the New Romanticism, David Gascoyne's "Miserere": these and many others offer the countless false notes that mar the writing of the period. It has been customary to point to a decay of "standards" as the cause of so much lamentable writing. Yet one cannot avoid asking why so many were drawn to this area of feeling with so little success. *Four Quartets* and Edwin Muir's later poems are among the few masterpieces from such ventures. Equally, George Barker, W.S. Graham and Vernon Watkins are among the few in this decreasingly ironic decade to essay the celebratory with convincing authority: the contrast between the poems in Watkins's first book and those in his second, *The Lamp and the Veil* (1945), shows how fragilely poised even his tone was.

Poetry that concerns itself with the war does not loom as large in the achievement of the decade as the war itself did in its history. The war was not at first seen in patriotic terms, though Hitler's early successes made it a war of survival. It was the Nazi's treatment of the Jews and of conquered peoples that contributed most strongly to the war's ideological content, but there is almost no poetry on this theme. The memory of World War I and the seeming betrayals that led to a second World War affected feeling very strongly, and there was a great fear of jingoism: "The truest statements about war are made under one's breath, and the most false on public platforms" Vernon Watkins wrote.[1] As Mildred Davidson has put it "the evils of warfare suddenly became side issues compared with the eternal themes of Love, Separation and Death."[2]

There was little fighting until 1940, and after that the war was somewhat stalemated for the British until the entry of Japan. There are few war poems from before this time. Sidney Keyes died at the end of the North African campaign in 1943 and finally gave Britain its first war poet hero. Relatively few in the forces saw action: of all the poets discussed in this book, only Keith Douglas, Bernard Gutteridge, Hamish Henderson, J.M. Russell, Alan Ross and Hugh Popham wrote poems during the war that reflected the experience of battle. The feeling of being trapped in time by the war, so that life was something that would begin when the individual was freed at the end of the war, is a common theme.

In spite of the dominance achieved by the poetry of Dylan Thomas, George Barker and their admirers, an equally important line of poetry in the decade is humanist, with a reassertion of traditional syntax and traditional forms. In its subduedly ironic tone and its emphasis on sensory impact and sensory perception, it continues the modification of ironic modernist poetry in the thirties. A common form of war poem is the meditative lyric, modern in its generally colloquial diction, but traditional in syntax, and owing a great deal formally to Auden and similar writers of the thirties. It is noteworthy that Auden emphasised the importance of Hardy to him as a poet of "syntax"[3]. Philip Larkin, in the late forties, was to begin to discover his own voice through the example of Hardy. Most of the war poetry is in this line, and notably that of Keith Douglas, Drummond Allison and Alan Ross. So too is that of Alun Lewis, though little touched by irony; while the lessons of the thirties are deliberately held to by the poets associated with Julian Symons's *Twentieth Century Verse* and George Woodcock's *Now*: Roy Fuller, Julian Symons, Ruthven Todd, H.B. Mallalieu and George Woodcock.

The tendencies so far discussed involved mainly the work of poets born between 1912 and 1918. In the situation created by the wartime demand for serious reading and the ironic outcome of paper rationing that anything printed would sell, the work of these writers flourished, though many of them were to cease publishing poetry before the decade was out, or shortly thereafter. However, when we turn to the generation born between 1918 and 1923, who came to maturity as the war began or in its early years, the situation is very different. It is instructive to list some of these writers: John Heath-Stubbs; Keith Douglas; Drummond Allison; Sidney Keyes; J.C. Hall; David Wright; Alan Ross; Gervase Stewart; Brian Allwood; Hamish Henderson; Alex Comfort; Philip Larkin; D.J. Enright; Donald Davie; Kingsley Amis; Dannie Abse; Vernon Scannell. The list might be extended to include William Bell (b.1924), closely associated in his career with other poets in the list. There are more names of those who died in the war or in early manhood than would generally be expected: Douglas; Allison; Keyes; Bell; Stewart; Allwood. There are also in contrast, some who emerged only later as among the most distinguished British writers: Larkin; Enright; Davie; Amis; Abse; Scannell. The latter group were all in their mid- or late twenties by 1950: none had produced memorable books by that time. The early work of most of them gives the appearance of writers groping for an idiom.

Most of those who found a fluent and individual idiom in the forties —Keyes, Heath-Stubbs, Comfort—were those who could comfortably go along with the resurgent admiration for Romantic poetry. Keyes died aged twenty-one, and Comfort published poetry infrequently after the decade ended. Their work in the forties seems inflated and superficial; while Stubbs, like his friend David Wright, had to turn his back on his early idiom in order to continue as a poet.

Though the nineteen-forties produced a welter of publication by new poets, it saw little poetry of permanent value from these poets who turned twenty around the beginning of the decade and who were in their late twenties when the decade ended. What is even more disturbing is the fact that, between the end of 1945 and the end of 1949, the only first book of any consequence by a poet born between 1924 and 1928 was J.M. Russell's *The Grinning Face* (1947). Such writers would have been in their early twenties during the last years of the decade. In brief, during the years 1940 to 1949 there was little poetry of note produced by writers born between 1918 and 1928—the poets whom one would have expected to leave their mark on the decade. There were the war poems of Keith Douglas, Alan Ross and Hamish Henderson; J.C. Hall's *The Summer Dance* (1951) and Michael Hamburger's *Flowering Cactus* (1950)—both bringing together poems from the forties; and the early books of John Heath-Stubbs. There were other poets writing who would eventually make fruitful careers; but it was clearly a bad time for beginners. Indeed, what is finally depressing about the forties is not the quality or quantity of good work produced during the decade: it is the stultification or misdirection of talent of this younger generation that war and the cultural situation produced.

The last years of the decade were the doldrums for English poetry, and several diagnoses have been offered from time to time. The most obvious one is that the unexpected decline in interest in poetry (and other serious writing), along with rising costs of publication that came with the end of the war, resulted in a drastic fall in the number of books of poetry published, particularly after publishers got burned financially in 1946 and 1947. This explanation is not entirely supported by the quality of the books actually published or of the poetry appearing in periodicals. The second and most favoured diagnosis, going back to the forties and fathered by *Scrutiny,* is that the decline in standards of taste and criticism had a devastatingly debilitating effect on creative writing. Yet D.J. Enright, a precocious contributor to *Scrutiny,* was well able to articulate this diagnosis (in *Focus,* 1, 1945) long before he found his own and different idiom as a poet. More pertinent is the distortion in poetic taste produced by the New Romanticism and the attendant resurgence of interest in Romantic poetry, along with the down-playing of the ironic mode. In particular, the growing adulation of Yeats turned younger writers to a model that it has seldom been fruitful to imitate. Such pressures were undoubtedly operative during the war years and account for many false starts— avowedly in the cases of Philip Larkin and Michael Hamburger. The nature of these pressures cannot be fully understood if thought of in purely literary terms: the situation comes to look like one of misguided taste—an effect, if anything, of the lack of standards as diagnosed by *Scrutiny.* It is only when the movement of taste is recognized as being a manifestation of a larger reorientation that it is properly perceived. John Wain recalled, in his autobiography *Sprightly Running* (1962), that, when he came to Oxford in the early forties, everyone was Christian. Like John Heath-Stubbs, he admired Charles Williams, who was lecturing there. It was this turning back to traditional and non-rational philosophies in the face of the shock of the war that gave rise to the cultivation of traditional and neo-Romantic modes in poetry in the early years of the decade. It was this that gave this change of taste its power.

After 1945, the situation was changed. Though the post-war years saw Dylan Thomas's *Deaths and Entrances* (1946) the most popular work of poetry of the period, for serious writers of poetry the neo-Romantic tendencies of the wartime period no longer exerted an important pressure. What was of concern to many younger writers was their relationship to the revolution in poetry brought about by Eliot and his generation, and the sense that to follow the directions laid down in that revolution now led to a dead end.

For the poets who came of age in the late twenties, the encounter with Anglo-American modernism had been liberating: it had seemed to provide the ideal form for the revolt against Victorian puritanism. They had found themselves able to adapt the new modes to native English forms and to their own realist preoccupations with the disintegrative forces they saw at work in their society. The ironic bent of modernism in English was completely in tune with their own predilections. The slightly younger Dylan Thomas, George Barker and David Gascoyne, in their early work, in many respects embraced the innovations of modernism in a more thoroughgoing way than did Auden and his contemporaries. However, the art of these younger writers was largely unironic, while their acceptance of Romantic poetry was obvious and constituted a reversal of the attitudes of Auden, MacNeice and others in the thirties. The wartime reaction to the cultural optimism that had been a frequent concomitant of modernism, especially in the twenties and early thirties, led to a further retreat from modernist models in the arts.

Nevertheless, the process of adjustment and absorption of modernism also involved a process of acceptance and acclimatisation that seemed to culminate immediately after the war in events like the award of the Order of Merit and the Nobel Prize to T.S. Eliot in 1948. Seeing the great Picasso exhibition in London at the end of the war, one could not help asking what further innovation was possible. The intervening years were to reveal answers; but, at the time, someone beginning in the arts must have had the sense that too many opportunities had been pre-empted. This was certainly the case for many of the poets who appeared subsequently in *New Lines*. The achievement of the great modern writers appeared as something that had to be circumvented rather than imitated, if a way forward was to be found to creative individuality.

The ambivalent relationship of British writers to modernism must be seen in the context of broader cultural developments in Britain in the first half of the twentieth century. England produced few writers of power in the Edwardian hey-day of its middle class. The remarkable writers to appear in London between 1880 and 1920 were Irish—Yeats, Shaw, Joyce; or American—James, Eliot, Pound; or even writers whose native tongue was not English, like Conrad. The British writers who flourished during that period were those whose work was directed to a moralistic, middle-brow audience—Bennett, Wells, Kipling. The notable exceptions were Hardy, Lawrence, Forster, and the brief poetic talent of Edward Thomas: they succeeded in making something new while they drew on the native power of English culture. Yet, with the partial exception of Lawrence, these writers were neither experimental nor outsiders from middle class life and its basic decencies. A thoroughly alienated artistic culture could not take hold in England: the nearest thing to emerge was Bloomsbury. In that measure one can understand why the various "isms"—"realism", "naturalism", "modernism" did not flourish in England, and why English culture remained so insular.

For many writers of the thirties, the situation outlined is related to their central subject, the decline of the middle class. Born into that class, they stepped outside in embracing a high-brow modernist art and a Left-wing political orientation. Their position was extremely ambivalent: they wrote of what their class had done to England with its materialism, its puritanism, and its bungling slaughter of youth in the Great War; at the same time they looked back nostalgically to a golden Edwardian childhood and the plenitude of a privileged liberal culture.

The writers of the forties came towards the end of this process; and, by the nineteen-fifties, the recognition that the old middle class culture has ended is one of the central recognitions of the "Movement". Though many writers of the forties began writing in the exciting days of the acceptance of modernism in the thirties, they did not inherit the radicalism of the *New Signatures, New Writing* poets. They could not feel betrayed by their ancestors or by the leaders of their class, because they did not belong to the class that felt betrayed. Thomas, Barker, Gascoyne, Fuller, Symons, Nicholson all came from the lower-middle classes and benefited from the increased opportunities for secondary education that came after World War I. They were not educated in the public schools and ancient universities of the upper-middle class establishment; while others, like Laurie Lee, W.S. Graham and Jack Clemo, had even less education.

Given the rootedness of British culture in social patterns, the upheavals produced by the two world wars and the changes attendant on growing economic, social and educational mobility were bound to produce a situation of cultural uncertainty. On the one hand, we find writers from outside the previously dominant upper-middle class drawn into an increasingly isolated metropolitan culture: it is this process that gave rise to Fitzrovia and to much that was rootlessly pretentious in the writing of the forties. This is the phenomenon that lies behind the lament over the collapse of "standards". On the other hand, the wartime cultivation of religious feeling in terms of inwardness and in isolation from social patterns went contrary to British cultural orientations, which were empirical and traditional.

Indeed, the irrational has never found a notable place in British intellectual life. This is not necessarily because the British are particularly rational. The irrational may be said to find its place in terms of the unspeakable and the unthinkable—in patterns of behaviour never brought to question. As Michael Hamburger wrote in his autobiography: "British culture was a way of life, not a set of edifying national exemplars that could be carried around in books."[4] Thinking about fundamentals is done in terms of the local and the particular and by relating questions to history and tradition. The larger emotional gestures and the larger abstractions found poor ground. Though "angst" was a word of common intellectual currency in the forties, British writers were too locked into the protecting certainties of middle class life (reinforced, if anything, by the war) to feel any profound sense of alienation from life. Decency was at once the measure and the ground of British feeling in this period. It is central to so much war poetry, and it had its fullest unironic expression in the work of Alun Lewis. The blandness of some of the lesser poetry of the period arises from this absence of irony: the war had taken away the pressures that induced the ironic socio-political perspective on middle class decency in the thirties.

A more obvious characteristic of the literature of the forties is its high valuation of sensitivity. Sensitivity may seem a *sine qua non* for the arts; but in the forties sensitive observation of the physical or the psychological seemed at once a sufficient and a necessary ingredient for a work of literature. We see this tendency satirised in Kingsley Amis's poem of the fifties, "Something Nasty in the Bookshop". The poems of Terence Tiller, Henry Reed's dramatic monologues, F.T. Prince's "Soldier's Bathing", the fiction of Denton Welch or L.P. Hartley, all show the over development of this quality, accompanied, in some cases, by the tone of self-admiration that Amis detects.

"Sensitivity" was first ostentatiously cultivated for its own sake in the nineties, the period in which the ambivalent relationship of the British middle classes to the arts took shape. It was the period in which the distinction emerged between high-brow and middle-brow art, both catering to publics that saw themselves as "serious". Virginia Woolf, herself an exponent of sensitive observation, saw the distinction in terms of an art that had designs on the reader and an art that did not. Behind this distinction lay the philistinism that valued art, if at all, only in moral terms. These stances were mirrored in their most schismatic form in the division between hearty and aesthete noted by Louis MacNeice as a pervasive feature of English public school and university life.[5] Allied with Victorian puritanism, these attitudes are the basis of the confrontation in Auden's *The Orators*

(1932) and the background to that Bloomsbury classic of debunking so popular with the writers of the thirties, Lytton Strachey's *Eminent Victorians* (1918).

Sensitivity is the badge of the alienated artist from Oscar Wilde to Cyril Connolly. An unattached sensitivity, cultivated for its own sake rather than as the concomitant of the exploration of significant experience, is a feature of much of the bad writing of the forties. Frequently such writing strikes one as a product of the metropolitan rootlessness of culture that reached excess in the period. Equally, it might be seen as a by-product of Anglo-American modernism, so distrustful of abstractions and so respectful of the "image". Yet the emphasis on sensitivity and perceptiveness can also be seen as a manifestation of a strength already noted—the rootedness of English cultural life in the particular. Ivy Compton Burnett, whose work flourished in the forties, replied late in life to the question "By wise one means what?" with ". . . perception, I think, and seeing things as they are . . ."[6]

In contrast to the cultivation of sensitive perception, a feeling for the emotive power of everyday things in all their plainness was shown by Hardy and later by Auden. It was to return to English poetry in the mature work of Philip Larkin. In the forties it is principally in regional writing and in writing about the war that *things* play a role that, without adjectival blandishment, derives strongly from their emotive significance as objects in our lives.

The patterns of everyday experience, so intimately entwined with patterns of culture in Britain, entered British writing in the first quarter of this century with an almost unconscious sense of the larger centrality of such experience and of the experiences of the British upper and middle classes. The two world wars destroyed that sense of centrality, and an awareness of this can be seen slowly developing in the forties, to emerge to consciousness in the writing of the fifties.

The place of the poetry of the forties in the history of British poetry in this century may partly be judged in terms of the careers that started then and continued and those that broke after early promise. Death took Alun Lewis, Keith Douglas, Sidney Keyes, Drummond Allison, Gervase Stewart, Brian Allwood and William Bell. It was soon to take Dylan Thomas, after a career whose slow disintegration is still a puzzle. Thomas, Barker, Gascoyne, Watkins and Raine had all begun their careers in the thirties: Barker and Watkins continued steadily as poets of stature, but Gascoyne's writing became more and more intermittent in the late forties and succeeding years. Kathleen Raine published no poetry to speak of from the early fifties to the late sixties. Yet these writers, who did so much to set the tone of the poetry of the decade, fared better than those who continued the pattern of writing found in *New Verse* and *New Writing:* Julian Symons, H.B. Mallalieu and D.S. Savage had ceased to publish poetry by the end of the decade; Ruthven Todd was to publish very little thereafter; and there was a considerable hiatus in the poetry writing of George Woodcock. Only Roy Fuller, of this group of writers, had a continuous career. The Apocalypse movement had died by 1943, and those associated with it had virtually closed their careers as poets during the decade or shortly thereafter: the exceptions were Norman McCaig and G.S. Fraser. Alex Comfort's last book of poetry for a long time appeared in 1951, while Laurie Lee's third and last volume was in 1953. Henry Reed's first book, *A Map of Verona* (1946) contains nearly all the poetry he has published. So many comparatively prolific careers of promise begun in the forties, or established in that decade, were over by 1953. Most of the casualties were among those who called themselves Romantics, though the continuers of a political, realist orientation survived little better.

Indeed, the careers begun in the forties (or the late thirties) that continued were few enough: Lawrence Durrell, Patric Dickinson, Roy Fuller, Anne Ridler, John Heath-Stubbs, W.S. Graham, Norman Nicholson, Alan Ross, Norman McCaig, G.S. Fraser, Sidney Goodsir Smith, David Wright, Terence Tiller, Charles Causley, Jack Clemo, R.S. Thomas and Patrick Kavanagh. Heath-Stubbs, Wright and McCaig all turned their backs on their earlier writing in order to find a viable mode in which to continue. Graham, R.S. Thomas, Causley, Clemo and Kavanagh were little known when the decade concluded, and would then have scarcely been regarded as typical of the period or its strengths.

Almost equally interesting is the list of careers that could not get started: Philip Larkin, Christopher Middleton and Vernon Scannell all published books that were false starts during the decade—books that very much reflected the worst shortcomings of the poetry of the period. Kingsley Amis's *Bright November* (1947) looks very weak beside his work of the fifties. The forties, in the early years so receptive to anything resembling talent, were in fact very inauspicious for the cultivation of a firm gift. The years that followed the war seemed even worse—and not merely in terms of the economic difficulties facing writers. By 1953 almost none of the periodicals mentioned in this book was still being published, and there was scarcely a literary magazine of any importance in existence in Great Britain.

This picture is not the one that presented itself to most poetry readers as the decade approached its end. The reputation of Dylan Thomas was at its height, and his influence on taste was enormous. The firm reputations were those of George Barker, David Gascoyne, Vernon Watkins, Kathleen Raine, Norman Nicholson and Lawrence Durrell. Lesser reputations were those of John Heath-Stubbs, Laurie Lee, Ronald Duncan, Terence Tiller, Alex Comfort, Henry Reed, Alan Ross and Roy Fuller. Among the celebrated dead were Sidney Keyes and Alun Lewis, though interest in their work dropped with the collapse of interest in war poetry shortly after the war ended. Much in evidence, though seldom in the best company, was Henry Treece. Those who spoke up for Welsh and Scottish nationalism (movements still with us) seemed on the silly fringe; while the verse drama (whose new writers left few works of any note) seemed an important revival. Keith Douglas's poetry was little known; and the work of Jack Clemo, R.S. Thomas and Charles Causley was scarcely known at all. Philip Larkin and Kingsley Amis were unknown outside their own circle of literary acquaintances; while Michael Hamburger was known mainly for his versions of Hölderlin and Baudelaire.

Renewal of interest in the forties will not involve, one hopes, a return to that view or a reversal of all judgements made against the decade. It is hard to imagine anyone finding the New Romanticism as important as it found itself. Yet the achievement of the decade in poetry of enduring value was greater and less contestable than has been allowed, as a listing of its outstanding books will show:

George Barker	*Eros in Dogma* (1944)
Charles Causley	*Farewell Aggie Weston* (1951)
Jack Clemo	*The Clay Verge* (1951)
Keith Douglas	*Collected Poems* (1951)
Lawrence Durrell	*A Private Country* (1943)
	Cities, Plains and People (1946)
Roy Fuller	*A Lost Season* (1944)
David Gascoyne	*Poems, 1937-1942* (1943)
W.S. Graham	*The White Threshold* (1949)
Patrick Kavanagh	*The Great Hunger* (1942)
John Heath-Stubbs	*Beauty and the Beast* (1943)
Patrick Kavanagh	*The Great Hunger* (1942)
Dylan Thomas	*Deaths and Entrances* (1946)
R.S. Thomas	*The Stones of the Field* (1946)
Vernon Watkins	*The Ballad of the Mari Llwd* (1941)

A few of these books were published shortly after the decade ended, but these contain mainly work written during the forties.

Can we point to some common features that reveal common strengths in the enduring writing of the decade? The books by

Thomas, Barker, Gascoyne, Watkins and Graham belong to the visionary, non-ironic mode that has always been felt to characterise the decade, and the work of Thomas, Barker and Graham exemplifies the overtly rhetorical tendencies so often deplored in the writing of the period. The work of Kavanagh, Causley and R.S. Thomas has a directness and a simplicity of involvement with the actual that was not a strength of most poetry of the forties; and, certainly for Thomas and Kavanagh, that strength goes along with their involvement with the life of a particular region. It would be hard, on the basis of the list, to say that the forties would have been a better literary decade had more of its poets continued the ironic, colloquial, realist mode exemplified by W.H. Auden. Only Fuller, and to some extent Durrell and Douglas, do so, despite the fact that this manner was the staple of much minor poetry.

Some obvious facts about the authors of these books present themselves. If we exclude Vernon Watkins, who left Cambridge in shock after a year, Keith Douglas and John Heath-Stubbs are the only products of the ancient universities. Indeed, few of the poets had any university education, and Kavanagh, Clemo and Graham had very little formal education at all. In this respect, the poets of the forties contrast with both the poets of the thirties and the poets of the Movement, nearly all of whom were Oxbridge products. Many of the poets on the list came from regions geographically and culturally remote from London: R.S. Thomas, Kavanagh, Clemo, Causley and Watkins all derived strength from regional culture. Indeed, the groupings point to a crisis in the cultural role of the metropolitan educational and literary centres; and the fact that the work of Causley, Clemo, R.S. Thomas and Kavanagh was so little known or esteemed during the decade, points to a shortcoming in contemporary valuations that originated largely in those metropolitan centres. In addition, Douglas and Heath-Stubbs are the only poets born after 1917 represented in the list—a reminder of how uncongenial the literary ethos of the decade proved to be for many of the better talents of their generation.

As early as 1950 Kenneth Allott said of the forties: "it is impossible to indict a whole poetic decade".[7] Indictments continue to come, and the decade is still under suspicion. Yet these indictments and suspicions arise from widely held if not very authoritative valuations made during the decade itself. These valuations and the associated climate of taste resulted in some work of enduring value going unnoticed while clearly meretricious work gained much attention. The task, to which this book has in part been addressed, is to see the poetry of the period free of its false valuations. When this is done, the poetry of the forties emerges as both rewarding and exciting. It is a decade worth returning to.

BIBLIOGRAPHY

BIBLIOGRAPHY

An attempt is made to give a comprehensive bibliography of all younger poets of any interest who began publishing in the nineteen-forties or in the years immediately preceding that decade, together with a descriptive bibliography of related material. For individual authors, all books of poems published in the British Isles up to and including 1983 are listed (though some discretion is exercised concerning small special editions of poems later collected, selections containing no new work and volumes of verse for children, published after 1950). Prose writings of relevance are listed selectively by author. Autobiographies, biographies and individual bibliographies are listed under the names of the authors to which they refer.

A guide to relevant bibliographies is to be found in *A Descriptive Catalogue of the Bibliographies of Twentieth Century British Poets, Novelists and Dramatists* by E.W. Mellown (New York: Whitson, 2nd ed., 1978). The publications of some of the smaller presses, including the Fortune Press, are described in *British Modern Press Books* by W. Ridler (London: Covent Garden, 1971). Full listings of books published by the Fortune Press and Editions Poetry London are contained in *R.A. Caton and the Fortune Press* by T. D'Arch Smith (London: Rota, 1983) and "Poetry London" by Alan Smith (*Antiquarian Book Monthly Review VI,* 4 & 5 (April & May 1979)).

Volume 20 (*British Poets 1914-1945*) and Volume 27 (*Poets of Great Britain and Ireland 1945-1960*) of the *Dictionary of Literary Biography* (Detroit, Gale) contain authoritative essays and bibliographies for many of the poets discussed in this book. Comprehensive bibliographies of individual poets, with biographical details and brief assessments, are contained in *Contemporary Poets* ed. J. Vinson (London: Macmillan, 1980). Earlier editions—*Contemporary Poets of the English Language* (London: St. James, 1970) and *Contemporary Poets* (London: St. James, 1975)—contain entries omitted from the later edition, some of which concern authors discussed in this book. (The bibliographies in the *Dictionary of Literary Biography* and *Contemporary Poets* provide a supplement and a check for this bibliography. Almost everything in this bibliography has been independently inspected, and the majority of it has been read. The *Dictionary of Literary Biography* and *Contemporary Poets* have been drawn on to supplement information on locations of manuscript collections.)

Manuscripts owned by the Arts Council, and lodged mainly in the British Library in London, are described in *The Arts Council Collec-*

tion of Modern Literary Manuscripts, 1963-1972 by J. Stratford (London: Turret, 1974). Supplementary to this is *Poetry in the Making: Catalogue of an Exhibition of Poetry Manuscripts in the British Museum* by J. Lewis (London: Turret, 1967), which contains more extensive descriptions of some of the manuscripts. The British Library holdings have been examined; and where material comes from the nineteen-forties, this is indicated in entries for individual authors. Some of the material, such as final typescripts for printing, is not as interesting as its description might suggest. The collections of manuscripts by Keith Douglas, David Gascoyne and Philip Larkin are of outstanding interest. The Dylan Thomas manuscripts in the Lockwood Memorial Library of the State University of New York at Buffalo, also of outstanding interest, were the basis of the edition of his *Notebooks*.

The following are contemporary critical surveys of the poetry and drama of the forties:

Spender, S.—*Poetry Since 1939* (London: Longmans, 1946)
Ross, A.—*Poetry 1945-1950* (London: Longmans, 1948)
Speaight, R.—*Drama Since 1939* (London: Longmans, 1947)
Trewin, J.C.—*Drama 1945-1950* (London: Longmans, 1951)

Auden and After by F. Scarfe (London: Routledge, 1942) gives a contemporary view from early in the decade of the work of Dylan Thomas, George Barker, David Gascoyne, Julian Symons, Roy Fuller and the Apocalypse poets. D. Stanford's *The Freedom of Poetry* (London: Falcon, 1947) contains essays on the work of Sidney Keyes, David Gascoyne, Alex Comfort, Lawrence Durrell, Nicholas Moore, Norman Nicholson, Wrey Gardiner, Kathleen Raine, Ruthven Todd and Anne Ridler, from a "New Romantic" viewpoint. A sense of how the literary scene appeared to a contemporary is given in *New Writing in Europe* by J. Lehmann (London: Penguin, 1940).

The following collections contain discussions of their development by poets dealt with in this book:

T.S. Eliot: A Symposium ed. R. March & Tambimuttu (London: Poetry London, 1948)
The Craft of Letters in England ed. J. Lehmann (London: Cresset, 1956)
Coming to London (London: Phoenix, 1957)
Writers on Themselves (London: B.B.C., 1964)
The Poet Speaks ed. P. Orr (London: Routledge, 1966)

Of related interest is Stephen Spender's *Life and the Poet* (London: Secker & Warburg, 1942), in which he gives a sense of the changing orientation of his generation.

The following memoirs are of special value for their illumination of the literary life of the forties. Those by J. Maclaren-Ross should not be regarded as uniformly accurate.

Davin, D.—*Closing Times* (London: Oxford, 1975)

Heppenstall, R.—*Four Absentees* (London: Barrie, 1960)

Lehmann, J.—*The Whispering Gallery* (London: Longmans, 1955)
—*I Am My Brother* (London: Longmans, 1960)
—*The Ample Proposition* (London: Eyre & Spottiswood, 1966)
—*In My Own Time* (Boston: Little, Brown, 1969) (A one-volume, slightly shortened version of the previous three volumes)

Maclaren-Ross, J.—*Memoirs of the Forties* (London: Ross, 1965)

Pudney, J.—*Home and Away* (London: Joseph, 1960)

Spender, S.—*World Within World* (London: Hamilton, 1951)
—*The Thirties and After* (London: Macmillan, 1978)

Leaves in a Storm: a book of diaries ed. S. Schimanski & H. Treece (London: Drummond, 1947)

Documents concerning Richard Hillary are:

Hillary, R.—*The Last Enemy* (London: Macmillan, 1942)
—"The Pilot and Peace" *World Review*, Oct. 1942

Koestler, A.—"The Birth of a Myth" *Horizon*, Apr. 1943 (reprinted in *The Yogi and the Commissar* (London: Cape, 1945))

Dickson, L.—*Richard Hillary* (London: Macmillan, 1950)

Information and opinions on poetry and verse drama on the radio by writers involved in its production are to be found in:

Arlott, J.—"Dylan Thomas and Radio" *The Adelphi* 30,2 (Feb, 1954)

Cleverdon, D.—*The Growth of Milkwood* (New York: New Directions, 1969)

Dickinson, P.—*The Good Minute* (London: Gollancz, 1965)

Heppenstall, R.—*Portrait of the Artist as a Professional Man* (London: Owen, 1969)

MacNeice, L.—"Introduction" to *Christopher Columbus* (London: Faber, 1944)
"General Introduction" to *The Dark Tower: and Other Radio Scripts* (London: Faber, 1947)

McWhinnie, D.—*The Art of Radio* (London: Faber, 1959)
Orwell, G.—"Poetry and the Microphone" in *Collected Essays*
        (London: Secker & Warburg, 2nd. ed., 1961)
British Radio Drama ed. J. Drakakis (Cambridge: Cambridge
University Press, 1981)

Accounts of the activities of important publishers of poetry are to be
found in:

Smith, T. D'Arch—*R.A. Caton and the Fortune Press*
        (London: Rota, 1983)
Smith, A.—"Poetry London" (*Antiquarian Book Monthly
        Review*, VI, 4 & 5 (April & May 1979))
Lehmann, J.—*Thrown to the Woolfs* (London: Weidenfeld &
        Nicholson, 1978)

Lehmann's autobiographies, listed above, also give an account of his
publishing activities with the Hogarth Press and from his own publishing house.

The important literary periodicals of the forties are discussed in the
text. The following is an attempt at a more comprehensive list of
periodicals that showed more than a passing interest in poetry in a
contemporary idiom. Included are periodicals from the thirties that can
be regarded as precursors of movements in the forties. One-issue publications are included if they seem to have been intended as the beginnings of periodical issue. Also included are symposia of more than
one issue, which were produced to evade the ban on new periodicals.
Periodicals, such as *Compass,* which consisted wholly or largely of
reprints, are excluded. In a few cases information is incomplete (or
possibly inaccurate) as not all issues are, for instance, dated, and complete runs of many periodicals are hard or impossible to locate.

Adam London (from No. 152): ed. M. Grindea (1941-   )
Arena London: ed. J. Davenport, J. Lindsay & R. Swingler
        (1949-1951)
Bell Dublin: ed. S. O'Faolain (1940-1954)
Bolero Oxford: ed. J. Waller (1938-1939)
The Booster (later *Delta*) Paris: ed. A. Perlès, L. Durrell, H.
        Miller & W. Saroyan (1937-1939)
Bugle Blast London: ed. J. Aistrop & R. Moore (1943-1947)
The Changing World London: ed. B. Wall & M. Harari (1947-
        1949)
Circus London: ed. J. Davenport
Citadel Cairo: ed. R.D. Smith (1942-?)
Comment London: ed. S. McLeod & V. Neuberg (1935-1937)

Contemporary Poetry and Prose London: ed. R. Roughton (1936-1937)

Cornish Review: Penzance ed. D.V. Baker (1949-1952)

Convoy London: ed. R. Maugham (1944-1946)

The Critic Cambridge: ed. C. Collins, W. Mankowitz, R. Williams (1947) (Continued as *Politics and Letters* (1948))

Delta (see *The Booster* above)

Focus London: ed. B. Rajan & A. Pearse (1945-1950)

Fords and Bridges Oxford & Cambridge: various editors (1936-1939)

Forum London: ed. M. Spark & D. Stanford (1949-1950)

Front Line London: ed. S. & B. Litvinoff (1946)

Gambit Oxford: various editors (1949-1950)

The Glass London: ed. A. Barrow (1948-1954)

Harvest London: ed. V. Stuart (1948-1950)

Here and Now London: ed. P. Alberry & S. Read (1941-1949)

Horizon London: ed. C. Connolly & P. Watson (1940-1950)

Imprint Cambridge: ed. J.M. Grundy (1949-1950)

Janus London: ed. R. Hutchins & J.R. Morley (1936)

Kingdom Come Oxford & Kenton: ed. J. Waller & others (Oxford); A. Rook, S.K. Schimanski & H. Treece (Kenton) (1939-1943)

Life and Letters Today London: ed. R. Herring (= R.H. Williams) (1935-1950)

London Forum London: ed. P. Baker & R. Gant (1946-1947)

Mandrake Oxford & London: ed. J. Wain, A. Boyars & others (1945-1956)

The Mint London: ed. G. Grigson (1946 & 1948)

Modern Reading London: ed. R. Moore (1941-1952)

The New Generation London: ed. P. Ratazzi (1946-1947)

New Poetry London: ed. N. Moore (1946)

New Road Billericay & London: ed. A. Comfort & J. Bayliss (1943, 1944); F. Marnau (1944, 1945); W. Gardiner (1949) (1943-1949)

The New Saxon Pamphlets (later *The New Saxon Review* (1945) & *Albion* (1946)) Edenbridge: ed. J. Atkins (1944-1947)

New Writing (as *Folios of New Writing* (1940-1941), *Daylight* (1941) *New Writing & Daylight* (1942-1946)) London: ed. J. Lehmann (1940-1946)

Nine London: ed. P. Russell, G.S. Fraser & I. Fletcher (1949-1956)

Now Marlow, Cambridge & London: ed. G. Woodcock (1940-1947)

Oasis London: ed. J. Bate & C. Nicholson (1942-1944) (Previously *X6,* typed and mimeographed)

Opus London: ed. D.V. Baker (begins at No. 8) (1941-1943)

Orientations Cairo: ed. G.S. Fraser

Orion London: ed. R. Lehmann, E. Muir & D.K. Roberts (1945-1947)

Orpheus London: ed. J. Lehmann (1948-1949)

Our Time London: various editors (1941-1949)

Outposts Blackpool: ed. H. Sergeant (1944-   )

Penguin New Writing London: ed. J. Lehmann (1940-1950)

Penguin Parade London: ed. D.K. Roberts (1937-1948)

Personal Landscape Cairo: ed. R. Fedden, L. Durrell & B. Spencer (1942-1945)

Phoenix Ayton: ed. C. Crawshaw, N. Hampson, J.A. Shaw & others (1939-1942)

Poetry Folios London: ed. A. Comfort & P. Wells (1942-1951)

Poetry London London: ed. M.J. Tambimuttu (1939-1949); ed. R. March & N. Moore (1948-1951) (1939-1951)

Poetry Quarterly Billericay & London: ed. W. Gardiner (1939-1953)

The Poetry Review London: ed. J. Gawsworth, M. Spark & others (1912-   ) & *Poetry of Today* (The *Poetry Review* New Verse Supplement) (1924-1947)

Poetry Scotland Glasgow: ed. M. Lindsay (1944-1945); ed. M. Lindsay & H. MacDiarmid (1947) (1944-1947)

Poets Now in the Services London: ed. A.E. Lowry

Politics and Letters (see *The Critic* above)

Prospect Little Chalfont: ed. E. Toeman (1944-1949)

Resistance London: ed. D. Stanford & D. West (1946)

Salamander Cairo: ed. K. Bullen & J. Cromer (1943)

Scottish Art and Letters Glasgow: ed. R. Crombie Saunders (1944-1950)

Scrutiny Cambridge: ed. F.R. Leavis & others (1932-1953)

Selected Writing London: ed. R. Moore & M.J. Tambimuttu (1942-1946)

Seven Taunton & Cambridge: ed. J. Garland & N. Moore (1938-1940); new series: London: ed. S. Tremayne (1941-1947)

Staples Modern Reading (a continuation of *Modern Reading* by its original publisher after *Modern Reading* transferred to Big Ben Books) (see above *Modern Reading*) (1946-1947)

The Townsman London: ed. R. Duncan (1938-1941) (continued as *The Scythe*)

Transformation London: ed. S. Schimanski & H. Treece (1943-1946)

Translation London: ed. N. Braybrooke & E. King (1945-1947)

Twentieth Century Verse London: ed. J. Symons (1937-1939)

Voices Tring: ed. D.V. Baker (1944-1947)

Wales Newton, Carmarthen, London: ed. K. Rhys (1937-1949)

The Welsh Review Cardiff: ed. G. Jones (1939 & 1944-1948)

The Wind and the Rain London: ed. N. Braybrooke (1942-1951)

The Windmill London: ed. E. Lane & R. Moore (1944-1948)

World Review London: ed. E. Hulton & others (1940-1948; new series, 1949-1953) (of interest only from 1948 onwards)

Writers of Tomorrow London: ed. P. Ratazzi (1944-1948)

Writing To-day London: ed. D.V. Baker (1943-1946)

The Year's Work in Literature London: ed. J. Lehmann (1949-1950)

Yellow Jacket London: ed. C. Fitzgibbon (1939)

The following are anthologies drawn from individual periodicals of the forties:

The Golden Horizon ed. C. Connolly (London: Weidenfeld & Nicolson, 1953)

Ideas and Places by C. Connolly (London: Weidenfeld & Nicolson, 1953) (Reprints Connolly's editorial "Comments" from *Horizon*)

Poems from New Writing ed. J. Lehmann (London: Lehmann, 1946)

English Stories from New Writing ed. J. Lehmann (London: Lehmann,1947)

The Pleasures of New Writing ed. J. Lehmann (London: Lehmann, 1952)

The Penguin New Writing 1940-1950 ed. J. Lehmann & R. Fuller (Harmondsworth: Penguin, 1985)

Personal Landscape ed. R. Fedden (London: Poetry London, 1945)

Salamander ed. K. Bullen & J. Cromer (London: Allen & Unwin, 1947)

The Importance of Scrutiny ed. E. Bentley (New York: Stewart, 1948)

A Selection from Scrutiny ed. F.R. Leavis (Cambridge: Cambridge University, 1968)

The Wind and the Rain: an Easter Book for 1963 ed. N. Braybrooke (London: Secker & Warburg, 1962)

The following anthologise work from many little magazines of the period:

Little Reviews Anthology ed. D.V. Baker (1943-1949, 5 vols.)

Histories of individual periodicals are:

> "Now: an heir of the Thirties" by G. Woodcock, *Modern Studies* 1,2 (1974)
> *Personal Landscape* by R. Fedden (London: Turret, 1966)
> "Poetry London" by A. Smith, *Antiquarian Book Monthly Review* VI, 4 & 5 (Apr & May, 1979)
> *The Moment of Scrutiny* by Francis Mulhern (London: New Left Books, 1979)

The special Cyril Connolly number of *Adam* (385-390, 1974/1975) contains material about *Horizon*. John Lehmann's autobiographies (see above) discuss his work as editor of *New Writing, Orpheus* and related periodicals. The 1963 reprint of *Scrutiny* (Cambridge University Press) contains "A Retrospect" by its principal editor, F.R. Leavis.

A brief survey of little magazines of the forties is given in *The Little Reviews 1914-1943* by D.V. Baker (London: Allen & Unwin, 1943), but the bibliographies of the five issues of his *Little Reviews Anthology* (see above) give much more information. *Periodicals 1979*, a catalogue issued by I.D. Edrich, 17 Selsdon Road, London E11 2QF, is easily one of the best sources of information on periodicals of the period. *English Literary Journals, 1900-1950* by Michael N. Stanton (Detroit: Gale, 1982) describes some of the periodicals listed in this bibliography and gives a valuable list of references. *An Author Index to Selected British Little Magazines, 1930-1939* by B.C. Bloomfield indexes some of the earlier periodicals listed above.

The following are poetry broadsheets or pamphlets published during the forties periodically or as series:

> *Caseg Broadsheets* (ed. B. Chamberlain & J. Petts) (1941-1942) (D. Thomas, A. Lewis, H.I. Bell, L. Roberts, B. Chamberlain)
> *Resurgam Younger Poets* (London: Favil Press, 1940-1944) (P. Baker, P. Ledward, B. Warr, D. Gibson, P. Scott, E. Litvinoff, A. Comfort, J. Atkins, L. Norris, B. Allwood)
> *Key Poets* (London: Fore Publications, 1950) (E. Sitwell, N. Cameron, J. Beeching, G. Barker, R. Swingler, J. Denwood, S. Snaith, D. Cooke, J. Lindsay, M. Carpenter)
> *The New Athenian Broadsheets* (1947-1951) (Mainly Scots poets)

Anthologies of contemporary writing, published in the forties, are:

> *The New Apocalypse* ed. J.F. Hendry & H. Treece (London: Fortune, 1939)

The White Horseman ed. J.F. Hendry & H. Treece (London: Routledge, 1941)

The Crown and the Sickle ed. J.F. Hendry & H. Treece (London: Staples, 1943)

A New Romantic Anthology ed. S. Schimanski & H. Treece (London: Grey Walls, 1949)

The Fortune Anthology ed. J. Bayliss, N. Moore & D. Newton (London: Fortune, 1942)

Auguary ed. A.M. Hardie & K.C. Douglas (Oxford: Blackwell, 1940)

Oxford and Cambridge Writing ed. A. Brown & D. Bain (Private pub.: Cambridge, 1942)

Middle East Anthology ed. J. Waller & E. de Mauney (London: Drummond, 1946)

A later anthology of Middle East writing is:

Return to Oasis: War Poems and Recollections from the Middle East, 1940-1946, ed. G.S. Fraser and others (London: Shepherd-Walwyn & Poetry London, 1980)

Contemporary anthologies of poetry are:

"5" ed. J.B. Donne (Oxford: Privately printed, 1949) (C.E.B. Brett, W.J. Harvey, J.D. James, J.M. Russell, J.B. Donne)

Air Force Poetry ed. J. Pudney & H. Treece (London: Lane, 1944)

An Anthology of Contemporary Northern Poetry ed. H. Sergeant (London: Harrap, 1947)

Contemporary Irish Poetry ed. R. Greacen & V. Iremonger (London: Faber, 1949)

Eight Oxford Poets ed. M. Meyer & S. Keyes (London: Routledge, 1941) (K.C. Douglas, G. Swaine, J. Heath-Stubbs, M. Meyer, R. Porter, D. Allison, J.A. Shaw, S. Keyes)

For Those Who Are Alive ed. H. Sergeant (London: Fortune, 1946)

For Your Tomorrow (London: Oxford, 1950) (Poems by men from public schools who died in World War II)

Irish Poems of Today ed. G. Taylor (London: Secker & Warburg, 1946)

Lyra ed. A. Comfort & R. Greacen (Billericay: Grey Walls, 1942)

Modern Scottish Poetry ed. M. Lindsay (London: Faber, 1946)

Modern Welsh Poetry ed. K. Rhys (London: Faber, 1944)

New Lyrical Ballads ed. M. Carpenter, J. Lindsay, H. Arundel
   (London: Poetry London, 1945)
Oasis—The Middle East Anthology of Poetry from the Forces ed.
   D. Saunders, V. Selwyn, D. Burke (Cairo: Salamander, 1943)
Oxford Poetry: 1942-43; 1947; 1948; 1949 (Oxford: Blackwell)
The Penguin Book of Contemporary Verse ed. K. Allott (London:
   Penguin, 1950)
Poems from Italy (London: Harrap, 1945)
Poems from the Desert (London: Harrap, 1944)
Poems from the Forces ed. K. Rhys (London: Routledge, 1941)
   & *More Poems from the Forces* ed. K. Rhys (London:
   Routledge, 1943)
Poems from India ed. R.N. Currey & R.V. Gibson (London:
   Oxford, 1946)
Poems of the Forces (London: Fortune, n.d. [1949])
Poems of the War Years ed. M. Wollman (London: Macmillan,
   1950)
Poems of This War ed. P. Ledward & C. Strang (Cambridge:
   Cambridge University, 1942)
Poetry from Cambridge in Wartime ed. G. Moore (London:
   Fortune, 1946)
Poetry from Cambridge 1947-1950 ed. P.M. Green (London:
   Fortune, 1951)
Poetry from Oxford in Wartime ed. W. Bell (London: Fortune,
   1945) & *More Poetry from Oxford* ed. W. Bell (London:
   Fortune, 1946)
Poetry from Oxford Michaelmas 1946—Trinity 1948 ed. N.
   Mawdsley (London: Fortune, 1949)
Poetry from Oxford Michaelmas 1948—Michaelmas 1949 ed. D.
   Williamson (London: Fortune, 1950)
Poetry in Wartime ed. M.J. Tambimuttu (London: Faber, 1942)
Poetry of the Present ed. G. Grigson (London: Phoenix,1949)
Poets of Tomorrow ed. J. Lehmann:
   First Selection (London: Hogarth, 1939) (P. Hewett, H.B.
      Mallalieu R. Todd, R. Waller)
   Second Selection: Cambridge Poetry 1940 (London: Hogarth,
      1940) (J. Bateman, S. Coates, A. Comfort, M.J. Craig, M.
      Holloway, N. Moore, J. Moreton, G. Scurfield, G. Stewart,
      E.V. Swart, T. Tiller)
   Third Selection (London: Hogarth, 1942) (L. Little, D.
      Gascoyne, L. Lee, A. Drinan, A. Harvey)
Proems (London: Fortune, 1938) (P. Evans, L. Durrell, R. Todd,
   E. Foxall, O. Blakeston, R. Heppenstall)

Sailing Tomorrow's Seas ed. M. Lindsay (London: Fortune, 1944)

Contemporary collections of popular verse of the forties are:

Airman's Song Book ed. C.H. Ward-Jackson (London: Sylvan, 1945)
Ballads of World War II ed. H. Henderson (Glasgow: Lili Marleen Club, 1947)

More recent anthologies are:

Poetry of the Forties ed. R. Skelton (London: Penguin, 1968)
Poetry of the Forties ed. H. Sergeant (London: Longmans, 1971)
The Terrible Rain: War Poets 1939-1945 ed. B. Gardner (London: Methuen, 1966)
The Poetry of War: 1939-1945 ed. I. Hamilton (London: Ross, 1968)

The last contains valuable "autobiographical statements" by some poets.

A full account of British history in the early twentieth century is *English History: 1914-1945* by A.J.P. Taylor (Oxford: Clarendon, 1965). There are innumerable books on the British role in World War II. The following give accounts of the aspects of the war that most affected the civilian population:

Calder, A.—*The People's War* (London: Cape, 1969)
Harrison, T.—*Living Through the Blitz* (London: Collins, 1976)

Major events and the style of life in the years after the war are described in *Age of Austerity* ed. M. Sissons & P. French (London: Hodder & Stoughton, 1963).

The Collected Essays, Journalism and Letters of George Orwell (4 vols.) (London: Secker & Warburg, 1968) gives particularly perceptive and intimate insights into the intellectual and social life of the forties. This is especially true of the "Wartime Diaries".

A retrospective view of the wartime experiences of a number of pacifists is given in *The Objectors* ed. C. Simmons (Isle of Man: Times Press, 1965). Statements by D.S. Savage, Julian Symons and George Woodcock to Conscientious Objection Tribunals are contained in *Now* No. 3 (Fall, 1940).

European Witness by S. Spender (London: Hamilton, 1946) gives a first-hand British impression of Europe immediately after the war.

Under Seige by R. Hewison (Weidenfeld & Nicolson, 1977) gives an account of artistic life in London from 1939 to 1945. Its "Notes on Sources" provides a valuable bibliographical aid. *Painting Since 1939* by R. Ironside (London: Longmans, 1948), *Music Since 1939* by R.H. Myers (London: Longmans, 1947) and *Ballet Since 1939* by A. Haskell (London: Longmans, 1946) survey three arts that flourished during the war years. *British Romantic Artists* by J. Piper (London: Collins, 1942) is symptomatic of an important change in orientation in the visual arts. A decidedly critical view of the New Romanticism in painting is given in G. Grigson's "Authentic and False in the New 'Romanticism' " (*Horizon* 99 (Mar, 1948)).

INDIVIDUAL POETS

Abse, Dannie (b. 1923)

Poetry	*After Every Green Thing* (London: Hutchinson, 1949)
	Walking Under Water (London: Hutchinson, 1952)
	Tenants of the House (London: Hutchinson, 1957)
	Poems, Golders Green (London: Hutchinson, 1962)
	D. Abse: A Selection (London: Vista, 1963)
	A Small Desperation (London: Hutchinson, 1968)
	Funland and other poems (London: Hutchinson, 1973)
	Collected Poems: 1948-1976 (London: Hutchinson, 1977)
	Way Out in the Centre (London: Hutchinson, 1981)
Prose	*A Poet in the Family* (London: Hutchinson, 1974) (Autobiography)
	A Strong Dose of Myself (London: Hutchinson, 1983) (Autobiography)
Editor	*Mavericks* (w. H. Sergeant) (London: Poetry & Poverty, 1957)
	Poetry and Poverty
Biographical	*The Poetry of Dannie Abse: Essays and Reminiscenses,* ed. J. Cohen (London: Robson, 1983)

Allison, Drummond (1921-1943)

Poetry	*The Yellow Night* (London: Fortune, 1944)
	The Poems of Drummond Allison, ed. M. Sharp (Reading: White Knight, 1978)

Manuscripts   British Library BM53713 (Poems)
                                      BMEg3797 (Prose
                                      Notebook)

Allwood, Brian (1920-1944)
  Poetry   *Now or Never* (London: Favil, 1944)

Amis, Kingsley (b. 1922)
  Poetry   *Bright November* (London: Fortune, 1947)
                               A Frame of Mind (Reading: Reading
                                   University School of Art, 1953)
                               The Fantasy Poets, 22: Kingsley Amis
                                   (Oxford: Fantasy, 1954)
                               A Case of Samples: Poems 1946-1956
                                   (London: Gollancz, 1956)
                               The Evans Country (Oxford: Fantasy,
                                   1962)
                               *A Look Round the Estate: Poems 1957-
                                   1967* (London: Cape, 1967)
                               Collected Poems 1944-1979 (London:
                                   Hutchinson, 1979)
  Prose   *Lucky Jim* (London: Gollancz, 1954)
                                   (Novel)
                               That Uncertain Feeling (London: Gollancz,
                                   1955) (Novel)
                               Socialism and the Intellectuals (London:
                                   Fabian Society, 1957)
                               What Became of Jane Austen (London:
                                   Cape, 1970) (Essays)
  Editor   *Oxford Poetry 1949* (w. J. Michie)
                                   (Oxford: Blackwell, 1949)
  Manuscripts   Lockwood Memorial Library, State
                                   University of New York, Buffalo
  Bibliography   *Kingsley Amis: a Checklist* by J.B. Gohn
                                   (Kent: Kent State, 1976)

Arlott, John (b. 1914)
  Poetry   *Of Period and Place* (London: Cape, 1944)
                               Clausentum (London: Cape, 1946)

Atkins, John (b. 1910
  Poetry   *Experience of England* (London: Favil,
                                   1942)
  Prose   *The Diary of William Carpenter* (London:
                                   Favil, 1943)
  Editor   *New Saxon Review (New Saxon Pamphlets)*

Baker, Peter
  Poetry   *The Beggar's Lute* (London: Favil, 1940)
  Publisher   Resurgam Press

Barker, George (b. 1913)
  Poetry   *Thirty Preliminary Poems* (London: Parton,
                                      1933)
                                  Poems (London: Faber, 1935)
                                  Calamiterror (London: Faber, 1937)
                                  Lament and Triumph (London: Faber,
                                      1940)
                                  Eros in Dogma (London: Faber, 1944)
                                  News of the World (London: Faber, 1950)
                                  The True Confession of George Barker
                                      (London: Fore, 1950; w. Part II,
                                      London: MacGibbon & Kee, 1965)
                                  A Vision of Beasts and Gods (London:
                                      Faber, 1954)
                                  Collected Poems, 1930-1955 (London:
                                      Faber, 1957)
                                  The View From a Blind I (London: Faber,
                                      1962)
                                  Dreams of a Summer Night (London:
                                      Faber, 1966)
                                  The Golden Chains (London: Faber, 1968)
                                  At Thurgarton Church (London: Trigam,
                                      1969)
                                  To Aylsham Fair (London: Faber, 1970)
                                  Poems of Places and People (London:
                                      Faber, 1971)
                                  The Alphabetical Zoo (London: Faber,
                                      1972)
                                  In Memory of David Archer (London:
                                      Faber, 1973)
                                  Villa Stella (London: Faber, 1978)
                                  Dialogues etc. (London: Faber, 1976)
                                  Seven Poems (Warwick: Greville, 1977)
                                  Anno Domini (London: Faber, 1983)
  Drama   *Two Plays* (London: Faber, 1978)
  Prose   *Alanna Autumnal* (London: Wishart, 1933)
                                  Janus (London: Faber, 1935)
                                  The Dead Seagull (London: Lehmann,
                                      1950)
                                  Essays (London: MacGibbon & Kee, 1970)
  Manuscripts   British Library 56257; University of Texas;
                                      Lockwood Memorial Library, State
                                      University of New York, Buffalo; Berg
                                      Collection, New York Public Library
  Biographical   *Homage to George Barker* ed. J. Heath-
                                      Stubbs & M. Green (London: Brian &
                                      O'Keefe, 1973)
  Bibliography   *Homage to George Barker* (above)

Bayliss, John (1919-1978)
Poetry

Indications (w. J. Kirkup & J.O. Thomas)
(London: Grey Walls, 1943)
The White Knight (London: Fortune, 1944)
Call Wind to Witness (w. C. Hamblett, A.
Lewis & E. Litvinoff) (London:
Capriole, 1945)
A Romantic Miscellany (w. D. Stanford)
(London: Fortune, 1946)
Venus in Libra (Walton on Thames:
Outposts, 1977)

Editor

The Fortune Anthology (w. N. Moore &
D. Newton) (London: Fortune, 1946)
New Road, 1943 & 1944 (w. A. Comfort)

Bell, William (1924-1948)
Poetry

Elegies (London: Fortune, 1945)
Mountains Beneath the Horizon (London:
Faber, 1950)

Editor

Poetry from Oxford in Wartime (London:
Fortune, 1945)
More Poetry from Oxford
(London: Fortune, 1947)

Bourne, David (1921-1941)
Poetry

Poems (London: Lane, 1944)

Brooke, Jocelyn (1908-1966)
Poetry

Six Poems (Jocelyn Brooke: Oxford, 1928)
December Spring (London: Lane, 1947)
The Elements of Death (Aldington: Hand &
Flower, 1952)

Bibliography

Jocelyn Brooke: A Checklist of his Writings
by A. Rota (London: Rota, 1963)

Bruce, George (b. 1909)
Poetry

Sea Talk (Glasgow: MacLellan, 1944)
Selected Poems (Edinburgh: Saltire, 1947)
Landscape and Figures (Preston: Akros,
1967)
Collected Poems (Edinburgh: Edinburgh
University, 1971)

Manuscripts

National Library, Scotland; Lockwood
Memorial Library, State University of
New York, Buffalo

Buxton, John (b. 1912)
Poetry

Westward (London: Cape, 1942)
Such Liberty (London: Macmillan, 1944)
Atropos (London: Macmillan, 1946)
Marriage Song for Princess Elizabeth
(London: Macmillan, 1947)

Capetanakis, Demetrios (1912-1944)
    Poetry & Prose w. Memoirs   *Demetrios Capetanakis: A Greek Poet in England* (London: Lehmann, 1947)

Causley, Charles (b. 1917)
    Poetry   *Farewell, Aggie Weston* (Aldington: Hand & Flower, 1951)

Survivor's Leave (Aldington: Hand & Flower, 1953)

Union Street (London: Hart-Davis, 1957)

Johnny Alleluia (London: Hart-Davis, 1961)

Underneath the Water (London: Macmillan, 1968)

Timothy Wintos (London: Turret, 1970)

Six Women (Richmond: Keepsake, 1974)

Collected Poems (London: Macmillan, 1975)

The Animal's Carol (London: Macmillan, 1975)

Here We Go Round the House (Leicester: New Broom, 1976)

Secret Destinations (London: Macmillan, 1984)

    Plays   *Runaway* (London: Curwen, 1936)

The Conquering Hero (London: Curwen, 1937)

Bendict (London: Muller, 1938)

How Pleasant to Know Mr. Lear (London: Muller, 1948)

    Prose   *Hands to Dance* (London: Carroll & Nicholson, 1951) (Stories) (New edition with autobiographical "Afterword", London: Robson, 1979)

    Manuscripts   University of Exeter (Notebooks, draft poems); Lockwood Memorial Library, State University of New York, Buffalo (1940's material)

Clemo, Jack (b. 1916)
    Poetry   *The Clay Verge* (London: Chatto & Windus, 1951)

The Map of Clay (London: Methuen, 1961)

Cactus on Carmel (London: Methuen, 1967)

The Echoing Tip (London: Methuen, 1971)

Broad Autumn (London: Methuen, 1975)

Prose

The Wilding Graft (London: Chatto & Windus, 1948) (Novel)
Confessions of a Rebel (London: Chatto & Windus, 1949) (Autobiography)
The Invading Gospel (London: Bles, 1958)
The Marriage of a Rebel (London: Gollancz, 1980) (Autobiography)

Coates, Stephen
Poetry

First Poems (London: Fortune, 1943)
Second Poems (London: Poetry London, 1947)

Comfort, Alex (b. 1920)
Poetry

France and Other Poems (London: Favil, 1941)
Three New Poets (w. R. McFadden & I. Serraillier) (Billericay: Grey Walls, 1942)
A Wreath for the Living (London: Routledge, 1942)
Elegies (London: Routledge, 1944)
The Song of Lazarus (Barnet: Poetry Folios, 1945)
The Signal to Engage (London: Routledge, 1947)
And All But He Departed (London: Routledge, 1951)
Haste to the Wedding (London: Eyre & Spottiswood, 1962)
All But a Rib (London: Beazley, 1973)
Coming together (New York: Crown, 1975)
Poems for Jane (London: Beazley, 1978)

Plays

In Egypt (London: Grey Walls, 1942)
Cities of the Plain (London: Grey Walls, 1943)

Prose

The Silver River (London: Chapman & Hall, 1938) (Diary)
No Such Liberty (London: Chapman & Hall, 1941) (Novel)
The Almond Tree: A Legend (London: Chapman & Hall, 1942)
The Powerhouse (London: Routledge, 1944) (Novel)
Art and Social Responsibility (London: Falcon, 1946) (Essays)

	Letters from an Outpost (London: Routledge, 1947) (Stories)
	The Novel and Our Time (London: Phoenix, 1948)
	On This Side Nothing (London: Routledge, 1947) (Novel)
	A Giant's Strength (London: Routledge, 1952)
Editor	*Lyra* (w. R. Greacen) (Billericay: Grey Walls, 1942)
	New Road 1943 & 1944 (w. J. Bayliss)
Bibliography	"Alex Comfort: a Bibliography in Progress" by D. Callaghan *West Coast Review,* 1969

Conquest, Robert (b. 1917)

Poetry	*Poems* (London: Macmillan, 1955)
	Between Mars and Venus (London: Macmillan, 1962)
	Arias for a Love Opera (London: Macmillan, 1969)
	Forays (London: Chatto & Windus, 1979)
Prose & Poetry	*The Abomination of Moab* (London: Smith, 1979)
Editor	*New Lines* (London: Macmillan, 1956)

Cooke, Dorian (b. 1916)

| Poetry | *Fugue for Our Time* (London: Fore, 1950) |

Corby, Herbert (b. 1911)

Poetry	*Hampdens Going Over* (London: Poetry London, 1945)
	Time in a Blue Prison (London: Fortune, 1947)
	Angel on My Shoulder (London: Fortune, 1948)
	Poems (London: Fortune, 1961)

Corsellis, Timothy (1921-1941)

Poetry	Selections in:
	Poems from the Forces ed. K. Rhys (London: Routledge, 1941)
	Poems of this War ed. P. Ledward & C. Strang (Cambridge: Cambridge University Press, 1942)
	More Poems from the Forces ed. K. Rhys (London: Routledge, 1943)

Craig, Maurice James (b. 1919)

| Poetry | *Some Way for Reason* (London: Heinemann, 1948) |

Currey, R[alph] N[ixon]
  Poetry

  Prose

  Editor

Dehn, Paul (1912-1976)
  Poetry

Dickinson, Patric (b. 1914)
  Poetry

Tiresias (London: Oxford, 1940)
This Other Planet (London: Routledge, 1945)
Indian Landscape (London: Routledge, 1947)
The Africa We Knew (Cape Town: Philip, 1973)
Poets of the 1939-1945 War (London: Longmans, 1960)
Poems from India (w. R.V. Gibson) (London: Oxford, 1946)

The Day's Alarm (London: Hamilton, 1949)
Romantic Landscape (London: Hamilton, 1952)
Quake, Quake, Quake (London: Hamilton, 1960)
The Fern on the Rock (London: Hamilton, 1965)

The Seven Days of Jericho (London: Dakars, 1944)
Theseus and the Minotaur (London: Cape, 1946)
The Stone in the Midst (London: Methuen, 1948)
The Sailing Race (London: Chatto & Windus, 1952)
The Scale of Things (London: Chatto & Windus, 1955)
The World I See (London: Chatto & Windus, 1960)
The Cold Universe (London: Chatto & Windus, 1964)
Selected Poems (London: Chatto & Windus, 1968)
More Than Time (London: Chatto & Windus, 1970)
The Wintering Tree (London: Chatto & Windus, 1973)
The Bearing Beast (London: Chatto & Windus, 1976)
Our Living John and other poems (London: Chatto & Windus, 1979)

Poems from Rye (Rye: Martollo, 1980)
Winter Hostages (Hitchin: Mandeville, 1980)
A Rift in Time (London: Chatto & Windus, 1982)

Prose
The Good Minute (London: Gollancz, 1965) (Autobiography)

Manuscripts
British Library 53786. University of Birmingham (Verse plays, translations, poems) (1940's material)

Douglas, Keith (1920-1944)
Poetry
Selected Poems (w. J.C. Hall & N. Nicholson) (London: Staples, 1943)
Collected Poems (London: Poetry London, 1951; new ed. Faber, 1966)
Complete Poems (London: Oxford, 1978)

Poetry & Prose
Alamein to Zem Zem (London: Poetry London, 1946; new ed. without poetry, Faber, 1966)

Prose
"Death of a Horse" *Citadel* (July, 1942) and *Lilliput* (July, 1944)
"The Little Red Mouth" *Stand* 9,2 (1970)
"Poets in This War" *Times Literary Supplement* 23 Apr, 1971 (written May, 1943)

Editor
Augury: An Oxford Miscellany of Verse and Prose (w. A.M. Hardie) (Oxford: Blackwell, 1940)

Manuscripts
British Library 53773-6; 56355-60; 57977 (Poems, diaries, letters, etc.); University of Leeds (Letters, poems); University of Texas. (All 1940's material)

Biography
Keith Douglas by D. Graham (London: Oxford, 1974)

Duncan, Ronald (1914-1982)
Poetry
Postcards to Pulcinella (London: Fortune, 1940)
The Mongrel and other poems (London: Faber, 1950)
Judas (London: Blond, 1960)
The Solitudes (London: Faber, 1961)
Unpopular Poems (London: Hart-Davis, 1968)
Man (London & Welcombe: Rebel, 1970-1974)
For the Few (Welcombe: Rebel, 1977)

	Auschwitz (Welcombe: Rebel, 1979)
	Man (I-V) (Welcombe: Rebel, 1981)
Verse Drama	*The Dull Ass's Hoof* (London: Fortune, 1940)
	This Way to the Tomb (London: Faber, 1946)
	Stratton (London: Faber, 1948)
	Our Lady's Tumbler (London: Faber, 1951)
Plays	*Collected Plays* (London: Hart-Davis, 1971)
Opera Libretto	*The Rape of Lucretia* (for B. Britten) (London: Boosey & Hawkes, 1946; Lane, 1946)
Prose	*All Men Are Islands* (London: Hart-Davis, 1964) (Autobiography)
	How To Make Enemies (London: Hart-Davis, 1968) (Autobiography)
	Obsessed (London: Joseph, 1977) (Autobiography)
Manuscripts	University of Texas

Durrell, Lawrence (b. 1912)

Poetry	*Quaint Fragments* (London: Cecil, 1931)
	Ten Poems (London: Caduceus, 1932)
	Bromo Bombastes (London: Caduceus, 1934)
	Transition (London: Caduceus, 1934)
	Proems (w. others) (London: Fortune, 1938)
	A Private Country (London: Faber, 1943)
	Cities, Plains and People (London: Faber, 1946)
	On Seeming to Presume (London: Faber, 1948)
	The King of Asine and other Poems by G. Seferis (w. B. Spencer & N. Valaoritis) (London: Lehmann, 1948) (Translation)
	The Tree of Idleness (London: Faber, 1955)
	Collected Poems (London: Faber, 1960; new ed., 1968)
	The Ikons (London: Faber, 1966)
	The Red Limbo Lingo (London: Faber, 1971)
	On the Suchness of the Old Boy (London: Turret, 1972)

Vega (London: Faber, 1973)

The Plant Magic Man (Santa Barbara: Capra, 1973)

Lifelines (Edinburgh: Tragara, 1974)

Collected Poems 1931-1974 (London: Faber, 1980)

Verse Drama   *Sappho* (London: Faber, 1950)

Prose   *The Black Book* (Paris: Obelisk, 1938; Olympia, 1959; New York: Dutton, 1969; London: Faber, 1972) (Fiction)

"Ideas about Poems" *Personal Landscape* 2 (Mar. 1942)

Prospero's Cell (London: Faber, 1945) (Travel)

Cefalu (London: Poetry London, 1947; later *The Dark Labyrinth,* London: Ace, 1958) (Fiction)

"Studies in Genius VI: Groddeck" *Horizon* XVII, 102 (June, 1948)

"Studies in Genius VIII: Henry Miller" *Horizon* XX, 115 (July, 1949)

A Key to Modern Poetry (London: Nevill, 1962)

Reflections on a Marine Venus (London: Faber, 1953) (Travel)

Bitter Lemons (London: Faber, 1957) (Travel)

The Alexandria Quartet: Justine 1957; *Balthazar* 1958; *Mountolive* 1958; *Clea* 1960 (London: Faber, 1962)

Art and Outrage (w. A. Perlès) (London: Putnam, 1959) (Letters)

Lawrence Durrell & Henry Miller (London: Faber, 1963) (Letters)

"The Other T.S. Eliot" *The Atlantic* Sep 1957

Spirit of Place (London: Faber, 1969) (Letters & Essays on Travel)

Interviews & Dialogues   "The Art of Fiction XXXIII, Lawrence Durrell" *Paris Review* 22 (Aut.-Win., 1959-60) (reprinted in *Writers at Work* (London: Secker & Warburg, 1963) (Interview)

The Big Supposer (w. M. Alyn) (London: Abelard-Schuman, 1973) (Dialogue)

Editor   *Personal Landscape* (w. R. Fedden & B. Spencer)

Manuscripts   University of California, Los Angeles;
                              University of Illinois, Urbana
Biographical   *My Family and Other Animals* by G.
                              Durrell (London: Hart-Davis, 1956)
                              My Friend Lawrence Durrell by A. Perlès
                              (London: Scorpion, 1961)
Bibliography   Bibliography by A.G. Thomas in *Lawrence
                              Durrell* by G.S. Fraser (London: Faber,
                              1968)

Farrar, James (1923-1944)
  Poetry and Prose   *The Unreturning Spring* (London: Williams
                              & Norgate,1950)

Fedden, Robin (1908-1977)
  Poetry   *The White Country* (London: Turret, 1968)
  Prose   *Personal Landscape* (London: Turret,
                              1966)
  Editor   *Personal Landscape* (London: Poetry
                              London, 1945) (Anthology)
                              Personal Landscape (w. L. Durrell & B.
                              Spencer)

Fletcher, Iain (b. 1920)
  Poetry   *A Homily to Kenneth Topley* (Tripoli:
                              Privately printed, 1945)
                              Orisons, Picaresque and Metaphysical
                              (London: Poetry London, 1947)
                              The Lover's Martyrdom (Oxford: Fantasy,
                              1957)
                              Motets (Reading: University of Reading,
                              1962)
                              A Milesian Intrusion (Nottingham: Byron,
                              1968)
                              Lauds: Four Poems (London: Stevens,
                              1980)

Fraser, G[eorge] S[utherland] (1915-1980)
  Poetry   *The Fatal Landscape*(London: Poetry
                              London, 1941)
                              Home Town Elegy (London: Poetry
                              London, 1944)
                              The Traveller Has Regrets (London:
                              Harvill & Poetry London, 1948)
                              Leaves Without a Tree (Tokyo: Hokuseido,
                              1956)
                              Conditions (Nottingham: Byron, 1969)
                              Poems of G.S. Fraser (Leicester: Leicester
                              University, 1981)

Prose

A Vision of Scotland (London: Elek, 1948)
"Some Notes on Poetic Diction", *Penguin
    New Writing* 37
The Modern Writer and His World
    (London: Verschoyle, 1953; revised,
    Pelican, 1964 & 1970)
"Keith Douglas" (British Academy
    Chatterton Lecture, 1956)
"The Poet and his Medium" in *The Craft
    of Letters in England* ed. J. Lehmann
    (London: Cresset, 1956)
Vision and Rhetoric (London: Faber, 1959)
Essays on Twentieth Century Poets
    (Leicester: Leicester University, 1977)
A Stranger and Afraid (Manchester:
    Carcanet, 1983) (Autobiography)

Editor

The Collected Poems of Keith Douglas (w.
    J. Waller: London: Poetry London,
    1951; w. J. Waller & J.C. Hall:
    London: Faber, 1966)
Alamein to Zem Zem by K. Douglas (w. J.
    Waller & J.C. Hall) (London: Faber,
    1966)
*Return to Oasis: War Poems and
    Recollections from the Middle East,
    1940-1946* (w. others) (London:
    Shepheard-Walwyn & Poetry London,
    1980)

Fry, Christopher (b. 1907)
Verse Drama

The Boy with a Cart (London: Oxford,
    1939)
The Firstborn (Cambridge: Cambridge
    University, 1946)
A Phoenix Too Frequent (London: Hollis
    & Carter, 1946)
The Lady's Not For Burning (London:
    Oxford, 1948)
Thor With Angels (London: Oxford, 1949)
Venus Observed (London: Oxford, 1950)
A Sleep of Prisoners (London: Oxford,
    1951)
The Dark is Light Enough (London:
    Oxford, 1954)
Curtmantle (London: Oxford, 1961)
A Yard of Sun (London: Oxford, 1970)

Prose

An Experience of Critics (w. others)
    (London: Perpetua, 1952)

Bibliography

"A Bibliography of Fry" by B.L. Schaer
& E.G. Prater *Tulane Drama Review* 4
(Mar, 1960)

Fuller, Roy (b. 1912)
Poetry

Poems (London: Fortune, 1939)
The Middle of a War (London: Hogarth,
1942)
A Lost Season (London: Hogarth, 1944)
Epitaphs and Occasions (London:
Lehmann, 1949)
Counterparts (London: Verschoyle, 1954)
Brutus's Orchard (London: Deutsch, 1957)
Collected Poems (London: Deutsch, 1962)
Buff (London: Deutsch, 1965)
New Poems (London: Deutsch, 1968)
Off Course (London: Turret, 1969)
To an Unknown Reader (London: Poem of
the Month, 1970)
Song Cycle for a Record Sleeve (Oxford:
Sycamore, 1972)
Tiny Tears (London: Deutsch, 1973)
An Old War (Edinburgh, Tagara, 1974)
From the Joke Shop (London: Deutsch,
1975)
The Joke Shop Annexe (Edinburgh:
Tragara, 1975)
An Ill-Governed Coast (Sunderland:
Ceolfrith, 1976)
Re-Treads (Edinburgh: Tragara, 1979)
The Reign of Sparrows (London: London
Magazine Editions, 1980)
More About Tompkins (Edinburgh:
Tragara, 1981)
House and Shop (Edinburgh: Tragara,
1982)
As from the Thirties (Edinburgh: Tragara,
1983)
New & Collected Poems (London: Secker
& Warburg, 1985)

Prose

"Poetry, Tradition and Belief" in *The
Craft of Letters in England* ed. J.
Lehmann (London: Cresset, 1956)
"From Blackheath to Oxford" *London
Magazine* N.S. 8,12 (Mar, 1969)
(Interview)
Owls and Artificers (London: Deutsch,
1971)

"Norman Cameron—Four Views" (w. others) *The Review* 27-28, Aut.-Win., 1971-2

Professors and Gods (London: Deutsch, 1973)

Souvenirs (London: London Magazine Editions, 1980) (Autobiography)

Vamp Til Ready (London: London Magazine Editions, 1982) (Autobiography)

Home and Dry (London: London Magazine Editions, 1984) (Autobiography)

Manuscripts   British Library 52618; Lockwood Memorial Library, State University of New York, Buffalo

Gant, Roland (b. 1919)
    Poetry   *Listen, Confides the Wind* (London: Fortune, 1947)

Gardiner, Wrey (1901-1981)
    Poetry   *Evening Silence* (Dawlish: Channing, 1937)

Cold Moon (Dawlish: Channing, 1938)

Sharp Scorpions (Billericay: Grey Walls, 1940)

The Chained Tree (Billericay: Grey Walls, 1941)

Questions of Waking (London: Fortune, 1942)

The Gates of Silence (London: Grey Walls, 1944)

Lament for Strings (London: Grey Walls, 1947)

Poems 1948-1954 (Tunbridge Wells: Russell, 1955)

    Masque   *The Last Refuge* (Billericay: Grey Walls, 1942)

    Prose   *The Colonies of Heaven* (Billericay: Grey Walls, 1942) (Autobiography)

The Once Loved God (London: Fortune, 1943) (Autobiography)

The Dark Thorn (London: Grey Walls, 1949) (Autobiography)

The Flowering Moment (London: Grey Walls, 1949) (Autobiography)

    Editor   *Poetry Quarterly*

Gascoyne, David (b. 1916)

Poetry

Roman Balcony (London: Temple Bar, 1932)

Man's Life is this Meat (London: Parton, 1934)

Poems by Benjamin Peret (w. Humphrey Jennings) (London: Contemporary Poetry & Prose; 1936) (Translation)

Hölderlin's Madness (London: Dent, 1938; Cass, 1969) (Translations & original poems)

Poets of Tomorrow (Third Selection) (w. others) (London: Hogarth, 1942)

Poems 1937-42 (London: Poetry London, 1943)

A Vagrant (London: Lehmann, 1950)

Night Thoughts (London: Deutsch, 1956)

Collected Poems (London: Oxford, 1965)

Collected Verse Translations (London: Oxford, 1970)

The Sun at Midnight (London: Enitharmon, 1970)

Three Poems (London: Enitharmon, 1976)

Early Poems (Warwick: Greville, 1980)

Prose

Opening Day (London: Cobden-Sanderson, 1933) (Novel)

A Short Survey of Surrealism (London: Cobden-Sanderson, 1935)

"The Unconscious: Spirituality: Catastrophe" by Pierre Jean Jouve *Poetry London* 4 (Translation)

"A Note on Symbolism" *Poetry Quarterly* 8,2 (Summer, 1946)

"Leon Chestov" *Horizon* XX, 118 (Oct, 1949)

Thomas Carlyle (London: Longmans, 1952)

Paris Journal (London: Enitharmon, 1978)

Journal 1936-37, Death of an Explorer, Leon Chestov (London: Enitharmon, 1980)

Manuscripts

British Library 56040-56060 (Notebooks 1937-1948); Berg Collection, New York Public Library; University of Tulsa, Oklahoma

Bibliography   "David Gascoyne: A Checklist" by A.
                                      Atkinson *Twentieth Century Literature* 6
                                      (1961)

Gawsworth, John (b. 1912) (Terence Armstrong)
  Poetry   *Collected Poems* (London: Sidgwick &
                                      Jackson, 1949)
                                      (For the extensive bibliography of this
                                      minor writer see the above.)
  Editor   *The Poetry Review*

Gee, Kenneth
  Poetry   *32 Poems* (London: Fortune, 1942)

Graham, W[illiam] S[idney] (b. 1918)
  Poetry   *Cage Without Grievance* (London: Parton,
                                      1943)
                                      Seven Journeys (Glasgow: MacLellan, 1944)
                                      2nd Poems (London: Poetry London, 1945)
                                      The Voyages of Alfred Wallace (London:
                                      Frushang, 1948)
                                      The White Threshold (London: Faber,
                                      1949)
                                      The Nightfishing (London: Faber, 1955)
                                      Malcolm Mooney's Land (London: Faber,
                                      1970)
                                      Implements in Their Places (London:
                                      Faber, 1977)
                                      Collected Poems (London: Faber, 1979)
  Prose   "Notes on a Poetry of Release" *Poetry
                                      Scotland* 3 (July, 1946)
  Manuscripts   National Library of Scotland

Greacen, Robert
  Poetry   *The Bird* (Dublin: Gayfield, 1941)
                                      One Recent Evening (London: Favil, 1944)
                                      The Undying Day (London: Falcon, 1948)
  Editor   *Lyra* (w. A. Comfort) (Billericay, Grey
                                      Walls, 1942)
                                      Northern Harvest (Belfast: McCord, 1944)
                                      Irish Harvest (Dublin: New Frontiers,
                                      1946)
                                      Contemporary Irish Poetry (w. V.
                                      Iremonger) (London: Faber, 1949)

                                      The Northman

Haggard, Stephen (1911-1943)
  Poetry   *The Unpublished Poems of Stephen
                                      Haggard* (Leeds: Salamander, 1955)
  Poetry & Prose   *I'll Go to Bed at Noon* (London: Faber,
                                      1944)

Hall, J[ohn] C[live] (b. 1920)
Poetry
    Selected Poems (w. K.C. Douglas & N.
      Nicholson) (London: Staples, 1943)
    The Summer Dance (London: Lehmann,
      1951)
    The Burning Hare (London: Chatto, 1966)
    The House of Voices (London: Chatto,
      1973)
Editor
    The Collected Poems of Keith Douglas (w.
      G.S. Fraser & J. Waller) (London:
      Faber, 1966)
    Alamein to Zem Zem by K. Douglas (w.
      G.S. Fraser & J. Waller) (London:
      Faber, 1966)

Hamblett, C.
Poetry
    Call Wind to Witness (w. J. Bayliss, A.
      Lewis & E. Litvinoff) (London:
      Capriole, 1942)
    Cactus Harvest (London: Fortune, 1946)
Editor
    I Burn for England (London: Frewin,
      1966)

Hamburger, Michael (b. 1924)
Poetry
    Poems of Hölderlin (London: Poetry
      London, 1943) (Translation)
    The Later Hogarth (London: Cope &
      Fenwick, 1945)
    Twenty Prose Poems of Baudelaire
      (London: Poetry London, 1947)
      (Translation)
    Flowering Cactus (Aldington: Hand and
      Flower, 1950)
    Decline, Poems by Georg Trackel (St.
      Ives: Latin, 1952) (Translation)
    Poems 1950-1951 (Aldington: Hand &
      Flower, 1952)
    The Dual Site (London: Routledge, 1958)
    Weather and Season (London: Longmans,
      1963)
    Feeding the Chickadees (London: Turret,
      1968)
    Travelling (London: Fulcrum, 1969)
    Home (Frensham: Sceptre, 1969)
    Travelling I-V (London: Agenda, 1972)
    Ownerless Earth (Manchester: Carcanet,
      1973)
    Conversations and Charwomen (Rushden:
      Sceptre, 1973)
    Real Estate (Manchester: Carcanet, 1977)

Palinode (Knotting: Sceptre, 1977)

Moralities (Newcastle: Morden Tower, 1977)

Paul Celan: Poems (Manchester: Carcanet, 1980) (Translation)

Variations: In Suffolk (Bedford: Sceptre, 1980)

Variations (Manchester: Carcanet, 1981)

Collected Poems (Manchester: Carcanet, 1984)

Prose

Reason and Energy (London: Routledge, 1957) (Criticism)

The Truth of Poetry (London: Weidenfeld & Nicolson, 1969) (Criticism)

A Mug's Game (Cheadle: Carcanet, 1973) (Autobiography)

Art as Second Nature (Manchester: Carcanet, 1974) (Criticism)

A Proliferation of Prophets (Manchester: Carcanet, 1983) (Criticism)

Manuscripts

University of Reading; Lockwood Memorial Library, State University of New York, Buffalo; University of Texas, Austin

Heath-Stubbs, John (b. 1918)

Poetry

Wounded Thammuz (London: Routledge, 1942)

Beauty and the Beast (London: Routledge, 1944)

Poems of Leopardi (London: Lehmann, 1946) (Translation)

The Divided Ways (London: Routledge, 1947)

The Swarming of the Bees (London: Eyre & Spottiswood, 1950)

Aphrodite's Garland (St. Ives: Latin, 1951)

A Charm Against the Toothache (London: Methuen, 1954)

The Triumph of the Muse (London: Oxford, 1958)

The Blue-Fly in My Head (London: Oxford, 1962)

Selected Poems (London: Oxford, 1965)

Satires and Epigrams (London: Turret, 1968)

Artorius (London: Enitharmon, 1973)

	Indifferent Weather (London: McKelvie, 1975)
	The Watchman's Flute (Manchester: Carcanet, 1978)
	Birds Reconvened (London: Enitharmon, 1980)
	Naming the Beasts (Manchester: Carcanet, 1982)
Verse Drama	*Helen in Egypt* (London: Oxford, 1958)
Prose	*The Darkling Plain* (London: Eyre & Spottiswood, 1950) (Criticism)
	Charles Williams (London: Longmans, 1955)
Editor	*The Faber Book of Twentieth Century Verse* (w. D. Wright) (London: Faber, 1953)
Manuscripts	Claude Collier Albert Memorial Library, State University of New York, Buffalo; University of Texas, Austin

Henderson, Hamish (b. 1919)

Poetry	*Elegies for the Dead in Cyrenaica* (London: Lehmann, 1948)
Interview	*The Poet Speaks* ed. P. Orr (London: Routledge, 1943)
Editor	*Ballads of World War II* (Glasgow: Lili Marleen Club, 1947)

Hendry, J[ames] F[indlay] (b. 1912)

Poetry	*The Bombed Happiness* (London: Routledge, 1942)
	The Orchestral Mountain (London: Routledge, 1943)
	The Ruins of Man (announced but not published)
	World Alien (Dunfermline: Borderline, 1980)
	Marimarusa (Caithness: Caithness Books, 1979)
Prose	"Dunbar the European" *Scottish Art and Letters* 5 (1950)
Prose	*Fernie Brae* (Glasgow: MacLellan, 1947) (Novel)
Editor	*The New Apocalypse* (w. H. Treece) (London: Fortune, 1939)
	The White Horseman (w. H. Treece) (London: Routledge, 1941)

The Crown and the Sickle (w. H. Treece)
(London: Staples, 1943)

Heywood, Terence (b. 1913)
Poetry   *How Smoke Gets in the Air: Architectonic*
(London: Fortune, 1952)

Hodgson, T[homas] R[ahilly] (1915-1941)
Poetry   *This Life, This Death* (London: Routledge,
1943)

Holloway, Geoffrey (b. 1918)
Poetry   *Rhine Jump* (London: London Magazine
Editions, 1974)

James, Diana
Poetry   *The Tune of Flutes* (London: Routledge,
1945)

Jennett, Sean (b. 1912)
Poetry   *Always Adam* (London: Faber, 1943)
The Cloth of Flesh (London: Faber, 1945)

Kavanagh, Patrick (1904-1967)
Poetry   *Ploughman and Other Poems* (London:
Macmillan, 1936)
The Great Hunger (Dublin: Cuala, 1942)
A Soul for Sale (London: Macmillan, 1947)
Come Dance with Kitty Stobling (London:
Longman, 1960)
Collected Poems (London: MacGibbon &
Kee, 1964)
Complete Poems (New York: Kavanagh,
1972)

Prose & Verse   *November Haggard, Uncollected Prose
and Verse of Patrick Kavanagh* (New
York: Kavanagh, 1971)

Prose   *The Green Fool* (London: Joseph, 1938)
Tarry Flynn (London: Pilot, 1948)
Collected Pruse (London: MacGibbon &
Kee, 1967)
Lapped Furrows (New York: Kavanagh,
1969) (Letters)
*Love's Tortured Hand: A Sequel to Lapped
Furrows* (New York: Kavanagh, 1978)
By Night Unstarred (Curragh: Goldsmith,
1978)

Manuscripts   National Library of Ireland
Biographical   *Beyond Affection: an Autobiography* by
Peter Kavanagh (New York: Kavanagh,
1977)

Bibliography

Keyes, Sidney (1922-1943)
Poetry

Plays & Prose
Manuscripts
Biography

King, Francis (b. 1923)
Poetry

Kirkup, James (b. 1918)
Poetry

Sacred Keeper by Peter Kavanagh
(Curragh: Goldsmith, 1980)
Garden of the Golden Apples by P.
Kavanagh (New York: Kavanagh, 1972)

The Iron Laurel (London: Routledge,
1942)
The Cruel Solstice (London: Routledge,
1944)
Collected Poems (London: Routledge,
1945)
Minos of Crete (London: Routledge, 1948)
British Library 54327 (Letter)
Sidney Keyes: a biographical enquiry by J.
Guenther (London: London Magazine
Editions, 1967)

The Rod of Incantation (London:
Longmans, 1952)

Indications (w. J. Bayliss & J. Ormond
Thomas) (London: Grey Walls, 1942)
The Cosmic Shape (w. R. Nichols)
(London: Forge, 1946)
The Drowned Sailor (London: Grey Walls,
1947)
The Creation (Hull: Lotus, 1951)
The Submerged Village (London: Oxford,
1951)
A Correct Compassion (London: Oxford,
1952)
A Spring Journey (London: Oxford, 1954)
The Descent into the Cave (London:
Oxford, 1957)
The Prodigal Son (London: Oxford, 1959)
The Refusal to Conform (London: Oxford,
1963)
Japanese Marine (Tokyo: Japan P.E.N.
Club, 1965)
Paper Windows (London: Dent, 1968)
White Shadows, Black Shadows (London:
Dent, 1970)
The Body Servant (London: Dent, 1971)
Broad Daylight (Frensham: Sceptre, 1971)
A Berwick Bestiary (Ashington: MidNAG,
1971)

Transmental Vibrations (London: Covent Garden, 1971)

Zen Garden (Guildford: Circle, 1973)

Scenes from Sesshu (London: Pimlico, 1978)

Zen Contemplations (Osaka: Kyoto, 1978)

Steps to the Temple (Osaka: Kyoto, 1979)

The Tao of Water (Guildford: Circle, 1980)

Fellow Feelings (Osaka: Kyoto, 1982)

To the Ancestral North (Tokyo: Asahi, 1983)

The Sense of the Visit (Taunton: Sceptre, 1984)

Verse Drama   *Upon This Rock* (London: Oxford, 1955)

Prose   *The Only Child* (London: Collins, 1957) (Autobiography)

Sorrow, Passions and Alarms (London: Collins, 1959) (Autobiography)

Larkin, Philip (b. 1922)

Poetry   *The North Ship* (London: Fortune, 1945; new ed. w. Intro., Faber, 1973)

XX Poems (No Pub. given, 1951)

The Fantasy Poets, 21: Philip Larkin (Eynsham: Fantasy, 1954)

The Less Deceived (Hessle: Marvell, 1955)

The Whitsun Weddings (London: Faber, 1964)

The Explosion (London: Poem of the Month, 1970)

High Windows (London: Faber, 1974)

Prose   *Jill* (London: Fortune, 1946; new ed. w. Intro., Faber, 1964) (Novel)

Contribution to "Four Conversations": Ian Hamilton *London Magazine* N.S. 4 (Nov, 1964)

All What Jazz? (London: Faber, 1970) (Record Reviews w. Intro.)

Required Writing (London: Faber, 1983) (Collected Shorter Pieces)

Interview   Interview with Dan Jacobson, *The New Review,* 1,3 (June, 1974)

Manuscript   British Library 52619 (Poetry Notebook) (1940's Material)

Bibliography   *Philip Larkin: a Bibliography* by B.C. Bloomfield (London: Faber, 1979)

Ledward, Patricia (b. 1920)
   Poetry   *Over the Edge* (London: Favil, 1940)
   Editor   *Poems of This War* (w. C. Strang)
                            (Cambridge:Cambridge University, 1942)

Lee, Christopher (b. 1913)
   Poetry   *Poems* (London: Hogarth, 1937)
                            The Secret Field (London: Fortune, 1940)
                            Remember Man (London: Fortune, 1942)
                            Under the Sun (London: Lane, 1948)
                            The Bright Cloud (Cambridge, Rampant
                                Lions, 1961)
                            The Veins of Meaning (London:
                                Enitharmon, 1980)

Lee, Laurie, (b. 1914)
   Poetry   Selection in *Poets of Tomorrow* (Third
                            Selection) ed. J. Lehmann (London:
                            Hogarth, 1942)
                            The Sun My Monument (London: Hogarth,
                                1944)
                            The Bloom of Candles (London: Lehmann,
                                1947)
                            My Many Coated Man (London: Chatto &
                                Windus, 1955)
                            [Selected Poems] (London: Vista, 1960)
                            Selected Poems (London: Deutsch, 1983)
   Verse Drama   *Peasants' Priest* (Canterbury: Goulden,
                                1947)
                            Voyage of Magellan (London: Lehmann,
                                1948)
   Prose   *Cider with Rosie* (London: Hogarth, 1959)
                            (Autobiography)
                          As I Walked Out One Midsummer Morning
                              (London: Deutsch, 1969)
                            (Autobiography)

Levertoff [later "Levertov"], Denise (b. 1923; emigrated to the United States
        in 1948. Only pre-1948 material is listed.)
   Poetry   *The Double Image* (London: Cresset, 1946)
                          Collected Earlier Poems (1940-1960) (New
                            York: New Directions, 1979)

Lewis, Alun (1915-1944)
   Poetry   *Two Poems* (Llanllechid: Caseg, 1941)
                          Call Wind to Witness (w. J. Bayliss, C.
                            Hamblett & E. Litvinoff) (London:
                            Capriole, 1942)

	Raiders' Dawn (London: Allen & Unwin, 1942)
	Ha! Ha! Among the Trumpets (London: Allen & Unwin, 1945)
	Selected Poems (London: Allen & Unwin, 1982)
Poetry & Prose	*Alun Lewis: Selected Poetry and Prose* ed. I. Hamilton (London: Allen & Unwin, 1966)
	A Miscellany of His Writing (Ogmore: Poetry Wales, 1982)
Prose	*The Last Inspection* (London: Allen & Unwin, 1942) (Stories)
	In the Green Tree (London: Allen & Unwin, 1948) (Stories & Letters)
Letters	"A Sheaf of Letters" *Wales* VII, 28 (Feb/Mar, 1945)
	Letters from India (Cardiff: Penmark, 1946)
	"Alun Lewis to Robert Graves" *The Anglo-Welsh Review* 16,37 (Spring 1967)
	Alun Lewis and the Making of the Caseg Broadsheets ed. B. Chamberlain (London: Enitharmon, 1970)
Bibliography	"Alun Lewis: A Select Bibliography" *Anglo-Welsh Review* 16 (Spring, 1967)

Lindsay, J[ohn] M[aurice] (b. 1918)

Poetry	*The Advancing Day* (Privately printed, 1940)
	Perhaps Tomorrow (Oxford: Blackwell, 1941)
	Predicaments (Oxford: Alden, 1942)
	No Crown for Laughter (London: Fortune, 1943)
	The Enemies of Love (Glasgow: Maclellan, 1946)
	Selected Poems (Edinburgh: Oliver & Boyd, 1947)
	Hurlygush (Edinburgh: Serif, 1948)
	At the Wood's Edge (Edinburgh: Serif, 1950)
	Ode for St. Andrew's Night and Other Poems (Edinburgh: New Alliance, 1951)
	The Exiled Heart (London: Hale, 1957)
	Snow Warning and Other Poems (Arundel: Linden, 1962)

	One Later Day and Other Poems (London: Brookside, 1964)
	This Business of Living (Preston: Akros, 1971)
	Comings and Goings (Preston: Akros, 1971)
	Selected Poems (London: Hale, 1973)
	Walking Without an Overcoat (London: Hale, 1977)
	Collected Poems (Edinburgh: Harris, 1979)
	Collected Poems (London: Lawrence & Wishart, 1983)
Prose	*The Scottish Renaissance* (Edinburgh: Serif, 1949)
	A History of Scottish Literature (London: Hale, 1977)
Editor	*Sailing Tomorrow's Seas* (London: Fortune, 1944)
	Modern Scottish Poetry (London: Faber, 1946; revised ed. 1966)
	Poetry Scotland

Little, Lawrence (b. 1921)
   Poetry   *Selection in Poets of Tomorrow* (Third Selection) ed. J. Lehmann (London: Hogarth, 1942)

Litvinoff, Emanuel (b. 1915)
   Poetry   *Conscripts* (London: Favil, 1941)
        Call Wind to Witness (w. J. Bayliss, C. Hamblett, A. Lewis) (London: Capriole, 1942)
        The Untried Soldier (London: Routledge, 1942)
        Crown for Cain (London: Falcon, 1948)
   Prose   "My East End Tenement" in *Writers on Themselves* (London: B.B.C., 1964)

McCaig [later MacCaig], Norman (b. 1910)
   Poetry   *Far Cry* (London: Routledge, 1943)
        The Inward Eye (London: Routledge, 1946)
        Riding Lights (London: Hogarth, 1955)
        The Sinai Sort (London: Hogarth, 1957)
        A Common Grace (London: Hogarth, 1960)
        A Round of Applause (London: Chatto & Windus, 1962)
        Measures (London: Chatto & Windus, 1965)

Surroundings (London: Chatto & Windus, 1966)

Rings on a Tree (London: Chatto & Windus, 1968)

A Man in My Position (London: Chatto & Windus, 1969)

Midnights (London: Poem of the Month, 1970)

Three Manuscript Poems (Exeter: Rougemont, 1970)

Selected Poems (London: Hogarth, 1971)

The White Bird (London: Chatto & Windus, 1973)

The World's Room (London: Chatto & Windus, 1974)

Tree of Strings (London: Chatto & Windus, 1977)

Old Maps and New: Selected Poems (London: Hogarth, 1978)

Inchadamph (Stirling: University of Stirling, 1978)

Equal Skies (London: Chatto & Windus, 1980)

A World of Difference (London: Chatto & Windus, 1982)

MacDonough, Donagh (1912-1968)
Poetry

Twenty Poems (w. N. Sheridan)
Veterans (Dublin: Cuala, 1941)
The Hungry Grass (London: Faber, 1947)
A Warning to Conquerors (Dublin: Dolmen, 1968)

Verse Drama *Happy as Larry* (Dublin: Fridberg, 1946)

McFadden, Roy (b. 1921)
Poetry

A Poem: Russian Summer (Dublin: Gayfield, 1942)

Three New Poets (w. A. Comfort & I. Serrailier) (Billericay: Grey Walls, 1942)

Swords and Ploughshares (London: Routledge, 1943)

Flowers for a Lady (London: Routledge, 1945)

The Heart's Townland (London: Routledge, 1947)

Elegy for the Dead of the Princess Victoria (Belfast: Lisnagarvey, 1953)

The Garryowen (London: Chatto &
Windus, 1971)
Verifications (Belfast: Blackstaff, 1977)
A Watching Brief (Belfast: Blackstaff,
1978)
Selected Roy McFadden (Belfast:
Blackstaff, 1983)

Mallalieu, H[erbert] B. (b. 1914)
Poetry
   A Letter in Wartime (London: Fortune,
1942

Marnau, Fred (b. 1920)
Poetry (German w.
translation)
   The Wounds of the Apostles (London: Grey
Walls, 1944)
Three Poems (w. W. Gardiner & N.
Moore) (London: Grey Walls, 1944)
Death of the Cathedral (London: Grey
Walls, 1946)

Editor
   New Road 3 & 4 (1945 & 1946)

Mathias, Roland (b. 1915)
Poetry
   Days Enduring (London: Stockwell, 1943)
Break in Harvest (London: Routledge,
1946)
The Rose of Tretower (Cardiff: Dock
Leaves, 1952)
The Flooded Valley (London: Putnam,
1960)
Absolom in the Tree (Llandysul: Gomer,
1971)
Snipe's Castle (Llandysul: Gomer, 1979)
*Burning Brambles: Selected Poems, 1944-
1979* (Llandysul: Gomer, 1983)

Prose
   Vernon Watkins (University of Wales,
1974)

Editor
   Anglo-Welsh Poetry 1480-1980 (w. R.
Garlick) (Ogmore: Poetry Wales, 1984)

Middleton, Christopher (b. 1926)
Poetry
   Poems (London: Fortune, 1944)
Nocturne in Eden (London: Fortune, 1945)
Torse: Poems 1949-1961 (London:
Longmans, 1962)
Nonsequences (London: Longmans, 1965)
Our Flowers and Nice Bones (London:
Fulcrum, 1969)
The Lonely Suppers of W.V. Balloon
(Manchester: Carcanet, 1975)

Fractions for Another Telemachus
  (Knotting: Sceptre, 1974)
Wildhorse (Knotting: Sceptre, 1975)
Eight Elementary Inventions (Knotting:
  Sceptre, 1977)
Pantaxanadu (Manchester: Carcanet, 1977)
111 Poems (Manchester, Carcanet, 1983)

Prose
  The Pursuit of the Kingfisher (Manchester:
  Carcanet) (1983) (Criticism)

Monahan, James (b. 1912)
Poetry
  Far from Land (London: Macmillan, 1944)
  After Battle (London: Macmillan, 1948)

Moore, Nicholas (b. 1918)
Poetry
  A Book for Priscilla (Cambridge, Epsilon,
  1941)
  The Island and the Cattle (London:
  Fortune, 1941)
  A Wish in Season (London: Fortune, 1941)
  The Cabaret, The Dancer, The Gentleman
  (London: Fortune, 1942)
  Buzzing Round with a Bee (London: Poetry
  London, 1942)
  Thirty-Five Anonymous Odes (pub.
  anonymously) (London: Fortune, 1944)
  Three Poems (w. F. Marnau & W.
  Gardiner) (London: Grey Walls, 1944)
  The War of the Little Jersey Cows (as by
  Guy Kelly) (London: Fortune, 1945)
  The Glass Tower (London: Poetry London,
  1946)
  Recollections of the Gala (London: Poetry
  London, 1950)
  Identity (London: Cadenza, 1969)
  Resolution and Identity (London: Covent
  Garden, 1970)
  Spleen (London: Menard, 1973)
  (Translation)

Prose
  Henry Miller (London: Opus, 1943)
  "A Difficult Poem" *Poetry London* X (on
  Wallace Stevens)

Editor
  The Fortune Anthology (w. J. Bayliss &
  D. Newton) (London: Fortune, 1942)
  *The PL Book of Modern American Short
  Stories* (London: Poetry London, 1945)
  Atlantic Anthology (w. D. Newton)
  (London: Fortune, 1945)

New Poetry

Nicholson, Norman (b. 1914)
Poetry

Selected Poems (w. K. Douglas & J.C. Hall) (London: Staples, 1943)
Five Rivers (London: Faber, 1944)
Rock Face (London: Faber, 1948)
The Pot Geranium (London: Faber, 1954)
A Local Habitation (London: Faber, 1972)
Hard of Hearing (London: Poem of the Month, 1974)
Cloud on Black Combe (Hitchin: Cellar, 1975)
Stitch and Stone (Sunderland: Ceolfrith, 1975)
The Shadow on Black Combe (Ashingdon: MidNAG, 1978)
Sea to the West (London: Faber, 1981)
Selected Poems 1940-1982 (London: Faber, 1982)

Verse Drama

The Old Man of the Montains (London: Faber, 1946)
Prophesy to the Wind (London: Faber, 1950)
A Match for the Devil (London: Faber, 1955)
Birth by Drowning (London: Faber, 1960)

Prose

Man and Literature (London: S.C.M., 1944)
"A Note on Allegory" *Focus One* 1945
"The Poet Needs an Audience" *Orpheus* 1, 1948
"Words and Imagery" in *T.S. Eliot: A Symposium* ed. Tambimuttu & R. March (London: Poetry London, 1948)
"The Image in My Poetry" *Orpheus* 2, 1949
"On Being Provincial" *The Listener* Aug 12, 1954, 248-9
William Cowper (London: Longmans, 1960)
"The Second Chance" in *Writers on Themselves* (London: B.B.C., 1964)
Contribution to *They Became Christians* ed. D. Morgan (London: Mowbray, 1966)
Wednesday Early Closing (London: Faber, 1975) (Autobiography)

Interview   *The Poet Speaks* ed. P. Orr (London:
                                   Routledge, 1966)
Editor   *Wordsworth: An Introduction & Selection*
                                   (London: Phoenix, 1949)
Manuscripts   British Library 56255 (Poems)

Norris, Leslie (b. 1921)
Poetry   *Tongue of Beauty* (London: Favil, 1942)
                                   Poems (London: Resurgam, 1946)
                                   The Loud Winter (Cardiff: Triskell, 1967)
                                   Ransoms (London: Chatto & Windus,
                                   1970)
                                   *Mountains, Polecats, Pheasants and Other
                                   Elegies* (London: Chatto & Windus,
                                   1973)
                                   Water Voices (London: Chatto & Windus,
                                   1980)
Editor   *Vernon Watkins: 1906-1967* (London:
                                   Faber, 1970)

Nott, Kathleen (b. 1910)
Poetry   *Landscapes and Departures* (London:
                                   Poetry London, 1947)
                                   Poems from the North (Aldington: Hand &
                                   Flower, 1956)
                                   Creatures and Emblems (London:
                                   Routledge, 1960)
                                   Elegies and Other Poems (Richmond:
                                   Keepsake, 1981)
Prose   *The Emperor's Clothes* (London:
                                   Heinemann, 1953)

Ormond, John (b. 1923)
Poetry   *Indications* [as by John Ormond Thomas]
                                   (w. J. Bayliss, & J. Kirkup) (London:
                                   Grey Walls, 1943)
                                   Requiem and Celebration (Llandybie:
                                   Davies, 1969)
                                   Definition of a Waterfall (London: Oxford,
                                   1973)
                                   Penguin Modern Poets 27 (w. E.
                                   Humphreys & J. Tripp) (London:
                                   Penguin, 1979)

Peake, Mervyn (1911-1968)
Poetry   *Shapes and Sounds* (London: Chatto, 1941;
                                   new ed. Village, 1974)
                                   The Glassblowers (London: Eyre &
                                   Spottiswood, 1950)

	The Rhyme of the Flying Bomb (London: Dent, 1962)
	A Reverie of Bone (London: Rota, 1967)
	Selected Poems (London: Faber, 1972)
	Rhymes without Reason (London: Methuen, 1974)
Prose	"The Glassblowers" *Convoy* IV (July 1946)
	Titus Groan (London: Eyre & Spottiswood, 1946)
	The Craft of the Lead Pencil (London: Wingate, 1946)
	"How a Romantic Novel was Evolved" in *A New Romantic Anthology* ed. S. Schimanski & H. Treece (London: Grey Walls, 1949)
	Gormonghast (London: Eyre & Spottiswood, 1950)
	Titus Alone (London: Eyre & Spottiswood, 1959)
Miscellaneous	*Peake's Progress: selected writings and drawings* (London: Lane, 1978)
Manuscripts	British Library
Biographical	*A World Away* by M. Gilmore (London: Gollancz, 1970)
	Mervyn Peake by. G. Smith (London: Gollancz, 1984)
Popham, Hugh (b. 1920)	
Poetry	*Against the Lightning* (London: Lane, 1944)
	The Journey and the Dream (London: Lane, 1945)
	Above Eskdale (London: Dropmore, 1946)
	Three Cantos from 'To the Un-born—Greeting' (London: Dropmore, 1946)
Porter, Roy	
Poetry	*World in the Heart* (London: Fortune, 1944)
Potts, Paul (b. 1911)	
Poetry	*The Lassoing of a Maverick* (1939)
	Instead of a Sonnet (London: Poetry London, 1944; Tuba, 1978)
Prose	*Dante Called You Beatrice* (London: Eyre & Spottiswood, 1960) (Autobiographical)

	To Keep a Promise (London: MacGibbon & Kee, 1970)
Prince, F[rank] T[empleton]	
Poetry	*Poems* (London: Faber, 1938)
	Soldiers Bathing (London: Fortune, 1954)
	The Doors of Stone (London: Hart-Davis, 1963)
	Memoirs in Oxford (London: Fulcrum, 1970)
	Drypoints of the Hasidim (London: Menard, 1976)
	Afterword on Rupert Brooke (London: Menard, 1976)
	Collected Poems London: Menard, 1978)
	The Yuan Chen Variations (New York: Sheep Meadow, 1981)
	Later On (London: Anvil, 1983)
Manuscripts	British Library 56258 (1947-1948)
Raikes, David (1924-1954)	
Poetry	*The Poems of David Raikes* (Oxford: Fantasy, 1954)
Raine, Kathleen (b. 1908)	
Poetry	*Stone and Flower* (London: Poetry London, 1943)
	Living in Line (London: Poetry London, 1946)
	The Pythoness (London: Hamilton, 1949)
	The Year One (London: Hamilton, 1952)
	Collected Poems (London: Hamilton, 1956)
	The Hollow Hill (London: Hamilton, 1965)
	Six Dreams (London: Enitharmon, 1968)
	Ninfa Revisited (London: Enitharmon, 1968)
	The Lost Country (London: Hamilton, 1971)
	On a Deserted Shore (London: Hamilton, 1973)
	The Oval Portrait (London: Enitharmon, 1977)
	Fifteen Short Poems (London: Enitharmon, 1978)
	The Oracle of the Heart (Dublin: Dolmen, 1979)
	Collected Poems 1935-1980 (London: Allen & Unwin, 1981)
Prose	"The Poet as Critic" *Poetry London* 2,8 (Nov/Dec, 1942)

"Are Poets Doing Their Duty?" *New Road* 1, 1943

"The Poet of Our Time" in *T.S. Eliot: A Symposium* ed. Tambimuttu & R. March (London: Poetry London, 1948)

"Michael Roberts and the Hero Myth" *Penguin New Writing* 39 (1950)

William Blake (London: Longmans, 1951; rev. eds. 1965, 1969)

Poetry in Relation to Traditional Wisdom (London: Guild of Pastoral Psychology, 1959)

Blake and England (Cambridge: Heffer, 1960)

Defending Ancient Springs (London: Oxford, 1967)

A Question of Poetry (Crediton: Gilbertson, 1969)

Blake and Tradition (London: Routledge, 1969)

Faces of Night (London: Enitharmon, 1972; scheduled for publication by Poetry London, 1946)

Farewell Happy Fields (London: Hamilton, 1973) (Autobiography)

The Land Unknown (London: Hamilton, 1975) (Autobiography)

The Lion's Mouth (London: Hamilton, 1977) (Autobiography)

The Inner Journey of the Poet (London: Allen & Unwin, 1982)

Manuscripts   British Library 52595-7 & Res. MS138; Lockwood Memorial Library, State University of New York, Buffalo; University of Texas; University of California, Irvine

Reed, Henry (b. 1914)

Poetry   *A Map of Verona* (London: Cape, 1946)

Lessons of War (London: Chilmark, 1970)

Drama   *Moby Dick* (London: Cape, 1947) (Radio Play)

The Streets of Pompeii (London: B.B.C., 1971)

Hilda Tablet (London: B.B.C., 1971)

Prose   "The End of an Impulse" *New Writing and Daylight,* Summer 1943)

Rhys, Keidrych (b. 1915)
  Poetry   *The Van Pool* (London: Routledge, 1942)
  Editor   *Poems from the Forces* (London:
                                   Routledge, 1942)
                                 More Poems from the Forces (London:
                                 Routledge, 1943)
                                 Modern Welsh Poetry (London: Faber,
                                 1944)

                       Wales

  Publisher   The Druid Press

Ridler, Anne (b. 1912)
  Poetry   *Poems* (London: Oxford, 1939)
                                 A Dream Observed (London: Poetry
                                 London, 1941)
                               The Nine Bright Shiners (London: Faber,
                               1943)
                               The Golden Bird (London: Faber, 1951)
                               A Matter of Life and Death (London:
                                 Faber, 1959)
                               Some Time After (London: Faber, 1972)
  Verse Drama   *Cain* (London: Poetry London, 1943)
                               The Shadow Factory (London: Faber,
                                 1946)
                               Henry Bly and Other Plays (London:
                                 Faber, 1950)
                               The Trial of Thomas Cranmer (London:
                               Faber, 1956)
                               *Who is My Neighbour? and How Bitter the
                               Bread* (London: Faber, 1963)
                               The Jesse Tree: A Masque (London:
                               Lyrebird, 1970)
                               The Lambton Worm (London: Oxford,
                               1979)
  Prose   "The Lustre Jug" *Transformation* [One]
                               "A Question of Speech" *Focus* 3 (1947)
                               Introduction to *Seed of Adam* by C.
                               Williams (London: Oxford, 1949)
                               Introduction to *The Image of the City* by
                               C. Williams (London: Oxford, 1958)

Roberts, Lynette
  Poetry   *Poems* (London: Faber, 1944)
                               Gods with Stainless Ears (London: Faber,
                               1951)

Rodgers, W[illiam] R[obert] (1909-1969)
Poetry   *Awake* (London: Secker & Warburg, 1941)
                          Europa and the Bull (London: Secker &
                              Warburg, 1952)
                          Collected Poems (London: Oxford, 1971)
Prose   *Ulstermen and their Country* (London:
                              Longmans, 1947)
Radio Features   *Irish Literary Portraits* (London: B.B.C.,
                              1972)
Interview   *The Poet Speaks* ed. P. Orr (London:
                              Routledge, 1966)
Biography   *W.R. Rodgers* by. D. O'Brien (Lewisburg:
                              Bucknell, 1970)

Rook, Alan (b. 1909)
Poetry   *Songs from a Cherry Tree* (Oxford: Halls,
                              1938)
                          Soldiers, This Solitude (London:
                              Routledge, 1942)
                          These are My Comrades (London:
                              Routledge, 1943)
                          We who are Fortunate (London:
                              Routledge, 1945)
Prose   *Not as a Refuge* (London: Drummond,
                              1948)

Ross, Alan (b. 1922)
Poetry   *Summer Thunder* (Oxford: Blackwell,
                              1941)
                          The Derelict Day (London: Lehmann,
                              1947)
                          Something of the Sea (London: Verschoyle,
                              1954)
                          To Whom It May Concern (London:
                              Hamilton, 1958)
                          African Negatives (London: Eyre &
                              Spottiswood, 1962)
                          North from Sicily (London: Eyre &
                              Spottiswood, 1965)
                          Poems 1942-1967 (London: Eyre &
                              Spottiswood, 1967)
                          A Calcutta Grandmother (London: Poem of
                              the Month, 1971)
                          Tropical Ice (London: Covent Garden,
                              1972)
                          The Taj Express (London: London
                              Magazine Editions, 1973)

	Open Sea (London: London Magazine Editions, 1975)
	Death Valley and Other Poems in America (London: London Magazine Editions, 1980)
Prose	"Arctic Convoy" *New Writing and Daylight* Autumn, 1944
	Poetry 1945-1950 (London: Longmans, 1951)
Interview	"A Conversation with Alan Ross" *The Review* 25 (Spring, 1971)
Editor	*The London Magazine*
Publisher	London Magazine Editions
Manuscripts	British Library 56352-54 (Typescripts of Poetry)

Russell, J.M. (b. 1925)
Poetry   *The Grinning Face* (London: Routledge, 1947)

Rye, Anthony (Samuel Youd) (b. 1922)
Poetry   *The Inn of Birds* (London: Cape, 1947)
                        Poems for Selbourne (London: Sidgwick & Jackson, 1961)

Savage, D[erek] S. (b. 1917)
Poetry   *Don Quixote and other poems* (London: Right Review, 1939)
                        The Autumn World (London: Fortune, 1939)
                        A Time to Mourn (London: Routledge, 1943)
Prose   *The Personal Principle* (London: Routledge, 1944)
                        The Withered Branch (London: Eyre & Spottiswood, 1950)
                        "Testament of a Conscientious Objector" in *The Objectors* ed. C. Simmons (Isle of Man: Times, [1965])

Scannell, Vernon (b. 1922)
Poetry   *Graves and Resurrections* (London: Fortune, 1948)
                        A Mortal Pitch (London: Villiers, 1957)
                        A Mask of Love (London: Putnam, 1960)
                        A Sense of Danger (London: Putnam, 1962)
                        Walking Wounded (London: Eyre & Spottiswood, 1965)
                        Epithets of War (London: Eyre & Spottiswood, 1969)

	Mastering the Craft (Oxford: Permagon, 1970)
	Selected Poems (London: Allison & Busby, 1961)
	Company of Women (Frensham: Sceptre, 1971)
	The Winter Man (London: Allison & Busby, 1973)
	The Loving Game (London: Robson, 1975)
	New and Collected Poems 1950-1980 (London: Robson, 1980)
	Winterlude (London: Robson, 1982)
Prose	"Coming to Life in Leeds" in *Writers on Themselves* (London: B.B.C., 1964)
	The Tiger and The Rose (London: Hamilton, 1971) (Autobiography)
	A Proper Gentleman (London: Robson, 1977) (Autobiography)
	Not Without Glory (London: Woburn, 1976) (Criticism)
Manuscripts	British Library 56071

Scarfe, Francis (b. 1911)
Poetry	*Inscapes* (London: Fortune, 1940)
	Forty Poems and Ballads (London: Fortune, 1941)
	Underworlds (London: Heinemann, 1950)
Prose	*Auden and After* (London: Routledge, 1942)
	Auden (Monaco: Lyrebird, 1949)

Scott, Tom (b. 1918)
Poetry	*Seeven Poems o Maister Francis Villon* (Tunbridge Wells: Russell, 1956)
	An Ode til New Jerusalem (Edinburgh: MacDonald, 1956)
	The Ship and Other Poems (London: Oxford, 1963)
	At the Shrine of the Unkent Sodger (Preston: Akros, 1968)
	Musins and Murgeonins (Thurso: Caithness, 1975)
	Brand the Builder (London: Ember, 1975)
	The Tree (Dumfermline: Borderline, 1977)
Editor	*The Penguin Book of Scottish Verse* (London: Penguin, 1976)

Scurfield, George
Poetry	*The Song of the Red Turtle* (London: Poetry London, 1941)

Sergeant, Howard (b. 1914)
   Poetry   *The Leavening Air* (London: Fortune, 1946)

The Headlands (London: Putnam, 1953)

Travelling Without a Valid Ticket (Bradford: Rivelin, 1982)

   Prose   *Tradition in the Making of Modern Poetry* (London: Britannicus Liber, 1951)

   Editor   *For Those Who Are Alive* (London: Fortune, 1946) (Poetry)

An Anthology of Contemporary Northern Poetry (London: Harrap, 1947)

Mavericks (w. D. Abse) (London: Poetry & Poverty, 1957) (Poetry)

Poetry of the Forties (London: Longmans, 1971)

Outposts

Serraillier, Ian (b. 1912)
   Poetry   *Three New Poets* (w. A. Comfort & R. McFadden) (Billericay: Grey Walls, 1942)

Short, John (b. 1911)
   Poetry   *The Oak and the Ash* (London: Dent, 1947)

Smith, Sydney Goodsir (1915-1975)
   Poetry   *Skail Wind* (Edinburgh: Chalmers, 1941)

The Wanderer (Edinburgh: Oliver & Boyd, 1943)

The Deevil's Waltz (Glasgow: Maclellan, 1946)

Selected Poems (Edinburgh: Oliver & Boyd, 1947)

Under the Eildon Tree (Edinburgh: Serif, 1948; rev. ed. 1954)

The Aipple and the Hazel (Edinburgh: Caledonian, 1951)

So Late into the Night (London: Russell, 1952)

Cokkils (Edinburgh: MacDonald, 1953)

Orpheus and Eurydice (Edinburgh: Macdonald, 1955)

Omens (Edinburgh: MacDonald, 1955)

Figs and Thistles (Edinburgh: Oliver & Boyd, 1959)

The Vision of the Prodigal Son (Edinburgh: MacDonald, 1960)

	Kynd Kitlocks Land (Edinburgh: MacDonald, 1965)
	Girl with Violin (London: Oxford, 1968)
	Fifteen Poems and a Play (Edinburgh: Southside, 1969)
	Gowdspink in Reekie (Loanhead: MacDonald, 1974)
	Collected Poems (London: Calder, 1975)
Verse Drama	*The Wallace* (Edinburgh: Oliver & Boyd, 1960)
Prose	*Carotid Cornucopia* (Glasgow: Caledonian, 1947; rev. ed. Edinburgh: MacDonald, 1964)
	A Short Introduction to Scottish Literature (Edinburgh: Serif, 1951)
Editor	*Merry Muses of Caledonia: Robert Burns* (w. J. Barke) (Edinburgh: MacDonald, 1982)

Spark, Muriel (b. 1918)

Poetry	*Fanfarlo* (Aldington: Hand and Flower, 1952)
	Collected Poems I (London: Macmillan, 1967)
Bibliography	*Iris Murdoch and Muriel Spark* by T.T. Tominaga & W. Schneidermeyer (Metuchen: Scarecrow, 1976)
Editor	*The Poetry Review*

Spencer, Bernard (1909-1963)

Poetry	*Aegean Islands and Other Poems* (London: Poetry London, 1946)
	The King of Asine and other Poems by G. Seferis (w. L. Durrell & N. Valaoritis, London: Lehmann, 1948) (Translation)
	The Twist in the Plotting (Reading: Reading University School of Art, 1960)
	With Luck Lasting (London: Hodder & Stoughton, 1963)
	Collected Poems (London: Ross, 1965)
	Collected Poems (Oxford: Oxford University Press, 1981)
Interview	*The Poet Speaks* ed. P. Orr (London: Routledge, 1966)
Editor	*Personal Landscape* (w. others)

Spender, Richard (1921-1943)

| Poetry | *Laughing Blood* (London: Sidgwick & Jackson, 1942) |

Parachute Battalion (London: Sidgwick & Jackson, 1943)

Collected Poems (London: Sidgwick & Jackson, 1944)

Stanford, Derek (b. 1918)

Poetry

A Romantic Miscellany (w. J. Bayliss) (London: Fortune, 1946)

Music for Statues (London: Routledge, 1948)

The Traveller Hears the Strange Machine: selected poems 1946-1979 (London: Sidgwick & Jackson, 1980)

Self Portraits (Bristol: Radcliffe, 1984)

Prose

The Freedom of Poetry (London: Falcon, 1947)

Christopher Fry (London: Neville, 1951)

Dylan Thomas (London: Neville, 1954)

Muriel Spark (London: Centaur, 1959)

Inside the Forties (London: Sidgwick & Jackson, 1977) (Autobiographical)

Editor

A Tribute to Wordsworth (w. M. Spark) (London: Wingate, 1950)

Resistance (w. D. West)

Stewart, Gervase (1920-1941)

Poetry

No Weed Death (London: Fortune, 1942)

Verse Drama

"The Two Septembers" *Transformation Three*

Summers, Hal (b. 1911)

Poetry

Smoke After Flame (London: Dent, 1944)

Hinterland (London: Dent, 1947)

Visions of Time (Aldington: Hand & Flower, 1952)

Burning Book and Other Poems (Lewes: Book Guild, 1982)

Symons, Julian (b. 1912)

Poetry

Confusions about "X" (London: Fortune, 1939)

The Second Man (London: Routledge, 1944)

A Reflection on Auden (London: Poem of the Month, 1973)

The Object of an Affair (Edinburgh: Tragara, 1974)

Prose

The Thirties (London: Cresset, 1960)

Critical Occasions (London: Hamilton, 1966)

	Notes from Another Country (London: London Magazine Editions, 1972) (Autobiography)
	Critical Observations (London: Faber, 1981)
Editor	*An Anthology of War Poetry* (London: Penguin, 1943)
	Twentieth Century Verse
Manuscripts	University of Texas, Austin

Tambimuttu, M[eary] J[ames] [Thurairajah] (1915-1983)

Poetry	*Out of this War* (London: Fortune, 1941)
	Natarajah (London: Poetry London, 1949)
Editor	*Poetry in Wartime* (London: Faber, 1942)
	T.S. Eliot: a Symposium (w. R. March) (London: Poetry London, 1948)
	Poetry London (Nos. 1-14)
	Selected Writing (w. R. Moore)
Publisher	Editions Poetry London (w. Nicholson & Watson)

Thomas, Dylan (1914-1953)

Poetry	*18 Poems* (London: Parton, 1934; Fortune, 1942)
	Twenty-five Poems (London: Dent, 1936)
	Deaths and Entrances (London: Dent, 1946)
	Collected Poems (London: Dent, 1952)
	The Poems (London: Dent, 1971)
Poetry and Prose	*The Map of Love* (London: Dent, 1939)
Verse Drama	*Under Milk Wood* (London: Dent, 1954)
Prose	"Answers to an Enquiry" *New Verse* 11 (reprinted in *A Casebook on Dylan Thomas* ed. J.M. Brinnin (New York: Crowell, 1960))
	Portrait of the Artist as a Young Dog (London: Dent, 1940)
	Quite Early One Morning (London: Dent, 1954)
	A Prospect of the Sea (London: Dent, 1955)
	Adventures in the Skin Trade (London: Putnam, 1955)
	"I am going to read aloud" *London Magazine* 3,9 (Sep, 1956)
	"Notes on the Art of Poetry" in *Modern Poetics* ed. J. Scully (New York: McGraw Hill, 1965)

	Early Prose Writings (London: Dent, 1971)
	Death of the King's Canary (w. J. Davenport) (London: Penguin, 1978)
	Collected Stories (London: Dent, 1983)
Letters	*Letters to Vernon Watkins* (London: Dent, 1957)
	Selected Letters (London: Dent, 1966)
	Twelve More Letters (London: Turret, 1969)
Notebooks	*The Notebooks of Dylan Thomas* (New York: New Directions, 1967)
Manuscripts	Lockwood Memorial Library, State University of New York at Buffalo; British Library 52903; Harvard College Library
Biographies and Memoirs	*Dylan Thomas in America* by J.M. Brinnin (London: Dent, 1956)
	The Life of Dylan Thomas by C. Fitzgibbon (London: Dent, 1965)
	Dylan Thomas by P. Ferris (London: Hodder, 1977)
	My Friend Dylan Thomas by D. Jones (London: Dent, 1977)
Bibliographies	*Dylan Thomas: a Bibliography* by J.A. Rolph (London: Dent, 1956)
	"Chronology of Composition" in *Entrances to Dylan Thomas* by R. Maud (Pittsburgh: University of Pittsburgh, 1963)
	Dylan Thomas in Print by R. Maud (Pittsburgh: University of Pittsburgh, 1970)

Thomas, R[onald] S[tuart] (b. 1913)

Poetry	*The Stones of the Field* (Carmarthon: Druid, 1947)
	An Acre of Land (Newtown: Montgomeryshire Printing, 1952)
	The Minister (Newtown: Montgomeryshire Printing, 1953)
	Song at a Year's Turning (London: Hart-Davis, 1955)
	Poetry for Supper (London: Hart-Davis, 1958)
	Judgement Day (London: Poetry Book Society, 1960)
	Tares (London: Hart-Davis, 1961)

The Bread of Truth (London: Hart-Davis, 1963)

Pieta (London: Hart-Davis, 1966)

Not That He Brought Flowers (London: Hart-Davis, 1974)

H'm (London: Macmillan, 1972)

What is a Welshman? (Llandybie: Davies, 1974)

Laboratories of the Spirit (London: Macmillan, 1975)

Frequencies (London: Macmillan, 1978)

Between Here and Now (London: Macmillan, 1981)

Later Poems (London: Macmillan, 1983)

Later Poems 1972-1982 (London: Macmillan, 1984)

Prose   "The Depopulation of the Welsh Hill Country" *Wales* 7 (Summer, 1945)

"Some Contemporary Scottish Writing" *Wales* 23 (Autumn, 1946)

"Replies to 'Wales' Questionnaire" *Wales* 23 (Autumn, 1946)

"Review of *Break in Harvest* by Roland Mathias" *Wales* 26 (Summer, 1947)

"A Welsh View of the Scottish Renaissance" *Wales* 30 (Nov, 1948)

Words and the Poet (University of Wales, 1964)

"The Creative Writer's Suicide" *Planet* 41 (January, 1978)

Selected Prose (Ogmore: Poetry Wales, 1983)

Tiller, Terence (b. 1916)

Poetry   *Poems* (London: Hogarth, 1941)

The Inward Animal (London: Hogarth, 1943)

Unarm, Eros (London: Hogarth, 1947)

Reading a Medal (London: Chatto & Windus, 1957)

Notes for a Myth (London: Chatto & Windus, 1968)

The Singing Mesh (London: Chatto & Windus, 1979)

Verse Drama   *The Death of a Friend* (Broadcast: unpublished, 1949)

Lilith (Broadcast: unpublished, 1950)

The Tower of Hunger (Broadcast: unpublished, 1952)

Todd, Ruthven (1914-1978) (Emigrated to the United States in 1947)

Poetry
Ten Poems (London: Constable, 1940)
Until Now (London: Fortune, 1942)
Acreage of the Heart (Glasgow: Maclellan, 1944)
The Planet in My Hand (London: Grey Walls, 1945)
Garland for the Winter Solstice: selected poems (London: Dent, 1961)

Prose
Tracks in the Snow (London: Grey Walls, 1947)

Biographical
Symons, J.—"Ruthven Todd" in *Critical Observations* (London: Faber, 1981)

Treece, Henry (1912-1966)

Poetry
38 Poems (London: Fortune, 1940)
Towards a Personal Armageddon (Illinois: Decker, 1941)
Invitation and Warning (London: Faber, 1942)
The Black Seasons (London: Faber, 1945)
The Haunted Garden (London: Faber, 1947)
The Exiles (London: Faber, 1952)

Prose
How I See Apocalypse (London: Drummond, 1946)
I Cannot Go Hunting Tomorrow (London: Grey Walls, 1946) (Stories)
"Notes on Poetry" *Transformation Three*
Dylan Thomas (London: Drummond, 1949; rev. ed. Benn, 1956)
"Apocalypse Revisited" *World Review* N.S. 29 (July, 1951)

Editor
The New Apocalypse (w. J.F. Hendry) (London: Fortune, 1939)
The White Horseman (w. J.F. Hendry) (London: Routledge, 1941)
The Crown and the Sickle (w. J.F. Hendry) (London: Staples, 1943)
Wartime Harvest (w. S. Schimanski) (London: Staples, 1943)
A Map of Hearts (w. S. Schimanski) (London: Drummond, 1944)
Herbert Read: an Introduction (London: Faber, 1944)
Air Force Poetry (w. J. Pudney) (London: Lane, 1944)

Bibliography

Leaves in the Storm (w. S. Schimanski)
(London: Drummond, 1947)
A New Romantic Anthology (w. S.
Schimanski) (London: Grey Walls,
1949)
Kingdom Come (w. S. Schimanski & A.
Rook) (No. 9 to conclusion)
Transformation (w. S. Schimanski)
Bibliography by A. Kamm in *Henry
Treece* by M. Fisher (London: Bodley
Head, 1969)

Wain, John (b. 1925)
Poetry

Mixed Feelings (Reading: Reading
University School of Art, 1951)
A Word Carved on a Sill (London:
Routledge, 1956)
Weep Before God (London: Macmillan,
1961)
Wildtrack (London: Macmillan, 1965)
Letters to Five Artists (London: Macmillan,
1969)
The Shape of Feng (London: Covent
Garden, 1972)
Feng (London: Macmillan, 1975)
Poems 1949-1979 (London: Macmillan,
1981)

Prose

Preliminary Essays (London: Macmillan,
1960)
Sprightly Running (London: Macmillan,
1962) (Autobiography)

Editor

Mandrake (1 & 2, 1945 & 1946)

Waller, John (b. 1917)
Poetry

The Confessions of Peter Pan (Oxford:
Holywell, 1941)
Fortunate Hamlet (London: Fortune, 1941)
The Merry Ghosts (London: Poetry
London, 1946)
The Kiss of Stars (London: Heinemann,
1948)

Editor

Collected Poems of Keith Douglas (w.
G.S. Fraser) (London: Poetry London,
1951) rev. ed. (w. G.S. Fraser & J.C.
Hall) (London: Faber, 1966)
Alamein to Zem Zem by K. Douglas (w.
G.S. Fraser & J.C. Hall) (London:
Faber, 1966)
Kingdom Come (1-8)

Waller, Robert (b. 1913)
  Poetry

Poets of Tomorrow (1st Selection) (w. others) ed. J. Lehmann (London: Hogarth, 1939)
The Two Natures (Aldington: Hand & Flower, 1951)

Watkins, Vernon (1906-1967)
  Poetry

Ballad of the Mari Lwyd (London: Faber, 1941)
The Lamp and the Veil (London: Faber, 1945)
The Lady with the Unicorn (London: Faber, 1948)
The Death Bell (London: Faber, 1954)
The North Sea (London: Faber, 1955) (Translations from Heine)
Cypress and Acacia (London: Faber, 1959)
Affinities (London: Faber, 1963)
Fidelities (London: Faber, 1968)
Uncollected Poems (London: Enitharmon, 1969)
Selected Verse Translations (London: Enitharmon, 1977)
Elegy for the Latest Dead (Edinburgh: Tragara, 1977)
The Ballad of the Outer Dark (London: Enitharmon, 1979)
The Breaking of the Waves (Ipswich: Golgonooza, 1979)

  Verse Drama

The Influences (Hayes: Bran's Headbooks, 1976) (Performed 1939)

  Prose

"W.B. Yeats—The Religious Poet" *Texas Studies in English* Win 1961/2
Yeats and Owen: Two Essays (Frome: Brans Head, 1981)

  Interview

The Poet Speaks ed. P. Orr (London: Routledge, 1966)

  Editor

Adventures in the Skin Trade by D. Thomas (w. Introduction) (London: Putnam, 1955)
Letters to Vernon Watkins by D. Thomas (w. Introduction) (London: Dent, 1957)

  Manuscripts

British Library 54157-54166 (Typescripts of Poetry) (1940's Material) (Catalogue of these manuscripts by R.E. Oldroyd—54167); National Library of Wales
National Library of Wales

Memoirs	*Vernon Watkins, 1906-1967* ed. L. Norris (London: Faber, 1970)
Bibliography	*Vernon Watkins 1906-1967* by. B. Jones (Welsh Arts Council)
	Two Swansea Poets: Dylan Thomas and Vernon Watkins (Swansea: Swansea Public Library, 1969)
	"Vernon Watkins: A Bibliography" by J. McCormick *West Coast Review* 4 (Spring 1969)

Welch, Denton (1915-1948)

Poetry	*Instruments, Poems and Fragments* (London: Enitharmon, 1976)
Poetry and Prose	*A Last Sheaf* (London: Lehmann, 1951)
	Denton Welch: Extracts from his published works ed. J. Brooke (London: Chapman & Hall, 1963)
Prose	*Maiden Voyage* (London: Routledge, 1943)
	In Youth is Pleasure (London: Routledge, 1944)
	Brave and Cruel (London: Hamilton, 1948)
	A Voice Through a Cloud (London: Lehmann, 1950)
	The Denton Welch Journals (London: Hamilton, 1952)

Witherby, Diana (b. 1915)

Poetry	*Poems* (London: Verschoyle, 1954)
	The Heat and the Cold (London: Deutsch, 1965)
	Collected Poems (London: Witherby, 1973)

Woodcock, George (b. 1912)

Poetry	*Six Poems* (London: Charles Lahr, 1938)
	The White Island (London: Fortune, 1939)
	The Centre Cannot Hold (London: Routledge, 1943)
	Imagine the South (Pasadena: Untide, 1947)
	"The Rediscovered Notebook" *Malahat Review* 31 (July, 1964)
	Notes on Visitations (Toronto: Anansi, 1975)
	The Kestral and Other Poems (Sunderland: Ceolfrith, 1978)
	Collected Poems (Victoria: Sono Nis, 1984)
Prose	"Time and the Poet" *Poetry London* 8 (Nov/Dec 1942)

The Writer and Politics (London:
  Porcupine, 1948)
Anarchism (London: Penguin, 1963)
The Rejection of Politics (Toronto: New
  Press, 1972)
Herbert Read (London: Faber, 1972)
"Now: an heir of the Thirties" *Modernist
  Studies* 1,2 (1974)
Letters to the Past (Toronto: Fitzhenry &
  Whiteside, 1982) (Autobiography)

Editor   *Now*

Wright, David (b. 1920)
Poetry   *Poems* (London: Poetry London, 1947:
                                       published 1949; completed 1943)
                                     Moral Stories (St. Ives: Latin, 1952;
                                       enlarged ed. London: Verschoyle, 1954)
                                     Monologue of a Dead Man (London:
                                       Deutsch, 1958)
                                     Adam at Evening (London: Hodder &
                                       Stoughton, 1965)
                                     Poems (Leeds: Leeds University, 1966)
                                     Nerve Ends (London: Hodder & Stoughton,
                                       1969)
                                     To the Gods the Shades (Manchester:
                                       Carcanet, 1976)
                                     A View of the North (Ashingdon:
                                       MidNAG, 1976)

Prose   "Keyes's Poetry" *London Magazine* 7,8
                                       (Nov, 1967)
                                     Deafness: A Personal Account (London:
                                       Lane, 1969) (Autobiographical)

Editor   *The Faber Book of Twentieth Century
                                       Verse* (w. J. Heath-Stubbs) (London:
                                       Faber, 1953)
                                     Mid-Century: English Poetry 1940-1960
                                       (London: Penguin, 1965)

Manuscripts   Arts North, Newcastle on Tyne; Rhodes
                                       University, Grahamstown, S. Africa

Yates, Peter (b. 1914)
Poetry   *The Expanding Mirror* (London: Chatto &
                                       Windus, 1942)
                                     The Motionless Dancer (London: Chatto &
                                       Windus, 1943)
                                     Light and Dark (London: Chatto &
                                       Windus, 1951)

Petal and Thorn: Selected Poems (London: Ward, 1983)

Verse Drama

The Assassin (London: Chatto & Windus, 1946)

The Burning Mask (London: Chatto & Windus, 1948)

REFERENCES

REFERENCES

Chapter 1

1   Horizon I, 2 (February, 1940).
2   Reed, Henry—"The End of an Impulse" (*New Writing and Daylight* (Summer, 1943)).

Chapter 2

1   Lehmann, J.—*New Writing in Europe* (London: Penguin, 1940) 146.
2   Spender, S.—*Life and the Poet* (London: Secker & Warburg, 1942) 11.
3   *Life and the Poet*, 96.
4   *Life and the Poet*, 110.
5   *The Evening Colonnade* (London: Bruce & Watson, 1973) 383.
6   *The Golden Horizon* (London: Weidenfeld & Nicolson, 1953) xiii.
7   *World Within World* (London: Hamish Hamilton, 1951) 293.
8   *Enemies of Promise* (London: Penguin, 1961) 271.
9   *Golden Horizon*, xii.
10 *Demetrios Capetanakis: a Greek Poet in England,* ed. John Lehmann (London: Lehmann, 1947) 104.
11 "Foreword" to *Poems from New Writing,* 1936-1946 (London: Lehmann, 1946) 5.

Chapter 3

1   Alvarez, A.—*The Shaping Spirit* (London: Chatto & Windus, 1958) 12.
2   "Romanticism and Classicism," *Speculations* (London: Routledge, 1924) 118.
3   Eliot, T.S.—*For Lancelot Andrews* (New York: Doubleday, 1929) vii.
4   Eliot, T.S.—"Tradition and the Individual Talent" in *Selected Essays* (London: Faber (3rd ed.), 1951) 21.
5   In *Kenyon Review,* December 1939. Quoted by Symons in *Notes from Another Country* (London: London Magazine Editions, 1972) 66-7.
6   *Essays and Studies,* XXII (Oxford: Clarendon, 1937).
7   Thomas, D.—"Letter to Richard Church" 9th December, 1955 in *Selected Letters* (London: Dent, 1966) 160-2.
8   "Coming to London" in *Essays* (London: MacGibbon & Kee, 1970).
9   Review of *The New Apocalypse, Seven* 8 (Spring, 1940).
10 "Art and Social Responsibility" *New Road,* 1944.
11 "Third Letter", *Poetry London* No. 3, November, 1940.

12   "Are Poets Doing Their Duty?", *New Road* 1943, 15.
13   "Correspondence", *Poetry London* No. 2, April, 1939, no page number.
14   Moore, N.—*Henry Miller* (London: Opus, 1943) 7.
15   *Lyra* ed. A. Comfort and R. Greacen (London: Grey Walls, 1942).
16   Baker, P.—*The Beggar's Lute* (London: Favill Press, 1940).
17   *I Am My Brother* (London: Longmans, 1960) 230.
18   "A Lost Talent", *Poetry Quarterly* 6, 2 (Summer 1944).
19   Durrell, L.—*The Black Book* (New York: Dutton, 1963).
20   "Preface" to reissue of *The Black Book,* 1963.
21   *The Black Book,* 227.
22   *The Black Book,* 185.
23   *The Black Book,* 99.
24   *The Black Book,* 207.
25   See Durrell, G.—*My Family and Other Animals* (London: Hart-Davis, 1956).
26   "A Landmark Gone", *Middle East Anthology,* ed. J. Waller and E. De Mauny (London: Drummond, 1946: first published as by Charles Norden in G.S. Fraser's Cairo Forces Quarterly, *Orientations* I, 1).
27   "The Poet Reviews Himself", *Personal Landscape,* 2,2, 19.
28   Durrell, L.—*The Big Supposer* (London: Abelard-Schuman, 1973) 27.
29   *The Big Supposer,* 125.
30   Seferis, G.—*On the Greek Style* (Boston: Little Brown, 1966).
31   "A Winter Journal", *Penguin New Writing* 32, 149.
32   *The Big Supposer,* 90.
33   *Prospero's Cell,* (London: Faber, 1945) 59.
34   *A Key to Modern British Poetry,* (Norman: University of Oklahoma, 1952) 23.
35   *A Key to Modern British Poetry,* 83.
36   *A Key to Modern British Poetry,* 162.
37   *A Key to Modern British Poetry,* 39.
38   *A Key to Modern British Poetry,* 43.
39   Perlès, A.—*My Friend Lawrence Durrell* (London: Scorpion, 1961) 41.
40   "Correspondence" *Poetry London* No. 2, April, 1939 no page number.
41   Durrell, L.—"Henry Miller", *Horizon* 115 (July 1949) 51.
42   *A Key to Modern British Poetry,* 26.
43   *A Key to Modern British Poetry,* 55.
44   *A Key to Modern British Poetry,* 86.
45   *Personal Landscape,* 1,4, 7-8.
46   *The Big Supposer,* 62.
47   *Personal Landscape* 1,2, 2.
48   *A Key to Modern British Poetry,* 198.
49   *Personal Landscape,* 1,2, 2.
50   Lawrence Durrell and Henry Miller: *A Private Correspondence* (London: Faber, 1963) 343.
51   *The Big Supposer,* 89.
52   *The Big Supposer,* 93.

53 "Christopher Marlowe" in *Selected Essays,* 3rd ed. (London: Faber, 1951) 118.

54 Ross, A.—"A Poet at the Cross Roads", *Poetry Quarterly* 10,1 (Spring 1948) 38-9.

55 *Personal Landscape,* 2,1,2.

56 "A Language by Itself" in March, R. and Tambimuttu (eds.)—*T.S. Eliot: a symposium* (London: Poetry London, 1948) 172.

Chapter 4

1 "The Lotus Eaters", *Now,* New Series No. 1, 3-4.

2 Diary 24 June, 1940: *The Collected Essays, Journalism and Letters of George Orwell* (London: Penguin, 1970) Vol. 2, 402.

3 Journal, September 4th, 1939: *Horizon* I,2 (February, 1940).

4 "Gladstone" *The Second Man* (London: Routledge, 1943).

5 "The Lotus Eaters", 7.

6 "Testament of a Conscientious Objector" in *The Objectors,* ed. C. Simmons (Isle of Man: Times Press, [1965]) 95.

7 Symons, J.—*Critical Occasions* (London: Hamilton, 1966) 195.

8 War-time Diary: 1941, 3rd July: in *Collected Essays, Journalism and Letters* Vol. 2, 459 & 461.

9 "Art and Social Responsibility", *New Road,* 1944.

10 "Art and Social Responsibility".

11 *Poetry Quarterly* 5,2 (Summer, 1943) 74-76.

12 Gardiner, W.—*The Dark Thorn* (London: Grey Walls, 1946) 11.

13 Treece, H.—*How I See Apocalypse* (London: Drummond, 1946) 22.

14 Read, H.—Poetry and Anarchism (London: Faber, 1938).

15 Woodcock, G.—"Now: an heir of the Thirties" *Modern Studies* 1,2 (1974) 21-30.

16 Woodcock, G.—*The Rejection of Politics* (Toronto: New Press, 1972).

17 The Rejection of Politics.

18 "Poetry Magazines of the Thirties: A Personal Note" *Tamarack Review* (October, 1973) 73.

19 *Poets of Tomorrow* (London: Hogarth, 1939) 44.

20 Woodcock, G.—*Notes on Visitations* (Toronto: Anansi, 1975) x.

21 *Declaration,* ed., T. Maschler (London: MacGibbon & Kee, 1957).

Chapter 5

1 MacNeice, L.—*Modern Poetry* (London: Oxford, 1938) 197.

2 All quotations from 1st edition, London: Lehmann, 1950.

3 All quotations from 1st edition, London: McKibbon & Kee, 1970.

4 "To George Barker, for his Sixtieth Birthday", in *Homage to George Barker,* ed. J. Heath-Stubbs and Martin Green (London: Brian & O'Keefe, 1973).

5   Graham, W.S. "Notes on the Poetry of Release", *Poetry Scotland,*
     Third Collection (July, 1946) 56-58.
6   MacLaren-Ross, J.—*Memoirs of the Forties* (London: Ross, 1965) 184
     and 183.
7   Quoted in *W.R. Rodgers* by D. O'Brien (Lewisburg: Bucknell, 1970)
     51. (No source given).
8   Orr, P.—*The Poet Speaks* (London: Routledge, 1966) 210.
9   *The Poet Speaks,* 209.
10   O'Brien, D.—*W.R. Rodgers*
11   Nemerov, H.—*Poetry and Fiction* (New Brunswick: Rutgers University
     Press, 1963) 206.

Chapter 6

1   "A Few Words of a Kind" (Caedmon Records, New York, TC 1043:
     see also "I am Going to Read Aloud", *London Magazine,* September,
     1956).
2   "Foreword" to *Adventures in the Skin Trade* by D. Thomas (London:
     Ace Books, 1961) 7.
3   Thomas, D.—*Letters to Vernon Watkins* (London: Dent, 1957) 20.
4   *Letters to Vernon Watkins,* 40.
5   *Letters to Vernon Watkins,* 31.
6   *Letters to Vernon Watkins,* 92.
7   Thomas, D.—*Selected Letters* (London: Dent, 1966) 115.
8   *Selected Letters,* 386.
9   Brinnin, J.M.—*Dylan Thomas in America* (London: Ace Books, 1956)
     95-96.
10   *Letters to Vernon Watkins,* 20-21.
11   *Letters to Vernon Watkins,* 116.
12   Deutsch, B.—*Poetry in our Time* (New York: Doubleday, 1963) 371-2.
13   *Selected Letters,* 289.
14   *Letters to Vernon Watkins,* 17.
15   *Letters to Vernon Watkins,* 123.
16   *Letters to Vernon Watkins,* 126.
17   *Quite Early One Morning* (New York: New Directions, 1960) 178-9.
18   Huddlestone, L.—"An Approach to Dylan Thomas", *Penguin New
     Writing* 35, 140.
19   "Note" to *Collected Poems* (London: Dent, 1952).
20   Jones, Daniel—*My Friend Dylan Thomas* (London: Dent, 1977) 57.
21   *My Friend Dylan Thomas,* 67.
22   *Selected Letters,* 380.
23   *My Friend Dylan Thomas,* 110.
24   *My Friend Dylan Thomas,* 110.
25   Davies, W.—*Dylan Thomas* (University of Wales, 1972) 26.
26   *Selected Letters,* 83.
27   Shapiro, K.—*In Defence of Ignorance* (New York: Vintage, 1965) 176.

Chapter 7

1   Scarfe, F.—*Auden and After* (London: Routledge, 1942) 155.
2   Fitzgibbon, C.—*The Life of Dylan Thomas* (London: Dent, 1965) 242.
3   Treece, H.—*How I See Apocalypse* (London: Drummond, 1946) 176.
4   Hendry, J.F.—"The Art of History", *Transformation* [One], 145 & 140.
5   Hendry, J.F.—"The Philosophy of Herbert Read", in *Herbert Read*, ed. H. Treece (London: Faber, 1944) 108.
6   Sorel, G.—*Reflections on Violence* (New York: Collier, 1961), 52.
7   *How I See Apocalypse*, 55.
8   Treece, H.—"Apocalypse Revisited", *World Review* N.S. 29 (July, 1951) 27.
9   *Apocalypse Revisited*, 26.
10 *Poetry London*, 3, 11.
11 *How I See Apocalypse*, 21.
12 *How I See Apocalypse*, 176.
13 "The Poetry of Nicholas Moore", *Poetry Quarterly* (Spring 1947).
14 Gardiner, W.—*The Dark Thorn* (London: Grey Walls, 1946) 37.
15 "The Art of History", *Transformation* [One], 141.
16 Comfort, A.—"Art and Social Responsibility" *New Road*, 1944, 19.
17 Comfort, A.—"Philosophies in Little", *Resistance* (October, 1946) 38.
18 Woodcock, G.—"The Poetry of Alex Comfort", *Poetry Quarterly* 9,2 (Summer, 1947), 111.
19 Gardiner, W.—*The Dark Thorn*, 32.
20 *The Dark Thorn*, 76.
21 *PQ* 7,3 (Autumn, 1945) 117.
22 *Outposts*, Special Centenary Number (Spring, 1974)
23 *New Verse* (May, 1939).
24 Maclaren-Ross, J.—*Memoirs of the Forties* (London: Ross, 1965)
25 *New Road* 1943, 12.
26 *A New Romantic Anthology*, ed. Stefan Schimanski and Henry Treece (London: Grey Walls, 1949) 80.
27 Gilmore, Maeve—*A World Away* (London: Gollancz, 1970) 64.
28 Quoted in Hewison, F.—*Under Seige* (London: Weidenfeld & Nicolson, 1977) 149.

Chapter 8

1   Muir, E.—*An Autobiography* (London: Hogarth, 1954) 51-52.
2   *An Autobiography*, 48-49.
3   Raine, K.—*Defending Ancient Springs* (London: Oxford, 1967) 29.
4   Orr, P. (ed.)—*The Poet Speaks* (London: Routledge, 1966) 271.
5   *Letters to Vernon Watkins* (London: Dent, 1957) 18.
6   Quoted in Mathias, R.—*Vernon Watkins* (University of Wales, 1974) 8.
7   *Letters to Vernon Watkins*, 17.

8   From a talk "Poetry and Experience" (October, 1961) quoted in
    Mathias, R.—*Vernon Watkins,* 70.
9   *The Poet Speaks,* 269.
10 *The Poet Speaks,* 267.
11 Mathias, R.—*Vernon Watkins,* 27-28.
12 Hamburger, M.—"Vernon Watkins, a Memoir" in *Vernon Watkins,
    1906-1967* ed. L. Norris (London: Faber, 1970) 50-51.
13 *Letters to Vernon Watkins,* 38.
14 *The Land Unknown* (London: Hamilton, 1975) 105.
15 *Faces of Night* (London: Enitharmon, 1972: scheduled for publication,
    1946) 3-4.
16 *Defending Ancient Springs,* 3.
17 *Defending Ancient Springs,* 13.
18 Raine, K.—*A Question of Poetry* (Crediton: Gilbertson, 1969; written
    1946).
19 *Faces of Night,* 73.
20 *Faces of Night,* 76-77.
21 *Faces of Night,* 70.
22 *Defending Ancient Springs,* 175.
23 *The Land Unknown,* 107.
24 *Defending Ancient Springs,* 82.
25 *Farewell Happy Fields,* 9.
26 *Poetry London* 5, 17, 23-25.
27 *The Land Unknown,* 182.
28 *The Land Unknown,* 40.
29 *The Land Unknown,* 92.
30 Raine, K.—*William Blake* (London: Longmans, 1951) 27.
31 *William Blake,* 24.
32 "In the Mirror: Diary Without Dates: extracts" in *An Idiom of Night*
    by P.J. Jouve (London: Rapp & Whiting, 1968) 10.
33 "Note on Symbolism" *Poetry Quarterly* 8,2 (Summer, 1946) 87.
34 *Poetry London,* 4, 112-114.
35 *Defending Ancient Springs,* 59.
36 Gascoyne, D.—*Paris Journal 1937-1939* (London: Enitharmon, 1978)
    126.
37 "In the Mirror", *An Idiom of Night,* 14.
38 British Library, BM:MSS 56041.
39 *Paris Journal,* 119.
40 *An Idiom of Night,* 41.
41 *Paris Journal,* 64.
42 *Paris Journal,* 79.
43 *Paris Journal,* 55.
44 See dates in *Poems 1937-1942* and in Manuscripts BM 56045 and
    56046, British Library.
45 *Defending Ancient Springs,* 48.
46 "Note on Symbolism."
47 "Leon Chestov" *Horizon* XX, 118 (October, 1944) 218.

48   "Leon Chestov" 219.
49   "Note on Symbolism" 86.
50   *Paris Journal*, 12.
51   *Paris Journal*, 128.
52   Gascoyne, D.—*Thomas Carlyle* (London: Longmans, 1952) 22.

Chapter 9

1   "Introduction" to *Irish Poems of Today* (London: Secker & Warburg, 1946).

2   *Wales*, January, 1944.

3   Letter to Henry Treece, 1 June, 1938 in *Selected Letters* (London: Dent, 1966) 199.

4   Jones, G.—*The Dragon Has Two Tongues* (London: Dent, 1968) 39.

5   *The Dragon Has Two Tongues*, 47.

6   *The Dragon Has Two Tongues*, 133.

6A   *The Dragon Has Two Tongues*, 46.

7   *The Dragon Has Two Tongues*, 41.

8   *Wales* 23 (Autumn, 1946) 22.

9   "A Welsh View of the Scottish Renaissance", *Wales* 30 (November, 1948) 603.

10   "Some Contemporary Scottish Writing", *Wales* 23 (Autumn, 1946) 98.

11   "Some Contemporary Scottish Writing", 102.

12   "The Depopulation of the Welsh Hill Country", *Wales* 7 (Summer, 1945) 75-77.

13   "A Welsh View of the Scottish Renaissance", 600.

14   Thomas, R.S.—*Words and the Poet* (University of Wales, 1964) 19.

15   *Wales* VII, 26 (Summer, 1947) 323.

16   *Words and the Poet*, 22.

17   *Words and the Poet*, 15.

18   Smith, S.G.—*A Short Introduction to Scottish Literature* (Edinburgh: Serif, 1951) 29.

19   *A Short Introduction to Scottish Literature*, 29.

20   Scott, A.—*The MacDiarmid Makars, 1923-1972* (Preston: Akros, 1972) 13.

21   "The Modern Makars" in *Scottish Poetry: A Critical Survey*, ed. J. Kinsley (London: Cassell, 1955) 268.

22   Scott, A.—"Goodsir Smith's Masterpiece: *Under the Eildon Tree*" (sic) in *For Sidney Goodsir Smith* (no ed. named) (MacDonald: Loanhead, 1975) 11.

23   *A Short Introduction to Scottish Literature*, 12.

24   "Introductory Note" to *For Sidney Goodsir Smith*, 9.

25   Fraser, G.S.—*Vision of Scotland* (London: Elek, 1948) 19.

26   *Vision of Scotland*, 20.

27   Muir, E.—*Scott and Scotland* (London: Routledge, 1936) 15.

28   Fulton, R.—*Contemporary Scottish Poetry* (Loanhead: MacDonald, 1974) 71.

29   Lindsay, M.—*Modern Scottish Poetry* (2nd Ed., Rev.; London: Faber, 1966) 19.

30   "Introduction" to *Two Decades of Irish Writing* (ed. D. Dunn) (Cheadle: Carcanet Press, 1975).

31   Kavanagh, P.—"From Monaghan to the Grand Canal", *Collected Pruse* (London: MacGibbon & Kee, 1967) 225.

32   Greacen, R.—*One Recent Evening* (London: Favill Press, 1944) 19-21. Quoted in *Northern Voices* by Terrence Brown (Dublin: Gill & MacMillan, 1975).

33   Quoted in *Northern Voices* by Terence Brown, from an exchange with Geoffrey Taylor, "Poetry Ireland", *The Bell* VI, 4 (July, 1943) 342.

34   Quoted in "W.R. Rodgers and John Hewitt" by Terence Brown in *Two Decades of Irish Writing*, (p. 92) from "Not Rootless Colonist", *Aquarius* 5 (1972) 91.

35   *Collected Poems* (London: MacGibbon & Kee, 1964) xiv.

36   "Self Portrait", *Collected Pruse*, 21.

37   "Literature and the Universities", *Collected Pruse*, 240.

38   "Suffering and Literature", *Collected Pruse*, 278.

39   "From Monaghan to the Grand Canal", *Collected Pruse*, 225.

40   "Self Portrait", *Collected Pruse*, 19.

41   "Pietism and Poetry", *Collected Pruse*, 245.

42   "Self Portrait", *Collected Pruse*, 13.

43   "From Monaghan to the Grand Canal", *Collected Pruse*, 227.

44   "Self Portrait", *Collected Pruse*, 13.

45   "From Monaghan to the Grand Canal", *Collected Pruse*, 223.

46   Heaney, S.—"The Poetry of Patrick Kavanagh" in *Two Decades of Irish Writing*, 106.

47   *I Can't Stay Long* (London: Deutsch, 1975) 15-17.

48   *Poets of Tomorrow* (Third Selection) (London: Hogarth, 1942) 45.

49   Orr, P. (ed.)—*The Poet Speaks* (London: Routledge, 1966) 156-8.

50   *Man and Literature* (London: S.C.M., 1943) 5.

51   *Wednesday Early Closing* (London: Faber, 1975) 202.

52   "On Two Contemporaries" in *Essays* (London: MacGibbon & Kee, 1970), 55-56.

53   *William Cowper* (London: Longmans, 1960) 5.

54   Clemo, J.—*Confessions of a Rebel* (London: Chatto & Windus, 1949) ix.

55   *Confessions of a Rebel*, 222.

56   *The Invading Gospel* (London: Lakeland, 1972).

57   *The Invading Gospel*, 35.

58   *The Wind and the Rain: an Easter Book for 1963* ed. N. Braybrooke (London: Secker & Warburg, 1962) 11.

59   *Here and Now*, 1.

60   Ridler, A.—"A Question of Speech" in *Focus* 3.

61   Review of *Poems, Seven* 8, 16.

62   Durrell, L.—*A Key to Modern British Poetry* (Norman: University of Oklahoma, 1952) 200.

63   *Transformation [One],* 201.

64   "The Parish and the Universe", *Collected Pruse,* 282.

65   Nicholson, N.—"On Being Provincial", *The Listener,* August 12, 1954, 248.

66   "On Being Provincial", 248.

Chapter 10

1   Eliot, T.S.—"Poetry and Drama" in *On Poetry and Poets* (London: Faber, 1957) 79.

2   "Introduction" to *Collected Plays* (London: Hart-Davis, 1971) viii.

3   "Introduction" to *Collected Plays,* ix-x.

4   Duncan, R.—*How to Make Enemies* (London: Hart-Davis, 1978) 129.

5   "Introduction" to *Collected Plays,* x.

6   Ridler, A.—"A Question of Speech" in *Focus* 3.

7   All quotations from Nicholson, N.—"The Poet Needs an Audience", *Orpheus,* 1.

8   Ross, A.—*Poetry, 1945-1950* (London: Longmans, 1951) 56.

9   Durrell, L.—*Reflections on a Marine Venus* (London: Faber, 1953) 180.

10   Durrell, L.—"The Other T.S. Eliot", *Atlantic,* 215, 5 (May, 1965) 63.

11   Durrell, L. and A. Marc *The Big Supposer* (London: Abelard-Schuman, 1973) 71.

12   *New York Times* February 6, 1955: cited in *Christopher Fry* by Emil Roy (Carbondale: University of Illinois, 1968) 49.

13   Cited in *Modern British Verse Drama* by W.V. Spanos from Fry's "Comedy", *Adelphi,* 27 (November, 1950) or *Tulane Drama Review* IV,3 (March, 1960).

14   "Notes on the Art of Poetry", in *Modern Poetics* ed. J. Scully (New York: McGraw-Hill, 1965).

15   Dickinson, P.—*The Good Minute* (London: Gollancz, 1965) 211.

16   Heppenstall, R.—*Portrait of the Artist as Professional Man* (London: Owen, 1969) 38-39.

17   *Portrait of the Artist as Professional Man,* 37.

18   MacNeice, L.—*Christopher Columbus* (London: Faber, 1944) 8 and 16.

19   *Christopher Columbus,* 12.

20   *Christopher Columbus,* 17.

21   Cleverdon, D.—*The Growth of Milk Wood* (New York: New Directions, 1969) 18.

Chapter 11

1   "Foreword" to *Penguin New Writing* No. 3, 8.

2   "Art and Social Responsibility", *New Road* 1944, 25.

3   Fuller, R.—*Professors and Gods* (London: Deutsch, 1973) 127.
4   *Opus,* No. 14 (Spring, 1943) 1.
5   *Poems from India* (Chosen by R.N. Currey and R.V. Gibson) (London: Oxford, 1946) viii.
6   Symons, J.—Preface to *An Anthology of War Poetry* (London: Pelican, 1942) viii.
7   *Professors and Gods,* 128-9.
8   *Professors and Gods,* 135.
9   In *The Poetry of War: 1939-1945* ed. I. Hamilton (London: New English Library, 1972) 155.
10   Introduction to *Components of the Scene* ed. R. Blythe (London: Penguin, 1966) 13.
11   *Poetry of War: 1939-1945,* 164-5.
12   *The Poet Speaks* (ed. P. Orr) (London: Routledge, 1966) 65.
13   Fuller, R.—Contribution to "Norman Cameron—Four Views", *The Review* 27-28 (Autumn-Winter, 1971-1972) 17.
14   *Professors and Gods,* 148.
15   *Professors and Gods,* 148.
16   Contribution to *The Poetry of War: 1939-1945,* 163-4.
17   Fuller, R.—"From Blackheath to Oxford", *London Magazine* N.S. 8,12 (March, 1969) 25.
18   *Professors and Gods,* 79.
19   "From Blackheath to Oxford" 30.
20   Fuller, R.—*Owls and Artificers* (London: Deutsch, 1971) 99.
21   *Owls and Artificers,* 128.
22   *Owls and Artificers,* 90.
23   Hamilton, I.—*A Poetry Chronicle* (London: Faber, 1973) 89.
24   Lewis, Alun—*In the Green Tree* (London: Allen & Unwin, 1948) 43.
25   Lewis, Alun—"Author's Note" to *The Last Inspection* (London: Allen & Unwin, 1942).
26   Scannell, V.—*Not Without Glory* (London: Woburn, 1976) 58.
27   Letter to Lynette Roberts, quoted in *Alun Lewis* by Alun John (University of Wales, 1970) 38.
28   Letter in *Alun Lewis and the Caseg Broadsheets* (London: Enitharmon, 1970).
29   *Horizon* 13 (January, 1941) 78.
30   *In the Green Tree,* 39.
31   From an unpublished journal, quoted in the "Introduction" to *Alun Lewis: Selected Poetry and Prose* ed. Ian Hamilton (London: Allen & Unwin, 1966) 52.
32   *In the Green Tree,* 47.
33   *In the Green Tree,* 51.
34   *In the Green Tree,* 36.
35   *In the Green Tree,* 52-3.
36   *In the Green Tree,* 35.
37   *In the Green Tree,* 41.
38   *In the Green Tree,* 47.

39   *In the Green Tree*, 57.
40   Letter to Lynette Roberts in *Alun Lewis* by Alun John, 39.
41   *The Poetry of War, 1939-1945*, 156.
42   *The Poetry of War, 1939-1945*, 157.
43   Fedden, R.—*Personal Landscape* (London: Turret Books, 1966) no page number.
44   Fedden, R.—"An Anatomy of Exile" in *Personal Landscape: an anthology of exile* (London: Poetry London, 1945) 7.
45   Letter to Anne Ridler, 1942 in *Spirit of Place* (London: Faber, 1969) 75.
46   *The Poet Speaks*, 236.
47   *Poetry Book Society Bulletin*, 37 (June 1963)
48   *The Poet Speaks*, 236 and 234.
49   See Graham, D.—*Keith Douglas* (London: Oxford, 1974) 148.
50   Letter to John Waller quoted in *Keith Douglas*, 148.
51   See Fraser, G.S.—"Passages from a Cairo Notebook" in *Leaves in a Storm*, ed. S. Schimanski and H. Treece (London: Drummond, 1947).

Chapter 12

1   Quoted in *The Poetry of War* ed. Ian Hamilton (London: New English Library, 1972) 10.
2   *I Am My Brother* (London: Longmans, 1960) 125.
3   *The Last Enemy* (London: Macmillan, 1942): page references are to the *Pan* edition, 1956.
4   Heath-Stubbs, J.—*The Darkling Plain* (London: Eyre & Spottiswood, 1950) 179.
5   Heath-Stubbs, J.—Letter to A. T. Tolley, 22 April, 1983.
6   Heath-Stubbs, J. "The Poetic Achievement of Charles Williams" *Poetry London* 4, 42-45.
7   *Poetry Quarterly* 9,2, 117.
8   Heath-Stubbs, J.—*Charles Williams* (London: Longmans, 1955) 10.
9   Introduction to *Selected Prose and Poetry* by G. Leopardi (London: Oxford, 1966) vii-viii.
10   Introduction to *Selected Prose and Poetry* by G. Leopardi, viii.
11   "Note on the Present Translation from the Canti" in *Selected Prose and Poetry* by G. Leopardi.
12   British Library MS54327.
13   Read, H.—"Publishing Keyes", *London Magazine* N.S. 7,8 (November, 1967) 55.
14   Letter to Richard Church in *Sidney Keyes: a biographical enquiry*—J. Guenther (London: Ross, 1967) 153.
15   *Minos of Crete* (London: Routledge, 1948) 164.
16   Wright, D.—"Keyes' Poetry", *London Magazine*, N.S. 7,8 (November, 1967).
17   Dust jacket of *Collected Poems*.

18   *Deafness* (London: Lane, 1969) 97.
19   *Deafness,* 97.
20   Introduction to *To the Gods the Shades* (Manchester: Carcanet, 1967).
21   *Deafness,* 97.
22   "Introduction" to *Mountains Beneath the Horizon* (London: Faber, 1950).
23   Graham, D.—*Keith Douglas* (London: Oxford, 1974) 219.
24   *Keith Douglas,* 218-219.
25   Hamilton, Ian—*A Poetry Chronicle* (London: Faber, 1973) 62.
26   *Keith Douglas,* 237.
27   *The Poetry of War,* 168-9.
28   "A Conversation with Alan Ross", *The Review* 25, 39.
29   *Poetry Quarterly,* 98-100 (Summer, 1978) 71.
30   *The Review,* 25, 50.
31   *The Review,* 25, 44.
32   Orr, P. (ed.)—*The Poet Speaks* (London: Routledge, 1966).
33   Fuller, R.—*Professors and Gods* (London: Deutsch, 1973) 135.
34   *Deafness,* 94.
35   Bell, W.—*Mountains Beneath the Horizon,* 14.

Chapter 13

1   See Larkin, P.—"Introduction" to 2nd ed. of *The North Ship* (London: Faber, 1973).
2   "Introduction", *The North Ship.*
3   Introduction to *Jill* (London: Faber, 1963) 19.
4   "Vernon Watkins: an Encounter and a re-encounter", in *Vernon Watkins 1906-1967* ed. L. Norris (London: Faber, 1970) 30; and "Introduction" to *The North Ship,* 9.
5   Hamilton, Ian—"Four Conversations" *London Magazine* (November, 1964) New Series 4,6, 72-77. (For details of *In the Grip of Light* see "Philip Larkin's *In the Grip of Light*" by A.T. Tolley, *Agenda* 22,2.)
6   See British Library MS 52619, which contains versions of many of these poems.
7   "Philip Larkin praises the poetry of Thomas Hardy" *The Listener* 25 July 1968, 111.
8   Jacobson, D.—"Philip Larkin" *The New Review* 1,3 (June 1974) 27.
9   Hamburger, M.—*A Mug's Game* (Cheadle Hulme: Carcanet, 1973) 105-6.
10   *A Mug's Game,* 128.
11   "Four Conversations", 80.
12   Abse, D.—*A Poet in the Family* (London: Hutchinson, 1974) 117.
13   *A Poet in the Family,* 153.
14   Stanford, D.—*Inside the Forties* (London: Sidgwick & Jackson, 1977) chapter 15.

15   Wain, J.—"Oxford and After", *Outposts,* 13 (Spring, 1949) 21-23.
16   Reed, H.—"The End of an Impulse", *New Writing and Daylight,* (Summer, 1943) 123.
17   Hobsbaum, P.—"Where are the War Poets?", *Outposts,* 61 (Summer, 1964) 23.
18   Wain, J.—*Preliminary Essays* (London: Macmillan, 1957) 159.
19   Enright, J.—*Conspirators and Poets* (London: Chatto & Windus, 1966) 58.
20   Orr, P. (ed.)—*The Poet Speaks* (London: Routledge, 1966) 48-49.
21   Davie, D.—Review of *Poets of the Pacific, Poetry London* 5,20, 26-29.

Conclusion

1   *A Little Treasury of Modern Poetry,* ed. O. Williams (New York: Scribners, 1952) 821.
2   Davidson, M.—*The Poetry and the Pity* (London: Chatto & Windus, 1972) 95.
3   Auden, W.H.—"A Literary Transferance", *Southern Review,* VI (Summer, 1940).
4   Hamburger, M.—*A Mug's Game* (Cheadle: Carcanet, 1973) 110.
5   MacNeice, L.—*The Strings are False* (London: Faber, 1965) 103.
6   Dick, Kay—*Ivy and Stevie* (London: Duckworth, 1971) 12.
7   Allott, K.—"Introductory Note" to *The Penguin Book of Contemporary Verse* (London: Penguin, 1950) 25.

NOTE
There are separate entries for authors and other literary figures and organisations, and for periodicals and anthologies. Books by specific authors, prose pieces and plays that are not whole books, and poems, are listed under authors, in that order. (Titles of sections of books of poetry are listed among poems.) Only books, plays or pieces of prose *named* in the text are indexed, but all poems quoted from or mentioned are indexed. The Index covers only the text from Chapters 1 to 13, and not prefatory or appended material. There are no entries for politicians, political parties, historical events, etc. Names of any kind that appear in quoted material are not indexed.

Chapters or sections of chapters devoted to a specific topic are indicated by putting their page numbers in bold type. Unpublished works appear with their titles in square brackets.

INDEX